THE YOUNG MR. WESLEY

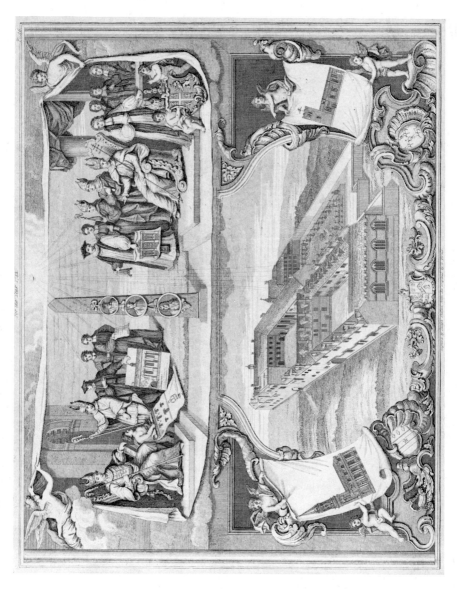

I LINCOLN COLLEGE IN THE EIGHTEENTH CENTURY

THE
YOUNG MR. WESLEY

A study of John Wesley and Oxford

---

by

V. H. H. GREEN, D.D.

Fellow and Senior Tutor of Lincoln College
Oxford

LONDON
EDWARD ARNOLD (PUBLISHERS) LTD.

First published in 1961

PRINTED IN GREAT BRITAIN BY
WESTERN PRINTING SERVICES LTD., BRISTOL

PREFACE

A NEW study of John Wesley might seem uncalled for. The spadework of an earlier generation of scholars, Luke Tyerman, John Telford, and J. S. Simon, has been supplemented by the researches of more recent historians, so much so that no ground might appear to remain untilled. This was my own feeling when I turned my attention to John Wesley. I had been struck by the comparatively little detailed work that had been done on the earlier period of John Wesley's career. The majority of historians with ample reason have concentrated on the later period of his life. Indeed the more important books that have dealt in comparatively recent times with his early life have been written in French and German, M. Léger's outstanding study, *La Jeunesse de Wesley*, published in 1910 (the copy which I read in the Bodleian Library in 1960 had not until then had any of its pages cut), and Professor Schmidt's first volume of his study of Wesley, published at Zürich in 1953. It became clear to me as I realized that there was nothing of any value to commemorate John Wesley's connection with my College that there might yet be room for an interpretation of his early life.

It was the more exciting to find that there was in fact considerable unpublished material which had never been adequately used by historians. The indefatigable editor of Wesley's *Journal*, Dr. Nathaniel Curnock, mentioned the Oxford diaries of John Wesley and gave an adequate summary of his first Oxford diary in his introduction to the *Journal*, but a very significant amount of material remained unquarried. Through the courtesy of Dr. Frank Cumbers, John Wesley's successor as the Steward of the Methodist Book Room and of the Conference of the Methodist Church to which this material belongs, I have been able to make full use of many unpublished documents, more especially the diaries that John Wesley kept between 1725 and 1735. I owe a very deep debt of gratitude to the Methodist Church for allowing me to make so free a use of its archives. It is fortunate that the Epworth Press will be publishing an edition of the first Oxford diary and an abridgement of the contents of the remaining Oxford diaries in addition to a revised edition of the *Journal*. I have deliberately refrained from making detailed bibliographical references to these manuscripts in the knowledge that the public will have

v

access to the material in published form. I have also to acknowledge most gratefully the kindness and helpfulness of their editor, the Reverend Wesley Swift, who saved me considerable time and trouble by placing many useful pieces of his own research at my disposal. He has had the good fortune to discover Wesley's fifth Oxford diary, which covers the period 7th September, 1734, to 28th February, 1735. I hope that those who read this book will turn ultimately to some of the sources which have made it possible. I have once again to thank the Rector and Fellows of my College for allowing me to make use of archives in the College's possession. Many of my colleagues have given me pieces of information, more especially Mr. Donald Whitton, who helped to unravel the location of rooms in the eighteenth-century College.

I cannot claim to have written a book that will in any significant fashion change the verdict of history on John Wesley, but I believe that there is sufficient new material to help in the understanding of his work and character, and to illuminate the working of the University itself in the early years of the eighteenth century. I have been more than aware of the difficulty of investing with any degree of life many of the minor characters who sometimes crowd the pages that follow, and I am conscious that in this I may well have failed. If the narrative is rather unexciting, and there is much that is dull and even tedious, I can only plead that in many respects John Wesley's life at Oxford was itself unspectacular and conventional. Yet in spite of this I think that I have been justified in throwing a little new light on one of the most distinguished sons of Oxford and Lincoln College and on the University with which he was closely connected in his formative years.

Finally I must thank again my friend, Mr. H. H. Brown, for his invaluable advice; he has saved me from many stylistic infelicities and the book has benefited greatly from his reading of it.

VIVIAN H. H. GREEN

CONTENTS

ILLUSTRATIONS

CHAPTER I

The Intellectual Background

THE Methodist movement can only be understood if its origins are considered within the religious and social framework of early eighteenth-century England, more especially of the University of Oxford where its main begetters spent their most formative years. The rise of Methodism has been interpreted as a reaction to the sloth of contemporary Anglicanism; but this does not explain satisfactorily the genesis of the movement nor attest its historical significance. The degeneracy of the Church of England in the eighteenth century has been overestimated as a result of later partisan writing, and its true position in the life of the nation at this time is only now being slowly revealed.[1] In fact the late seventeenth and early eighteenth century was a critical period in the history of the Church since it witnessed the beginning of the first genuinely critical attitude to Christian theology.[2] The Methodist movement was possibly less of a reaction to contemporary religious activity, or the lack of it, than an answer to a problem the outward expression of which was theological and philosophical in content, but it was an answer expressed in practical rather than in intellectual terms.

An important attempt was made to establish the rational basis of Anglican theology in the last half of the seventeenth century. In part this was a probable reaction to the violence and eccentricity of theological developments which had occurred during the period of the Civil Wars and which continued under the Commonwealth. It was a significant sequel to prevailing Calvinism. The Cambridge Platonists were the avant-garde of such a movement. In their writings, influenced by Plato's belief in ideas, they tended to exalt the function of reason in leading the way to truth.

[1] As, for instance, by Dr. Norman Sykes in his *Church and State in England in the 18th Century* (1934). Cf. also the evidence of the *Visitations of Archbishop Herring*, edited by S. L. Ollard.

[2] See, *inter alia*, G. R. Cragg, *From Puritanism to the Age of Reason* (1950); R. N. Stromberg, *Religious Liberalism in 18th Century England* (1954); N. Sykes, *From Sheldon to Secker* (1959), 140–87; and for the Continental scene, P. Hazard, *The European Mind* (1680–1715) (trs. 1953).

There was, they argued, a 'reason in things', originating with the rational Creator of the Universe, in which human beings share; 'the judgement of reason is the reason of our minds', Benjamin Whichcote commented, 'perceiving the Reason of things'.[1] 'To go against reason is to go against God; it is the self-same thing, to do that which the reason of the case doth require and that which God Himself doth appoint; reason is the divine governor of man's life; it is the very voice of God.'[2] The Cambridge Platonists did not deny the necessity of revealed truth,[3] and in the last analysis reason was for them tinged with a mystical meaning. Yet in stressing that reason confirmed the assurance of faith,[4] they paved the way for its rehabilitation. Men were not merely wearied by the high passions engendered by past theological debates; they were discovering within the realm of secular thought and scientific experiment that patient reasoning achieved more than dogmatic declarations.

John Locke and Sir Isaac Newton were the most distinguished writers though not necessarily the most representative, who sympathized with such developments. Locke was theologically a Unitarian;[5] his philosophical thinking was to lead easily both to deism and to scepticism; but the certainty of God's existence was the foundation of his *Essay Concerning Human Understanding*. 'Reason', he wrote there,[6] 'is natural *revelation*, whereby the eternal Father of Light, and Fountain of all knowledge, communicates to mankind that portion of truth which he has laid within the reach of their natural faculties. *Revelation* is natural *reason* enlarged by a new set of discoveries communicated by God immediately, which reason vouches the truth of, by the testimony and proofs it gives that they come from God.' Locke was indeed at one with the coming school of theologians when he argued that religion should be reduced to its basic essentials; if only the obscurantist ideas which had enveloped the Christian religion were eliminated, religious truth could be clearly discerned and appreciated.

The harmonious relationship of faith and reason to which Locke paid homage had its complement in the marriage of science and theology to

---

[1] B. Whichcote, *Aphorisms*, 33.

[2] *Op. cit.*, 76. Cf. p. 40, 'In the use of Reason and the exercise of virtue we enjoy God.'

[3] Cf. J. Smith, *Select Discourses*, 61.

[4] R. Cudworth, *The Intellectual System of the Universe*, 11, 517 ff.

[5] See H. McLachlan, *The Religious Opinions of Milton, Locke and Newton* (1941), though the author's conclusions seem somewhat extreme.

[6] *Essay*, iv, 9, 4.

which Newton with most contemporary scientists held steadfast. The deeper penetration of nature's secrets and the apparent order which they suggested strengthened his belief in the omnipotence and omnicompetence of God. 'When I wrote my treatise about our system', he told Richard Bentley, 'I had an eye upon such principles as might work with considering men, for the belief of a Deity.'[1] Newton may not have been theologically orthodox; but most of his fellow-scientists, more particularly Robert Boyle and John Ray,[2] were strong Christians whose faith was strengthened by the apparent order and design which their experiments revealed. 'The consideration of the vastness, beauty, and regular motions of the heavenly bodies, besides a multitude of other phenomena of nature and the subserving of most of these to men, may justly induce him as a rational creature to conclude that this vast, beautiful, orderly, and (in a word) many ways admirable system of things, that we call the world, was framed by an author supremely powerful, wise and good, can scarce be denied by an intelligent and unprejudiced considerer.'[3] The masterful Richard Bentley, who gave the first of a series of lectures, founded by Boyle to promote such ideas, essayed to confute unbelief, that 'labyrinth of nonsense and folly', by using recent scientific knowledge. 'There are other books extant which they must needs allow of as proper evidence; even the mighty volumes of visible nature, and the everlasting tables of right reason, wherein if they do not wilfully shut their eyes they may read their own folly written by the finger of God in a much plainer and more terrible sentence, than Belshazzar's was by the hand upon the wall.'[4]

Contemporaries did not use the word reason in the modern sense of it; and for its orthodox advocates its meaning was often invested with significant qualifications. These scholars had no wish to apply rational criticism to scriptural studies; for while there had been important advances in the field of biblical scholarship and while the ground was being prepared, as by the French Catholic, Richard Simon, for the beginnings of textual criticism, no genuine attempt was made to 'rationalize' the Scriptures. No orthodox theologian would have argued, as some deists did, that reason removed or made unnecessary the mysteries of faith. Reason, Robert

[1] Newton, *Opera*, iv, 429.
[2] See C. E. Raven, *John Ray* (1942).
[3] Boyle, *Works*, v, 515 ff.
[4] R. Bentley, *The Confutation of Atheism, Eight Sermons Preached at the Honourable Robert Boyle's Lecture* (1693), 16.

South commented, 'proves the revelation of it [the Word of God contained in the Scriptures] by God; but, then having done this, here it stops, and pretends not to understand and fathom the nature of the thing revealed'.[1] Reason showed that revelation was revelation and made plain its content, but it could not decide ultimately whether that which was revealed was to be accepted or rejected as true. In Locke's words 'revelation cannot be admitted against the clear evidence of reason'. In Latitudinarian opinion it was reason's function to assess whether divine revelation was authentic historically; it had its part to play in interpreting such revealed truth. Stillingfleet, for instance, 'proved that the Mosaic history must be true because it was reasonable, and he established the credibility of the whole idea of revelation on purely rational grounds. Yet, though willing to show that revelation has the support of reason, he was careful to insist that its authority is ultimately greater.'[2] The interpretation of revealed truth lay within the scope of man's reasoning power; but once historic authenticity has been established it was not thought permissible to repudiate revelation. Reason meant therefore little more than the exercise of the intellect and an orderly, logical process of thought, not precisely defined. It had something in common with the *intellectus agens* of the medieval scholastics and it was perhaps a sign of the times that Henry Wharton should have unearthed and published the treatise of a fifteenth-century[3] English bishop, Reginald Pecock, whose confidence in human reason had wrought his condemnation and downfall.[4]

The application of this rational treatment to dogmatic theology harbingered an excessive optimism. Many orthodox writers believed that no one could doubt the divine authorship and inspiration of the Scriptures once the evidence had been clearly presented. The 'pretences of the atheist', Stillingfleet declared, were 'weak, ridiculous and impertinent'.[5] The content of the Holy Scriptures admittedly contained some things that were above human reason, but nothing that was contrary to it. Indeed reason seemed so to clarify the statements of scripture that reason-

---

[1] South, *Sermons*, i, 368.

[2] G. R. Cragg, *From Puritanism to the Age of Reason*, 69.

[3] *A Treatise proving Scripture to be the Rule of Faith, writ by Reginald Peacock, bishop of Chichester, before the Reformation about the year 1450* (1688). This was republished and edited by J. L. Morison in 1909.

[4] See V. H. H. Green, *Bishop Reginald Pecock* (1945), 113–43; E. F. Jacob, *Reynold Pecock* (1951) and E. H. Emerson, 'Reginald Pecock, Christian Rationalist', *Speculum* (1956), 235–42.

[5] Stillingfleet, *Origines Sacrae*, 392.

able men would be better placed to ascertain without difficulty the principles of Christian belief.

The late seventeenth-century theologians were, then, not merely optimistic about the remarriage of faith and reason but too hopeful about the impact that this was likely to have on the Church. They believed that it would make even less likely any recrudescence of Roman Catholicism, which was still regarded as the most intellectually obscurantist of religious faiths.[1] It would also help to eliminate the accretions and superstitions which in the course of centuries had served to split the unity of the Church and to conceal the real essentials of the Creed. It would undoubtedly controvert doubters and unbelievers. It is not difficult to see in such optimism new hopes for a new age, and in the decline of such hopes material for future criticism of the contemporary Church.

The Latitudinarian theologians had not, however, perceived the possible drift of their own presuppositions in the hands of less skilled and less professional students of theology. They had stopped short of applying rational criticism to the *arcana* of religion; they held that there was an irreducible element of mystery which could not be so treated. There were, however, some who were unready to adopt this sage procedure. What grounds were there for admitting the supremacy of reason and yet forbidding ingress into every chamber of human experience? The Latitudinarians believed that if only men were able to examine Scripture patiently and reasonably, they would see how admirable and reasonable were its claims; their followers and critics found that these notions were fallacious. Deism may indeed be traced to the writings of Lord Herbert of Cherbury, but in its spread it was in a part a natural development of certain ideas implicit in the theology of the Latitudinarians, more particularly the importance they attached to the natural judgement of the human mind.

The writings of contemporary Socinians and Arians testified to this. The Socinians, for instance, found that the doctrine of the Trinity was not well founded in Scripture. In other words they refuted the claim which the Latitudinarians had stressed that rational investigation of Scripture only enhanced and clarified the teaching of the Church. Such anti-Trinitarianism was but the first step in the discarding of dogma and the creation of a

[1] It is worth recording that the anti-Romanism of the High Churchmen of the period may be explained in part as a sequel to the experience of those restored Anglicans who had been obliged to spend a period of exile in a Roman Catholic country.

natural or rational religion; 'a good life', the author of a tract entitled *Brief Notes on the Creed of St. Athanasius*, published in 1689, had remarked, 'is of absolute necessity to salvation, but a right belief in those points that have always been controverted . . . is in no degree necessary'.[1] The so-called Arianism of the period was a deduction from Socinianism. Its chief advocate, the learned, industrious and eccentric William Whiston, held that Christ, being created by God, must be inferior to Him; Christ was less than God and if divine yet separate from him. Such anti-Trinitarianism slid almost imperceptibly into Unitarianism; Christ then became the highest and noblest of human creatures and no more than that.

The way was now open for the propagation of plain Deism. The deists who constituted a by no means homogeneous group of writers and pamphleteers were themselves better suited to destructive than to constructive criticism. Where the Socinian and the Arian had been chiefly concerned with examining religion in the light of a literal interpretation of the Bible, the deist examined religion itself in the light of rational enquiry. The conclusions to which they came, expressed for instance in such books as Anthony Collins' *Discourse of Freethinking*, John Toland's *Christianity Not Mysterious*, and Matthew Tindal's *Christianity as Old as Creation* were cumulatively devastating. The deist criticized the Church and its beliefs on the ground that the latter represented accretions welded on the truths of natural religion in order to preserve the vested interests of the priesthood. He pointed out apparent inconsistencies in the Christian scheme of things, the unreasonable supposition, for instance, that God should have confined his attention and his revelation to such a relatively unimportant people as the Jews. It was equally absurd, it was also urged, to read into the character of Christ, just and good man as he undoubtedly was, the superhuman qualities that had been claimed for him by orthodox tradition. The dogma and ritual of the Church had been invented to safeguard its ministers and interests. What was left after all this had been said was the natural religion which provided man with an adequate and sensible guide to living. The deists profess, so Dr. Clarke allowed, 'to believe only so far as 'tis discoverable by the light of nature alone, without believing any Divine Revelation'. Faith became no more than a 'firm persuasion built upon substantial reasons'.[2] The objections which the deists raised against institutional religion are now familiar enough; indeed they appear to-day very naïve. Yet their ultimate impact was significant. This was not because

[1] Quoted in Stromberg, *Religious Liberalism in 18th Century England*, 38.
[2] Toland, *Christianity not Mysterious*, 138.

their influence was particularly wide or extensive; indeed the reverse was largely true. It was because in some small way an effective challenge had been offered to Christian belief itself. The Church was in fact confronting a crisis as serious as that of the cleavage represented at the Reformation; in some sense it was even more vital, for whereas the Reformation created bitterly hostile Christian groups divided about ecclesiastical organization and liturgy rather than the fundamentals of belief, this late seventeenth- and early eighteenth-century movement was directed against Christianity itself. It was a meagre growth and in due course it practically disappeared, but it prepared the ground for future criticism.

It is, however, important to observe that deism had itself severe intellectual limitations. It suffered from the same uncritical acceptance of certain premisses as did its opponents. If it declared that the dogmatic teaching of the Church and its interpretation of Christian revelation were unacceptable to the intelligent man, it emphasized strongly that belief in a creative deity was indispensable to morality and civic virtue. It was neither agnostic nor atheistic. The spearhead of its criticism must seem to the modern sceptic somewhat blunted. Moreover, it lacked any creative or uniform articles of belief; as a movement it proved to be singularly inchoate. In his *Christianity As Old As Creation*, Matthew Tindal, a fellow of All Souls and originally an undergraduate of Lincoln, where he had been a pupil of the later Non-juror, George Hickes, tried to formulate a constructive deism; but his book revealed the defects and the illogicalities of the deistic position. It was easily answered by orthodox writers. Their penetrating criticism of deism had, however, a significant by-product. In showing the falsity of its basic assumptions, the orthodox critics did more to reveal the inadequacy of natural religion put forward by the deists than to justify the necessity of a revealed religion. The way was thus open for the sceptic or agnostic, such as David Hume, who would find belief in either a natural or a revealed religion equally unacceptable.

The orthodox response to the important intellectual challenge thus offered took three main directions; but it is first worth underlining the seriousness of the challenge itself. It is difficult to trace a clear connection between the pamphlets and writings of the obscure pedagogues who championed the deistic position and the feeling of anxiety about the Church and contemporary religion which pervaded the comments of so many high-minded and deep-thinking men at that time; but there was a connection between the concern with the state of the Church and the spread of unbelief. It was not that the Church was neglectful of its duty or that religion was everywhere at a low ebb;[1] but that many anxious Christians believed rightly that irreligion and indifference were making progress and wrongly accounted the Church responsible for this. 'No age', Daniel Defoe wrote in 1722, 'since the founding and forming the Christian Church, was ever like, in open avowed atheism, blasphemies, and heresies, to the age we now live in.' 'I suppose', said Dean Swift, 'it will be granted that hardly one in a hundred among our people of quality or gentry appears to act by any principle of religion; that great numbers of them do entirely discard it, and are ready to own their disbelief of all revelation in ordinary discourse. Nor is the case much better among the vulgar, especially in great towns.'[2] These comments reflected a commonly taken opinion which recurred throughout the century.

It may be suggested that the distinction between this and earlier ages can be overstressed. It is reasonable to suppose that for many people religious belief had for long been only an aspect of the conventions of society which they accepted without question; the decline in the power of ecclesiastical sanctions and the comparative freedom of the press no longer made it necessary to coat secular forms with religious faith. Yet there is an essential difference between this and earlier ages. Until the closing years of the seventeenth century the majority of Europeans had accepted a conventional religious belief; now in every class a considerable minority abandoned their faith. Why this occurred is much too big a problem to discuss here. Many of the factors that we associate with increasing secularism at a later date, more especially scientific discoveries in the realms of geology and mechanics, were not noticeably operative at this period; indeed science seemed to support rather than to deny the credal statements of the churches. There was nothing in the behaviour, belief or organization of the churches to generate irreligion; it was rather the fruit of certain significant social and intellectual developments. No one in the period was able to explain it satisfactorily. Some connected the growing indifference to religion with the freedom of the press[3] and the permitted

---

[1] It must be added that the Church of England was essentially a middle- and upper-class society, and that it had never to any marked extent won the love or respect of the working classes.

[2] Swift, 'Project for the Advancement of Religion', *Works*, 11, 175.

[3] The Convocation of Canterbury thought the 'late excessive growth of infidelity, heresy and profaneness' primarily a result of the freeing of the press and the end of the danger of popery, which fostered differences among Protestants (*A Representation of the Present State of Religion, unanimously Agreed upon by a Joint Committee of Both Houses of Convocation of the Province of Canterbury*, 1711).

publication of deistic writings.[1] There was perhaps some truth in this; but deism was itself an aspect of the growing spirit of criticism as well as a contribution to it. Basically the divorce between religion and the people became more marked. Indeed, it may be argued that the gap has never been closed. Here a little, there a little was done to bring back a sense of religion; the Evangelicals, the Tractarians, the Roman Catholics, the Methodists, all did something, but the ultimate effect was less than many of their historians have claimed. This is not to belittle what was attempted or achieved, but simply to suggest that the early years of the eighteenth century saw the effective opening of the religious crisis, and that all the attempts that have so far been made to cope with it have been historically only very partially successful.

What was the intellectual response to the crisis in the first half of the eighteenth century? Deism and scepticism in part originated in the confident optimism of the late seventeenth- and early eighteenth-century thinkers with their stress on the coincidence of faith and reason. It was only natural therefore that the proponents of Christian rationalism should have continued to believe that their original position held good, and that the implicit defect of the deist position lay in its latent irrationalism. Continued belief in the correlation of faith and reason was not a monopoly of any one school of churchmanship. Charles Leslie, the Non-juror, observed that 'God never required any man to believe anything that did contradict any of the outward senses'.[2] The High-Church Jacobite, Bishop Atterbury, pronounced that the Church 'desires nothing more than to be tried at the bar of unbiased reason, and to be concluded by its sentence'.[3] Indeed their position was perhaps summarized by the statement of the orthodox dissenter, Philip Doddridge, that 'It is certainly the duty of every rational creature to bring his religion to the strictest test, and to retain or reject the faith in which he has been educated, as he finds it capable or incapable of rational defence.'[4]

There was then a continued belief in the efficacy of a rational defence of

[1] The licensing system ended between 1693 and 1695, but publications containing matter that could be construed as seditious or blasphemous were liable to condemnation. In fact the deists suffered very little persecution; Thomas Woolston in 1729 and Peter Annet in 1762 suffered penalties for blasphemy. Arthur Bury's *The Naked Gospel* was condemned to be burned at Oxford in 1690; but an attempt to introduce a law for the repression of such literature in 1721 failed.

[2] Leslie, *Theological Works*, ii, 'The Socinian Controversy Dismissed'.

[3] Atterbury, *Sermons*, iii, 29.

[4] Doddridge, *Correspondence and Diary*, II, 423.

the Christian faith as a stream of published works, for the most part un-distinguished, showed clearly enough. Indeed the fertility of the writers of religious works and the reading public they enjoyed proves the continued interest taken by the literate public in religious matters. When Henry Dodwell wrote his *Christianity Not Founded on Argument* in 1743, his work was traduced by the critics on the ground that he was challenging Christianity at its most vital apologetic point, what a modern writer has termed 'the rational and positive demonstration of its historical truth and logical consistency'. 'A constant and sincere observance of all the laws of reason', Samuel Clarke asserted in his Boyle lectures, '. . . will unavoidably lead a man to Christianity.'

Yet in plain, human experience the deist writings showed, if nothing else, that this was not necessarily so. They had indicated that there were illogicalities and inconsistencies which obscured rather than clarified the declarations of Scripture. It was his appreciation of the very genuine intellectual difficulties implicit in unorthodox criticism which led Joseph Butler to write the ablest apologetic work of his time, *The Analogy of the Christian Religion*. Butler approached the problem of religion from the standpoint of the scientific critic; he would probe, as the deists had probed, the claims made by religion with the pen of meticulous judgement. He confessed the difficulties of revealed as of natural religion; he found nature confused and contradictory. Nature did not reveal, as it had done for Newton earlier and was to do for Archdeacon Paley later, the hand of a greater designer; it simply pointed to the obscurity and mystery of the design. Butler established Christianity on the only terms upon which it can probably be established intellectually, not on certain proof but on probability.

In line with Butler, the philosophical Bishop of Cloyne, George Berkeley, had in *Alciphron* perceived the impossibility of putting forward an unanswerable intellectual proof of religious truth. He ventured the proposition that matter is illusory and God the sole reality. Berkeley was less persuasive than Butler; but both Butler and Berkeley, suggesting the inadmissibility of the claims made earlier in the century for the co-identity of revelation and reason, realized that Christianity was not intellectually reprehensible. They put forward intellectual arguments for its acceptance, but they were different from those ventilated by the Latitudinarians and their followers. In certain ways Butler's apology has never been surpassed, but neither Butler nor Berkeley had more than a small public. They were indeed somewhat lonely figures, and for the most part the exponents of Christian intellectualism reverted to the earlier tradition.

Berkeley's *Alciphron* was published in 1732; Butler's *Analogy* in 1736. The flight from reason had in fact already begun, and it is within the fideism of the non-rationalists with their insistence on personal experience and the assurance of truth and salvation which this provided that the third response to the religious crisis of the period is to be found. The phrase 'non-rationalist' is more accurate than anti-rationalist, for most of those who felt that the content of faith lay in personal experience rather than rational argument did not deny the validity of the latter; they simply believed that it was irrelevant to the assurance of salvation. William Law indeed came to the conclusion that to trust in reason was in some sense a denial of the 'witness of the Holy Spirit'. 'If you are afraid of reason hurting your religion, it is a sign that your religion is not as it should be. . . . Complain therefore no more of want of evidence; neither books, nor study nor learning is wanted.' The authentic Christian experience, 'common cause of humility, self-denial, renunciation of the world, poverty of the spirit, and heavenly affection', provided the only sure ingress to Christian truth.

Methodism partook of similar nutrition. John Wesley was never himself opposed to the use of reason to justify Christian truth nor did he question its validity,[1] but he became convinced that the Christian experience was the fuller and finer witness to Christian truth, and ultimately that assurance of salvation was the gift of the Holy Spirit. In this way Methodism was a valid response to the challenge to religion and was indeed largely conditioned by it. It is only as a response to such a challenge that its rise becomes intelligible. It was not historically nor purposively simply an attempt to deal with the defective sense of duty of a too-comfortable Anglican Church, but yet another attempt, and in some ways the most successful, to defeat spreading infidelity and indifference and to bring a sense of real religion to the people. It was an attempt to combat growing unbelief by the religion of personal experience; but it by-passed the intellectual challenge which had originally promoted it. This was in no way surprising. John Wesley was a man of wide reading but of increasingly circumscribed intellectual interests. Neither he nor his companions were creative thinkers; he had the pen of a ready writer, but

[1] He never discarded the respect for reasonable argument and logical thinking which he had learned at Oxford; in abridging John Norris' *Reflections* he seems deliberately to have suppressed criticisms of the scholastic disputations and sterile syllogisms of University education.

much of what he wrote[1] consisted of abridgements or condensations of books already in print. The remainder of his work lacked originality and profundity. His response to the challenge of the contemporary situation had been to inculcate personal holiness in himself and his companions, and to take the message of the Gospel and of goodwill to the prisoners in Oxford gaol. He offered in fact nothing that could satisfactorily meet the intellectual difficulties of his time and it would have been very surprising if Methodism had gained a real hold in the eighteenth-century University of Oxford.

His work found its genuine expression in bringing a sense of religion to the lower middle classes, often bored by the conventionality and aridity of current Anglican worship, and to the working classes who for geographical reasons sometimes lay outside the influence of the parochial system and whose interests in any case the Church of England had long neglected or ignored. In this way Methodism, together with the Evangelical movement inside the Church of England, contributed to a revival of religion which had significant social and political consequences. Too much must not, however, be claimed for it. It is doubtful whether in fact, as Lecky and Halévy claimed, Methodism saved England from the consequences of a French revolution. The stress that it laid on personal religion and the total reliance that it placed on the Scriptures led to an evasion of the intellectual challenge. By the very nature of its social grouping it was closely related to the continuance of the existing social structure which did much to condition its habit of thought. Yet when all this has been said Methodism was a movement of great historical significance, and what it was it owed initially to the genius of one man, John Wesley, who habitually described himself as a fellow or former fellow of Lincoln College in the University of Oxford.

[1] See Richard Green, *A Bibliography of the Works of John and Charles Wesley* (1896).

CHAPTER II

The Oxford Background

(i) Introduction

OXFORD UNIVERSITY in the first half of the eighteenth century was suffering from the lassitude which in the history of institutions so often follows a period of energy and action. During the seventeenth century scholarship had flourished and intellectual activity had been keen; under the impulse of the constitution provided by Archbishop Laud in 1634–6, the University was by comparative standards an effective and learned society. In spite of the discord and disruption caused by the civil wars and the commonwealth, it had continued to retain its reputation. The Colleges were for the most part full and though often disturbed by the domestic conflicts which form a feature of most inbred societies they were prosperous. The University had played a prominent part in the violent religious and political controversies of the time. A society which was then and long continued to be a stronghold of the Church of England was naturally aligned to the group of politicians most devoted to the Church and to the Crown. The critics of the Church and the opponents of the Crown were out of favour and liable to lose their fellowships. Many of the Heads of Colleges and fellows were probably time-servers, sedulous in stressing their loyalty to the government in power; but the devotion to Crown and Church also represented a genuine attachment to principle which, as during the difficult reign of James II, led to quickened resentment at arbitrary interference with the University's freedom of action. It is moreover plain that by identifying itself with religious and political orthodoxy the University was giving an opportunity to the growing number of dissidents in religion and politics to question its effectiveness as a home of learning and morality. Many of the most determined attacks on the University came from men who had an axe to grind. In recognizing the lowered spiritual and academic temperature of the eighteenth-century University, it is also necessary to remember that the University continued to fulfil many of its essential functions in an adequate fashion.

Indeed the chief point about the history of the University in the first

half of the eighteenth century was not its inadequacy as a home of learning and scholarship nor its failure to educate the young, but the bad press
it received as a result of its political and religious standing. It was equally
unpopular with politicians of the Whig establishment and the literary
publicists of the coffee houses. Its later history shows only too well that
the University may easily be regarded by any group of politicians as
politically suspect, and it has been, and still is, repeatedly the object of
embittered criticism by angry *alumni* whose abuse is usually equalled only
by their ignorance. This was the situation in the first half of the eighteenth
century. After 1714 there was a kind of alliance between the Whig politicians who suspected that the University's independent politics harboured
pro-Jacobite sympathies and the deistic writers who resented the University as a seat of clerical privilege, power and partisanship. They concealed
their attacks in the guise of standing for learning and justice; 'whether', as
Nicholas Amhurst put it, 'in their present unregulated state, they are not
the nurseries of pedantry instead of sound learning, of bigotry instead of
sound religion; whether their statutes . . . are not generally perverted, or
partially executed; whether the publick discipline is not wretchedly
neglected, and the publick exercises confin'd to nonsensical jargon, and the
mere burlesque of true knowledge'.[1] The critics of the University were
assisted by the fact that there were undoubted elements of truth in their
charges, but their words must not be taken, as historians have tended to
take them, as truth. They wished to discredit the University to ensure
that it might follow a subservient political line and because they wished to
undermine its championship of orthodox Anglicanism.

There thus poured forth from the presses a series of vituperative and
scurrilous attacks, some of them comparatively well-informed but all
intended to bring the existing institution into disrepute and to further
plans for its reform. Perhaps the most disinterested critic was the Cornish-
man, Humphrey Prideaux,[2] a graduate of Christ Church. A great admirer
of the then dean, Dr. Fell, he had studied under the orientalist, Dr.
Pococke, and was rewarded by the patronage of the Earl of Nottingham,
who presented him to the rectory of St. Clement's, Oxford, in 1679, and
a prebendal stall at Norwich Cathedral in 1681. For a time he divided his
duties between Oxford and Norwich, arousing some ill-will at the College
by his censorious efficiency; but in 1685 he severed his connection with the

[1] *Terrae-Filius* (1721), 5.

[2] For a sketch of Prideaux's life see R. W. Ketton-Cremer, *Norfolk Assembly*
(1957), 63–91.

University. 'I have hearkened to proposals that have been made to me of marriage, and because they are such as are very advantageous', he had decided to accept them. He was appointed to the archdeaconry of Suffolk and soon quarrelled with the new Dean of Norwich, Dr. Fisher, whom he described as 'good for nothing but his pipe and his pot'; but in 1702 he succeeded to his place and showed himself an efficient administrator and a stern disciplinarian as well as an acrimonious critic of his bishop.

This elderly, captious and critical scholar was ready to supply ammunition for an attack on his University; 'I nauseate Christ Church', he had said on being offered Pococke's chair, and 'I have an unconquerable aversion to the place'. His letters to John Ellis show there was a strand of personal rancour in his ill-temper which his later sufferings from the stone may have increased. The dons were no better than 'dunces and knaves' who preached 'most scandalous duncecall sermons'. Pembroke was the 'fittest College in town for brutes' while men from Balliol habitually haunted 'a dingy, horrid, scandalous ale-house' and 'by perpetual bubbering add to their natural stupidity to make themselves perfect sots' This biased critic who had not been for any length of time in Oxford since he attended Dean Fell's funeral in 1686 recommended a limitation on the tenure of life fellowships since elderly dons (and deans, one might add) were liable to be overtaken by sottishness or spleen. Useless fellows might be relegated to an institution which with a rare flash of humour he named 'Drone Hall'. Dean Aldrich described Prideaux (because of certain typographical errors in a published work, for which indeed the author was only in part responsible) as an 'inaccurate, muddy-headed man', and his criticisms of the University must be received cautiously. They were in fact founded on his fear that its orthodoxy was likely to be impugned by deists and the like. He believed that the University could better fulfil its function as a home of religion and learning if its studies were revised and its teachers were made more efficient; to this end he proposed to increase further the powers of the heads of Colleges and to make arrangements at the beginning of every parliament for new legislation. The old man pressed his plans upon Townshend and upon an Archbishop already harried by other demands.

Detestation of the religious orthodoxy of the University appeared most forcibly in the strongly worded criticisms of the deist writer, John Toland. Toland was not an Oxford graduate, but he had lived in Oxford during 1694-5, and he had no doubt that the University should be made politically dependent and freed from its clerical stranglehold by the setting-up of a royal visitation. 'Why may not Oxford . . . be reformed or purg'd by a Royal Visitation tomorrow, as Aberdeen was the other day, or as Oxford itself was at the Reformation?' It was his belief that only by such means could 'Barbarism, and Ignorance, Turbulency and Sedition' be 'banish'd out of that delicious spot'; he looked forward to the time 'when public lectures in all faculties are frequented (as elsewhere) under pain of expulsion, when the fruits of private lectures are seen in publick exercises, and that instead of the bare Editors of old books, they become the authors of new ones'.[1]

Perhaps the most stringent critic was Nicholas Amhurst, a Merchant Taylors' scholar whose fellowship at St. John's was allegedly terminated for libertinism and misconduct in 1719. Amhurst cherished a violent hatred for his former Society, especially for the President, Dr. Delaune, by no means a man of impeccable character, whom he attacked in vitriolic prose. Indeed much of his argument was founded on his experience of St. John's, and he did not easily forget or forgive the rough usage to which he believed himself to have been subjected. Amhurst's criticisms appeared in *Terrae-Filius*, written after his expulsion from his College, which was widely read and believed. It was an uneven publication, hard-hitting and shrewdly analytical of some of the worst defects of contemporary University education; but it was maliciously propagandist and viciously satirical. It was intended to discredit the University and to prepare the way for a much-needed reformation.

For Amhurst the University was a thoroughly reactionary, corrupt and treacherous society. It was governed by statutes which were outmoded and oaths which could be no longer regarded as effective; its revenues were founded on endowments and bequests which were no longer executed. Its academic exercises were a series of meaningless futilities.[2] Its lecturers did not lecture and its professors made no attempt to teach. 'I have known', he writes, 'a profligate *debauchee* chosen professor of *moral* philosophy; and a fellow, who never look'd upon the *stars soberly* in his life, professor of *astronomy*: we have had *history* professors, who never read anything to qualify them for it, but *Tom Thumb, Jack* the *gyant-killer, Don Bellianis of Greece* . . . we have had likewise numberless professors of *Greek, Hebrew,* and *Arabick,* who scarce understood their mother tongue.'[3] He compared the heads of Colleges with the directors of the South Sea

[1] J. Toland, *The State Anatomy of Great Britain* (1717).
[2] *Terrae-Filius*, 105–9, 227–34.
[3] *Op. cit.*, 47–8.

Company.[1] The University no longer had any claim to be regarded as a home of scholarship and learning, for its curriculum was completely outmoded. The 'sciences and arts have declin'd in Oxford, in proportion as their *fineries* were increased'.[2] Such learning as there was was deliberately obscurantist and intended to prevent the enquirer from reaching the truth. 'At least, whatever portion of *common sense* they enjoy themselves, they take especial care to keep it from those under their tuition, having innumerable large volumes by them, written on purpose to obscure the understanding of their pupils, and to obliterate or confound all those impressions of right and wrong which they bring with them to the university.'

The responsibility for this sad state of affairs, which lay in part[3] with the out-of-date constitution of the University (and the inducement which a fellowship gave to a life of indolence and ease),[4] lay with the knavish politics of the place and the predominance of the High-Church tradition. A Whig stood no chance of preferment at Oxford. 'To call your self a Whig at Oxford, or to act like one, or to lie under the suspicion of being one, is the same as to be *attainted* and *outlaw'd*; you will be discourag'd and brow-beaten in your own college, and disqualify'd for preferment in any other: your company will be avoided and your character abused; you will certainly lose your degree, and at last, perhaps, upon some pretence or other, expell'd.'[5] The way to get on at Oxford was to cultivate disloyalty.

'If he will but laugh at oaths to his King, and think those sacred to the university, all is like to go well with him . . . if he gets drunk, he must be sure to talk treason, and damn the Whigs: if he loves a w—re, as long as he does but love the church as well, he may enjoy both . . . and from step to step he goes through the favour of all his mother's *best* children to a college living.'[6]

The University for Amhurst was plainly a nest of traitors; 'they never talk so much of *loyalty*, as when they are preaching up treason and rebellion'.[7]

[1] *Terrae-Filius*, 59 ff.
[2] *Op. cit.*, 25.
[3] *Op. cit.*, 105.
[4] He would have a limit on the length of tenure of fellowships (*op. cit.*, 217–19).
[5] *Op. cit.*, 175.
[6] *Op. cit.*, 44.
[7] *Op. cit.*, 26.

C

He associated all this with the University's attachment to the High-Church tradition. Amhurst did not put forward avowed free thought, but he adopted a distinctly anti-clerical tone and an aversion to the University's High-Church views. 'Ill-minded priests in all ages', he wrote, 'wrapt up the amiable *truths* of religion in a cloud of hard names, and cooked them up like *French ragouts*, with so many different ingredients, that no body knows what to make of them.'[1]

> ' If the cause of High-Church be not the very worst in the world, it is impossible that it should ever fail, being so strongly surrounded with temporal encouragements without, and secured with early-imbib'd prejudices within . . . and its only enemies are beggarly *truth* and naked *honesty*.'[2]

Amhurst's journalistic efforts with their unerring perception of where the enemy cause was weakest must be treated cautiously, but the effect of his criticisms was considerable. 'Methinks it could not do any great hurt to the universities', he wrote at the start of his series, 'if the old fellows were to be jobed at least once in four or five years for their irregularities, as the young ones are every day, if they offend.'[3] He could rest assured that the old fellows had been 'jobbed' and that the University had once more been held up to ridicule and contempt.

The commonly accepted opinion of Oxford found expression in a comedy written by a young graduate of Wadham, James Miller, *The Humours of Oxford*, which John Wesley amused himself by reading soon after its publication. The plot is an involved and farcical rigmarole, and the Oxford characters who appear are singularly unattractive. They include Haughty, a don described as 'an imperious, pedantick unmannerly Pedagogue, of a vile life and vicious principles', and a friend of his, Conundrum, full of counterfeit learning and punning but fundamentally a hypocrite who liked nothing better than to get into the bed of a young Oxford 'jilt', Kitty.[4] There was an Oxford scholar, Ape-Hall, played in

---

[1] *Terrae-Filius*, 8.

[2] *Op. cit.*, 234.

[3] His appeal is indeed to the young reader: 'Why should a poor undergraduate be called an *idle rascal*, and a *good for nothing blockhead*, for being perhaps but twice at Chapel in one day, or for coming into college at ten or eleven o'clock at night . . . whilst the grey-headed doctors may indulge themselves in what debaucheries and corruptions they please, with impunity, and without censure.' (*Op. cit.*, 3.)

[4] 'He's as unintelligible as Welsh Puddle. . . . He is more fond of making a quibble, than making himself understood. . . . When I came to his Chamber, I found him

the theatre by Mr. Cibber and depicted as a typical 'smart', a 'trifling ridiculous fob, affecting Dress and Lewdness, and a Contemner of Learning'.

'I have flourished my Studies. . . . I have been a downright drudge to 'em . . . what between Dressing, Dancing, Intriguing, the Tennis-Court and Tavern, I am so completely taken up . . . my first two years, I had a good-for nothing, musty Fellow for a Tutor, who made me read Latin and Greek. . . .'

'Why,' he exclaims of the don, 'he is a Fellow of A College; that is to say, a Rude, Hoggish, Proud, Pedantick, Gormandizing Drone—a drearing, dull Sot, that lives and rots, like a Frog in a Ditch, and goes to the Devil at last, he scarce knows why.'

Further he is 'a furious High-Churchman, with nothing but Ignorance, which is the Mother of their devotion'.

In one scene the Vice-Chancellor finds the two dons the worse for drink.

'In what manner must we expect to be talk'd of by the world . . . it must inevitably be our Ruin, if not seasonably put a Stop to,' he declares, 'and this Place which is the daily parent of so many brave and bright spirits . . . instead of being a Seminary of learning and good Manners, would degenerate into a Nursery of Ignorance and Debauchery.'

In the fourth act the don, Haughty (played at the Theatre Royal by Mr. Harper), sang the following song:

> What Class in Life, tho' ne'er so great
> With a good Fellowship can compare?
> We still dream on at our old rate
> Without perplexing Care. . . .
>
> An easier Round of Life we keep
> We eat, we Drink, we Smoak, we sleep
> And then, then, then
> Rise and do the same again.

It was hardly surprising that Miller's play should have created some consternation in Oxford where it was thought some of the characters

---

entrench'd amongst a Parcel of musty old Books, like a Bug in a Bedstead—with half a Dozen Woollen Nightcaps on his Head; a short black Pipe in his Mouth; a great pair of Spectacles on his Nose; and a Book in his hand.' (*The Humours of Oxford* (1730), 47.)

were easily identifiable. It at least finished his own chances of promotion as far as the University was concerned, nor did his Bishop regard the dramatic productions which came from the pen of this playwright and parson as wholly satisfactory recommendations to preferment.[1]

There can be little doubt that long before Gibbon and other famous men added their own particular chorus of denunciation the public had learned to associate the University with good if coarse-mannered living, with neglect of scholarship and with reactionary principles. While there were some grounds for all these charges, it was the University's association with politics and religion which accounted for the publicity given to its other defects. Few ever considered whether it was not failing to provide a home of scholarship and a school of culture.

(ii) *The University and Politics*

Politics did much to condition the history of the University in the eighteenth century and accounted for the reputation or lack of it which it enjoyed in the outside world. The majority of the dons subscribed to what was currently called the High-Church tradition and hoped to maintain the predominance of the Anglican Church and the hereditary succession. They had greeted the accession of the Stuart Churchwoman Anne with effusive gallantry and basked in the patronage she had showered, even if she would not act as an instrument of Oxford High Churchmanship. The accession of George I was welcomed by only a few interested partisans; some were vocally in favour of the Pretender but would have been unlikely to raise a sword to support him.

> 'That there were Oxford men who, when out of the country, would drink the health of the Duke of Ormonde everyone, including the government, knew, but the University occupied no place in the Pretender's conspiratorial plans.'[2]

The government, however, thought otherwise, and instead of seeking to buy the favour of the majority who were sitting on the fence, it withdrew its patronage from all but the convinced supporters of the Whig administration. As a result the majority of the Oxford residents outside those Colleges, Wadham, Merton, Exeter and Christ Church, where the

---

[1] Cf. 'Well, happy are those Gentlemen that can send their Sons to *Oxford* for Education; for they are in as fair a way to come to Preferment.' (*Op. cit.*, 53.)

[2] W. R. Ward, *Georgian Oxford, University Politics in the Eighteenth Century* (1958), 150 ff., to which I am much indebted for what follows in this section.

government had a majority of supporters, remained critical of the Whig regime and fostered a spirit of political independence. The scene was indeed very confused; but there was a separation between the University and the political establishment which had a detrimental effect on the University's domestic life, fostering dissension in the Colleges and corrupt elections.

The first reaction of official opinion had favoured the Hanoverian succession:

> 'The gentlemen here who were rampant four days ago,' Dr. Stratford of Christ Church wrote on 2nd August, 1714, 'begin to turn upon their heel very quickly. Delaune [the President of St. John's] ordered King George to be prayed for yesterday morning in St. John's Chapel, when it was objected that it was not certain the Queen was dead. "Dead," says he, "she is as dead as Julius Caesar."'

At the ordinance on Wednesday night the President of Trinity toasted the Earl of Oxford. Delaune said then, 'He is out, what do you toast him for? What have we to do with him?'[1] The Vice-Chancellor, Dr. Gardiner, led loyal opinion being 'very zealous to pay his duty to the King'; but buttered poems and addresses brought comparatively small return, and loyalty became more reluctant. With a strange lack of wisdom, the victorious politicians dispensed their patronage on political lines; if this did not encourage Jacobitism, it discouraged the government's somewhat lukewarm supporters from undertaking strong measures to repress disaffection.

There was a rising tide of criticism sufficient to alarm the ministers. In fact the University was about to feel the cold shoulder of political disapproval, as its critics and opponents seized the reins of power and patronage. A fellow of St. John's hinted in a University sermon 'at some of our modern tyrants and usurpers . . . meaning particularly ye present Elector of Brunswick'. Dr. Hayward of the same College was reported to have said that 'K. George had suspended his favours at present from ye University by some representations'. Neither the undergraduates (or for that matter the junior fellows of Colleges), nor the townsmen of Oxford were averse to making use of opportunities for displaying the nature of their sympathies or for having a riotous evening. The convenient proximity of Restoration Day (29th May) and the new King's birthday (28th May), followed by the Pretender's birthday (10th June), afforded pretexts for trouble.

[1] *Hist. MSS., Comm. Portland MSS.*, vii, 197, 198.

On 28th May, 1715, the Constitution Club, a small but talkative group of Whig residents, met at the King's Head to celebrate the royal birthday. A bonfire was lit, a crowd collected, and the disaffected scholars, who had thronged the houses and streets near the tavern, continued throwing up their caps, scattering money amongst the rabble, and crying 'Down with the constitutioners', 'Down with the Whigs'; 'No G[eorg]e; Ja[me]s for ever. . . .' The mob not unnaturally got out of hand, broke all the illuminated windows they could find, and sacking the Presbyterian meeting-place, seized its pulpit to use it as the main source of fuel for a bonfire at Carfax. The next day they broke windows which were not illuminated to commemorate the restoration of Charles II.

These riots provided the government with an excuse to strengthen its hold on the University. The Vice-Chancellor and the Heads of the Houses took precautions to prevent a recurrence of trouble; but a series of minor incidents kept alive the government's suspicions of the University's loyalty. As a loyal officer commented in a moment of exasperation: 'I never was in such a damned, villanous, hellish place.' The flight of the University's Chancellor, Ormonde, and the subsequent election of his brother, Lord Arran, aroused distrust, more especially as Arran's inauguration was carried out amidst great rejoicing. The government decided to divert Colonel Pepper's regiment to Oxford, where it arrived early on the morning of 9th October; subsequently ten or eleven suspected Jacobites were arrested, though the leading suspect, Colonel Owen, got over Magdalen wall in his nightshirt. On 28th October Brigadier Handasyde's regiment was quartered in the city, and Oxford was placed virtually in the hands of the military.

> King George, observing with judicious eyes
> The state of both his universities,
> To Oxford sent a troop of horse; and why?
> That learned body wanted loyalty.
> To Cambridge books he sent, as well discerning,
> How much that loyal body wanted learning.[1]

When the Constitution Club sought to celebrate King George's birthday in 1716, there was again the promise of riot; and when it seemed as if the Junior Proctor was about to intervene, the Club's steward, Richard Meadowcourt of Merton, halted the proceedings by proposing the royal

[1] John Wesley was sufficiently intrigued by this rhyme to copy it out in his first Oxford diary.

toast. Later, Meadowcourt was fined 40s. by the Senior Proctor, John White of Christ Church, and put in the Black Book, an action which had the effect of debarring him from the master's degree until he had satisfied the proctorial authorities. The University Whigs made much of this and other persecutions in an effort to win popular support; but their temerity made even the moderates anti-ministerial in feeling. When a young fellow of Jesus of Whig sympathies, Peter Maurice, preached a University sermon which seemed heterodox in some of its statements, it was not only the moderate Tory, Dr. Delaune, but the Whig professor of Divinity, John Potter, who together condemned him. The moderate Whigs, ready as they were to support the politics of the ministry, fought shy of encouraging any movement which might seem to imperil the Church. The authorities grumbled; but there was no further trouble until 30th October, 1716, the birthday of the Prince of Wales. On this day the Constitution Club decided to celebrate the occasion with a dinner at the Star Inn to which they invited a number of officers. It was later asserted that the Major of the regiment commanded his soldiers to break the windows of all townsmen who had failed to engage in loyal illumination. 'Come in, Boys, and drink, and then go out and do it again.' Trouble naturally followed, leading to some violence. The Whigs refused to believe that the soldiers had initiated the trouble, though it was very likely so, and the University's loyalty was further impeached. 'If', as Archbishop Wake wrote to Dr. Gardiner, the Vice-Chancellor, 'there be no disaffection in ye Universitys to the present government . . . I may truly say you are very unfortunate in the reports wch. everywhere spread abroad.'

Rumours of disloyalty served the interests of the University's critics who were not slow to seek to persuade the government to curb further its privileges. It is not altogether easy to analyse the ingredients of this onslaught; but it is important to observe that it set the tone for the recurrent criticisms levelled at the University until the middle of the nineteenth century, and indeed did much to determine historical judgements passed on the eighteenth-century University. Doubtless many of the supporters of the Hanoverian regime had exaggerated notions about the extent of Jacobite opinion in the University, but all the evidence would suggest that Jacobitism of action amongst graduates and undergraduates had in it little more than verbal disloyalty.

The prospect of a Statute to regulate the Universities became suddenly and alarmingly close. Early in 1716 Townshend, after consulting with Prideaux, Cowper, the Lord Chancellor, the Lord Chief Justice and the

Archbishop,[1] considered a bill for controlling the Universities, and the suggestion was renewed after the October riots in Oxford. The bill as then drafted proposed that the Crown should have the right to nominate to all offices in the Universities and Colleges, from Heads of Houses to commoners, for a limited period of years. This was a singularly ruthless document which would have placed the Universities at the mercy of the political party then in power. Moreover, the extent to which as a result of fertile pamphleteering the Universities appeared to many to have become nurseries of sedition is revealed by the ready support which men of moderate views were ready to give the bill. Archbishop Wake, for instance, replying to the remonstrances of the Warden of All Souls, felt that the government was acting judiciously. The government, however, again held its fire as Cowper persuaded the ministers that it would be better to postpone the presentation of the bill until the Occasional Conformity Act had been repealed. The possible presentation of the bill and a visitation of the Universities were still under discussion in 1718 and 1719. It was only the rejection of the Peerage Bill and the consequential division within the ministry which ended all prospects for the proposed Universities measure.

It is hardly surprising that threatened government action augmented the unpopularity of its adherents in the University, roused the indignation of the moderates who resented the threat to their independence, and stimulated the hot-headed to inexpedient and rash criticism. But the group of government supporters, though small, was arrogant. Gathered together in the Constitution Club, they asserted their loyalty loudly and whenever the slightest evidence presented itself unearthed latent treason.

The majority of Oxford graduates remained reluctant to adopt the subservient line taken by members of the Constitution Club, albeit there is little to suggest that their dislike of the existing regime was in any practical way linked with treasonable activity. There was a spate of indignant ripostes to the hostile pamphleteers. John Allibond's *Seasonable Sketch of an Oxford Reformation* was designed to show that Toland and his colleagues were like the regicides of 1648. The Warden of All Souls, a controversialist by nature, defended his tenure of the Vice-Chancellor's office which had coincided with the troubles of 1715–16. But defence by interested partisans made inevitably less impact on popular opinion than the more widely spread attacks. There were a few who found it difficult to keep silent under provocation. Among them the Professor of Poetry,

[1] On Wake's attitude see Norman Sykes, *William Wake*, II, 132–4.

Thomas Warton, who had already revealed his anti-Hanoverian sympathies in a satirical ballad, *The Turnip Hoer*, preached the University Sermon on Restoration Day (29th May) in the course of which he stated that Justice beareth all things, hopeth all things, and *restoreth* all things; subsequently Meadowcourt and his friends denounced him for sedition to the Vice-Chancellor and the Secretary of State. Earlier, the Principal of Brasenose, Robert Shippen, whose brother, William, was the proto-Jacobite leader in the House of Commons, had moved in Convocation in December, 1717, what amounted to a vote of censure of the King's German policy:

> 'This the only infelicity of his Majesty's Reign,' so he observed with due caution, 'that He is unacquainted with our Language and constitution, and it is therefore the more Incumbent on His British Ministers to inform Him, that our Government does not stand on the same foundation with His German dominions.'

Shippen's resolution was rejected by 189 votes to 96, a sure indication that moderate opinion was still in control at Oxford.

Although the government had by the third decade of the century abandoned the idea of direct control over the University, the ministers were still anxious and angry about the extent of political dissent in the University. If they wished to win support, two courses were open to them; they could bring pressure to bear in internal College affairs, partly by interest, partly by the influence of College visitors, or they could dispense patronage. As a result of the use which was made of the first of these courses, there opened an extremely complex, exceptionally unscrupulous and often indecisive series of College disputes,[1] by means of which the Whig residents sought to secure control over their governing bodies. The final effect of these struggles made certain Colleges ministerial strongholds, more especially Jesus, Merton, Wadham, Christ Church and Exeter. Other Colleges which were sometimes the scene of fierce conflict remained divided or, as was the case with Lincoln, continued to be independent Tory in opinion and composition. In spite of the animus to which these disputes had given rise the results were politically inconclusive.

There remained patronage. Skilfully employed at the very start of the reign, it might at least have forestalled the opposition of the moderates to the government. In fact, however, the only significant beneficiaries of the new regime were its partisans. Potter became Bishop of Oxford. John

---

[1] W. R. Ward, *Georgian Oxford*, esp. 97–118.

Wynne, the Principal of Jesus, was given the see of St. Asaph in 1715. Robert Clavering, a former undergraduate of Lincoln and a fellow of University College, was appointed to a canonry of Christ Church and the Regius Professorship of Hebrew in the same year, *en route* for the see of Llandaff (and the more congenial deanery of Hereford) and eventually the bishopric of Peterborough. Most of the other appointments of Oxford men to the episcopal bench made in the first half-century were also of safe government partisans.

When the number of Heads of Houses, professors and fellows of Colleges is considered, it would seem that Oxford received less than its share of patronage. The sensible Bishop of London, Edmund Gibson, upon whom for a time Walpole placed so much reliance in ecclesiastical matters, realized that government patronage would best foster a sense of loyalty, and with this in mind he persuaded the government to institute a scheme which might, had it had effective government support, have done much to strengthen a genuine and in many ways admirable association between the government and the University. A plan was put into operation for creating, at Oxford and Cambridge, what were to be known as the Whitehall preacherships. Twelve chaplains from each University were to be appointed for a month to officiate in the King's chapel at Whitehall; for their services each was to receive £30 and, presumably, the expectation of future preferment. But, more important, twenty young men were to be given places at the government's expense in each University and there to be trained in Modern History and Modern Languages in order that they might be employed after graduation in the royal service. The King endowed a Regius Professorship of Modern History in 1724 to provide for their teaching; out of his stipend of £400 the professor had to pay for instructors in Modern Languages.

This interesting project started well. The newly appointed professor, David Gregory, was more conscientious than many of his successors, sending annual reports to the government on the capabilities of his scholars. But all these plans failed, less because of lack of enthusiasm in the University than because the government was unwilling to make any real use of the scholars whom it had selected and caused to be trained. Gregory could not fight government indifference and in 1736 received the reward of his loyalty by nomination to the deanery of Christ Church. His successor, William Holmes, expressed his readiness to make 'His Majesty's benefaction to the University effectual', but since the government never actually employed any of the fourteen scholars he named, he could with a clear conscience devote himself to his duties as Vice-Chancellor and as President of St. John's, a post which he had held since 1728.

It is not without significance that Holmes had been elected to the headship of his College in 1728, for it showed that the governing political opinion was steadily winning more ground in Oxford, as moderation prevailed. A new generation of Whig dons was appearing, men like Conybeare, Burton of Corpus, Fanshawe of Christ Church, less sycophantic, ready to sustain the independence of the University; but ready also to support the ministerial cause in academic and political elections.

The political climate of Oxford, however, remained unsympathetic towards the ministry. There was no notion of genuine disloyalty to the Crown; but the electors of Oxford, for the most part ordained ministers, felt more keenly about their independence and that of the Church, with the result that less than their fair share of the considerable patronage at the disposal of the Crown and ministry fell to their lot. It was not until the reign of George III that Oxford once more became the favoured apologist of both Crown and Church, and the loyal son of both. It was hardly accidental that Lord Lichfield should have been succeeded as Chancellor in 1772 by Lord North.

The story of the part that Oxford played or ceased to play in national politics has been emphasized, because it did so much to condition its intellectual and ecclesiastical history. It was not merely that the bitter and unseemly squabbles inside so many of the Colleges tended to destroy respect for the fellows; but learning and creative writing were discouraged, and a parochialism of attitude was fostered which continued to influence the University's attitude to the outside world until the reforms in the middle of the next century. It was this rather than the lack of learning and research which lowered the intellectual temperature of the place. In these circumstances the reputation of the University sank lower than it had ever done. It became associated in the popular mind with treasonable opinion, loose living, lack of scholarship and Laodicean religion.

(iii) *The University and Religion*

The religious tradition of the University was also unpopular with the leading authorities in the state in the first half of the eighteenth century. This was partly, perhaps mainly, because of the support which High

Churchmen had given to the notion of passive obedience,[1] with its implied criticism of the Hanoverian dynasty and its lingering devotion to the prince over the sea.[2]

It was, however, not simply a matter of politics. The theological learning of Oxford supported ideas that were in many quarters regarded with dislike, and were believed by some to be definitely untenable. The majority of its dons would have subscribed to learned but somewhat controversial High-Churchmanship. This did not mean that they would have identified themselves with the Non-jurors,[3] though some of the more devout High Churchmen, John Wesley among them, greatly sympathized with their theology. It does suggest, however, that the contemporary religious feeling of Oxford was equally unsympathetic towards Latitudinarianism and Erastianism, Enthusiasm and Pietism. It drew its spiritual nourishment from patristic studies which had been its principal contribution to research in the seventeenth century, and from a theological and catholic tradition which embraced both Richard Hooker and William Laud. Its academic performance dated back to the previous century; but the works of Grabe[4] and Potter[5] showed that its interest in patristic learning was not moribund.

Thus while the religious life of its College chapels was conventional and in many ways arid, the University stood theologically for a conception of the Church, its officers and its sacraments, more in accord with the teaching of the Caroline divines than with that of the fashionable Latitudinarian

---

[1] The College library at Lincoln is for instance exceptionally rich in literature relating to Sacheverell, showing the interest shown by contemporaries in the issues he had raised.

[2] In his first diary John Wesley copied out a contemporary rhyme which obviously reflected his own sympathies:

> In Cana's Town our Lord was pleas'd
> With Bridal Folk to dine,
> And to compliment the Ruler's Feast
> Turn'd Water into Wine
> But when for Joy of George's Birth
> Our Rulers mounted your Theatre
> Heaven would not countenance your Mirth,
> But turned the claret into water.

[3] J. H. Overton, *The NonJurors* (1902); H. Broxap, *The Later Non-Jurors* (1924); George Every, *The High Church Party, 1688–1718* (1956).

[4] *Spicilegium SS. Patrum ut et hereticorum seculi post Christum natum*, 2 vols. (1714). Cf. p. 273.

[5] See p. 38.

writers. Its teaching on the great questions of revelation and reason, on dogma and miracle, on the Trinity, was conventionally orthodox; the books recommended by its tutors were more likely to be Bull and Pearson, Sprat and Atterbury, Smalridge and South than Clarke, Tillotson and Locke.[1] It thus became suspect not merely as a home of political dissent but of potential priestcraft and sacerdotalism, criticized by the Latitudinarians for its suspicion of reason and science, and attacked by the deists as a home of academic, political and religious reaction. It rejected the amorphous conception of the Church implied in Benjamin Hoadly's famous sermon and in the Bangorian controversy was violently hostile to him.

In the main, then, the University was on the defensive, and its critics, albeit often opposed to each other, were likely to have the ear of the influential public. A review of the sermons preached before the University would suggest that orthodoxy and an avoidance of extremes were expected of its preachers. Its officials might sympathize with the aims of John Wesley and his companions, but they could not accept the demonstrative pietism and enthusiasm with which they became associated. The University, through the infiltration of government supporters into some of the Colleges, was kept constantly aware of the dangers presented by the growing intrusion of theological points of view which were not specifically its own; yet a continuous tradition linked the patristic learning of the Caroline dons with the famous Dr. Routh, President of Magdalen from 1791 until his death in 1854, whose studies were so much in line with those of the century in which he was born.

It feared both the neo-Arianism of Samuel Clarke and Whiston, and the deism of Tindal and Toland. What might happen if an unorthodox cleric was elected to the headship of a College had been shown by the fate of Exeter under Arthur Bury, who wrote a book, *The Naked Gospel*, which had raised the question as to whether the doctrine of the Incarnation was a necessary part of Christianity.[2] Fear of the infiltration of deism among the undergraduates was widespread. 'My brother', wrote Nicholas Stevens, a young fellow of Trinity, who became a deist, 'I take to be a sceptical Christian, and therefore while he hopes Christianity may be true, does not care to give so much countenance to Deism, or to say he

[1] See the lists of Wesley's own reading which must have been in many ways typical of other young dons of his generation, pp. 305 ff.

[2] See C. W. Boase, Introduction to the *Register of Exeter College* (1894), cxxviii–cxxxiii.

doubts of the truth of Christianity.'[1] John Wesley's brother, Samuel, published a hard-hitting reply to Stevens' arguments.[2] In 1730 *Fog's Weekly Journal* complained that Magdalen was infested with deists on the strength of the expulsion of two members of the College; 'On Friday, June 12,' Hearne wrote, 'Mr. Pescod, a young M.A. & Demy of Magd. Coll., Mr. Lisle, Mr. Wells & Mr. Barnes, three Bach. Demys of the same Coll., were convened before the President &c., and on Thursday morn, June 18, Pescod and Wells were expelled the College for Blasphemy and other vile Practices.'[3] While deistic and similar writings were less dangerous than they appeared to be, there can be little doubt that the University feared the spread of unorthodoxy as the circular letter from the Vice-Chancellor and Heads of Houses in 1729 showed.[4]

To many Whig politicians and Latitudinarian Bishops the teaching and standpoint of the University, coupled with its support of clerical privilege, seemed politically dangerous, academically old-fashioned and, to use a term unknown to contemporary writers, reactionary.

(iv) *The Scandal and Achievement of Oxford*

The vituperative attacks on the University would have been less harmful if there had not been a measure of truth in the picture of slothful and self-indulgent living and indifference to learning which most of them portrayed. Yet because there were scandals, it should not be thought that self-indulgence and loose living were typical of all or even of a majority of the senior members of the University. At every period its social life tends to reflect contemporary custom. It is therefore not surprising in an age marked by 'deep potations' and heavy gambling that senior and junior common rooms should in some respects mirror these things. Dr. Delaune, the President of St. John's, reputed an exceptionally heavy gambler, for instance, was so heavily in debt that he converted to his own use, if but temporarily, the income received from the sale of Clarendon's *History*. Evidence of heavy drinking abounds. Richard Graves, who matriculated at Pembroke in 1732 and later became a fellow of All Souls, described the cliques of undergraduates who existed at his College. One,

---

[1] Quoted in A. Léger, *La Jeunesse de Wesley* (1910), 30–1*.

[2] *Two Letters from a Deist to his friend concerning the Truth and Propagation of Deism in opposition to Christianity* (1730), printed in full in Léger, *op. cit.*, 28*–47*.

[3] Hearne, *Collectanea*, x, 297. Robert Wells of Grantham had originally entered Lincoln College as a commoner on 2nd May, 1726.

[4] See p. 147–8.

'a set of jolly, sprightly young fellows . . . drank ale, smoked tobacco, punned and sung bacchanalian catches the whole evening', while another, consisting of gentlemen commoners, 'treated me with port-wine and arrack-punch; and now and then, when they had drank so much as hardly to distinguish wine from water, they would conclude with a bottle or two of claret. They kept late hours, drank their favourite toasts on their knees, and, in short, were what were then called "bucks" of the first head.'[1] There were naturally graver irregularities; but these were the inevitable concomitants of a masculine and celibate society. It is unlikely that the morals of undergraduates in the first half of the eighteenth century were noticeably worse than they were at earlier or later dates. It may be rather more unusual to find the breath of scandal touching the senior common rooms, more especially as the majority of the dons were in Anglican orders; but many of the University clergy had neither then nor later a deep sense of vocation to the Christian ministry. Given the conditions of a fellowship, this is not altogether curious. A fellowship provided a means of security as well as comparative comfort, but it nearly always entailed ordination and celibacy. Nor is it surprising that absence of vocation should not seldom have resulted in scandal. There were fellows of Colleges who made use of the facilities offered by the fair ladies of the town, or were obliged to satisfy their passions by irregular unions. If there was also an element of sexual perversion, this was perhaps made the more probable by the essentially masculine nature of University society. Hearne, not always a trustworthy guide, mentioned the case of John Pointer, a chaplain of Merton College, accused of 'sodomitical practises' and 'advised to go off from the College, and forbid reading Prayers as Chaplain there any more'.[2] He proceeded gloomily: 'This and other Vices are becoming so common in England, being spread from beyond sea and from a most loose Court at London where there is no Religion, that they are not by many looked upon as sins.'

Oxford society was, however, much perturbed by the state of affairs revealed at Wadham College after a charge of homosexuality had been levelled against the Warden, Robert Thistlethwayte, in 1739.[3] On Saturday,

---

[1] R. Graves, *Recollections of some particulars in the life of the late William Shenstone* (1788), 15–16.

[2] Hearne, *Collectanea*, xi, 133.

[3] See, for instance, a very outspoken pamphlet, *A faithful Narrative of the Proceedings in a late affair between the Rev. John Swinton and Mr George Baker both of Wadham College, Oxford* (London, 1739).

3rd February, 1739, the Warden had summoned an undergraduate of the College, William French,[1] to his lodgings and behind locked doors had made passionate approaches to him. When French eventually emerged for supper at six, he seemed much disturbed, and astonished his friends by calling the Warden the worst of scoundrels and by saying that he could get him expelled from the College. His friends thought that he had taken leave of his senses and warned him that if he continued to talk in that way he would be turned out of the College. Eventually one of them, George Baker,[2] persuaded French to reveal what had occurred. French was himself distraught because he feared that if he protested, he would be sent down without a degree, nor was he ready to talk to his tutor, the Rev. John Swinton, who he rightly believed would side with the Warden. Baker himself sent for two of the fellows, Mr. Stone and Mr. Watkins, the latter a former associate of John Wesley's,[3] who advised French to apply to the Vice-Chancellor. The latter told him to get a *testimonium* from his College. This involved getting a signature from the Warden, who had so far been kept in the dark. When Thistlethwayte learned what was happening, the unhappy man begged French to keep quiet, saying that they would both be ruined. 'My Dear,' he said, 'I'll give you any Thing; nay, all that I am worth in the world, if you will not expose me.' But neither the young man nor his father who had come to Oxford nor the majority of the fellows would agree to this course. Indeed further evidence from the Warden's butler and barber showed that he had made similar attempts on their persons, kissing them and 'tickling' their breeches. The barber had at last let fly, knocking the Warden back into his chair with the words 'Damn you—you Son of a Bitch, what do you mean?' Thistlethwayte, subsequently arraigned at the Assizes, broke his bail and fled the country.

The only one of the fellows who had been suspiciously loyal to the Warden had been French's tutor, John Swinton, who was soon shown to be guilty of similar offences, having kept one of the servant's boys, 'lousy, ragged and filthy as he was', in his rooms for some days for the purpose of sexual play. The boy was, however, young and easily browbeaten into denying what he had previously alleged. Although the evidence suggests that Swinton was guilty, his accuser was forced to publish an apology, and was bound over to keep the peace. The Warden died in France and was

[1] Of Merriott, Somerset, 1736. B.A. 1740.
[2] S. of Nicholas B. of Chiselborough, Som. Matric. March, 1734; B.A. 1737.
[3] See pp. 74, 113, 114, 136, 177, 212.

subsequently buried in St. Mary's Church, Dover, but Swinton went on to hold various preferments. A *cause célèbre* should not be allowed to suggest that this was anything but an exceptional offence, but the publicity may well have alarmed some of the more anxious parents. More austere contemporaries were worried by the prevalence of gambling, drinking and luxury, and the consequent tendency to dissipation to which these gave rise.

Ample illustrations abound then to prove that the University, neither in its junior nor its senior common rooms, was wholly free from loose living; but it would be absurd to state that because of a few such instances that it was given over to this particular form of self-indulgence. Such cases made the headlines, then as now, just because they were unusual. There is no reason to suppose that the average undergraduate did not live decently according to the conventions of the period, studied, if not intensely, at least sufficiently, and performed his other exercises; the mass of the undergraduates were neither 'bucks' nor 'smarts'. The majority of the dons were not the coarse-grained clerics billowing in their gowns as depicted by the caricaturist; they did not neglect their ministerial duties, were more conscientious as tutors than is often supposed, and took an interest in politics and theology, particularly where the latter had a political connotation. If to a more recent generation their performance of tutorial duties seems perfunctory, the common understanding of what a fellowship entailed may help to explain this. There is nothing in fact to suggest that the eighteenth-century don was a man of more scandalous character than his successors,[1] or that the average undergraduate was a much better or worse man.

The more serious and better sustained charge of ignorance and inefficiency remains. There is much evidence to indicate that as a centre of scholarship and study the University was in some ways in decline. The government of the University, as laid down by the Laudian statutes of 1636, consisted of three assemblies, the Hebdomadal Board which was virtually the governing council of the University composed of the Vice-Chancellor (selected from the Heads of the Colleges), the proctors and the Heads of Colleges; Congregation mainly composed of residents, the powers of which had become increasingly attenuated; and Convocation

---

[1] An examination of the Senior Common Room at Lincoln (see pp. 88–96), though a society less quarrelsome than that of some other Colleges, supports this statement; it was certainly free from the bickering and personal disputes typical of the next century (see, for instance, V. H. H. Green, *Oxford Common Room, passim*).

or Magna Congregatio which consisted of all those who retained their names on the books of their College. While the latter had no right to initiate legislation, it had the power to reject legislation presented to it. In fact, however, the University was governed by a small group of Heads of Houses. While there were some praiseworthy exceptions, many of these were undoubtedly men of mediocre capacity. Hearne's comments were so often inspired by his political opinions that they must be accepted only with caution; but none can read his pages without feeling that many of the Heads of Colleges lacked the qualifications required for their office. Hearne with his instinctive condemnation of the Whig partisan, Dr. Gardiner of All Souls, the lecherous Dr. Shippen of B.N.C., of Warden Holland of Merton 'common called *dull John* from his stupidity', had a Whig counterpart in Amhurst whose *Terrae Filius* provides a recipe for a College head; take, he said, a 'old heavy country parson' from whom had been extracted 'all Remains of common sense and common honesty' or a 'plotting, intriguing, rakish, drinking' fellow who could be drilled into a 'rigid disciplinarian'. The reality may have been less sombre than Amhurst or Hearne would lead us to believe, but the government of the University was more distinguished by torpor than by intelligence, and for this the Heads of the Colleges bear great responsibility.

The fundamental defect of the early eighteenth-century University lay in the lack of any real incentive to research, more especially as far as its junior members were concerned. The examination system, if not quite the elaborate farce that it had become by the end of the century, had little merit. The actual procedure for obtaining the degrees of B.A. and M.A. was governed by careful regulations designed to ensure a regular series of examinations and disputations; but in fact they would appear already to have become futile. Some were beginning to question the continued hold which the study of Aristotle and Formal Logic had on the curriculum, but no effective change was made until the reforms at the beginning of the next century. Thus the average undergraduate had little stimulus to read outside the mechanical exercises set by his tutor, nor were tutors and lecturers under much pressure to teach or to do original work.

The teaching inside and outside the Colleges had become very perfunctory. There were for the greater part of the period sixteen professorial chairs, supplemented by the foundation of the Regius chair of modern history in 1724. One chair, White's professorship of philosophy, was automatically attached to the senior proctorship. The majority of the other chairs were held by men who were already busy in other posts. John

Potter held the chair of divinity with the bishopric of Oxford; his successor, George Rye, was archdeacon of Oxford. John Fanshawe, who succeeded him, was no doubt a scholarly man and for six years held both the chairs of divinity and Greek; but as a Regius professor he was a ministerial nominee who was concerned with promoting the interests of his patrons. College heads held the Lady Margaret chair of divinity as well as the Regius chair of modern history. In spite of James Hurdis'[1] attempt at a later date to answer the aspersions that Gibbon made against the professoriate in his *Autobiography*, there is little to suggest that these professors did in fact lecture or carry out the work of instruction. While Amhurst's statements must be received cautiously, his comments at this point ring true:

> 'Yesterday morning at nine a clock the bell went as usually for lecture. . . . I went to the schools, big with hopes of being instructed . . . and having saunter'd a pretty while along the quadrangle, impatient of the lecturer's delay, I ask'd the *major* (who is an officer belonging to the schools) whether it was usual now and then to slip a lecture or so; his answer was, that he had not seen the face of any *lecturer* in any faculty, except in *poetry* and *musick*, for three years past. . . . Every *thursday* morning in term time there ought to be a *divinity* lecture in the *divinity* school: two gentlemen of our house went one day to hear what the learned professor had to say upon that subject; these two were joined by another *master of arts* . . . the doctor . . . was very much surprised to find that there was an audience. He took two or three turns about the school, and then said, *Magistri, vos non estis idonei auditores; praeterea, juxta legis doctorem Boucher, tres non faciunt collegium-valete;* and so went away.'[2]

'The silence of the Oxford professors,' wrote Edward Gibbon, 'which deprives the youth of public instruction, is imperfectly supplied by the tutors, as they are styled, of the several colleges.' Yet if he condemned the second of his tutors, Dr. Winchester, who 'well remembered that he had a salary to receive, and only forgot that he had a duty to perform' as totally neglectful, he described his first tutor, Dr. Waldegrave, formerly of Lincoln College, as 'a learned and pious man, of a mild disposition, strict morals and abstemious life'.[3] It is easy to see why many of the tutors

[1] J. Hurdis, *A word or two in vindication of the University of Oxford and of Magdalen College* (1800), 36, 41.
[2] N. Amhurst, *Terrae-Filius*, 51.
[3] See p. 131-3.

appeared to be negligent. The syllabus was unrelated to any approaching examination; its content was unlikely to seize the imagination of the average undergraduate or spur the tutor to research. He taught mechanically rather than sedulously, and if a pupil preferred the attractions of the tavern or the chase he did not feel that it was incumbent on him to demand his attention. It is almost equally easy to understand why the majority of the professors ceased to lecture. It was by no means apparent what duties or obligations were attached to a professorial chair, and since much at least of what the professors would have lectured on would have been irrelevant to the curriculum of the University they could hardly have expected to have commanded a large audience. Indeed it may be surmised that the system of lectures broke down because no one really wanted to attend. For the busy man whose stipend as a professor was small, such lectures might have been rightly regarded as a waste of time.[1] It is clear that the failure to establish a teaching chair in modern history was at least in part the responsibility of the government which had endowed it but provided no real stimulus for the professor to teach.

It is surprising that, given these conditions, so much teaching was done, so much was read by undergraduate and don alike, that in so much the light of learning and research was kept burning, if a trifle dimly. Not all the professors failed to lecture. James Bradley, who became Savilian Professor of Astronomy in 1722 and with unusual single-mindedness resigned his ecclesiastical preferments, did not at first live in Oxford; but in 1732 he moved to a house in New College Lane and delivered lectures to comparatively large audiences in the Ashmolean Museum. Professorial lectures, save those delivered by the professors of poetry, were, however, exceptional. While the evidence is not easy to adduce, it appears that many tutors in the Colleges tried to do their duty conscientiously. Wesley spoke appreciatively of his tutor at Christ Church and himself proved a most conscientious tutor at Lincoln. Whitefield's tutor at Pembroke was solicitous and kind. Richard Edgeworth, who went to Corpus as a gentleman commoner in 1761, described his tutor as 'excellent' and under his supervision he applied himself 'assiduously not only to my studies . . . but also to the perusal of the best English writers, both in prose and verse'. Many undergraduates used their time at the University to read widely in classical and other literature. Richard Graves was at first associated in his early

---

[1] Such was the complaint of Edward Nares, an early nineteenth-century professor of modern history. Cf. G. Cecil White, *A Versatile Professor. Reminiscences of Rev. Edward Nares* (1903), 236–7, 245.

days at Pembroke with 'a very sober little party, who amused themselves in the evening with reading Greek and drinking water. Here, I continued six months, and we read over Theophrastus, Epictetus, Phalaris's Epistles, and such other Greek authors as are seldom read at school.'

In fact the University continued to be the home of scholarship and learning in spite of some intellectual decline. The contemporary conception of a fellowship at a College was different from that of our day; it was, like a scholarship, an award already earned by a reputation for scholarship. It was not intended as a means to further research or to the production of learned work. A few of the fellows acted as tutors in their Colleges but many of the rest were only infrequently resident; it was no part of their plan to remain fellows for the remainder of their lives. As soon as a College living appeared vacant they forsook Oxford with suggestive speed. As a result of this College fellowship system parochial life was enriched by some well-read parish priests. The existing fellowship system certainly paid too little attention to intellectual merit, but the standard of conversation and reading in the Oxford Senior Common Rooms was not as low as satirists supposed it to be. It is impossible to read Hearne's *Collectanea* without glimpsing something of the intellectual curiosity of early eighteenth-century Oxford, particularly in the field of antiquarian studies, and if a survey of Wesley's life at Oxford does nothing else, it reveals the comparatively civilized society in which he moved. The attention paid by historians to virulent quarrels among the dons would sometimes lead one to believe that they were engaged in nothing but intrigue, but there was a better side to life in a Senior Common Room. A study of the contemporary catalogues of the College libraries would show a readiness to buy widely.

An interest in learning ordinarily manifests itself in the production of scholarly books. Any judgement made about book production at this period must be cautious. The intellectual interests of the eighteenth-century don were different from those of his twentieth-century successor; nor are all twentieth-century professors fertile in the making of books. Oxford, however, lacked classical scholars of the genius of Richard Bentley as Christ Church found to its cost in the Phalaris controversy. Save for Thomas Shaw's observations on the Middle East,[1] a book which

---

[1] Shaw had been chaplain to the English factory at Algiers. He held the professorship of Greek (1741–51) with the principalship of St. Edmund Hall as well as the livings of Godshill, Isle of Wight, and Bramley, Hants. His *Travels or observations relating to several parts of Barbary and the Levant* was published in 1738; there was a supplement in 1746.

went into three editions,[1] the professors of Greek were silent. The Civil lawyers as also the Camden professors of ancient history appear only to have succeeded in producing a single pamphlet in each faculty.[2] The Margaret professors of divinity were too absorbed in the affairs of the University and their Colleges[3] to publish more than the occasional sermon.[4] If this were all that could be said in extenuation of University scholarship at this period, it would be slight indeed. The future primate, John Potter, was, however, an industrious and conscientious patristic and classical scholar who throughout a busy life continued to study and to write.[5] His successor, George Rye, made little impact and had completed his publications[6] before his accession to the professorial chair.

More significant work was, curiously enough, being done in the field of Oriental studies and science. Even Robert Clavering, who was preferred to the chair of Hebrew for his support of the ministry, had at least contributed something to his subject.[7] His successor, Thomas Hunt, who held the chairs of Hebrew and of Arabic, was a sound Oriental scholar,[8]

[1] The third edition was published in 1808.

[2] Henry Brooke's *An appeal to the publick, from an unappellate tribunal; or an impartial enquiry into the rise, progress and extent of visibatorial power* (1740), and Sedgwick Harrison's *An Account of the late election for the University of Oxford together with some incidental remarks on the printed poll* (London, 1722).

[3] William Delaune, professor from 1715 to 1728, became President of St. John's and his successor, Thomas Jenner, professor until 1768, was later President of Magdalen.

[4] Jenner published *Charity and compassion towards men, the occasion of thanksgivings to God, a sermon at the meeting of the governors of the Worcester infirmary* (1752).

[5] As a young fellow of Lincoln he published in 1694 *Variantes Lectiones et Notae ad Plutarchi librum de Audiendis Poetis; et ad Basilii Magni Orationem ad Juvenes.* There followed later *Lycophronis Chalcidiensis Alexandra, cum Graecis Isaaci Tzetzis commentariis &c cura et opera* (1697), a second edition dedicated to Graevius appearing in 1702; *Archaeologia Graeca*, 2 vols. (1697–8); *Clementis Alexandrini Operao quae extant, recognita*, 2 vols. (1715); his theological treatises were published after his death in three volumes in 1753.

[6] Two sermons—*The supremacy of the crown and the power of the church asserted and adjusted* (1714), and *A sermon at the consecration of John Potter, Bp. of Oxford* (1715). Also *A treatise against the nonconforming nonjurors, in answer to the objections which Mr Dodwel and others have brought against the Church of England*, 2 vols. (London, 1719).

[7] *R. Mosis Maimonidis Tractatus duo. 1. De Doctrina Legis, sive educatione puerorum. 2. De Natura et ratione Poenitentiae apud Hebraeos*, being the third and fifth chapters of the first book of the *Yad hachazakah* (Oxford 1705).

[8] *A Fragment of Hippolytus from two Arabic MSS in Bodleian Library* (Vol. IV of Parker's *Bibliotheca Biblica*, 1728); *De Antiquitate, elegantia, utilitate, linguae Arabicae* (1739), his inaugural lecture as Laudian Professor of Arabic; *A Dissertation on Proverbs vii, 22, 23* (1743); *De usu dialectorum Orientalium* (1748), a prefatory discussion to his

defended vigorously by Sir William Jones in 1771 against the aspersions brought against his scholarship a decade earlier by Duperron. John Gagnier, who began his career as a canon regular of the Abbey of St. Genevieve, came to England where he took Anglican orders and received the patronage of Bishop Lloyd of Worcester; subsequently he taught Hebrew at Oxford and in 1724 was made Lord Almoner's professor of Arabic. Although Hearne had only a slight regard for his scholarship, he was in fact a prolific writer and an adequate Oriental scholar.[1] Finally Kennicott, perhaps the most distinguished Hebraist of his age, matriculated at Wadham in 1743–4 and became a fellow of Exeter in 1747. A pupil of Hunt's, most of his life was to be spent in the collation of Hebrew manuscripts.

The University could also boast of the achievements of some of its scientific professors. The professors of medicine added little of distinction to their subject,[2] but astronomy and botany had exponents of international reputation. The Savilian professor of geometry from 1704 to 1742 was the Astronomer-Royal, Edward Halley, a universal genius and an attractive man of whose discoveries even the layman to-day is not unaware.

---

lectures as professor of Hebrew; he translated but did not publish a History of Egypt by Abd Al Latif. Kennicott edited posthumously his *Observations on several Passages in the Book of Proverbs*. Hunt also edited the works of Bishop Hooper of Bath and Wells, and second edition of Thomas Hyde's *Historia veterum Persarum*.

[1] In 1706 he published an edition of the fictitious Joseph Ben Gorion's *History of the Jews* in the original Hebrew with a Latin translation and notes; *L'Eglise Romaine convaincu de dépravation, d'idolatrie, et d'antichristianisme* (The Hague, 1706); *Vindiciae Kircherianae, sive Animadversiones in novas Abrahami Trommii Concordantias Graecas versionis LXX, vulgo dictae interpretum* (1718); issued in folio Abū Al-Fidā's *Life of Mahomet* in Arabic with a Latin translation and notes in 1723; prepared an edition of the same author's *Geography* but only a specimen 72 folio leaves was actually printed in 1726–7 (see *Journal des Savants*, 1727). In 1732 he wrote in French a life of Mahomet, 2 vols., Amsterdam, reprinted in 3 vols. in 1748; and translated into German in 1802–4. He contributed Book 3 to Comte Henri de Boulainvilliers' *La Vie de Mahomed* (1730). He was also the author of 'Lettre sur les Médailles Samaritaines' (in 'Nouvelles de la République des Lettres' in *Journal de Trevoux* (1705), latinized in Ugolinus, *Thesaurus Antiquitatum*, vol. xxviii, 1283); *Tabula nova et accurata exhibens paradigmata omnium conjugationum Hebraicarum* (1710); *Carolina, Ecloga in diem natalem Willielminae Carolinae, serenissimae Principis Walliae* (1719); *Liber Petra Scandali de principio et causa schismatis duarum ecclesiarum Orientalis et Occidentalis, ex Graeco Arabice redditus,* 1721; *Animadversiones in novam Josephi Gorionidis*.

[2] William Woodford, professor from 1730 to 1759, made no published contribution to the subject. His predecessor, Joshua Lasher, wrote *Pharmacopaeus et chymicus symmystae seu pharmacopoeia chymica* (1698 and 1706).

His successor, Nathaniel Bliss, who had been rector of St. Ebbe's since 1736, though less distinguished, was a competent observer, and made communications of scientific import, including observations on Jupiter's satellites in 1742.[1] James Bradley, though owing his early interest in the subject to a scientifically minded uncle rather than his tutors at Balliol, was one of the founders of modern astronomy. This singularly honest and fair-minded cleric whom Halley described in 1717 as 'eruditus iuvenis, qui simul industria et ingenio pollens his studiis promovendis aptissimus natus est'[2] was the discoverer of the aberration of light and nutation.[3] Two of the professors of botany, Gilbert Trowe and Humphrey Sipthorp, made little impact on their subject, but John Jacob Dillenius, who held the chair from 1734 to 1747, had a reputation which extended well outside Oxford.

A list such as this cannot indicate exactly what Oxford contributed to the intellectual life of the nation in the eighteenth century, but it may suggest that the common dismissal of the University as a home of sloth and intrigue is not wholly justified. The way in which the junior members of a University are affected by its ethos is something strangely impalpable and difficult to define. At least there is some evidence, and further research might reveal more, to show that in spite of the well-founded charges made against its learning and efficiency the University continued to contribute to the cultural life of the Church and nation. It is unfortunate but true that reformers always seek to depict the institution they believe they have reformed in blacker colours than the unreformed society originally deserves; their zeal habitually exceeds their discretion.

[1] Bradley's *Miscellaneous Works and Correspondence*.

[2] *Phil. Trans.*, xxx, 853.

[3] See Bradley, *Miscellaneous Works and Correspondence* (Oxford, 1832), and Rigaud, *Life of Bradley*.

CHAPTER III

The Home Background

WHEN John Wesley was elected a fellow of Lincoln College, Oxford, on 17th March, 1726, he had behind him six years' experience of Oxford life which formed a useful and significant preparation for his subsequent tutorial and pastoral work. Yet the influence of his family background, more especially the impact of that dominant personality his mother, was the paramount factor in his early development. The parsonage houses at Epworth and Wroot did not merely provide a family circle, sometimes disturbed by inner tensions but ultimately tied by strong affections; they represented a religious background of mingled churchmanship, of a strong High-Church tradition diluted at source by nonconformity which had been long abandoned by his father and mother.

John's father, Samuel Wesley, if descended from a sixteenth-century primate of Ireland, had been brought up in the Nonconformist tradition at a time when nonconformity had only just escaped from the penumbra of Anglicanism, and carried with it appropriate penalties. Samuel's father and grandfather had been ejected from their livings in 1662,[1] and Samuel was at first intended for the dissenting ministry. His wife's forebears were also of vigorous Nonconformist stock. Her father, Dr. Samuel Annesley, of gentle and even noble lineage,[2] had been a prominent Nonconformist divine, if more moderate in his views than the elder John Wesley,[3] and had been ejected from his living of St. Giles, Cripplegate;[4] subsequently

[1] A. G. Matthews, *Calamy Revised* (1934), 521. Bartholomew Wesley had been ejected from the livings of Charmouth and Catherston Leweston, Dorset; subsequently he practised as a physician, dying in 1670–1. His son, John (who predeceased his father), was ejected from Winterborne Whitchurch, Dorset, and suffered imprisonment. He was a stern Puritan: 'He had most diabolically railed in the pulpit against the late King and his posterity; had extolled Cromwell and said that David and Solomon came far short of him. . . .'

[2] He was a nephew of the Earl of Anglesey; his grandfather (on his mother's side), John White, was a well-known lawyer and M.P. for Southwark.

[3] Wood, *Athenae Oxonienses*, iv, 510.

[4] A. G. Matthews, *Calamy Revised*, 13. Annesley, who died in 1696, was much esteemed by his contemporaries, among them Defoe, who 'wrote a pathetic and

he became minister of a meeting-house in St. Helen's Place, Bishopsgate. Samuel Wesley and Susanna Annesley[1] had discarded their original Non-conformity before marriage, but the Puritan impress was not lost, for the habits of early piety, deeply ingrained, are not easily thrust aside. The ethical impulses and the disciplined austerities of the household at Epworth testify to a powerful Puritan strain.

Since Samuel Wesley was originally intended for the dissenting ministry, he attended a number of dissenting academies before he entered Exeter College, Oxford, as a poor scholar or servitor in August, 1683. According to his son, he had already begun to doubt the dissenting faith in which he had been brought up.

'Some severe invectives being written against the Dissenters,' his son wrote many years later, 'Mr. S. Wesley, being a young man of considerable talents, was pitched upon to answer them. This set him on a course of reading which soon produced an effect different from what had been intended. Instead of writing the wished-for answer, he himself conceived he saw reason to change his opinion, and actually formed a resolution to renounce the Dissenters and attach himself to the Established Church. He lived at this time with his mother[2] and old aunt, both of whom were too strongly attached to the Dissenting doctrine to have borne, with any patience, the disclosure of his design. He, therefore, got up one morning at a very early hour, and, without acquainting any one with his purpose, set out on foot to Oxford and entered Exeter College.'

The high Anglican tradition of Oxford University confirmed the doubts already latent in his mind, with the result that he was ordained deacon at Bromley by Bishop Sprat on 7th August, 1688. The ingredients in his change of allegiance are not obscure. It was in part a psychological reaction to an environment with which he had grown increasingly out of sympathy; the influence of his former headmaster, Henry Dolling, of

---

melodious elegy on his death'. His funeral sermon was preached by Dr. Daniel Williams, the founder of the Library which still bears his name (*Arminian Magazine*, (1792), 33–8).

[1] Annesley had twenty-four children, but only a son and two daughters, Susanna and Elizabeth (married to the eccentric publisher, John Dunton) survived him. One daughter, unknown to him, was married to Oates' colleague, the infamous Thomas Dangerfield.

[2] She was apparently a niece of Thomas Fuller, the church historian. She survived her husband and latterly was helped financially by her son, Samuel.

Dorchester Grammar School, cannot be discounted.[1] His life at the dissenting academies had convinced him that there was a substantial degree of cant and insincerity in nonconformity. His experience was unfortunate but confirmed by the subsequent contact with dissenters.[2] Moreover the cause which had brought distress to his father and grandfather was intellectually weak. He was drawn to the traditionalism of Anglican orthodoxy, more especially to the vigorous and patriotic loyalty so characteristic of the Church of England under the later Stuarts. His emotional and intellectual inclinations were closely, even mystically, attached to a fervent royalism which constituted the deepest of all his attachments. A child of the Restoration—he was born in 1662—he came to Oxford in the heyday of its royalist orthodoxy. He witnessed King James' betrayal of the Church of England, but his daughters, Mary and Anne, embodied those traditions in Church and State which in the elder Wesley's belief had made England the beloved country that for him it so undoubtedly was. The would-be dissenting minister blossomed into the loyal Anglican; henceforward he was a stern opponent and a somewhat undiscerning critic of dissent. It is possible that he realized that the Church of England promised more in the way of preferment to an aspiring cleric, but Samuel was never obviously an ecclesiastical careerist. The liturgy, loyalty and piety of late seventeenth-century Anglicanism, finding reflection in the learning and zeal of Oxford, were more decisive factors in Samuel Wesley's change of allegiance. These blended with a Nonconformist background to give the household at Epworth something of its distinctive quality.

If Samuel Wesley ever hoped for a rich reward he was unfailingly disappointed. Soon after his ordination he resigned a comparatively lucrative

[1] Samuel Wesley's first book, the oddly entitled *Maggots: or Poems on Several Subjects never before handled*, published in 1685, was dedicated to Dolling.

[2] He recalled his experiences at a gathering in Leadenhall Street in 1693 where the majority were dissenters: 'A little after we went to supper: but then the scene was changed; and they all fell a railing at *Monarchy*, and blaspheming the memory of king *Charles* the *martyr*, discoursing of their *calves-head club*, and producing or repeating some verses on that subject. I remember one of the company told us of a design, that they had at their next *calves-head feast*, to have a cold pye served on the table, with either a live *cat* or *hare*, I have forget whether, enclosed; and they contrived to put one of their company who loved *monarchy*, and knew nothing of the matter, to cut it up; whereupon, and on the leaping out of the *cat* or *hare*, they were all to set up a shout, and cry, *Halloo, old puss! to the* honour of the *good old cause*, and to shew their affection to a *commonwealth*.' (S. Wesley, *A Defence of a Letter concerning the Education of Dissenters in their private Academies*, 4.)

naval chaplaincy worth £70 a year, to marry on a curacy worth only £30. In 1694 John Sheffield, the Marquis of Normanby, whose chaplain he then was (and to whom in 1701 he dedicated his *History of the Old and New Testament*), suggested to the Archbishop of Canterbury that he might be a suitable candidate for an Irish bishopric; but neither a mitre nor even a prebendal stall came his way. He had hardly the qualities, good and bad, thought desirable in an eighteenth-century bishop. He was obstinate, passionate, partisan and pedantic; nor was a very genuine piety necessarily a recommendation at that time. He was indeed treated kindly by the Archbishop of York and the Bishop of Salisbury, but his pastoral experience was confined to dreary Lincolnshire villages, interrupted only by attendance in London as a proctor in Convocation.

He was appointed to the Lincolnshire living of South Ormsby in 1690 and subsequently by the Crown to the living of Epworth in 1695. Legend asserted that he had made himself unpopular at South Ormsby by rebuking the mistress of a local magnate, John Saunderson, later Earl of Castleton;[1] but his appointment to Epworth, a living in the gift of the Crown, was a reward for his loyalty to the monarchy, expressed in his mediocre literary compositions. He lived his remaining thirty-eight years at Epworth, holding it from 1725 with the more poorly endowed rectory of nearby Wroot. He would indeed have gone elsewhere and cherished the idea of mission work in India, China, or even Abyssinia, but no effective opening occurred.[2] It became plain that his life's work was to be spent on the chill Lincolnshire flats. 'Most of my friends', he told the Archbishop of York after a particularly bad period in 1705, 'advise me to leave Epworth if e'er I should get from hence. I confess I am not of that mind, because I may yet do good there; and 'tis like a coward, to desert my post because the enemy fire thick upon me. They have only wounded me yet, and I believe CAN'T kill me.'

His principal distraction from parochial troubles, debt and household

[1] John Wesley asserted that the nobleman in question was the Marquis of Normanby and that his father resented the fact that his mistress sought to be on visiting terms with Mrs. Wesley. 'Coming in one day, and finding this intrusive visitant sitting with my mother, he went up to her, took her by the hand, and very fairly handed her out. The nobleman resented the affront so outrageously as to make it necessary for my father to resign the living.' It seems most unlikely that the nobleman in question was Lord Normanby in view of the elder Wesley's friendly contacts later; and much more likely that his appointment to Epworth was a reward for his patriotism.

[2] Adam Clarke, *Memoirs of the Wesley Family*, 96–8.

worries was literary work. For a time he supplemented his income by journalism, contributing to his brother-in-law John Dunton's *Athenian Gazette*.[1] After the *Gazette* came to an end in 1696, he continued to write and publish the mediocre verses which poured in such profusion from his pen; some of these, on the battle of Blenheim, earned him a short-lived sinecure as chaplain in Colonel Lepell's regiment from the Duke of Marlborough. In 1693 his magniloquent and egregious life of Christ in verse was published; in spite of its stilted sonority and some execrable versifying, it proved moderately popular. His *magnum opus* was a learned and prolix work on the book of Job which engaged most of his leisure for some decades and was published shortly after his death. 'It is very prettily bound', Queen Caroline, to whom it was dedicated, told John Wesley when he presented it to her; but very few can ever have plodded through its varied and useless learning. It lay in all its classic erudition profoundly still-born; 'Poor Job! It was his eternal fate to be persecuted by his friends', Bishop Warburton commented. 'His three comforters passed sentence of condemnation upon him, and he has been executed in effigy ever since. He was first bound to the stake by a long catena of Greek fathers: then tortured by Pineda; then strangled by Caryll and afterwards cut up by Wesley and anatomized by Garnet. He was ordained, I think, by a fate like Prometheus, to lie still upon his dunghill, and have his brains sucked out by owls.' Samuel Wesley had only a minor place in the literary history of early eighteenth-century England; but he genuinely loved scholarship and found a true solace in the writing of verse. There can be little doubt that his children were themselves powerfully influenced by the atmosphere of scholarship and poetry which emanated from their father's study.

It was indeed fortunate that the rector of Epworth could find release and relief from parochial clamour. The swampy island of Axholme was a remote outpost of civilized England, hardly approachable by road.[2] Before it had been drained by the Dutch engineer, Cornelius Vermuyden, in the early seventeenth century, it was frequently covered by water. Even in the summer boats laden with corn floated over Haxey Cross to the River Idle. From Westwoodside to Hatfield Woodhouse the water was usually three feet deep; much ground in the parish of Owston was

---

[1] John Dunton had married Mrs. Wesley's sister. On Samuel Wesley and his family, consult Maldwyn Edwards, *Family Circle* (1946), *passim*.

[2] The fullest description of Axholme remains. W. B. Stonehouse, *The History and Topography of the Isle of Axholme* (London, 1839.)

flooded. Epworth standing on a small hillock was thus often isolated from the mainland; it is the 'best uplandish town for building in one streate in the Isle', Leland had commented in the sixteenth century. In 1626 Cornelius Vermuyden began the work of drainage, thus uncovering much fertile land; yet, even so, in winter the waters from the neighbouring rivers, the Idle, the Trent and the Don, often penetrated the low-lying moorland while here and there bogs and fens held impenetrable sway, as round the island of Lindholm. Moreover, if the drainage made Epworth less remote from the mainland, the operation itself caused ill-feeling which gave rise to long-lasting lawsuits and occasional acts of savage violence. The fensmen were tough, independent, crude and barbarous; they resented interference with their traditional way of life. By the terms of Vermuyden's contract with the Crown, the lands reclaimed from the waters were to be divided into three lots; a third went to the Crown, a third to the tenants of the manors in which the reclaimed lands were situated, and a third to Vermuyden himself. Vermuyden, however, sold his shares to several of his countrymen, who thus became partners or participants in the enterprise. This caused great ill-feeling and constant trouble, the echoes of which survived to the elder Wesley's day.

His parishioners were as uncouth and independent-minded a set of peasants as could be found in England; but they were not all peasants. Samuel Wesley was not as isolated from social contacts as has been sometimes suggested; his son's diary makes it plain that there was a flourishing social life, dinners, dancing and visits, which brought the Wesleys into contact with the richer yeomen families of the district, more especially the Maws and the Pindars, and with the most important family in the neighbourhood, the unpopular Popplewells of Temple Belwood. Robert Popplewell, who died in 1720, was a self-made man, a yeoman's son who had made a fortune out of the troubles caused by drainage. Yet, among peasants and fishermen, yeomen farmers and country gentry, Samuel Wesley like his fellow-rectors of the island parishes, among them his friend, Joseph Hoole[1] of Haxey, remained an outsider whose activities were more likely to create resentment than to win approval.

It was thus improbable that a man of Samuel Wesley's temperament and strong views could long remain at peace with his hard-headed and suspicious flock. He was conscientious enough to win their dislike, insufficiently gracious to earn their affection. In an attempt to rebuke their

[1] His brother, Nathaniel, was for a time Wesley's curate (L. Tyerman, _Samuel Wesley_, 392).

moral lapses, he sought to apply a penitential discipline,[1] strangely anticipating what his son so unwisely was to attempt in Georgia. Although a homely man, fond of a tobacco[2] and a jest, he was a rigorist where duty was concerned. When his diocesan, William Wake, the Bishop of Lincoln, took a confirmation at Epworth, involving eight hundred candidates from the deaneries of Corringham and Manlake, Wesley told the bishop that it would have been more proper 'for every parish to have come by themselves and none to have been confirmed but those whose name had been given in by the ministers'.[3] His parishioners vented their irritation in insult and abuse, maiming his cattle, hurting his dog, and even perhaps by firing his crops and rectory.

Samuel Wesley also aroused the hostility of the better born and more literate. Neither his dislike of dissent,[4] which according to his son led him to write the speech which Henry Sacheverell used in his own defence,[5] nor his political Toryism made him universally liked. In the general election of 1705 there were four candidates for the county of Lincolnshire, the sitting members, Sir John Thorold and Mr. Dymoke,[6] Colonel Whichcott and Mr. Bertie. Samuel Wesley promised that he would not oppose Thorold but refused to assist Dymoke; instead he said that he would help Colonel Whichcott, who lived in the neighbourhood. On his return from London, he discovered that Whichcott and Bertie were invoking the support of the dissenters whereas Thorold and Dymoke were

---

[1] Cf. M. Edwards, *Family Circle*, 14, 24.

[2] This was a habit which he had developed at Oxford; cf.

> In these raw mornings, when I'm freezing ripe,
> What can compare with a tobacco pipe?
> Primed, cock'd and touch't, 'twould better heat a man
> Then ten Bath faggots or Scotch warming pan.

[3] Norman Sykes, *William Wake*, i, 173–4.

[4] See *A Letter from a Country Divine to his Friend in London, concerning the Education of Dissenters in their Private Academies . . . offered to the Consideration of Parliament for Religion* (1702). This provoked an angry riposte from Samuel Palmer and further pamphlets by Wesley, *Defence* (1704) and *Reply* (1707). In this controversy he had the support of Bishop Wake; though Wake was in 1710 not best pleased to hear that the stout controversialist had been elected a proctor (Sykes, *Wake*, i, 153–4).

[5] J. Wesley, *History of England*, iv, 75. It is difficult to believe that the elder Wesley was alone responsible for its composition and easier to suppose that it was a collective work in which, in addition to Sacheverell himself, Smalridge and Atterbury took a part.

[6] It is interesting to notice that both Thorold and Dymoke were related to future fellows of Lincoln College; cf. pp. 89–94.

firmly for the Church. Straightway he abandoned Whichcott and gave
all his support to Thorold and his companion. The election was everywhere peculiarly violent, nor was Epworth immune from party feeling.

'I went to Lincoln,' so Wesley told Archbishop Sharp, 'on Tuesday
night, May 29, and the election began on Wednesday the 30. A great
part of the night our Isle people kept drumming, shouting and firing of
pistols and guns under the windows where my wife lay, who had been
brought to bed not three weeks. A clergyman met me in the Castle-
yard, and told me to withdraw, as the Isle men intended me a mischief;
another told me that he had heard near twenty of them say, if they got
me in the Castle-yard, they would squeeze my guts out. When they
knew I had got home, they sent the drum and mob with guns &c as
usual to compliment me until after midnight. One of them passing by
on Friday evening, and seeing my children in the yard, cried out "O
ye devils, we will come and turn you all out of doors a begging
shortly."'

The various strands of opposition were thus fused in a common onslaught. Mr. Pindar, of Owston, a friend of Whichcott, demanded the
immediate repayment of a loan of £30 and when this was not forth-
coming had the rector lodged in the debtors' gaol at Lincoln. In this
calamity he showed courage and good sense. His imprisonment marked
the peak of his unpopularity. While he was never to be free from trouble,
at last his parishioners became more ready to tolerate him.

All his life he was dogged by debt. No assessment of John Wesley can
be made which does not take into account the comparative penury in
which he and his brothers and sisters lived. Yet it was comparative. In
1705 Mrs. Wesley told Archbishop Sharp that she had never wanted
bread; 'but, then, I had so much care to get it, before it was eat, and to
pay for it after, as has often made it very unpleasant to me'. For the most
part the rectory did not lack servants; and Samuel Wesley spent money in
travelling to London to attend Convocation. But he was constantly and
chronically in debt. Friends came as constantly to his assistance; the Archbishop of York, the Bishop of Salisbury, Lady Northampton. South
Ormsby had been valued at £50 a year; Epworth was worth £130 a
year, and to this he added in 1724 the £50 from Wroot. This was more
than many incumbents received at this time. It is true that there were
exceptional expenses resulting from the destruction of the rectory by fire,
partially in 1702 and totally in 1709, which involved him in expensive
rebuilding and refurnishing. But the real root of Samuel Wesley's con-

tinuous financial troubles lay nearer home. As his wife was forced to admit, he lacked worldly wisdom. Her brother, who was in the service of the East India Company, had entrusted him with the conduct of certain business while he was abroad; but the rector had failed hopelessly. In extenuation Susanna told her angry brother that he must own 'I was mistaken when I thought him fit for business.' 'He is', she added, 'one of those who, our Saviour saith, are not so wise in their generation as the children of this world.' His saga of financial troubles was never to end. 'I know not when we have had so good a year, both at Wroote and at Epworth as this year,' Emily told her brother John on 7th April, 1725, 'but instead of saving anything to clothe my sister or myself, we are just where we were.'

It was indeed fortunate that Samuel Wesley had a wife of such sterling quality. Where he was weak, she was invariably strong, business-like, practical, efficient, determined. She was a woman of the highest capacity, but her very masterfulness, if it strengthened the discipline of family life, must have diminished domestic peace. Though Dr. Annesley's daughter was as intransigently orthodox as her husband, he was not a little put out to discover that during his absence on proctorial duties in London she had been holding a service and taking prayers at the rectory for a congregation that numbered as many as two hundred. There is little doubt that she had as keen a conception of duty as her husband. She saw to the education of her children and instilled in them a code of conduct which was never wholly lost. Her life was punctuated by a round of constant childbearing, but she found time to read pious literature as well as to superintend the household. She was certainly the stronger partner of the two; she kept her husband's feet firmly on the ground.

The relationship between a couple in many ways so unlike, more especially where one was obstinate and the other strong-willed, could not be continuously harmonious. Susanna Wesley once remarked that she and her husband rarely thought alike. Shortly before John's birth, an incident occurred which threw a strange light upon the elder Wesley, the memory of which was not quickly forgotten. The rector happened to notice that his wife omitted to repeat the 'Amen' to the prayer for King William III. He called his wife to his study and asked her why she failed to do so.

'I was a little surprised at the question, and don't well know what I answered, but too well I remember what followed. He immediately kneeled down and imprecated the divine vengeance upon himself and

E

all his posterity if ever he touched me more or came into a bed with me before I had begged God's pardon and his, for not saying Amen to the prayer for the Kg.'[1]

In spite of his refusal to share his bed with his wife, they went to the Communion together next morning. Samuel Wesley remained completely firm and impenitent, even when the King's death on 8th March led to the accession of Queen Anne (for whom Mrs. Wesley as a loyal supporter of the Stuarts would certainly have been ready to say the 'Amen'). He left Epworth for London, saying that he would seek a service chaplaincy. The incident displays a tenacity to principle and a lack of consideration which illuminates the strained relationship which arose between the rector and his parishioners, as with his children. Susanna Wesley was worried and upset at her husband's precipitate departure from her bed and his parish. 'I'm more easy in the thoughts of parting', she told her confidante, Lady Yarborough, who lived at Snaith Hall, 'because I think we are not likely to live happily together', but she added, 'I have six very little children, which though he tells me he will take good care of, yet if anything should befall him at Sea we should be in no very good condition.' For her part, Susanna Wesley kept her ground; she regarded the late king no more loyally than before. 'I've unsuccessfully represented to him the unlawfulness and unreasonableness of his Oath; that the Man in that case has no more power over his own body than the Woman over her's; that since I'm willing to let him quietly enjoy his opinions, he ought not to deprive me of my little liberty of conscience.' Through Lady Yarborough, she sought the advice of the Non-juror George Hickes, who told her that he could hardly conceive that the Archbishop of York or the Bishop of Lincoln would uphold her husband. These contacts are of interest if only as indicating the High-Church toryism of John Wesley's background. Towards the end of the summer Samuel came home, intending to stay only a few days before departing for ever, but he stayed on and the fire which destroyed part of the rectory[2] served to bring the disastrous episode to a close. Indeed, the pregnancy which resulted from the reconciliation of Samuel and Susanna was terminated by the birth of John Benjamin Wesley, to give him his full name, on 17th June, 1703.[3]

[1] See the correspondence in R. Walmsley, 'John Wesley's Parents', *Proc. W.H.S.*, xxix, 50–7.

[2] 'Fired by one of my servants.'

[3] When John Wesley and his father were in London on November 30, 1733, his father told him the circumstances leading to his birth.

The memory of this unhappy quarrel always remained, but neither this nor subsequent arguments between husband and wife should be taken to mean that the Wesley household was not fundamentally happy and united. The rector was a man of moods and for all his quirks enjoyed the love of his wife and children; he was probably happier in the intimate circle of his own household than in his parish. If his attitude towards even his own family, more especially towards Hetty, may appear disagreeable and even cruel, it was because of his abiding attachment to principle. He refused, as other idealists have done, to allow principle to be overridden by affection. His wife spoke of him in loving language. The children were not unhappy at Epworth and were a united family, all the more so because they were thrown upon their own resources by the isolation of the island. If in winter the mists circled its watery marshes, in summer when clouds raced over the blue sky it appeared to those who lived there beautiful and prosperous. To an eighteenth-century man like Wesley, its watery expanses and flat fields were no defects. It is impossible to read his early diaries without feeling that when the scene changes to Epworth his spirits rise, for he is back at home in a familiar and well-loved framework.

John Wesley was the fifteenth child and the second surviving son of his parents. This is in itself significant. It serves to underline the physical stamina of his mother, whose life was so much overshadowed by recurring pregnancies from which she emerged in no way debilitated but rather the more determined and devoted. The pattern of the household into which John was born helped to establish the way in which his life was to develop. His elder brother Samuel was twelve years older than himself; his particular position in the family imposed on him a responsibility and sense of obligation of which he never divested himself. Age and sex gave him a position which he never lost; he was confidant, adviser, a kind of substitute father-figure. As his father weakened and his mother aged, his stature increased. His very responsibility in a household so interrupted by childbirth and burdened by financial worries provided a freedom which his brothers and sisters lacked. He became an orthodox High Anglican of Jacobite inclinations, a better poet than his father, a careful scholar, a sensible divine, but he was perhaps less bound to the Lincolnshire flats than the other members of the Wesley household; he was more a man of the world, the product of Westminster and Christ Church, the protégé of Bishop Atterbury and Lord Oxford.

It is worth noting that until Charles was born in 1707, the household was predominantly female; Samuel, entered at Westminster in 1704, the year after John was born, spent most of his time away at boarding-school. John's formative years were spent in the midst of a sisterhood in a household dominated by a matriarch; Emilia, born in 1691; Susanna (Sukey), born in 1695; Mary (Molly), born in 1696; Mehetebel (Hetty), born in 1697; Anne (Nancy), born in 1702. His two remaining sisters, Martha (Patty) and Keziah (Kezzy), were born after John. Thus when John was four years old, his daytime companions were girls aged sixteen, twelve, eleven, ten and five. His games were bound to be girlish amusements; nursery life had to be shaped by the dominant sex. Mrs. Wesley did not believe that her children should mix freely with the children of the parish. There was a decisive streak of femininity in John's character (and to some extent in that of Charles also). His neatness, his meticulous, at times fussy, concern with detail, his personal sensitivity, his histrionic approach, must have been in part conditioned at this early age. While he was well-liked by his fellow-men, he seems always to be more at home in female society. The influence of the sisterhood was without doubt pervasive.

To this must be added the personality of his mother, and the close affection which bound John to her. The wide range of her interests, her considerable if narrow knowledge of theology, the help she gave her husband in the parish, even to the extent of provoking the curate's wrath, all these additional to her domestic and material cares, bear witness to her extensive competence. Her children were taught to act strictly and honestly; they were brought up to respect learning. They were obliged to experience if not poverty at least austerity; they were unfamiliar with luxury or self-indulgence. John Wesley was conditioned early to a Spartan existence. The figure of his mother was never far from his mind in Oxford and in Georgia. His inability to make a proposal of marriage to the women with whom he was in love represented the psychological impact of all this; none of them reached the standards he associated with her. When he was face to face with the need for a decision he could not take the step which seemed to savour of a betrayal.

There was little question that Mrs. Wesley ruled the household. In reply to a query which John put to her in later life, she explained at length, in a letter that has been very frequently quoted, the principles on which she had brought up her children. Life was disciplined according to a regular routine. 'When turned a year old (and some before), they were taught to fear the rod, and to cry softly, by which means they escaped abundance of correction which they might otherwise have had.' They sat with their parents at meal times and 'were suffered to eat and drink [small beer] as much as they would, but not to call for any thing'. If they wanted anything, they were allowed to whisper their requirements to the maid. They were not permitted either to be finicky or greedy over their food. They were absolutely forbidden to eat anything between meals and if one of them dared 'to go into the kitchen to ask anything of the servants . . . they were certainly beat'.

Mrs. Wesley believed that the fundamental factor in a child's development was obedience. 'The first thing to be done is to conquer their will, and bring them to an obedient temper . . . the subjecting of the will is a thing which must be done at once, and the sooner the better.' 'When a child is corrected,' she continued, 'it must be conquered, and this will be no hard matter to do, if it be not grown headstrong by too much indulgence. And when the will of the child is totally subdued, and it is brought to revere and stand in awe of the parents, then a great many childish follies and inadvertences may be passed by.' This method provided the 'only strong and rational foundation of a religious education', since self-will was the evident root of all sin and misery.

This regime, so different from that favoured by twentieth-century educationists and psychologists, if austere, was not cruel. Obedience was rewarded by genuine affection; punishment was just, not arbitrary. The circumstances of the household at Epworth, the very size of the Wesley family, doubtless made a measure of discipline and order necessary and even salutary; nor would educationists of Wesley's own day have demurred at the emphasis laid by Susanna Wesley on obedience and the submission of the will to the requirements of the good life. Yet it is well to note that the system was bound to shape the children's future development. They were trained early in book-learning and prayer. For six hours a day the indefatigable mother taught her children to read and write. All play was very strictly regulated. 'There was no such thing as loud talking or playing allowed of. . . . Rising out of their places, or going out of the room, was not permitted, except for good cause; and running into the yard, garden, or street, without leave, was always esteemed a capital offence.' Their mother regulated their religions life with equal precision. She believed sincerely that she was training her children to follow the will of God; but in the first instance she was subordinating their wills to her own. Likewise, their ideas of God were in the main the ideas which Susanna placed before them.

These two features, the femininity of his early environment and the thorough training to which he was subjected by his mother, were of the first importance in John Wesley's development. It was inevitable that though some of the children would in later life react against their mother's domination, all were to a marked degree dependent upon her. The girls, highly educated by the standards of their time, pressed for an independence and a responsibility of which they were at the same time genuinely afraid. Their married lives were almost uniformly disastrous, as was John's own. Their short ventures away from Epworth always failed and soon they homed to the gaunt rectory. Hetty's indiscretion was never fully forgiven by her father, but she yearned to be taken back into the family. Martha (Patty), who succeeded Hetty as a governess or companion to a Mrs. Grantham, soon resigned. Kezzy's time as a pupil-teacher at Lincoln proved a period of ill-health and debt; at length she came back too to Epworth. In some respects the brothers were less tied, more especially Samuel as the eldest; but even in their development the powerful, loving, counselling and warning figure of Susanna Wesley was never far away.

This was the background to John's early life. The only other significant incident of his early years was his rescue from the burning rectory in 1709. In later life he attached great importance to the event as his mother had done at the time. He believed strongly in the providential element in his personal history, and looked back to his rescue as a manifestation of God's purpose. Yet, being only six years old at the time, he can hardly have thought at once in those terms. More immediately, the fire led to the dispersal of the children to the houses of kindly neighbours in the district, a course which gave Susanna much anxiety since it brought about an unpleasing relaxation of the usual discipline to which the children were submitted.

'They were left at full liberty to converse with servants, which before they had always been restrained from; and to run abroad to play with any children, good or bad. They soon learned to neglect a strict observance of the Sabbath; and got knowledge of several songs and bad things, which before they had no notion of. That civil behaviour which made them admired when they were at home, by all who saw them, was in great measure lost; and a clownish accent, and many rude ways were learnt, which were not reformed without some difficulty.'

Yet we need hardly fear that Susanna Wesley's methods proved ineffective in getting rid of these ill-habits.

When he was eleven years old he went to Charterhouse, then situated in London, as a foundation scholar on 28th January, 1714, on the nomination of the Duke of Buckingham, the Lord Chamberlain of the House-hold.[1] There is inadequate evidence to show how Charterhouse influenced the young boy,[2] but as he later acted as a steward at the founder's day dinner on 12th December, 1727,[3] his memories cannot have been alto-gether unpleasant. It was said that he liked to exercise himself even at that time in talk and argument. One of the ushers at Charterhouse, Andrew Tooke, was impressed by seeing Wesley engaged in haranguing boys younger than himself.[4] John himself later asserted that freed from the restraint of discipline at home, he became somewhat negligent, but he admitted that at school he 'still read the Scriptures, and said my prayers morning and evening'.[5] His account is coloured by his later experience, though some relaxation of effort would be hardly surprising.

In any case the home remained the most powerful influence in his life. Although no letters from this period of his life survive, he was a constant correspondent. He was certainly interested in and affected by the 'super-natural' visitation to which the rectory was subjected when he was four-teen and fifteen years old. The trouble occurred first on 1st December, 1716, when his sisters, Susanna and Nancy, heard strange knockings; other sounds like groans and the crashing of bottles were heard by his sisters and by the servants. The rector's man, Robert Brown, heard someone come 'slaring' through the garret to his chamber, rattling by his side, as if against his shoes, though he had none there; at other times walking up and down stairs, when all the house were in bed, and gobbling like a turkey cock. The rector did not at first hear these sounds himself nor did his children tell him. When he first heard the knockings, his wife suggested that they might be made by rats; but the knocking was too regular and

[1] Samuel Wesley's former patron, the Marquis of Normanby, had been created Duke of Buckingham in 1703. Like his protégé, he was the writer of much indiffer-ent verse; 'a writer', as Dr. Johnson later described him, 'who sometimes glimmers but rarely shines'.

[2] See 'John Wesley and the Charterhouse' in *Proc. W.H.S.*, 1949–50, 20–1, 25–30. Wesley's first surviving letter of 3rd November, 1721, was addressed to Ambrose Eyre, the treasurer of Charterhouse (*Letters*, i, 4).

[3] See R. Birley, 'John Wesley as a Steward at the Founder's Day Dinner' in *Proc. W.H.S.* (1949–50), 56–7.

[4] A letter to the Rev. Thomas Coke, LL.D., and Mr. H. Moore by 'An Old Mem-ber of Society', quoted in L. Tyerman, *Life of Wesley*, i, 20.

[5] Wesley, *Works*, i, 92. Tyerman's comment, 'John Wesley entered the Charter-house a saint and left it a sinner', is absurd special pleading. Cf. his own comment in a letter of 9th February, 1750: 'I have not found God so present with me for so long a time, ever since I was twelve years old.' (*Letters*, iii, 30.)

persistent. One night the noises became so loud that it was impossible to sleep; the Wesley's dog, a mastiff, which on first hearing the visitant had barked, now simply whined and shivering showed every sign of fear. Another evening there was a great noise behind the kitchen door, the latch of which kept being lifted up, although Emily tried to keep it down; 'it was lifted up, and the door pushed violently against her, though nothing was to be seen on the outside'.

The visitant was evidently politically conscious. When the elder Wesley prayed for King George I, and his son, it made a great noise. On three occasions, Samuel found himself powerfully pushed by an invisible agency 'once against the corner of my desk in the study, a second time against the door of the matted chamber, a third time against the right side of the frame of my study door, as I was going in'. The noises became worse, more especially after Mrs. Wesley had hired a villager, John Maw, to blow a horn through the house to scare the rats, should they be the cause of the trouble. 'Old Jeffery', as Emily dubbed their visitor after one who had died in the house, haunted them by day and by night. There were knockings, the swishing as of a nightgown, the sound of steps made by someone wearing jack-boots, the banging of doors, the shattering of glass, the splintering of wood, the pouring of coins on a floor, but all without any outward physical manifestation, though Robert Brown insisted that the grinder had once moved of its own accord. Samuel Wesley was sufficiently perturbed by these disturbances to postpone a visit to Joseph Hoole of Haxey, whom he subsequently invited to spend a night at the rectory to learn his opinion of the visitations. At first it seemed as if Old Jeffery was not going to oblige, but then came the familiar sound, like the 'turning of a windmill when the wind changes' or the winding-up of a jack.

There followed a period of quiet, but on 24th January, 1717, it again made its presence felt by knocking when the rector prayed for the king; In the main it operated as before, but Nancy told her brother Samuel of an incident rather less easy to accept. One night she was sitting on the press bed in the nursery, playing cards with her sisters. Robert Brown was also in the room. 'The bed on which my sister Nancy sat', John wrote subsequently, 'was lifted up with her on it. She leapt down and said, "Surely old Jeffery would not run away with her." She was persuaded to sit down again but had scarcely done so before the bed was again levitated several times successively a considerable height, upon which she left her seat, and would not be prevailed upon to sit there any more.' 'Old

Jeffery' had long ceased to terrify; he had become a nuisance and a bore. The younger Samuel, full of curiosity, demanded accounts from his sisters, which they dutifully gave, but his mother probably reflected what the family now felt when she wrote, 'I cannot imagine how you should be so curious about our unwelcome guest. For my part, I am quite tired with hearing or speaking of it.' Then suddenly the visitations ended as abruptly as they had begun.

What did they signify? Mrs. Wesley said that she had heard unusual noises long before old Jeffery commenced operations; and much later, in 1750, Emily seemed to imply to her brother that she was still in contact with her former visitant; but these comments must be received with reserve. There seemed no obvious physical explanation. Samuel wondered whether it was the maid or the manservant who had only come to the house recently; but his mother told him that their fright was too real to be assumed. Other evidence seemed to acquit Robert Brown. Could it have been a neighbour? Samuel Wesley had apparently been preaching against the way in which some of his parishioners indulged in witchcraft; earlier his parishioners had not been averse to playing tricks on the rector and his family. The timing and the occasion, as well as the long continuance, of the hauntings, would however seem to argue against an outside cause. The rector and his wife at first wondered whether it could be one of their own children; suspicion seems to have fallen on Hetty, who was 'particularly troubled'. She was the only one of the sisters who never spoke of these mysterious occurrences; but such accounts as we have make it impossible for her to have been the conscious executant. Her mother had suggested that rats would explain the phenomenon. Certainly on one occasion when there was a noise under the bed in the nursery, Mrs. Wesley looked under it and 'something ran out pretty much like a badger, and seemed to run directly under Emily's petticoats, who sat opposite to me on the other side'. Twice Robert Brown saw a similar creature: 'one night, being ill, he was leaning his head upon the back kitchen chimney . . . with the tongs in his hands, when from behind the oven-stop, which lay by the fire, somewhat came out like a white rabbit'. The rector also commented on some feeble squeaks that he heard 'a little louder than the chirping of a bird; but not like the noise of rats.'

All these events were extraordinarily well authenticated. The rector was neither an unduly superstitious nor an over-credulous man. When Sukey first told him, he was very angry. 'Sukey,' he said, 'I am ashamed of you; these boys and girls fright one another; but you are a woman of sense and should know better. Let me hear of it no more.' Later after he had experienced some weeks of persistent haunting he would only say, 'It would make a glorious penny book for Jack Dunton; but while I live I am not ambitious for anything of that nature.' The rest of the family came to accept Old Jeffery's presence in a very matter-of-fact way. They were no longer alarmed. One of John's sisters said that when she was brushing the floor she often heard sweeping being done behind her, and only regretted that the visitant would not take the broom itself into his or its hands.

Still they were naturally much concerned to explain what it was all about. They feared that it might be a portent of death. They had originally refrained from informing the rector because they were afraid that it might refer to his own imminent decease. He himself thought that it might indicate that Samuel had died, and when Samuel did not write home for a while, both husband and wife were seriously concerned that this might be so, though the spirit had not complied with the rector's request to give a positive answer. Mrs. Wesley thought that it might very well refer to the death of her brother in India.

John Wesley developed decided views of his own. He was not at home when the incidents occurred, but his brother Samuel kept him fully informed. When he went home in 1720 he made a careful enquiry into everything that had happened. He discussed the affair with all whom he could in 1726. With the care which marked all his actions, he kept all the material and used it for an article in the *Arminian Magazine* in 1784.[1] He did not doubt that the incident was supernatural in causation; a later experience at the rectory in 1726 confirmed his original impression.[2] He came to believe that the visitation was intended to bring home to his father the sinfulness of his desertion of his wife in 1702. 'I fear his vow was not forgotten before God.' He founded this belief on the violent knocking which occurred when his father prayed for the Hanoverian king in family prayers; but it was strange that so many years had elapsed before Old Jeffery decided to take action, and strange too that the action was not in the first instance directed against the rector.

---

[1] *Arminian Magazine* (1784), 548–50, 606–8, 654–6.
[2] See p. 106. In 1768 he commented, 'The English in general and indeed most of the men of learning in Europe, have given up all accounts of witches and apparitions. I am sorry for it; and I willingly take this opportunity of entering my solemn protest against the violent compliment which so many that believe the Bible pay to those that do not believe it.' (*Journal*, 25th May, 1768.)

It is impossible to advance an adequate explanation. The events had all the characteristic features of haunting by so-called poltergeists; a home recently constructed, a young woman at the age of puberty, violence and mischief. Yet a natural explanation might equally well be put forward. What is important is the effect that the hauntings had on the impressionable mind of the young adolescent at Charterhouse. They served to arouse his interest in similar phenomena, to buttress his natural credulity, to confirm his awareness of the unseen world.[1]

In 1720 John Wesley was now seventeen and on the verge of manhood. He was eager and enthusiastic, scholarly minded[2] and pious by inclination. Unless he had reacted against the atmosphere of his home he would hardly have been otherwise. Throughout life he remained at heart a conformer or, perhaps it would be better to say, that throughout life he tried to conform to the standards so firmly held at Epworth. Where the world seemed amiss, it was because it lacked the qualities which he associated with his home. It is true that in time to come his religious life would undergo a reorientation, that he would to some extent shed the high-anglicanism, diluted at source by vestiges of nonconformity, which had been the order of the day at Epworth, but his mature religious ideas evolved out of the logical and spiritual background of Epworth, reinforced perhaps by his experiences at Oxford and Georgia. Whatever his father's deficiencies, he was a dutiful pastor. He heard his father talk of and may himself have experienced the work of small religious societies; he had seen how his father sought to discipline the erring members of his flock. There had been ingrained in him a regularity of life and a habit of prayer which he never lost. Respect for learning and scholarship, intelligent observation, were the concomitants of a household the head of which was a scholar and poet, albeit of a mediocre order, and where the presiding genius was a woman of true piety with an interest in theology supported by reading. There was a genuineness of purpose which none could mistake. This does not indicate that the household at Epworth was unduly solemn; there were visits to the local fairs, cards, dancing and other amusements were enjoyed; but always there was a powerful awareness of vocation.

In other ways, too, John Wesley was obviously influenced by his youthful environment. He cannot have failed to observe the ignorance

[1] Cf. pp. 64–5, 168n.
[2] In 1719 Samuel Wesley told his father that John 'is with me, and a brave boy, learning Hebrew as fast as he can'.

and barbarity of the Lincolnshire peasantry; disorder, violence and immorality made their presence felt, even within the fastnesses of the rectory itself.

He must have realized, if as yet unconsciously, that the teaching of the Church was of limited effect, even within the circles of the educated, much more so among the labourers and their families. He did not question then or later the social structure of society. Following the example of his father, he remained a lifelong Tory in the widest sense of that word and an unquestioning admirer of monarchy; but the problem of instilling religion and morality, order and obedience, among the lower classes must have been brought home to him at an early age. He learned, too, to be courageous. He had heard how his father faced the ugly local mob; and he must surely have experienced the jeers of the local children. The experience stood him in good stead when in later years he faced hostile crowds. He knew also the fear of God; it was the first lesson his mother taught him and the one that he would never lose. It was an ever-present obsession which conditioned his whole existence; and if the deity of whom he learned through the vivid teaching of the prophets and apostles and by the experience of prayer reflected some of the characteristics of his parents, this only served to make his religious experience more realistic. At least until 1738, and to some extent after that date, he was to seek the spiritual security and the self-authenticating authority which as a young child he had known at his mother's knees.

All these features may have been modified by six years in the rough and tumble of an eighteenth-century boarding-school, but in principle they had imprinted themselves indelibly on young John Wesley. Heredity and environment had served to fashion him. But the influence of Oxford was to be equally decisive in his development, if in rather a different way.

CHAPTER IV

John Wesley at Christ Church, 1720–6

JOHN WESLEY came up to Oxford, an earnest, high-minded young man, to one of the most diversified societies in existence, for Christ Church, then under the direction of Dean Boulter, was not merely the largest but the most distinguished College in the University. He was placed under the supervision of tutors with whom his relations were uniformly friendly. The first was George Wigan, whom Thomas Hearne described as 'a great and very good tutor·. . . a disciplinarian and a sober, studious, regular and learned man',[1] but Wigan retired, as John told his mother,[2] to his country living, that of Old Swinford, near Stourbridge, where he died over fifty years later in 1776. Wesley was in fact much more intimate with his successor, Henry Sherman. He was a conscientious, kindly man, a friend of John's brother, who agreed to take Wesley on the same terms as Wigan. 'He told me', Wesley wrote, 'he would never take any more of me than he had done, but would rather add something to than take from what little I had.' A friendship developed between the young man of twenty and the older man of thirty-two which survived into Wesley's early days at Lincoln.

Another friend with whom he sat often and corresponded much when he was away from Oxford was Jonathan Colley. Colley had taken his degree from B.N.C., but later went to Christ Church where he acted as

---

[1] *Collectanea*, ed. H. E. Salter, xi, 55. Wigan's departure seems to have been the cause of some dissension in Christ Church. Cf. Canon Stratford's comment to Harley: 'Your old tutor quitted his place of power. There was general joy upon his dimission, and I am afraid he is the most contemptible man that ever was in the place. They durst not offer, after all their menaces, to pass any censure upon Wigan. . . .' (29th December, 1725, *Portland MSS.*, vi, 412.) On 1st January, 1726, he wrote again: 'I think I told you that they were forced to drop the business of Wigan. He is come off with flying colours, but upon his being left out from being rhetorick, some of the mutineers there have made a couplet,

> Would you have all as dull as he that does preside,
> Keep Sherman in, and Wigan lay aside.'　　　　(*Op. cit.*, vi, 413.)

[2] 23rd September, 1723, *Letters*, i, 5.

Chantor or Precentor, in addition to holding the small living of Cassington from 1718 to his death in 1738. In 1725 he was forty-eight, a conventional High Churchman of pronouncedly Tory if not Jacobite sentiments, and a stern critic of William Bradshaw, the Whig Dean foisted upon the College by the government, after Boulter's preferment to the archbishopric of Armagh in 1724. He had given outward expression to these views by setting a penitential anthem for Sunday, 28th May, the day appointed for the celebration of the King's birthday, which so enraged the Dean 'that after service he sent for and reprimanded him'.[1] He was friendly with Hearne and Canon Stratford,[2] but Hearne thought some of his theological views so eccentric that he did not hesitate to call him 'crazed', 'an apocalyptical Man, being much given to Books upon the Revelation, reading, besides Mede, other Things that he meets with upon that Subject', and in particular a commentary written by Daubuz which he was convinced was the 'most learned Book by much that he ever read'.[3] It may not have been accidental that Wesley was later reading both Mede and Daubuz[4] and there can be little doubt that he was influenced by Colley at this time.

There is no information available about Wesley's studies as an undergraduate but he doubtless performed conscientiously the barren[5] exercises necessary for his degree. He was evidently a young man of scholarly inclinations. At Charterhouse he developed a liking for Latin verse which he fostered at Oxford; one of his earliest surviving compositions is a conventional, romantic series of verses translated from the Latin which he sent his brother, Samuel, then an usher at Westminster.

Throughout his career as an undergraduate and indeed as a young graduate he was dogged by a shortage of money. When he described how a friend of his lost his cap and wig as he was standing at a coffee-house door, he could afford to add: 'I am pretty safe from such gentlemen; for unless they carried me away, carcass and all, they would have but a poor purchase.' His father could not give him very much help. His brother Samuel was certainly generous; he asked Sherman to transmit to John the

[1] Hearne, *Collectanea*, ix, 310.

[2] *Op. cit.*, ix, 390; x, 59; xi, 15.

[3] *Op. cit.*, ix, 197. In another place (xi, 189) Hearne's editor, Dr. H. E. Salter, attributes this work incorrectly to Danbury.

[4] He read the *Works of the Pious and Profoundly Learned Joseph Mede* in 1730; and Charles Daubuz' *A perpetual commentary on the Revelation of St. John* in 1734.

[5] In later life, he described them as 'an idle, useless interruption of useful studies', 'horribly shockingly superficial', 'an execrable insult upon common sense'.

rent of the rooms to which he was entitled as a Student of Christ Church (but in which he did not reside). John had his exhibition of twenty pounds a year from Charterhouse, and a studentship from his Oxford College. But he was still often short of cash and obliged then as later to borrow money from friends, among them almost certainly his tutor, Mr. Sherman. Indebtedness had been so long a familiar feature of life at Epworth that it must have weighed less with John than it did with some of his contemporaries; but he was anxious about the state of his finances. 'Dear Jacky,' his mother told him, 'be not discouraged. Perhaps, notwithstanding all, we shall pick up a few crumbs for you before the end of the year.' His mother hoped for help from her brother, Samuel Annesley, who was supposed to be returning to England from India, where he had been in the service of the East India Company. She made a journey to London on purpose to meet him but he failed to materialize. His parents may have believed that Wesley did not always spend such money as he had too wisely. 'I wish', his mother told him on 24th November, 1724, 'you would save all the money you can conveniently spare, not on a visit [to the family at Wroot], but for a wiser and better purpose,—to pay debts, and make yourself easy.'

Even if his means were so narrow at this period of his life that he wore his own hair, and that too long, to save the charges of a barber, he revelled too much in society to live the life of a recluse. Many of his friendships dated from his undergraduate days at Christ Church.

His surviving letters indeed afford no more than occasional glimpses of the sort of young man he then was. He was clearly concerned with his health. At this period of his life he suffered much from bilious catarrh, which occasionally incapacitated him, and later he suspected that he had consumption. He awoke on 16th July, 1733, and was horrified to find himself spitting blood; 'O Eternity,' he wrote, and, then, 'spare me for this company' (presumably the Holy Club); but in later life he knew neither pain nor sickness. Apart from Providence, he attributed this good health to 'constant exercises and change of air', continuously good sleep in which he could indulge at will, early rising, 'having constantly for above sixty years, risen at four in the morning', and absence of worry.

In fact he owed much of this to Dr. Cheyne's *Book of Health and Long Life*, which he read when its fourth edition appeared in 1725.

'He refers', he told his mother, 'almost everything to temperance and exercise. . . . He entirely condemns eating anything salt or high-seasoned, as also pork, fish and stall-fed cattle; and recommends for drink two pints of water and one of wine in twenty-four hours, with eight ounces of animal and twelve of vegetable food in the same time.'[1]

Wesley was greatly influenced by Cheyne's advice and later read his other works. Cheyne himself described how on coming to London he had lived a gay life until his health gave way, with the result that he decided to live more temperately and as a result acquired a new and more serious view of things and a deeper sense of religion.[2] In his book he advised all who lived a sedentary life

'. . . to use as much abstinence as they possibly can either by lessening one half of their usual quantity of animal food and strong liquors, 'till such time as they regain their wonted freedom and indolence; or by living a due time wholly upon vegetable diet, such as sago, rice, pudding and the like, drinking only a little wine and water'.[3]

He praised the use of exercise, more especially riding,

'. . . the most manly, the most healthy, and the least laborious and expensive of spirits of any, shaking the whole machine, promoting a universal perspiration and secretion of all the fluids . . . and thereby, variously twitching the nervous fibres, to brace and contract them, as the new scenes amuse the mind.'[4]

He stressed the evils of luxury and the benefits of early rising.

'Those who live temperately, will necessarily sleep but little. . . . Valetudinary, studious and contemplative people, ought to go to bed by eight, nine, or ten at latest, and rise by four, five or six.'[5]

Cheyne's prescriptions may be said to have determined Wesley's future regimen.

Wesley's letters confirm his continued interest in the supernatural and

---

[1] *Letters*, i, 11.

[2] Cheyne's autobiographical remarks occur in his *English Malady* (4th edn., 1734), 325–64. See also J. M. Bulloch, *Dr. George Cheyne* (1930); *Letters to Lady Huntingdon*, ed. C. F. Mullett (1940), and *Letters to Samuel Richardson*, ed. C. F. Mullett, University of Missouri Studies, XVIII (1943).

[3] Cheyne, *Essay of Health and Long Life* (4th edn., 1725), 36. Cf. 'Water alone is sufficient and effectual for all the purposes of human wants in drink. Strong liquors were never designed for common use.' (*Op. cit.*, 43.) Another book which he read later, *A Treatise of Health and Long Life*, by Leonard Lessius and Lewis Cornaro also strongly advocated abstinence. Cornaro (d. 1566) said that an egg a day was sufficient food; he lived to be a centenarian. Cheyne praised the work in a letter to Richardson.

[4] *Op. cit.*, 95.

[5] *Op. cit.*, 84.

the comparable credulity and naïveté of his outlook. He described at some length the seizure of a young man by the devil,[1] vouched for by the late Bishop of Raphoe, a curious occurrence which befell an undergraduate of Christ Church called Barnesley,[2] and his own eagerness to visit a house near Oxford[3] reputed to be haunted.

After Wesley had graduated as a bachelor of arts in 1724, he remained in Oxford, presumably using his rooms in Christ Church, to fulfil the exercises necessary for the master's degree. He had also to come to a decision about his future. There was every likelihood that he would follow his father's and brother's examples and be ordained. He hoped for a vacant College fellowship which would provide much-needed financial security as well as the opportunity for further reading and study until marriage or preferment brought his tenure to a close. It might mean the holding of a College office and the supervision of pupils but this was not inevitable. It could be held concurrently with a curacy at Epworth. Otherwise it was difficult to see what the future had in store for him. Although his father was relatively well known, he was not in contact with aristocratic or episcopal patrons; not in receipt of preferment himself, holding political views unsympathetic to the established government, it was unlikely that his son could hope for patronage. His elder son, Samuel, was to find his close associations with Jacobitism a barrier to advancement. If patronage had been offered, John Wesley might conceivably have accepted it; in much later life he subscribed himself a chaplain to the Countess of Buchan.[4] After graduation he prepared himself for ordination, widened still further the range of his reading and study, and waited for the opportunity of a fellowship.

[1] *Letters*, i, 6, 13–14. The story was told him by his friend, Robert Harrison, whose father, an Irish clergyman, heard it from the Vicar-General; another friend of later days, Henry Hamilton, was the son of the Archdeacon of Raphoe.

[2] *Op. cit.*, i, 10. Barnesley (probably William B., who matriculated at Christ Church in May, 1723) was walking in the fields near Oxford when he and his friends saw something cross their path 'like a man or woman in light grey, but of so thin a substance that they could plainly see through it'. Later Barnesley learned that his mother had died that very evening at the same time as they had seen the apparition.

[3] *Op. cit.*, i, 14. Cf. p. 168n.

[4] 'Except a few from curiosity, and *some hoonurable women* the congregation was very mean. There was a Scotch Countess of Buchan, who is carrying a pure rosy vulgar face to heaven.' (H. Walpole writing from Bath to John Chute, 10th October, 1766.) She was Agnes Stewart, who married Henry, Earl of Buchan, in 1739, and died in 1778.

F

Both his parents had hoped that he would be ordained, though their immediate reaction to ordination in 1724–5 was characteristically different. His father stressed the need for further study, especially of the languages, Greek and Hebrew, which would enable him to understand the Scriptures more satisfactorily. His mother was much more concerned with the practical aspect. 'Mr. Wesley', she wrote, 'differs from me, and would engage you, I believe, in critical learning, which, though accidentally of use, is in no wise preferable to the other.' His father had originally thought that John should delay ordination until he was certain that this was his vocation.

'As to what you mention of entering into Holy Orders, it is indeed a great work, and I am pleased to find you think it so. As to the motives you take notice of, my thoughts are; if it is no harm to desire getting into that office, even as Eli's sons, to eat a piece of bread; yet certainly a desire and intention to lead a stricter life, and a belief that one should do so, is a better reason: though this should, by all means, be begun before, or ten to one it will deceive us much afterwards. . . . But the principal spring and motive, to which all the former should be only secondary, must certainly be the glory of God, and the service of his Church in the edification of our neighbour.'

Mrs. Wesley believed that there should be no delay. 'I think the sooner you are a deacon the better, because it may be an inducement to greater application in the study of practical divinity, which of all other studies I humbly conceive to be the best for Candidates for Orders.'

There is little doubt that John Wesley prepared himself conscientiously for ordination, more so than the majority of the candidates in his time; it was the result of the training which he had received at his home, but it was also a tribute in its way to the influences to which he had been subject at Christ Church. In January, 1725, he sought his father's advice as to suitable commentaries on the Bible. His father replied that the Bible was its own best commentary:

'. . . for the several Paraphrases and Translations of it in the Polyglot, compared with the Original, and with one another, are, in my opinion, to an honest, devout, industrious, and humble man, infinitely preferable to any comment I ever saw. But Grotius is the best, for the most part, especially on the Old Testament.'[1]

[1] J. Whitehead, *John Wesley*, i, 384–5.

He was reading Grotius and Wake's *Catechism* on the day of his examination for orders.[1] He took his father's advice to heart, and the Greek Testament continued to be his constant companion; in May, 1725, for instance, he studied St. Matthew's Gospel. He also continued with Hebrew and paid some attention to the Old Testament; on Sunday, 27th June, 1725, he read through twenty chapters of the book of Job. He supplemented his reading of the Scriptures with many general theological works, more especially the patristic writings, some of which he was translating in April.[2] He thus had a substantial fund of theological and scriptural knowledge at his disposal when he was made a deacon in September, 1725.

He was indeed increasingly concerned with the outward practice of religion and the inner spiritual life. He made a note of the sermons he had heard, attended the Divinity disputations, and from time to time observed that he had talked of religious matters with his friends. His mother commented appreciatively on what seemed to her the greater seriousness of his attitude:

'. . . the alteration of your temper has occasioned me much speculation. I, who am apt to be sanguine, hope it may proceed from the operations of God's Holy Spirit, that, by taking off your relish for earthly enjoyments, he may prepare and dispose your mind for a more serious and close application to things of a more sublime and spiritual nature . . . now, in good earnest, resolve to make religion the business of your life. . . . I heartily wish you would now enter upon a strict examination of yourself, that you may know whether you have reasonable hope of salvation by Jesus Christ. . . .'[3]

This piece of advice, with its Pauline echoes, made an impact on John Wesley's stern if sensitive spirit. His mother had called into being a challenge which penetrated deep into his subconscious, arousing a self-questioning spectre that would not be laid. It is of interest to note that his diary already begins to record occasional bouts of introspection and self-examination. As he put away Bishop Bull's *Companion* which he had been reading the evening before his ordination, he noted down what seemed to him his most salient faults, boasting, greed of praise, intemperate sleep,

[1] 16th September, 1725.
[2] See Appendix I on 'Wesley's reading'.
[3] Whitehead, *op. cit.*, i, 385–6.

detractions, lying, heat in arguing.[1] There is little doubt that his ordination was a landmark in his spiritual development.[2]

He was ordained to the diaconate by Bishop Potter of Oxford on Sunday, 19th September, 1725. His father's objections to early ordination had been quickly overruled, partly because he realized that with the additional responsibility of Wroot he could well do with his son's help[3] and partly by his wife's powerful advocacy of the wisdom of an early ordination. He had hoped that Wesley could have been made deacon on Trinity Sunday, 1725, but this project did not materialize owing to family circumstances which kept Wesley in Oxford. John himself had not thought them a serious obstacle; 'I might have taken Bugden [Buckden] in Huntingdonshire, where Bishop Reynolds [of Lincoln] ordained, in my way', and so, he added, have saved the two guineas which would have to be expended on letters dimissory. He called on the kindly Bishop Potter at Cuddesdon on Wednesday, 25th August, wrote out his testimonial and was examined for orders on Thursday, 16th September, presumably by one of the bishop's chaplains and subscribed to the Thirty-nine Articles the next day. He noted the fact of his ordination[4] succinctly in his diary, and added that during the afternoon of 19th September he walked in the gardens of Trinity College and heard Dr. John Bear, formerly of Exeter College, preach on the Holy Ghost teaching the Apostles all truth.[5] His life's ministry had begun.

Six months lay between his ordination to the diaconate and his election to a fellowship at Lincoln. His life was now relatively well-documented as a result of the daily diary that he kept; there is much that it does not tell us.

[1] 18th September, 1725.—Bishop George Bull's *A Companion to Candidates for Orders, or One Great Importance of the Priestly Office* (1714). He was advising a young man preparing for ordination to read it thirty years later (19th February, 1755, *Letters*, iii, 125).

[2] The Roman Catholic writer Maximin Piette contended that his ordination rather than his conversion was the crucial event in his spiritual development. Cf. his *John Wesley in the Evolution of Protestantism* (1937), 306.

[3] He already had a curate in the local schoolmaster, William Romley, the father of John Wesley's future critic; but like other eighteenth-century incumbents he did not expect to take all the services in his parishes himself.

[4] Eleven deacons and eight priests were ordained (*Subs. and Ordinations, Dioc. of Oxford, 1712–26*, fol. 57).

[5] By marrying the mother of Wesley's friend, Dr. Burton, he had become the latter's father-in-law. He was previously curate at Bray, near Maidenhead. He was 'a good-natured man, and a good Scholar . . . small, & of a low voice'. (Hearne, *Collectanea*, ix, 29.)

Wesley was singularly reticent when it came to expressing his own opinions. He noted down his principal occupations, the books he read, the people he saw, sometimes particularizing as to the hour and in his later diaries to the minute; but he rarely expressed his personal opinion or commented upon the people whom he met. Now and again we learn of the topic of his conversation but only very infrequently the views that he or his friends put forward. In spite of the reviews of his spiritual development, the element of self-criticism and the resolutions to live well which make up the majority of the entries in cipher in his first diary, his early diaries remain strangely impersonal. Perhaps they epitomized the man himself. Although they appear open, revealing, straightforward, they also suggest dark recesses where it is difficult, if not impossible, to penetrate with any degree of certainty. Yet the diary henceforward provides a daily framework for John Wesley's life which has hitherto been lacking.[1]

Until his election to a fellowship at Lincoln College in March, 1726, he lived at Oxford, only varying his life by visits to his friends in the Cotswolds with whom, for instance, he spent the greater part of the Christmas holidays of 1725–6. If he was ordained to a curacy at Epworth, it may seem strange that he did not visit his home during this period, even if he corresponded regularly with his parents; but, quite apart from the expense of travelling which he could ill afford, he may very well have not wished to lose any opportunity of a fellowship.

He did not spend the first months of his ministry in any particular cure of souls, but helped in the parishes round Oxford when the opportunity presented itself. He preached his first sermon at the village church of South Leigh, near Witney, on Sunday, 26th September, 1725, but strangely enough made no mention of the fact in his diary, though he preserved his carefully written-out sermon notes. Later in the year, apart from the services he conducted at his friends' churches in the Cotswold villages of Buckland, Broadway and Stanton, he took duty at Fleet Marston and Winchendon, Shipton, where he took a wedding and a funeral, Thame, Binsey, Weston and the Oxford churches of St. Peter and St. Thomas. The resultant fees enabled him to supplement his income, and when there were no such demands for his services, he listened to the University sermon at St. Mary's. He was much affected by a sermon from Mr. Strait, of Magdalen, which he heard the Sunday before his election at Lincoln.

[1] There is a gap in the diary as the volume covering the period, 20th February, 1727, to 29th April, 1729, is still missing.

'Never forbid the Scriptures to any one,' the preacher urged, 'and never mock at them or use their phrases lightly.'

The greater part of his time was spent in further study. Indeed the extent of his reading reveals a picture of University life in the early eighteenth century very different from that usually portrayed. There were few days when he did not devote some hours to the study of the Greek Testament, and the biblical bent of his interest can already be discerned. But he was also engaged in reading and making notes on the somewhat heavy lumber of contemporary theological works; the sermons of Bennet, Norris, Smalridge and Atterbury, Hickes on Schism, Watts on Predestination, Ellis on the Thirty-nine Articles, Fiddes on Morality, Hutcheson's *Enquiry into Ideas of Beauty and Virtue*, books by Whiston, Berkeley and Wake. He does not often record the topics of conversation with his friends, but over breakfast and tea they certainly concerned themselves with the serious questions of the day. Fascinated by the problem of predestination,[1] the doctrine of which he vigorously repudiated, he talked of it with his Christ Church contemporary, John Rigby.[2] With another Christ Church contemporary, Edmund Bateman,[3] who was preparing for ordination, he discussed the problem of 'loving creatures' before they walked round Christ Church meadows. Another autumn day he was at New College, involved in argument, probably with his friend, 'Robin' Griffiths, as to whether the Old Testament can be said to contradict the New. Church discipline was the theme of a conversation on All Saints' Day, 1725.

His reading and conversation were not, however, narrowly theological. Indeed the breadth of his reading at this period was very impressive, more especially as he later consciously and resolutely abandoned the study of secular literature. It must, then, have been at this time that he garnered in a tenacious memory the wide general knowledge that he displayed in later life.[4] Sometimes he went to read in the Bodleian Library; at other

[1] On 29th July, 1725, he wrote to his mother: 'That God should be the author of sin and injustice . . . is a contradiction to the clearest ideas we have of the divine nature and perfections' (*Letters*, i, 22–3). He was reading Watts on predestination on 27th September, 1725.

[2] Matric. May, 1719; B.A. 1723, M.A. 1725. He and Thomas Horne were made deacons in Cuddesdon Church in May, 1732.

[3] Matric. April, 1720; B.A. 1723, M.A. 1726; ord. deacon by the Bishop of Oxford in September, 1726; Tutor Ch. Ch., 1731; D.D. 1736.

[4] Ronald Knox's comment, 'On the other hand he was . . . a complete Philistine about literature, as about everything else that belonged to this world' (*Enthusiasm*, 447), basically correct as it may be, needs to be modified.

times he made use of his College library where, for instance, he scanned Paolo Sarpi's history of the Council of Trent on 17th June, 1725, presumably in Sir Nathaniel Brent's translation. Classical literature continued to afford him continuous intellectual entertainment.[1] The poems of Horace were for a long time to give him pleasure, and later he used to declaim them to himself on his long rides through the countryside. 'Translated half an oration in Tully' was how he spent part of a Saturday in July, 1725, and another Saturday, indulging an intellectual recreation which fascinated him for years to come, he 'writ a copy of Latin verses'. One winter's day he amused himself by translating part of the fifteenth chapter of Proverbs into Latin verse. He perused the standard classical literature of his day, including Cluver's book on *Italia Antiqua*, and the Aeneid of Virgil, the Satires of Juvenal, and the work of Xenophon, Cornelius Nerpos, Epictetus and Anacreon. A few days before his election at Lincoln, he read through almost all the plays of Terence.

He was clearly interested in current classical and philosophical questions, reading with attention some of the works relating to the Phalaris controversy which raged round the formidable figure of Dr. Bentley.[2] He was also concerned with the philosophical views of Locke, Hutcheson and the critical problems they raised.[3] A reference in his diary and a letter to his mother show that he was impressed by Berkeley's *Three Dialogues between Hylas and Philonous*, though he found his arguments unacceptable.

His reading at this period took him down many different avenues of English literature. His first entry in his diary, on 5th April, 1725, referred to his perusal of Nahum Tate's translation of Fracastoro's poem, *Syphilis*;[4] on 3rd June, 1725, he 'learned ye Geography of ye first book of Milton'. He read the poems of Milton, Spenser, Cowley, Waller, Herbert, Prior and Leonard Welsted in the period preceding his election to a fellowship;[5] Burnet's *History of the Reformation and History of his own Times*,

---

[1] Cf. p. 255.

[2] Viz. R. Johnson's *Aristarchus Anti-Bentleianus* (1717) and Charles Boyle's *Dr. Bentley's Dissertations on the Epistles of Phalaris . . . examined* (1698).

[3] Viz. his reading of Henry Lee's *Anti-Scepticism: or, notes upon each chapter of Lock's Essay* (1702) on 12th October, 1725.

[4] *Syphilis, or a Poetical History of the French Disease* (1686); an edition of the Latin poem, edited by Charles Peters, was published in 1721.

[5] On the day after his ordination he wrote out a copy of verses on the death and funeral of the Duke of Marlborough for his friend, Thomas Burcombe, of Christ Church.

Clarendon's *History of the Great Rebellion*, and Thomas Salmon's recent *Review of the History of England* showed his interest in history.

His scientific and medical interests[1] were also represented in his reading. He was a keen observer, concerned with the interrelationship of natural phenomena, and even in later life he wrote a number of semi-scientific tracts,[2] though in this as in so much else his attitude was uncritical. He saw no opposition between scientific discovery and religious belief, but thought rather that the former sustained the latter, as his perusal of Ditton's *Discourse*[3] seemed to indicate. Among other works at this period of his life he studied Halley's book on Magnetism and Gravity, Keill's *Principia*, Boyle's *Chemistry* and James Drake and Daniel Le Clerc's *History of Physick*.

In a time when there was little or no fiction to afford a vicarious outlet for the imagination, poems and plays could alone take the reader into the world of fantasy. John Wesley had now and for some time to come a passionate interest in plays and in the theatre, as his visits to London demonstrate. He not only read the plays of Shakespeare, *Othello* and *Henry IV*, during these months, but many others—Ben Jonson's *The Silent Woman*, Nathaniel Lee's *Theodosius* and the tragedies of Nicholas Rowe, of which he was particularly fond, *The Ambitious Stepmother*, *Jane Shore* and *The Fair Penitent*. His interest in plays, more especially in tragedy, was not merely a recreation. It provided an outlet for feelings and interests which he otherwise carefully repressed. There was a histrionic streak in his character,[4] and he liked to see himself playing a part. Three or four times in May and June, 1725, he noted in cipher in his diary that he had 'acted an hour'.

He was already somewhat uneasy at the extent to which he was

[1] On 9th July, 1725, he was translating ten pages of 'specifick Remedies' for his tutor, Mr. Sherman.

[2] *The Desideratum: or Electricity Made Plain and Useful* (1760) which was an account of various experiments, and of the curative properties of electricity.

[3] Humphrey Ditton was a mathematician (d. 1715); Wesley was reading the appendix to Ditton's *Discourse concerning the Resurrection of Jesus Christ*.

[4] Horace Walpole heard Wesley preach at Lady Huntingdon's Chapel in Bath on 5th October, 1766, and wrote acutely if critically to John Chute that 'I have been at one opera, Mr. Wesley's. They have boys and girls with charming voices, that sing hymns, in parts, to Scotch ballad tunes. . . . Wesley is a lean, elderly man, fresh-coloured, his hair smoothly combed . . . wondrous clean, but as evidently an actor as Garrick. He spoke his sermon, but so fast and with so little account, that I am sure he has often uttered it. . . . There were parts and eloquence in it, but towards the end he exalted his voice and acted very ugly enthusiasm.'

attracted to lighter reading, and often the word 'idleness', self-accusatory in tone, is to be found when he lists any books of this type. On 4th October, 1726, he resolved that he would read no light book that week except on Saturday. He realized that whereas his friends in the Cotswolds liked to read plays, and to attend the theatre, his mother would hardly have approved of all his choice of light literature. His over-scrupulous conscience was burdened by the necessity to reach a decision; but he remained as yet irresolute between inclination and what he conceived to be duty.

His reading left him ample time for talk and social recreation. His diary shows him constantly at the coffee-house where he breakfasts with his friends, drinks tea and reads the news. An entry in his diary for 9th March, 1725, gives a list of seventeen College friends. This includes seven from Christ Church including his tutor, Henry Sherman, Edmund Bateman, Walter Ward,[1] Fielder Hammond,[2] William Burman,[3] Emanuel Langford[4] and Edward Shuckburgh.[5] John Burton, who was a young fellow of Corpus, was a powerful influence at a later date. Urbane, pious and intelligent, this public-spirited young man won the esteem of so unlikely a person as Nicholas Amhurst for his attempt to introduce more modern studies, including Newton and Locke, into the Oxford curriculum. In 1725 he was appointed (without his seeking according to himself but not so according to others) to the vicarage of Buckland, near Faringdon, which he was able to hold with his fellowship and where Wesley occasionally did duty for him. Hearne, who respected his learning, thought him ambitious and described him as a 'busy man . . . always speeching of it in a very dull flat way in the Convocation House';[6] Hearne suggested, probably unjustly, that Burton's tenure of the Pro-proctorship and mastership of the Schools which won Amhurst's admiration[7] had been

---

[1] Matric., Ch. Ch., 16th November, 1719, aged 18; B.A. 1723, M.A. 1726, D.D. 1741. Subsequently rector of Biddenden, Kent, and prebendary of St. Paul's, d. 1755.

[2] Matric., Ch. Ch., December, 1720, aged 17; B.A. 1724, M.A. 1727.

[3] Matric., Ch. Ch., B.A., M.A., ord. priest at Oxford in September, 1726.

[4] Matric., Ch. Ch., 1721; B.A. 1726, M.A. 1728. Ord. deacon at Oxford, September, 1726.

[5] Son of Sir Charles Shuckburgh. Matric., Ch. Ch., 28th November, 1722, aged 18; B.A. 1726. Rector of Bromshall, Stafford, d. 1730.

[6] Hearne, *Collectanea*, x, 5.

[7] 'A gentleman who bears such a general, good character, both as to learning and probity.' (*Terrae-Filius*, xix.)

indiscreet.[1] Another Corpus friend was Thomas Pollen.[2] Others in the list included Walter Frank[3] of Merton, a son of the Archdeacon of Bedford, Richard Woodesdon of Magdalen, who later became the Master of the Free School of Kingston-on-Thames, Richard Watkins[4] of Wadham, later Rector of Clifton Campville, and Henry Pitt[5] of Exeter, a relative of the future minister. 'Robin' or John Griffiths, who was a son of his friend, the vicar of Broadway; his early death eighteen months later deeply shocked Wesley.[6] There were also three men from his future College, two Northerners, Thomas Bayliff[7] and Robert Bulman,[8] and a future minor canon of Westminster, Thomas Persehouse.[9] This list is by no means exhaustive. 'Had company to breakfast' was a familiar entry, and a list of those with whom he breakfasted at his or their invitation would include in addition to those named above, John Ditcher and Charles Potter,[10] Thomas Aldersey,[11] Luke Gwynne,[12] John Rigby, Robert Harrison, Samuel Payne,[13] John Inglis,[14] and Thomas Eedes,[15] all from Christ Church; and Ambrose Lisle,[16] a young fellow of Magdalen.

[1] Hearne, *op. cit.*, x, 213.

[2] Son of Edward P., of Lincoln. Matric., C.C.C., 1717, aged 15; B.A. 1721, M.A. 1724, later rector of Little Bookham.

[3] Matric., Merton C., 23rd March, 1721; B.A. 1725.

[4] Matric., Wadham C., 4th April, 1720; B.A. 1723, M.A. 1726, fellow 1727-39, d. 1776.

[5] Son of Christopher P., of Blandford, and brother of Christopher, the rector of Pimperne and translator of Virgil and Vida (whose *Art of Poetry* Wesley was reading on Christmas Eve, 1725). Matric., Exeter C., 10th October, 1722, aged 16; Petrean fellow, 1724, B.A. 1727, M.A. 1729, d. 1733.

[6] See p. 115.

[7] Born at Newcastle-on-Tyne, entered aged 15, 2nd February, 1721.

[8] Son of George B., of Newcastle-on-Tyne, entered 11th April, 1724.

[9] Son of Humphrey P., curate of Knightsbridge, entered 19th May, 1724, aged 17.

[10] Son of Christopher P., of Holywell, Oxford. Matric., Ch. Ch., 9th December, 1720, aged 19; B.A. 1724, M.A. 1727.

[11] Matric., Ch. Ch., 21st March, 1721.

[12] Matric., Ch. Ch., 13th December, 1722, aged 17; B.A. 1726. There was also a Francis Gwynne, who was at Christ Church in 1717 and subsequently became a fellow of All Souls.

[13] Matric., Ch. Ch., December, 1722, aged 18; B.A. 1726, M.A. 1729.

[14] Matric., Ch. Ch., 1717; B.A. 1720, M.A. 1723.

[15] Matric., Magd. H., 1715, aged 18; Ch. Ch., B.A. 1719.

[16] Matric., Hart. H., 1715, aged 15; fellow of Magd. C., 1723-8; barrister-in-law of the Middle Temple, 1725; died abroad 1728. There was also a demy of Magd., Thomas Lisle, who matric. in 1725. The first is more likely to have been Wesley's acquaintance.

Occasionally he went to the local taverns, treated by his friend, John Ditcher of Christ Church, at the King's Head, the day after he was ordained, or sitting at the Greyhound[1] with Edward Winnington. Chess and cards helped to pass the time; 'sat at Mr C[olley] played at cards', he notes on 15th October. 'Played an hour at backgammon with Harrison'[2] is another entry. 'Sat at ombre' with Sherman, his former tutor, and Bateman, he commented one winter's evening. On another occasion he 'played an hour at billiards'. He did not yet own a horse and kept his spare, athletic frame in trim by walking round Christ Church meadows, to Binsey, to Littlemore. Once at least he went with his friend Richard Woodesdon of Magdalen on the river. He attended the horse races in Port Meadow in August.[3] Sometimes he played royal tennis, 'three sets on September 10th, two hours on September 21, two hours on September 30th and six sets on October 5th'.

Most of his friends were, as one would expect, men of his own age and standing, young graduates undertaking the exercises which would bring them their masters' degree or recently elected to a fellowship. Henry Pitt, for instance, introduced him to two of his young friends in Exeter, Richard Barford and Charles Vinicombe, and in the Senior Common Room to the aged Rector of Exeter, Matthew Hole, who pleased Wesley by his compliments.[4] Apart from Sherman and Colley in Christ Church, his contacts with the senior members of the University were relatively slight, but he had breakfast with the learned antiquarian, Dr. Tanner, a canon of Christ Church, on 12th September. Another senior Christ Church acquaintance was William Le Hunte, a Student of Christ Church, who served as proctor in 1724 and was later vicar of Kidderminster. Robert Leybourne, of B.N.C., was another don with whom he was friendly.[5]

There is perhaps little enough to be gleaned from such a list. Except for Burton none of them played a very significant part in his future career, and he lost contact with most of them as they disappeared into the obscurity of eighteenth-century parish life. It is possible to surmise from

[1] Formerly at the corner of Long Wall.

[2] Son of an Irish clergyman from Westmeath. Matric., Ch. Ch., 21st October, 1723, aged 21.

[3] Cf. Hearne, *Collectanea*, ix, 9 (24th August), 185 (27th August).

[4] Matthew Hole became a fellow of Exeter in 1663, was elected Rector in 1716, and died in 1730, aged 90. Among the various sins which Wesley noted down on Good Friday, 1726, he entered 'flattery of Dr. Hole'.

[5] See p. 108, 136.

the relatively little evidence at our disposal that they were men of similar tastes to himself, earnest,[1] serious, studious and religious. It is moreover of some significance that while the majority of his friends were drawn as one would expect from Christ Church, many came from other Colleges. The eighteenth-century College, like its modern equivalent, tended to be something of a closed society. That Wesley should have had a range of acquaintances drawn from a number of Colleges is a tribute to his sociable nature.

Meanwhile he was working on the themes which he intended to make part of his master's degree, more especially the problem of reasoning in the brute creation, which he talked over during the autumn and winter of 1726 with Burton of Corpus and his friend Bateman, and which he later discussed with his friends, the Kirkhams, at their home in the Cotswolds.

The problem of his future career had still to be settled. The possibility of a fellowship at Lincoln College had been raised in the early summer of 1725, but for long the outcome remained uncertain. The College had three fellowships, the tenure of which was limited in the first instance to natives of the diocese of Lincoln. The outgoing fellow, John Thorold, was cousin of the Member of Parliament for the county whom Wesley's father had championed in 1705, a wealthy and pious young man who was in later life to do much to forward John's work.[2] He resigned on 3rd May, 1725, and it was not long before the question of Wesley's candidature was raised.[3] His father was an acquaintance and neighbour of the Rector of Lincoln, John Morley, who held the living of Scotton, near Gainsborough, where he was often in residence. The elder Wesley immediately set about pressing his son's claims. At the beginning of August, 1725, he visited John

---

[1] There is no indication of any breach of University regulations in Wesley's career except for the ambiguous entry in his diary for 27th September, 1725, 'taken by Mr. B. without a hat'. The regulations laid down that every graduate had to wear a gown and square cap when walking about the University. By contravening this regulation, Wesley laid himself open to a proctorial fine (for the first offence) of 1s. 8d.

[2] The baronetcy had been created in 1642. John Thorold, of Marston and Cranwell, and of Syston Park, near Grantham, was born in 1703, entered Lincoln as a gentleman commoner in 1721 and was elected to a Lincoln fellowship on 23rd June, 1724. He apparently refused to draw any stipend. He succeeded to the baronetcy in 1748, and died in 1775. See also p. 94. In 1883 the family's estates were said to consist of 12,533 acres in Lincolnshire, bringing in an annual revenue of £17,652.

[3] On 13th March, 1725, his father had written that 'Mr. Downes has spoken to Dr. Morley about you, who says he will inquire of your character' (L. Tyerman, *Samuel Wesley*, 393).

Thorold's father at Gainsborough, 'and shall again, by God's leave, be there to-morrow, and endeavour to make way for you from that quarter'. About the same time he told his son that he had waited on Rector Morley 'and found him more civil than ever. I will write to the Bishop of Lincoln[1] again, and to your brother, Samuel,[2] the next post.' It was obviously intended that these two should bring such influence as they could to bear on the College.

The father's plea made some impression on Dr. Morley, who was well aware of the elder Samuel's honesty and scholarship. At any rate on the afternoon of 16th August John noted that he had called at Lincoln. Subsequently he breakfasted there on 23rd August and again on the 26th. There followed a long period of uncertainty. It soon became evident that his candidature was not making the headway for which his parents had hoped. 'As', his father wrote to him, 'to the Gentlemen Candidates you write of—does anyone think the devil is dead, or so much as asleep, or that he has no agents left? Surely virtue can bear being laughed at.' This letter suggests that Wesley's seriousness or other factors may already have raised a smile among some of the fellows of Lincoln who favoured other possible candidates. His father, writing again on 19th October, 1725, urged him to bear patiently with his opponents, while his mother told him, 'If it be a weak virtue that cannot bear being laughed at, I am sure it is a strong and well-confirmed virtue that can bear the test of a brisk buffoonery.'

Whatever the raillery which Wesley had to undergo in the Senior Common Room of Lincoln, he became with the evident support of the Rector a frequent guest in the College. He himself realized that his candidature was not universally approved. On 26th August, after breakfasting at the College, he had later in the day visited Lisle at Magdalen, where they talked about 'detraction', very likely with regard to his candidature at Lincoln. After he had breakfasted at the College again on 29th August, he grimly set down the condemnatory words 'idle talk'. He was at the College shortly after his ordination, but there seems then to have followed a longish interval during which he did not visit Lincoln until 5th December.

[1] This was Richard Reynolds, Bishop of Lincoln, and Visitor of the College from 1723 to 1744.

[2] Writing to his brother on 21st March, 1726, John ascribed much of his success to his influence: 'that success, which I owe chiefly, not to say wholly, to your interest' (*Letters*, i, 27).

Early in the new year, 1726, he called on the Rector who had told him previously that the election would not take place until Candlemas; when the fellows met they postponed a decision until 17th March. Meanwhile he was getting increasingly anxious about the situation and discussed it with his older friend, William Le Hunte, towards the end of January. However, there were now indications that what opposition there had been was beginning to disappear as the fellows perceived that there was much to be said in Wesley's favour on personal and other grounds.

His religious and political views were such as would certainly appeal to his future colleagues. His High-Churchmanship carried with it a dislike of the Hanoverian regime which suggested an inclination to flirt with Jacobitism, but his inherent sense of loyalty and dislike of Roman Catholicism would never have made him a Jacobite in fact. In June, 1734, he was to preach what was construed as a 'Jacobite' sermon before the University which was much criticized; but he had taken the precaution of getting the Vice-Chancellor to approve the text before he preached it, and 'may therefore', as his brother Charles told Samuel Wesley the younger, 'bid Wadham, Merton, Exeter and Christ Church do their worst'. Yet, after conversing with his friend Pollen of Corpus 'against King George'[1] on 14th December, 1725, he had thought fit to include among his resolutions the following Saturday evening one not to detract 'against the King'. He was, however, especially in his early years, in close touch with those whose sentiments were conversationally critical of the Hanoverian dynasty and its agents. He may have been acquainted with the Jacobite Non-juror, Thomas Hearne, who had many friends in Lincoln.[2] Two days before his ordination he was talking with Sherman[3] at breakfast about passive obedience, and vindicated Sacheverell. At New College on 5th November, 1725, a significant day, he talked, presumably with Robin Griffiths, of passive obedience and engaged in 'evil speaking' of Walpole; when he breakfasted with Lord

---

[1] This, and other comments of a similar nature, were written in cipher in his diary.

[2] On 2nd February, 1726, he had breakfast at Hearne's and sat with him the next day; but this may have been another Mr. Hearne (elsewhere he speaks of an acquaintance, a Mr. Hearne of London). Dr. Salter asks whether the entry for 21st January, 1730, 'Wellesley talked with me about Bilstone's treason and said 'twas much to my honour', referred to John Wesley (*Collectanea*, xi, 479), but Wesley was in London on that day.

[3] Sherman's own sympathies were probably high Tory; Sherman 'spoke to us', the Non-Juror, John Byrom, noted in his journal during a visit to London on 2nd January, 1726.

Dupplin on 14th February, 1727, they talked of Walpole and Lord Bolingbroke, though no doubt somewhat more circumspectly than on the occasion a year previously, when he and others had been talking against the government in Burman's rooms. On 31st January, 1726, he listened to Dr. Owen preaching the annual sermon in commemoration of King Charles, 'and Saul was consenting to his death'. He was the more affected by the sermon which Dr. George Coningsby, the Vice-Principal of St. Mary Hall, preached on a similar anniversary in 1727, so much so that he made a comparatively lengthy summary of its conclusions in his diary.[1] In his sermon Coningsby had praised Charles I with flattery that fringed on treason; he was a 'prince . . . not alien by birth' who 'preferred to dignities in the church men of true worth and learning'. 'From such expressions K. George (as he is stiled)', Hearne added, 'was look'd upon as reflected upon for preferring such as he does & the Revolution branded.'[2] One, Francis Ayscough, of Corpus, referred the matter to the Vice-Chancellor, the President of his own College, Dr. Mather, and Coningsby was called to explain his sentiments before a committee of Heads of Houses and doctors. The preacher glibly explained he had lost his notes, an excuse which did not save him from being suspended from preaching before the University for two years, a sentence for which Lord Townshend thanked the authorities.

All the various difficulties relating to Wesley's election at Lincoln were in any case being smoothed out. On 11th March, 1726, he sat with his Lincoln friend, Thomas Persehouse, and two fellows of the College, John Brereton and Richard Hutchins, having previously written a theme at the Rector's. The next evening he reviewed his life and resolved never to rush his prayers, to rise at daybreak and to reflect twice each day on what he intended to do and once a day on what he had done. Monday, 14th March, seems to have been the crucial day. He breakfasted with Brereton at the College, read in the Bodleian and then underwent some form of examination in Horace and Homer later in the morning. During the

---

[1] 'No exception to be made from a general rule, unless either by the lawgiver or from the reason of the thing. St. Paul's reasons are against it, as is the very idea of government; for supremacy, limited or unlimited, implies a last resort, and from that last resort there lies no appeal. So that to assert both supremacy and resistance, that is a farther appeal, is a palpable contradiction. If God be the origin of all power, then is the supreme governor his vice-gerent. If his vice-gerent, then he has no superior, but him from whom his authority is derived, and if he has no superior but God, then there can be no appeal from him to any but God himself.'

[2] Hearne, *Collectanea*, ix, 263, 266, 268.

afternoon he called on the Rector and later at a mutual friend's, Mr. Le
Hunte's, he talked again with three of the fellows, Tottenham, Vesey and
Brereton. Three days later, 17th March, he was elected 'unanimo con-
sensu' to the vacant fellowship; he underlined the entry of his election in
his diary and added the letters which called for thanksgiving to God,
'V.F.' After the election he 'waited on ye Fellows severally' and dined
with them that evening. There was rejoicing when the news reached
Epworth: 'I think myself obliged to return great thanks to Almighty
God, for giving you good success at Lincoln', his mother told him. 'Let
whoever be pleased be the instrument, to him and to him alone the glory
appertains.' 'What will be my own fate before the summer be over, God
knows; *sed passi graviora*', his father began somewhat gloomily, but then
brightening at the strange good fortune, finished with a flourish, 'Wherever I am, my Jack is Fellow of Lincoln.'

In spite of the success which had crowned his efforts, a feeling of dissatisfaction persisted. When shortly after the 'conversion' of May, 1738,
John Wesley looked back over his earlier spiritual development, he recalled that in his early years at the University he 'said his prayers both in
public and private, and read, with the Scriptures, several other books of
religion, especially comments on the New Testament'. But he added that
he had no 'notion of inward holiness; nay, went on habitually, and for the
most part very contentedly, in some or other known sin: indeed, with
some intermission and short struggles, especially before and after the Holy
Communion, which I was obliged to receive thrice a year'. At the time of
his ordination there was a change, a more compelling realization of the
need for a change of life. As a result of reading Thomas à Kempis, 'I
began to see that true religion was seated in the heart, and that God's law
extended to all our thoughts as well as words and actions.' He added that
at the time he thought that à Kempis was too strict, and this is borne out
by his comments in a letter that he wrote to his mother on 28th May,
1725.

'I can't think that when God sent us into the world He had irrever-
sibly decreed that we should be perpetually miserable in it. . . . What
are become of all the innocent comforts and pleasures of life, if it is
the intent of our Creator that we should never taste them? A fair
patrimony, indeed, which Adam has left his sons, if they are destined
to be continually wretched! . . . Another of his tenets, which is indeed
a natural consequence of this, is that all mirth is vain and useless, if
not sinful. . . . And he seems to carry the matter as much too far on

the other side afterwards, where he asserts that nothing is an affliction to a good man, and that he ought to thank God even for sending him misery.'[1]

By 1738 he had come to believe that these apparently sensible and pertinent objections were somehow ill founded, but even so he recognized the influence which à Kempis had already wielded in his life. To this he added the influence of 'a religious friend, which I never had till now'.[2] The result of all these things, epitomized in his ordination itself, was that

'I began to alter the whole form of my conversation, and to set in earnest upon a new life. I set apart an hour or two a day for religious retirement. I communicated every week. I watched against all sin, whether in word or deed. I began to aim at, and pray for, inward holiness!'[3]

This was in his own words Wesley's spiritual state when he was elected at Lincoln. Autobiographical statements of this kind, more especially when they are made under the stress of a recent emotional experience, are notoriously untrustworthy. Yet Wesley's portrayal of his spiritual development is by and large supported by the evidence of his diary and letters. Whether he was justified in deploring its inadequacies is entirely another matter upon which the historian is hardly called to make a judgement. It will appear that Wesley was obsessed by the notion of moral imperfection; like Martin Luther at an earlier date, he sought an infallible authority by which he could direct his life. If he was aiming for holiness, then he was dissatisfied with his efforts.

His diary is studded with short entries made in cipher which are avowals of past failure and resolutions to do better in future. Many of these self-critical confessions were made on Saturday night, preparatory to his attendance at holy communion the following morning. They owed something to his reading in ascetical theology but most to the scrupulous temperament of Wesley himself. He found life pleasurable and as he commented when reading à Kempis this seemed to him part of the divine plan. 'If our taking up the cross implies our bidding adieu to all joy and satisfaction, how is it reconcilable with what Solomon so expressly affirms of religion—that her ways are ways of pleasantness and all her paths peace?' But he had a nagging suspicion that he was falling below the

[1] *Letters*, i, 16.
[2] See p. 206.
[3] *Journal*, i, 466-7.

G

standards required of him by God. Shortly before his ordination his mother, it will be recalled, commended his greater seriousness of purpose; and we cannot acquit that good lady of encouraging the introspective self-examination to which her son so constantly submitted himself.

There were recesses in his soul into which he alone could peer. 'Hide nothing', he told himself, but the spiritual insight into his own character was sometimes curiously limited. He looked so constantly into a spiritual mirror that ultimately he failed to recognize some of the defects it revealed. Faced with the possibility of spiritual disaster, he became preoccupied, perhaps too much so, with the problem of finding a solution to his own inadequacy. He was not particularly worried by problems of belief or doctrine. It was the simple problem of failing to live a Christian life as he saw it.

Yet when the cipher entries are unravelled, many of the failings which he noted with such regularity seem relatively trivial; for instance, idleness, lying, heat in arguing, levity, detraction and intemperate sleep. There is almost some lack of imagination in the repetition of such phrases. What in truth did they amount to? Idleness, perhaps the most frequent self-accusatory word, was usually associated with Wesley's lighter reading; yet idle in the accepted sense of the word he never was, nor never could be. 'Told a lie', he writes at least twice, but he meant much more than to tell an untruth; to Wesley the word implied misrepresentation and intellectual dishonesty. He was certainly sometimes heated in argument; he himself noted that he had argued warmly over a trifle, probably with Burman,[1] the evening of the day he was ordained. From early youth he had taken a stand on principle and possessing a lucid and logical mind he was apt to challenge loose thinking on the part of others; in the subsequent argument he occasionally became heated and bitter. He had displayed 'devilish anger', he wrote on 1st March, 1726. Levity less censured in his early diary than later was the opposite of that seriousness of purpose which fought a winning battle in Wesley's mind. Detraction, a curious word of which he was strangely fond, must stand for that criticism of others, what he termed elsewhere rash censures, contemning others. Intemperate sleep is susceptible of more than one interpretation. Generally Wesley merely intended to convey that he had over-indulged in sleep; immoderate was a more suitable adjective to indicate what he meant. He was already indeed concerned with early rising, another of the customs

---

[1] Cf. a later entry, for 13th November, 1725, when he reproached himself for his 'unchristian usage of Burman'.

which became wellnigh an obsession with him. But he could also mean the passing fancies, the sexual hallucinations, of the dream world: the 'unclean thoughts' he adumbrated in a review of his failings on 29th January, 1726.[1]

Wesley had recourse to resolutions or rules of life, modelled as it would appear from later references on Jeremy Taylor's *Rules and Exercises of Holy Living*. He recalls himself to regular devotion, to prayer and humility, to work for at least six hours every day, to rise in the mornings at five o'clock, to fast every Wednesday in the month, to eliminate impurity of thought by thinking of God's omnipresence.[2] The very day after his ordination he resolved to reflect twice every day; on 24th October, 1725, he vowed that he would read over the last week's resolution every day. He must commit his failures and his resolves to paper. It was almost as if he wished to talk to himself, to reassure himself in his battle against the forces of evil. Time and time again, sometimes the very day after the original resolution, he was forced to admit 'breach of vow or resolution'.

When therefore John Wesley became a fellow of Lincoln College, there was present a definite element of spiritual uncertainty, nor could he have stated then what the future held in store. Conscientious, earnest, studious, sociable, he was about to begin another stage in his career. He determined that it should not be an unavailing one. 'Removing soon after to another College', he wrote in 1738, 'I executed a resolution which I was before convinced was of the utmost importance, shaking off at once all my trifling acquaintance. I began to see more and more the value of time. I applied myself closer to study. I watched more carefully against actual sins; I advised others to be religious, according to that scheme of religion by which I modelled my own life.' Although he had there epitomized the experience of some four or five years, he yet made it plain, and rightly so, that an epochal period in his life was just about to begin.

[1] Cf. the juxtaposition of the words in the confession of 1st December, 1725 'Intemperance in sleep: sins of thoughts: hence useless or sinful anger.'
[2] Cf. especially the review of 1st December, 1725, 29th January and 12th March, 1726.

CHAPTER V

Lincoln College during John Wesley's Time

LINCOLN COLLEGE, Oxford, with which John Wesley was to be associated until his marriage brought his tenure of his fellowship to a close in 1751, was a small society which had been founded by Richard Fleming, Bishop of Lincoln, in 1427, to supply learned clerics to combat the menace of the Lollard heresy. It was situated in the narrow Turl which debouches into the High Street by All Saints' Church, only recently rebuilt to the design of Dean Aldrich, and it consisted then, as it still does, of two small quadrangles which in addition to rooms for fellows and undergraduates housed a fifteenth-century dining-hall and a fine Chapel which had been built partly through the munificence of a former Visitor of the College, John Williams, Bishop of Lincoln, in 1630-1. The College library was located in the former Chapel on the north side of the front quad and above the panelled[1] Senior Common Room where the fellows of the College met to drink their wine after dinner, to make their wagers[2] and to pass the time in gossip and discussion. Behind the College there was a pleasant garden called the Grove adorned by fruit trees and shrubs;[3] to the east side of this a small cottage-like building was built in 1739 to house six undergraduates.

The College was not rich. Its endowments, by comparison with those enjoyed by most other Colleges, were small. It possessed a little property in Oxford; seven or eight houses and three inns in the parish of All Saints, the Split Crow, the Maidenhead, and, most important of all, the Mitre, which was leased at an annual rental of £4 13s. 4d. in 1726 to Mr. Dod-

---

[1] I take the opportunity to correct a statement in my *Oxford Common Room* (1957), 17; the panelling is almost certainly of oak, not of chestnut.

[2] On 22nd March John Wesley lost a wager of a shilling to Fielder Hammond, of Christ Church.

[3] Viz. entries in the accounts: in 1734, Johnson, the gardener, received £3 2s. 11d. and £4 6s. 9d.; in 1738 money was expended on trees for the garden and the Grove, on gravel, for 'new pulling the codling hedge': in 1749-50, for a garden roller, flower roots, four laurestinus bushes for the Grove and for making a 'new Eppalice'.

84

well.[1] There was also some other property, a few houses, stables and gardens situated in and near Oxford. In the near neighbourhood of Oxford the College owned a farm at Littlemore (let to Allen at a rental of £3 6s. 8d.), a farm and mill at Iffley, land at Combe and Twyford, farms at Policot and Ashendon (where its distinguished tenant was Richard Grenville), Petsoe and Eckney, Botley (Berks), and Charlbury; it owned some property in Standlake, Berrick and Chalgrove. Further afield it possessed land at Little Smeaton in Yorkshire and at Whitstable in Kent.[2] But though it was not a wealthy College, it was quietly prosperous during the first half of the eighteenth century. There was only one year, 1744, in which the Calculus or annual account showed a deficit, and this was because of unusually heavy expenses on building. Between 1725 and 1751 the annual expenses varied between £940 9s. 4¾d. (in 1747) and £1,184 10s. 3½d. (in 1737) while the income ranged from £1,609 18s. 11¾d. (an unusually high figure due to a benefaction in 1737) to £1,021 6s. 3½d. There was generally a useful if not very substantial balance.

College life, for all the political and religious vicissitudes of the past two centuries, was still rooted in its medieval framework. The obit days of its principal benefactors continued to be remembered, not indeed by the masses and services as had been originally intended, but by special allowances paid to fellows in residence at the time of the commemoration.[3] The accounts show that on average there were about six of the twelve fellows resident, sometimes in the summer fewer than this. Another relic of the past was the small allowances paid to the fellows on different religious festivals.[4] More recent commemorations were indicated by the two

[1] Dodwell was replaced *c.* 1735 as tenant by Bernard and *c.* 1743 by Austin.

[2] Viz. a typical item in the accounts indicates the visits of College officials to these properties, e.g. in 1731 'our expenses in visiting our estate at Whitstable, £14 14s. 6d.' Mr. Robinson's and Mr. Farrer's expenses to the College living of Winterbourne in 1734, £9 10s.; Mr. Hutton's and the bursar's expenses to Berrick in 1738, 2s.

[3] Viz. on 16th November (Walter Bate) and 16th January (Bishop Beckington) they received 6d.; on 21st March (John Crosby), 11th April (Cardinal Beaufort), 8d.; on 10th January (Archdeacon Darby), 23rd February (John Southam), 26th February (John Forrest), 29th March (Archbishop Rotheram), 23rd August (Bishop Audley), 10th October (Bishop Smith) and 29th (William Dagville), 1s. The Rector received double allowance (originally because he was the celebrant at the commemorative mass).

[4] Originally the statutes prescribed an addition to the allowance for commons (i.e. for the common table) on these days which were known as 'gaudies'. By the sixteenth century they implied only small money payments to the Rector and

shillings and fourpence allocated for a bonfire on 29th May (Restoration Day) and 5th November.

A fellowship was financially a share in the common revenues of the College computed according to what a fellow had by right, irrespective of whether he was in residence or not, and by what he enjoyed by reason of his residence in College. The extremely complicated financial machinery of an eighteenth-century College, made the more tangled by the difficulty of ensuring that what was put down on paper actually represented the true facts of the case, does not make it easy to reckon what the sum total of a fellow's income was likely to have been.[1] It was made up of many allowances which were rooted in the College's medieval foundation. The chief of these, known as provision, was dependent upon residence. A fellow also received commons (i.e. a share in the common table), obit money,[2] and gaudy money. He was given an allowance of two shillings a quarter for the laundress, a shilling for the barber, and slightly variable amounts for vinegar, brawn, and oysters,[3] and poundage.[4] Each fellow also received a small dividend. Whether in residence or not, he was entitled to a share of the fines or renewal of leases which occurred annually; these indeed made up the major fraction of his fellowship, and

---

fellows; a note was kept of their residence on such days. The days and the allowances were: The Conception of the Blessed Virgin Mary (2d.), Christmas (8d.), Epiphany (4d.), Purification (2d.), Quinquagesima (2d.), Annunciation (2d.), Easter (8d.), Ascension (4d.), Pentecost (8d.), Corpus Christi (4d.), St. Mildred (2d.), Assumption (2d.), St. Bartholomew (4s. *inter presentes*), Nativity (2d.), St. Michael (2d.), Dedication of St. Michael's, Oxford (2d.), All Saints (4d.), Dedication of All Saints', Oxford (4d.). The place of the old gaudies was taken in the eighteenth century by certain days on which by College order special payments were made for a College dinner and for a supply of wine at dinner, e.g. Easter Day, Christmas Day, the two Chapter days, 6th May and 6th November.

[1] See Appendix 2.

[2] See p. 185n[2].

[3] An alleviation for the severities of Lent was provided by the benefaction (1526) of William Fettiplace of Childrey to Queen's College. He gave Lincoln certain rights of supervision over the execution of his will which Queen's bought up for a yearly quit-rent of 6s. 8d. The proceeds of this quit-rent were devoted to the purchase of oysters in Lent, but ultimately commuted to a money payment. Although the College continued to buy a collar of brawn, this too was represented by a commutation.

[4] This was a percentage charged on certain items of each person's expenditure in the buttery and kitchen. The proceeds served to meet some establishment charges and to make up the stipends of some officials.

account for the very variable sums of money that he received from year to year. Finally through the recent bequest of Nathaniel, Lord Crewe, the Bishop of Durham, the Rector received £20 and the fellows £10 each a year in augmentation of their stipends.[1] As against this each fellow had to pay his subscription to the Senior Common Room, and if he were living in College, the share of its expenses, and his battels. The affairs of the Common Room were regulated by itself, not by College meetings, and if the subscription did not cover all its expenses,[2] the remainder was shared out among the residents.[3] Every fellow was entitled to his rooms free of rent, and if he were absent a rental from these rooms when they were otherwise occupied. If he was a tutor he received fees from his tuition, and similarly if he held College office as a moderator he enjoyed an additional emolument.

A fellow was not therefore a rich man—indeed, if he were rich he was debarred by the statutes from being elected to a fellowship—but he enjoyed an adequate income in pleasant surroundings as long as he remained unmarried. He very often supplemented his income by taking parochial work elsewhere, but, again, he was not permitted to hold his fellowship with a cure of souls, bringing in more than a certain limited annual income. When the College was founded, three churches had been appropriated, one of which, St. Mildred's, had been pulled down completely; the other two, All Saints' and St. Michael's, were staffed by chaplains often appointed in the eighteenth century from among the College fellows. Two parishes, Combe and Twyford, had been annexed to the Rectorship, and were also often served by fellows of the College; the chaplain of Combe received £30 a year. None of these chaplaincies, however, counted as livings. A College fellow ordinarily looked forward to preferment to a living which would not merely give him an opportunity for marriage but in general promised a richer reward than did a fellowship. It was at this period that a Livings Fund was established for the purchases of advowsons, which would provide a possible avenue of retirement or preferment for a College fellow; that of Great Leighs in

---

[1] His bequest to the College amounted annually to £474 6s. 8d.—£160 for the Rector and fellows; £40 for the four chaplains of the College cure of souls; £240 for twelve exhibitioners; £28 13s. 4d. for four Trappes scholars; £20 for four Marshall scholars and £5 13s. 4d. for the Bible Clerk.

[2] The chief expenses were coal, candles, pipes, and an almanack; occasionally glasses. A rule laid down that if any member took a candle from the Senior Common Room he should forfeit a bottle of wine.

[3] Thus in 1731 Wesley's share amounted to 9s. 4d.; in 1734 to 13s.

Essex had been bought in 1726 for £800 and that of Winterborne Abbas and Winterborne Steepleton in Dorset in 1735 for £935.

At the time of Wesley's election the governing body of the College consisted of a Rector and twelve fellows; many of the latter were non-resident and only appeared at the two major College meetings on 6th May and 6th November, and not always then, to request further leave of absence. The Rector, John Morley, was himself a Lincolnshire man, though originally of Trinity and Pembroke Colleges, who had been a fellow of the College since November, 1689; since 1711 he had also been able to hold (by dispensation) the Lincolnshire living of Scotton, near Gainsborough, where he was a near neighbour of Wesley's father. In the fellowship election of 1725–6 that 'generous man', as Wesley called him, was a strong supporter of his young comrade from Lincolnshire; John Wesley himself respected and liked Morley. Writing to Anne Granville on 17th June, 1731, he excused his delay in replying to her letter by reason of the 'death of one of the best friends I had in the world' (Morley died at Scotton on 12th June), while two days later he told Mrs. Pendarves, ''Tis but a few days since that I had a little share in your misfortune in parting with a sincere friend. But I shall go to him again, if he does not return to me, though he is gone a longer journey than Selima, I hope as far as Paradise.'[1] Morley was a 'worthy, honest man', who had been a 'great Tutor at the College' until his elevation to the rectorship and subsequent marriage made him indolent.[2] In politics he was an active if moderate Tory who used his interest to defeat the government's supporters,[3] though he proved a bitter opponent of the Jacobite Dr. King in the election of 1722.[4]

There were eleven fellows at the time of Wesley's election. One of the fellows was appointed by the Visitor to the College, the Bishop of Lincoln; throughout Wesley's tenure of his fellowship this was William Vesey, who was elected in 1703 and retained his fellowship until his death at the age of seventy-eight in 1755. A studious bachelor, his antiquarian interests brought him into friendly contact with Thomas Hearne. They often talked together on the past history of the College and the topo-

---

[1] *Letters*, i, 89.
[2] *Collectanea*, ed. H. E. Salter, x, 427.
[3] W. R. Ward, *Georgian Oxford* (1958), 117, 133.
[4] *Op. cit.*, 126. He brought pressure to bear on the members of his College to vote against King, 'being especially savage', Dr. Ward notes, but 'failed to prevent the majority of second votes being cast for King'.

II JOHN MORLEY, RECTOR OF LINCOLN, 1719–31
Thomas Photos, Oxford

graphy of Oxford: Vesey 'told me', wrote Hearne, 'he thought he had found in their College Writings that the Spicery in Oxford was in All-Hallows parish'.[1] In September, 1728, Vesey showed Hearne the College Register and in subsequent conversation Hearne suggested to Vesey that the historical passages in Thomas Gascoigne's manuscript *Dictionarium Theologicum*, then housed in the College library, should be printed;[2] but neither Vesey nor Tottenham, another fellow whom Hearne knew, was eager that he should undertake this task.[3] The College, however, owed Vesey an immense debt for transcribing many of the College charters and documents, some of which, among them the original charter of foundation, have since been lost. The books in the College library also still bear witness to his conscientious care. Vesey was for a time one of Wesley's closest friends in College.

Most of the other fellowships were attached to regions, the first preference in an election being given to candidates from these localities. Wesley, for instance, was elected to a Lincolnshire fellowship. In the sixteenth century, Edward Darby, Archdeacon of Stow, had endowed three fellowships, one of which had subsequently become the Visitor's fellowship, but the other two were given to natives of Northamptonshire or Leicestershire and the archdeaconry of Stow. These were held, in 1726, by Euseby Isham, who later succeeded Morley as Rector, and Thomas Vaughan, who elected in 1715, remained a fellow until his death in 1747. The Somerset or Wells fellow was John Tottenham, who resigned in 1730, when he was succeeded by Peter Davis of Christ Church. The Lincolnshire fellows were Wesley, Michael Robinson and Charles Dymoke; the latter was related to the Dymokes of Scrivelsby Court who by tradition supplied the champion at the coronation. The fellows of the Lincolnshire diocese were Knightley Adams, who had been elected as far back as 1700, Richard Hutchins, another future Rector, who died in 1781, and William Lupton. Lupton died in 1726 and was succeeded in the Yorkshire fellowship by Lewis Fenton. The remaining fellows connected by birth with the county or diocese of York were Benjamin Mangey, whose brother, Dr. Thomas Mangey, won some distinction as a theologian and preacher, and John Brereton.

[1] *Collectanea*, x, 1–2.
[2] *Op. cit.*, x, 49–50.
[3] Excerpts were again reprinted by Thorold Rogers in *Loci e Loco Veritatum* (1881), but a full edition, repairing some of Rogers' inaccuracies, is promised by Mrs. Maxwell.

None of these fellows had played or was to play a prominent part in either the life of the Church or of the University. John Tottenham, who was a friend of Hearne's and in the early days of his fellowship an intimate of Wesley's, became a canon of Wells and was vicar of Cheddar from 1729 to 1740. William Lupton, who had been a fellow since 1698, a protégé of the College's former Rector and benefactor, Nathaniel, Lord Crewe, had been a preacher at Lincoln's Inn Chapel, Lecturer at the Temple Church and held a prebendal stall at Durham. He printed a number of sermons,[1] one of which, asserting the doctrine of eternal punishment, won him some publicity.

'He was', Hearne commented, 'a studious Man, a good Scholar, and a good Preacher; but, I am told, there is something (I know not what) that is very singular, whimsical, and odd in his Will. He was a Man of a sickly Constitution, and he would be frequently complaining of his Health when he lived in Oxford, where he used to keep in very much on that account.'[2]

Dr. Lupton, who had so justly appreciated the unhealthy character of the Oxford climate, was the only one among the fellows who was at all widely known outside Oxford. The College's failure to elect Lupton as Rector in 1719 in preference to Morley to some extent alienated its patron,

[1] Viz.: *The Necessity and Measures, the Excellency and Efficacy of Works of Charity Represented* (preached before the Lord Mayor and Aldermen at St. Bridget's Church, 8th April, 1713); *National Sins Fatal to Prince and People* (preached before the House of Commons at St. Margaret's, Westminster, 30th January, 1724); *The Eternity of Future Punishment Proved and Vindicated* (preached before the University of Oxford, 24th November, 1706); *The Omniscience of God* (preached before Nathaniel, Bishop of Durham, in his Chapel at Stene, 2nd October, 1720); *A Sermon preach'd before the Sons of the Clergy* (at St. Paul's, 5th December, 1717); *The Resurrection of the Same Body* (preached before the University of Oxford, 2nd April, 1711); *A Discourse of Murther* (preached at Lincoln's Inn, 1725); *A Sermon preached at St. Dunstan's in the West* (on Friday, 16th December, 1720, being a day appointed by His Majesty for a General FAST; and particularly for beseeching God to preserve us from the PLAGUE); *The Temporal Advantages of Religion* (preached before Nathaniel, Lord Crewe, Bishop of Durham, in his chapel at Stene, being the anniversary of his consecration, his lordship having then been FIFTY YEARS A BISHOP, 1721); *Christian Conversation*, a farewell sermon at St. Dunstan's-in-the-West, 20th March, 1726.

[2] *D.N.B.*, xii, 289; Hearne's *Collectanea*, ix, 243. He incorrectly stated that Lupton had relinquished his fellowship long ago. On Crewe's irritation with the fellows at their election of Morley see *Portland MSS.*, vii, 255-9, 262. I have to thank Mr. J. B. Lawson for drawing my attention to this.

Nathaniel, Lord Crewe, and led to a diminution of the benefaction it had hoped from him.

The remainder, all of whom were in orders, were either destined to end their days as College fellows or as country parsons. Knightley Adams went to the College living of Great Leighs in Essex, succeeding there another fellow of the College, John Brereton, who had also in his time acted as chaplain of All Saints' Church, Oxford. Lewis Fenton went to another College living, the advowson of which had been purchased recently, that of Winterborne Abbas and Steepleton in Dorset. Samuel Adams, who followed Knightley Adams in 1742, was later vicar of Twyford, the rectorial living.

The period following the Restoration had on the whole been prosperous. Its most distinguished Rector had been a former fellow, Nathaniel, Lord Crewe,[1] who moved from the bishopric of Oxford to that of Durham: ecclesiastical time-server and political sycophant as he may have been, and sorely tried as he was by the College's behaviour in 1719, he yet proved a benefactor. Many of Lord Crewe's exhibitioners came from the north of England, and were enabled to enter Lincoln through his generosity. His protégé, William Lupton, given the task of commemorating the fiftieth anniversary of his lordship's consecration as a bishop, praised not without some justification

'. . . the Beneficial Use, which this *Noble* Hand hath made of *Riches*. . . . His Generous and Lasting Provisions for the *Education of Youth*, the *Advancement of Learning*, and the *Defence and Propagation of Religion*, Cannot be Concealed, and shall never be Forgot. Blessed the Man, who thus Cultivates and Inricheth his Countrey, by his Passage through it!'[2]

It was the College's good fortune that Crewe should have had as successors men as capable as Thomas Marshall, a pioneer in Anglo-Saxon studies, who bequeathed to the College his precious collection of pamphlets of the period of the Civil War, and Fitzherbert Adams, who helped to enrich the interior of the Chapel and Common Room. It had also elected as fellows some of the future luminaries of the Non-juring movement; John Kettlewell and George Hickes, the Non-juring bishop of Thetford, had been among them. Its political tradition was certainly Tory, if not completely uniform at all times, and clearly not Jacobite.

The fellows of the College were still governed by its fifteenth-century

[1] See C. E. Whiting, *Nathaniel, Lord Crewe.*
[2] W. Lupton, *The Temporal Advantages of Religion* (1721), 27.

statutes. College affairs were settled at meetings of the fellows in residence; it was here that elections to fellowships and scholarships were made. No eighteenth-century minute exists of these meetings save of the formal appointment to College offices and leaves of absence given to fellows at the two principal meeting days, 6th May and 6th November. At the May Chapter they appointed the preacher for the Feast of All Saints (at All Saints' Church), immemorially the Rector; at the same time fellows were nominated to preach on the Feast of St. Michael (at St. Michael's) and at the Dedication of All Saints. In November the Subrector, Bursar and Librarian, and the Moderator of Classes were elected; the Greek Lecturer, who was nominated by the Rector, was responsible for giving instruction in the Greek Testament. The fellows also elected a Claviger, who held one of the three keys of the College treasury. Two fellows were appointed to preach sermons at Combe in Lent. At the meeting on 22nd December, the Bursar presented the accounts and if these proved acceptable the Calculus was then signed by the Rector and fellows who were then in residence.

The life of an Oxford fellow in the early eighteenth century was on the whole leisurely and peaceful, if sometimes disturbed, though not to any extent in Lincoln, by occasional and protracted personal quarrels. The better rooms in the College were reserved to the resident fellows. When John Wesley came into residence he chose at the College meeting on 6th May, 1726, the rooms situated in the second quad overlooking the Turl,[1] which had been formerly occupied by his friend, Bayliff. The resident fellows dined in Hall at 12 noon,[2] retiring to the Senior Common Room afterwards. The even tenor of existence was interrupted by occasional feast days, of which the Gaudy on All Saints' Day would seem to have been the most opulent.[3] At its inception the College had been a religious

---

[1] See Appendix 3, 'John Wesley's rooms in Lincoln College'.

[2] The hour for dinner steadily became later; the Rector dined at the more fashionable hour of 1 p.m.

[3] The accounts provide for the purchase of additional wine on the feast days; Christmas Day, Candlemas Day, Easter Day, 6th May, Whitsunday, Michaelmas Day, All Saints, Audit Day (22nd December); the greatest expenditure was on All Saints' Day (1738–9, £4 14s. 6d.; 1741–2, £2 9s.). Certain other days also seem to have been marked by additional wine; these were occasions on which the College tenants traditionally presented capons (Mather on 19th December, Foulkes on 2nd February, Huckwell on 19th March, Astrey on 29th May, Houghton on 5th November); but it is not clear whether the tenant had already commuted the capons into a money payment or not.

foundation, and all of its fellows in Wesley's day were in Anglican orders. Morning and evening prayer were said in Chapel daily; and the Holy Communion was regularly if infrequently celebrated there.[1] Later during Wesley's time as a fellow, though after he had ceased to be resident, the College ordered the scholars to read the lessons at Morning and Evening services, with the proviso that 'for the greater solemnity' fellows in their surplices should read the lessons on Sundays, holidays and their eves.

The demands which teaching (or indeed study) made upon a fellow's time were comparatively small. If he wished he could engage in informal instruction of men from his own or other Colleges, which would add to his stipend. The complicated series of exercises which led to a University degree were already conventional and meaningless. No undergraduate had to pass anything in the least similar to a modern examination before he became a bachelor of arts. It was, however, realized that the University existed to foster scholarship and to train those who came to it in intellectual exercises. It was to this end that the College appointed annually a Moderator of Classes and a Greek Lecturer. The former presided over the disputations which were supposed to convey instruction in logic and philosophy, while the latter was obliged to teach the rudiments of the faith and comment on the Greek Testament. Certainly one and sometimes two fellows acted as tutors. It seems unlikely that those who were appointed to the Moderatorship and the Greek Lecturership had themselves to be in residence if there were fellows living in College ready to do their work, but if there was no one the Rector was entitled to summon a fellow to reside as indeed he did in Wesley's case.[2] A College order of 1770 evidently describes contemporary practice, which had probably existed unchanged since Wesley's day. On every day of the four weeks following the November Chapter day, excepting Sundays, there were to be undergraduate exercises which are listed as follows: 'Disputations on Mondays, Wednesdays, and Fridays; a Greek (Testament) Lecture on Tuesdays and Thursdays; Declamations and Themes on Saturdays.' No one was to be excused attendance at any of these 'upon any pretence whatever'. Similar exercises were to be performed on the same

[1] This can again be gauged from the accounts: 25th December, Wine for Chapel, 1s. 0d.; 7th March, Wine for ye Sacrament 1st Sunday in Lent, 2s. 0d.; 18th April, Easter Day, Wine in Chapel, 2s. 6d.; Whitsunday, 2s. 6d.; 24th October, Wine in ye Chapel, 2s. 6d. There are also regular references to the washing of surplices. It is interesting to observe that in 1755 Arthur Annesley, a former gentleman commoner of the College, presented an altar-cloth of rich velvet with a set of cushions.

[2] See p. 122–3.

days of every week in full term from Ash Wednesday to the Commemoration of Benefactors in the third week of the Act Term, in July. Attendance was only excused on Chapter Days and the day of the Assize Sermon.
In other seasons of the year, as there were likely to be fewer resident, no
declamations would be required of the undergraduates, but all 'that are
in Town carry up their Themes on Saturdays in Full Term'. There was to
be a Greek (Testament) lecture once a week, while disputations were to
take place twice a week, if there were four in a class, or once if there were
fewer. It may be doubted if these stipulations had ever been effectively
carried out.[1] Yet it would be incorrect to suggest that the College took no
interest in teaching its undergraduates or had no love of learning. It is an
indication of its conscientiousness that year after year it employed John
Gagnier as its Hebrew Master during Wesley's time.

It was then a comparatively scholarly and gentlemanly society. John
Thorold of Cranwell, whom Wesley succeeded as a fellow and with
whom he was later friendly, was a country gentleman, scholar and author
of evangelical works on the Scriptures as well as a benefactor to his old
College. This 'new star of righteousness' as Grace Granville described
Thorold to Lord Lansdowne in November, 1738,

> '. . . has a very plentiful fortune . . . a married man and five children.
> He preaches twice a week, Mondays and Fridays, reads a chapter out
> of the Bible, and then explains every verse of it. He has got a young
> gentleman from Oxford to live with him, who follows his example.'[2]

Another of the fellows, Euseby Isham, later Rector, the brother of Sir
Justinian Isham, was a member of a well-known Northamptonshire
family. A friend of Hearne, he had similar antiquarian interests and after
he became rector began to gather materials for a history of the College, 'in
the manner of Dr. Savage's Ballio-Fergus', a project which proved still-

---

[1] E.g. 6th May, 1748, the College ordered that 'over and above, what other
Satisfaction, the Subrector may think fit to require, the sum of one shilling shall
immediately be put on the Name of every Undergraduate who shall neglect to
Narrate in his Turn; and the sum of Two shillings and Sixpence on the Name of
everyone, who shall neglect to bring in his Theme on Saturdays'. (*Col. Reg.*, iii,
fol. 12.)

[2] Lady Llanover, *Autobiography and Correspondence of Mrs. Delany*, ii, 8; John
Thorold published *A View of Popery or Observations on the Twelve Articles of the Coun-
cil of Trent presented to the Consideration of Ingenuous Romanists* (1766); *Scripture
interpreted by Scripture, or the Doctrine of the Trinity deduced from the Old and New
Testaments* (1770). In 1773 he gave the College £100 to augment the stipend of the
Bible Clerk.

born.[1] Another fellow was Hearne's correspondent, John Tottenham, from whom the Oxford annalist tried to elicit information about the character of Dr. Kidder, the Bishop of Bath and Wells (Tottenham had become a canon of Wells), and topics of historical and antiquarian interest.

'Yesterday,' Hearne wrote, on 11th February, 1727, 'call'd upon me Mr. Tottenham, Fellow of Linc. Coll., & read part of a letter he had rec'd from Dr. Archer, Archdeacon of Taunton, in wch the Dr. offers to send me some things relating to Glastonbury, if they would be of service. . . . He is look'd upon as honest, and so is Mr. Tottenham.'

Two years later Hearne happened to meet Tottenham as he was walking back from Beckley on Magdalen Bridge, 'it being an extraordinary fine day', and Tottenham told him that Archer promised to send him 'some MSS papers of good value'.

Hearne provides one further glimpse of College life at this time. The College was the patron and the incumbent of All Saints' Church at the end of the Turl. The acting Chaplain was the senior fellow, John Brereton, who had already aroused Hearne's wrath by opposing the publication of excerpts from Gascoigne; 'notwithstanding now that I have printed them they prove very useful and are extremely well received by good men such as are lovers of truth, and would have virtue flourish, and vice and wickedness exposed'. Hearne was provoked further by Brereton's unwillingness to restore some of the monuments belonging to the Church 'now lying next the street without the church'. He secured the support of the Rector, Euseby Isham, of Vesey and Richard Hutchins, but when he met Brereton as he was entering the churchyard and rather unwisely congratulated him on the decision to restore the stones, Brereton 'fell into a passion and used very scurrilous language, which is what I have been several times told he also hath used more than once before upon the same occasion'.[2] In general, however, the society which John Wesley was shortly to join was easy-going and good-tempered.

The number of residents, apart from the fellows living in College, was small. A list in Wesley's handwriting of members of the College gives 38 men, while bursarial lists for 1725 and 1727 respectively give 40 and 46 men in residence. Entrants were few and some were surprisingly

[1] *Collectanea*, xi, 206.
[2] *Op. cit.*, xi, 60.

young,[1] but the average age seems to have been much as to-day.[2] Undergraduates in the eighteenth century were classed according to their social
status; but Lincoln, which was never a fashionable college, housed no
noblemen. It had a few gentlemen commoners who paid substantially
larger fees[3] for the privilege of membership of the Senior Common
Room and living in better rooms in the College at higher rentals. 'A
gentleman-commoner,' wrote Amhurst, 'if be a man of fortune, is soon
told, that it is not expected from one of his form to mind exercises: if he
is studious, he is morose, and a heavy bookish fellow: if he keeps a cellar
of wine, the good-natur'd fellows will indulge him, tho' he should be too
heavy-headed to be at chapel in a morning.' These strictures, well sustained as they may have been in a number of cases, do not seem to have
been true as far as the gentlemen commoners at Lincoln in Wesley's
time were concerned. It was normal for a gentleman commoner to give
a piece of silver to the Senior Common Room on his departure.[4]

The undergraduates consisted of scholars and exhibitioners, usually
elected by the College after matriculation, commoners, servitors and the
Bible clerk. The former were in enjoyment of a small emolument provided out of endowments; Lord Crewe had recently made provision
for the election of scholars and exhibitioners who received £20 and £10
a year respectively. The servitors still performed menial tasks, waiting at
table in the hall.[5] The Bible clerk or Bibliotista had a special room, one of

---

[1] At Lincoln the numbers were: 1725, 5; 26, 17; 27, 6; 28, 7; 29, 3; 30, 8; 31, 11;
32, 8; 33, 11; 34, 8; 35, 7.

[2] An analysis of the 91 who entered the college between 1725 and 1735 shows
that 1 entered at 13, 1 at 14, 2 at 15, 12 at 16, 27 at 17, 28 at 18, 13 at 19, 5 at 20,
1 at 22, and 1 at 28. Thus only 16 out of the 91 were under 17.

[3] Thus whereas an ordinary commoner paid 20s. 6d. on admission (5s. to Domus,
3s. to the Bursar, 4s. to the Manciple, 2s. 6d. to the Cook, 2s. to the Bible clerk,
2s. to the Porter, 1s. to the Scrape-Trencher, and 1s. to the Rector's servant), a
gentleman commoner paid £2 10s. 10d. (9s. 4d. to Domus, 4s. to the Bursar, 10s.
to the Manciple, 5s. to the Bible clerk, 7s. 6d. to the Cook, 5s. to the Porter, 2s. 6d.
to the Scrape-Trencher, and 8s. for six napkins), in addition to £4 for a treat. His
tuition fees were also higher, £2 a quarter by comparison with the £1 and £1 11s. 6d.
charged a commoner and 10s. 6d. charged a servitor. He paid also 2d. a week extra
towards the fire in hall in addition to the normal charges levied on a commoner,
viz., 1s. 10d. to Domus, 2s. 1d. to the Manciple, 4d. for the Cook, per week; and
also paid his share of the Senior Common Room expenses.

[4] The list included in 1730 two candlesticks and snuffers from J. Thorold, a decanter
from H. Hamilton, a salver from W. Thorold, two sauceboats from Westley Hall,
twelve forks from J. Westley and a decanter from Richard Morgan.

[5] Every servitor who did not serve a table in hall had to pay 3d. a week.

the smallest, in the Chapel quad and was responsible for the care of the Chapel, ringing the bell and lighting the stairs and performing certain other tasks for which he received fees. Like the servitors he only paid ten shillings and sixpence a quarter for his tuition.[1]

The commoners' fees were made up of a series of dues which are in no way easy to disentangle. He had to pay, in addition to tuition, which normally came to £4 a year, an admission fee and caution money; he also paid 4s. 3d. a week from which 1s. 10d. was allocated to Domus to pay the stipend of the Moderator and Lecturer. If the amount contributed in this way by the undergraduates to the Moderator's salary of £3 a term was insufficient, the deficit was added to what had been expended on fuel and candles and divided equally among the bachelors and commoners.[2] Of the remaining 2s. 5d., 2s. 1d. went to the Manciple and 4d. to the cook. Every undergraduate had also to pay a rental for his chamber, the amount depending on whether he was sharing and where his room was situated; better rooms cost as much as £6 a year, but a garret could be rented for 15s. He ordinarily took over the furniture at valuation; if he were a wealthy man he might spend a considerable sum on improvements for which the College at the end of his tenure would compensate him to the extent of a third of the cost. Mr. Howson paid the upholsterer £5 10s. 6d. for work done in his rooms, and the son of Wesley's neighbour at Epworth, Robert Pindar, £6 7s. Each undergraduate and bachelor had also to pay for his battels or provisions, a sum varying according to the needs of the individual.

The other requirements depended much on personal taste and the amount of the allowance that the man had at his disposal. Necessarily he must have heat and light, with coals at 4s. a sack; Pindar spent 4s. 6d. on candles. Each undergraduate had also to have a cap and gown—a gentleman commoner of Lincoln paid £2 10s. for two silk gowns—and to pay the costs of a barber and of a wig unless, like John Wesley, he preferred to save money by wearing his own hair. Mr. Black paid 12s. 6d. for

[1] So, for instance, Edward Browne paid £1 11s. 6d. to John Wesley for three quarters' tuition in June, 1731.

[2] In the first quarter of 1731 the candle bill amounted to £9 10s. 6d., and fires in hall to £5, amounting in all to £14 10s. 6d. This was then divided among the 28 commoners—9s. each—and the 12 servitors—4s. 6d. each, giving a profit of 15s. 6d. to the College. In this quarter the fees for the moderators and lecturers were 3s. 2d. short but in subsequent quarters there was an excess of revenue over expenditure. The relative individual figures for heat and light in the remaining three quarters were 2s. 6d., 2s., and 3s. 8d., the servitors paying half this sum in each case.

H

shaving in 1728 while a wig varied enormously in cost, the more expensive being as much as £3. Tailors' bills varied according to the man's tastes and funds. Howson paid the seamstress 18s. 6d., Pindar 11s. 1d., Black £1 1s. 8d. Mr. Charlton paid 12s. for a hat, while young John Wesley, recently elected a fellow, paid 15s. Mr. Black's buckskin breeches and gloves cost £1 13s.; Wesley paid 5s. for a pair of gloves. He also paid 13s. 6d. for a pair of black silk stockings, 6s. 6d. for two pairs of thread, and 5s. for two pairs of worsted. Black paid his shoemaker £1 2s., Wesley paid 8s. 6d. for a pair of boots. Among other items in Wesley's accounts may be mentioned £1 1s. for a bureau, 6s. for spoons, 4s. for a picture, 3s. 6d. for a chafing-dish and charcoal, 10s. 6d. for napkins and towels, and 2s. 6d. for a penknife and a comb. Postage, laundering and the fees involved in the various exercises for the degrees[1] were other necessary levies on the undergraduate's purse. Some undergraduates and young graduates had their own horse but most hired a horse from time to time when they wished to take a journey.[2] Many undergraduates remained in College the whole year through, nor was there the exodus at the end of each term which is now so familiar a feature of University life.

The more detailed personal bills of a Lincoln undergraduate, David Locock, for 1742–3 survive. They show that he spent £3 13s. 1d. on various items of clothing, among them a velvet hunting-cap (14s.), a pair of gloves (1s. 4d.), two pairs of knitted hose (8s.), a square cap with a best tuft (6s. 6d.), two handkerchiefs (6s. 9d.) and four long cravats (18s.). The hire of a horse from Mr. Dry at the Eastgate for ten days cost him 15s. Between 1st and 24th January, 1743, he had bought some sixteen bottles of port at 2s. a bottle. His bill for shoes amounted to £1 13s. 6d., while on books and stationery he had expended £2 1s. 1d.[3] He had also borrowed from one Mr. Ryder sums amounting to £3 5s., in addition to a brown grogram waistcoat, a white dimity waistcoat, and a pair of white cotton stockings. When Mr. Locock left the College, the furniture in

---

[1] Mr. Long paid 15s. to 'answer under bachelor' in 1723, and all the various exercises carried their own fees. Wesley purchased 'Quodlibets at the auction' for 2s. 2d. The taking of a degree also entailed the payment of a fee.

[2] Mr. Charlton's horse cost him £7 8s., its shoeing 1s. 6d. and saddlery £1 11s. Fifteen days' upkeep amounted to 15s. Wesley's accounts include 2s. 6d. for spurs, 6d. for a lash for a whip and various amounts for hiring a horse, e.g., 2s. to take him to Combe, or to Abingdon; 4s. 6d. to Burton's parish of Buckland.

[3] This included Xenophon's *Expeditio Cyri* (18s.), Scheiber's *Compendium* (1s.), Cotton's *Works* (3s.) and Dionysius' *Geogr.* (2s. 6d.). On the other hand Pindar's book bill was £4 19s. 6d., Howson's £3 8s. 6d., and Black's £8 7s.

his room, consisting of one oval broken table, four prints and two maps, five matted bottom chairs, a bed, a bolster, blankets and sheets, and one wig block were valued at £4 4s.

The undergraduate's existence, punctuated as it might be by Chapel, Hall and occasional academic exercises, could be as varied as his expenses. He might spend his time in the coffee-house, reading the news and talking with his companions; he might follow the 'toasts' of the town in Christ Church Walk and Merton Mall, or bid fair to imitate the fast and elegant young noblemen of Christ Church.

'He saw, though he could not agree they had a vast deal of learning, that they had very good linnen; not abundance of wit, indeed, but very rich lace, red stockings, silver-buttoned coats, and other things, which constitute a man of taste in Oxford. . . . They were continually crying, Dick, prithee let's burn this damn'd brown wig of thine; get thee a little more linnen. . . . Dick, says one, did you never see miss Flavia, one of our top toasts?'

On the other hand, and often forgotten by the historian of the eighteenth-century University, there were the visits to the Bodleian and the College libraries and the time spent with the College tutor. Some College tutors might be inefficient and slack but there were conscientious men, like John Wesley, who took their duty seriously and tried to educate the men under their supervision. 'In the English colleges', Wesley wrote much later in his life, 'every one may reside all the year, as all my pupils did; and I should have thought myself little better than a highwayman if I had not lectured them every day in the year but Sundays.' There is no reason to believe that Wesley's conscientious devotion to duty was regarded as in any way extraordinary in the Oxford of his day; it was his religion rather than his learning that aroused public curiosity.

CHAPTER VI

The Young Fellow of Lincoln College, 1726–9

JOHN WESLEY was admitted to his fellowship on 27th March, 1726; on 19th April he was given leave of absence until 29th September. On 6th May he was nominated to preach the patronal day sermon at St. Michael's, and subsequently he held a number of other College offices.[1] Henceforward his life for many years was to be intimately associated with Lincoln. The statutes laid down that every fellow should proceed to the degree of bachelor of divinity within seven years of taking his master's degree; but one fellowship, founded by John Crosby in 1476, the so-called canonist fellowship, was free from this liability. Since Wesley failed to proceed to the B.D., he was elected to this fellowship on 13th July, 1736, when he was in Georgia, and continued to hold it until his resignation in 1751. As late as June, 1741, Wesley enquired about the exercises necessary for the B.D. degree.

Above all else, his fellowship provided financial security.[2] 'I reckon my fellowship near sixty pounds a year. Between forty and fifty it will infallibly cost to live at College, use what management I can.' Shortly after his election, his father had unexpectedly sent him a bill on Dr. Morley for twelve pounds, which he had paid to the Rector's use at Gainsborough; so that, 'now several of my debts are paid and the expenses of my treat defrayed, I have above ten pounds remaining; and if I could leave to stay in the country till my College allowance commences, this money would abundantly suffice me till then.' We have already commented on the difficulty of disentangling the complex financial machinery of the College, and the sum of sixty pounds mentioned by Wesley in his

---

[1] It might be convenient to mention the offices he held. He was appointed to preach the sermon at St. Michael's in 1726 and 1732; was Claviger in 1726–7, 1731–2; lecturer in logic, 1726–30; in Greek, 1726–7, 1729–34; in Philosophy, 1730–5; nominated to preach the sermon on All Saints' Day in 1734, 1743 and 1749; and Lent preacher at Combe in 1731, 1737 and 1743. It was possible for a substitute to undertake these duties.

[2] See Appendix 2.

letter to his brother, in December, 1726, was the amount that he would enjoy if he was resident in College.¹ Absentee fellows did not receive the so-called *provisio* nor did they get all the allowances. Wesley received nothing until he came into residence in the middle of the sixth week of the fourth term, 1726. On 23rd November, 1726, he received a statement from the Bursar which actually left him in debt to the College. His allowances for the term amounted to £2 13s. 0¾d., of which *provisio* accounted for £1 11s. 10¾d.² But he owed money for battels, mainly for the second and fourth terms,³ as well as £2 for admission to the Senior Common Room and 2s. 1¾d. for his share of the Common Room expenses. He was thus in debt to the College to the tune of £3 2s. 10¾d., though he also received from the College his share of the fines amounting in all to £2 10s. 10¾d.⁴ This situation changed as soon as he became resident.⁵

The young man who had just been elected a fellow of Lincoln had many facets to his character. He was eager and enthusiastic, gay without being frivolous. He still enjoyed the diversions of life; he noted for future reference, in cipher it is true, the steps of a new dance, 'a grip and a gink with the other foot. . . . Walk a little faster. . . . First salute her, then bow, and hand her to a chair.'⁶ Into the same notebook he copied a verse on the 'fair Belinda' that had attracted his attention:

> Belinda has such wondrous charms
> 'Tis Heaven to lie within her arms
> And She's so charitably given
> She wishes all mankind in heaven

together with a verse, slightly tinged with ribaldry, purporting to be part

¹ As the College account year ran from 6th November to 6th November, it is not always easy to adjust the information the accounts supply as to residence, more especially as the whole year was divided into four terms. Wesley, however, came back into residence, shortly before the beginning of what we should to-day call the Michaelmas Term, 1726.

² *L.C. Bursar's Day Book*, 1725–6, fol. 27.

³ For the second term £2 7s. 6d. and for the fourth term £1 5s. Wesley paid the Bursar on 23rd November, 1726 (*op. cit.*, fol. 34).

⁴ W. Hart's fine (28th September, 1726) of which Wesley's share came to 1s. 6¾d.; Widow Tuckey's fine (14th October, 1726)—£1 12s. (*op. cit.*, fol. 46), and Mop's fine from which Wesley received 17s. 4d. (*op. cit.*, fol. 47).

⁵ See Appendix 2.

⁶ I have to thank Mr. Wesley Swift for drawing my attention to this, as indeed to many other points in the first Oxford Diary.

of the Provost of Aberdeen College's translation of the Bible:

> Absalom was hanged in a tree
> Crying the Lord have Mercy
> Joab came by, full angry was He,
> And run his spear up his arsy.

This was the young man who loved to play the flute and twice at Christmas, 1726, paid a shilling to Mr. Austin, the lutanist.

Yet there was another, far more serious side. His entries in his diary and account book were made with meticulous care, though not with the thoroughness which marked the later journals. All the items of his personal expenditure were chronicled with minute exactitude, 4d. for breakfast, 1s. 10d. for pins, needles, threads and ribbon, 4d. for the upholsterer, 1s. 2d. for cards at Mr. Colley's, 1s. to the man who brought and set up his bedstead, 3s. 6d. for brandy, lemons and sugar, 3d. for tobacco at the Common Room, 1s. 6d. for a key to the College garden. Although he may sometimes have been dissatisfied with himself he was in his daily conduct already a master of method. In reality an intense earnestness, lacking at times a human touch,[1] was veiled by a surface sociability. His father had observed his son's mental inelasticity and expressed his concern. 'I like your way of thinking and arguing,' he had written on 1st September, 1725, 'and yet I must say, I am a little afraid of it. He that believes without or against Reason, is half a Papist, or Enthusiast. He that would meet Revelation by his own shallow Reason, is either half a Deist or an Heretic. O my dear! steer clear between this Scylla and Charybdis.'[2]

John Wesley never escaped completely from the temptation to 'bend' others to his will and to 'manage' others for their own good, though doubtless he believed that he served God in so doing. Time and time again he questioned himself about his own motives and condemned his own shortcomings; but he only glimpsed dimly the temptations involved in directing other people's lives. It was during the three years following his election that the more ascetic and religious side of his character gained the gradual ascendancy, for, try as he would, he did not find it an easy

---

[1] Ronald Knox noticed what his many biographers do not seem to have suspected, that in his later life 'He was too much absorbed by the sense of divine mission to be really interested in human contacts, except where these directly illustrated it.' (*Enthusiasm*, 443.)

[2] L. Tyerman, *Samuel Wesley*, 395; but his version has been corrected.

matter to blend a love of this present world with what he believed to be the teaching of his master.

His fellowship may not have changed very perceptibly the rhythm of his existence; but it introduced him to a congenial and cultured society. 'In ye Common Room' became a frequent insertion in his diary. Two days after his election he dined with Tottenham and won the game of cards that followed. In the ensuing weeks he breakfasted and dined with other resident fellows, Isham, Hutchins, and Vesey. 'I never knew a college besides ours', he wrote proudly to his brother less than a month after his election, 'whereof the members were so perfectly satisfied with one another and so inoffensive to the other part of the University. All I have yet seen of the Fellows are both well-natured and well-bred; men admirably disposed as well to preserve peace and good neighbourhood among themselves, as to promote it wherever else they have any acquaintance.'[1] On 6th April, two days after writing this letter, he obliged one of his new colleagues, William Vesey, by reading prayers for him in the College Chapel, and on Easter Monday (11th April) rode with Isham and Hutchins to meet Tottenham at Handborough.

In other ways the pattern of his existence remained the same. The day after his election at Lincoln he had breakfast at Merton, probably with Walter Frank, and later studied Hebrew Grammar and read Clarendon's history; in the afternoon he went for a walk. He continued to read voraciously: Prideaux's *Connection*, Beveridge, Norris, Smalridge, Dryden's *Miscellanies*, Milton. His removal to Lincoln had brought a further widening of his circle of acquaintances, but he kept up with friends of older vintage, often breakfasting with his former tutor, Sherman. He gave his friend, Potter, the first-hand impressions of his new College, and dined with Pitt at Exeter, where he found the talk in the Common Room 'rambling'. On 13th April he supped with Burton and on Sunday read prayers for him at Buckland. He sat with John Ditcher at the King's Head. As in his earlier days, he took his exercise by walking, going for instance to Binsey on 12th April.

He was at Oxford over Easter, 1726, reflecting (in cipher) on religious resolutions in his diary for Good Friday,[2] and attending church 'till near eleven' on Easter Sunday; a week later he began the long walk to

---

[1] *Letters*, i, 30.

[2] 'Breach of resolution, in devotion, want of mortification, sleep, idleness, sins, flattery of Dr. Hole [the rector of Exeter whom he had met at Pitt's], lying detraction.'

Epworth, which he reached on Saturday, 23rd April. He liked walking, but the walk to Epworth represented the emptiness of his purse rather than choice. He was pleased to find that all was well at the rectory, and the following day he twice read prayers for his father.

In spite of the undercurrents which occasionally disturbed the life of the parish and rectory, the summer of 1726 was something of an idyll. John Wesley had returned to Epworth as a fellow of an Oxford College, possessed of a stipend and a reputation for scholarship. His father found him an invaluable assistant in his labours on the book of Job; he acted, too, as a curate in the watery wastes of Wroot. His mother rejoiced in the serious and sensible son who would readily accompany her on her visits and read to her during the long summer evenings; his sisters too were pleased with the eligible young bachelor who had now returned from Oxford. Some of them were already married, and Wesley noted in his diary the visits that he made to their homes; Sukey had married a local farmer, Richard Ellison, 'a coarse, vulgar, immoral man', as Wesley's sister described him, who lacked religion, good nature and good manners. Anne (Nancy) had married a local land surveyor, John Lambert. She gave birth to a son during the summer; John was a godfather and danced at the party which followed the christening ceremony. Hetty was recently married to a plumber, William Wright, a union marked from the start with unhappiness. The others, Kezzy, Patty, Molly, Emily, if not un-touched by romance, were still at home to welcome their brother, to listen to his reading of Lewis' poems and Scarron's plays,[1] to give him their confidence and seek his counsel, and with him to make hay, stack turfs, and to gather fruit. On two consecutive days he picked elder flowers and roses.

Once more, and for a longer period than for many years past, his life became even more sociable than it had been at Oxford. The social re-sources of Epworth and its neighbourhood were limited but there were few families of any substance in the neighbourhood with whom the Wesleys were not on visiting terms, Aaron Maw and the other members of his clan, Miss Kitty Hargreaves and her mother, Mr. Harper, the apothecary, who was many years later to become Emily's husband, Mr. Popplewell of Temple Belwood, Mr. Pindar of Owston, his hostility to Wesley's father apparently long forgotten, one son an undergraduate at Lincoln and another soon to join him, the local clergy, Mr. Hoole of Haxey, and the schoolmaster, Mr. Romley. There was a constant inter-

[1] *The Whole Comical Works of Mons. Scarron*, 4th edn., 2 vols., 1727.

change of visits; he dined with Pindar and drank tea with Pennington; he took his mother to sup with Mrs. Barnard and her daughters. He visited friends in the neighbouring villages, Finningley, Luddington, Laughton and Auckley, sometimes taking services in the local churches; and he went further afield to enjoy the delights of Bawtry fair or to visit his friends the Becudas at Doncaster, and Mr. Darntry and Mr. Echard at Gainsborough.

Life passed pleasantly during the summer of 1726, bathing in the river with Mr. Thompson, and in dallying with fair Kitty Hargreaves. Sometimes he went shooting,[1] and once bagged three plovers. He indulged in a spate of light reading, and read a number of Restoration plays, frothy, slightly scandalous comedies and tense, sentimental and pathetic tragedies. When he wished he could escape from the busy household into the shade of the arbour which he had recently made in the garden. Here he worked and talked with his friends. 'Cut stakes, made two benches in the arbour', he noted in his diary. Here, too, he read the heavy tomes that he had presumably borrowed from his father's library. When he tired of reading, he could continue making his *camera obscura* (he had already constructed one when he was at Oxford), work for his father in the garden or make a table in the garret, or, a more civilized task, compose Latin verse. 'I would not have you leave off making verses,' his mother told him, 'rather make poetry sometimes your diversion, though never your business.'

There was indeed no lack of diversions. Towards the end of August, he accompanied the local antiquary, George Stovin, Mr. Buck and Mr. Oughtibridge on an archaeological expedition to Lindholm in the middle of Hatfield waste; legend spoke of a hermit who had once lived there and had the power to conjure up demonic forces. The investigators found the hermitage or cell in a sadly dilapidated condition; but at the east end there stood a stone that was said to mark the hermit's grave. After measuring this they walked home, but returned the following Saturday when, with the consent of the occupier, Richard Howlegate, they raised the stone with levers and digging underneath discovered a skull and some bones. They brought their finds home and that evening John Wesley 'sat up late' telling his family of his experiences.[2]

---

[1] His accounts include, in addition to 3s. 4d. paid for shoes at Wroot, 13s. 4d. for 'powder and shot'.

[2] Mr. Stovin's account was submitted to the *Gentleman's Magazine* in 1747 (xvii, 23). In some particulars he seems at fault; he speaks of Samuel Wesley as one of

He had occupied himself during the morning of the day of this expedition in copying out an account of the strange disturbances which had affected Epworth Rectory some years previously, consulting his father's diary and making enquiries of his mother and sisters. It was another indication of his continuing interest in the supernatural, shortly confirmed by an unusual experience. On Tuesday evening, 13th September, 1726, Wesley wakened suddenly a little before ten and was surprised to see the bedroom door slowly open, shut and then open and finally shut again loud and distinctly. His dog, Tony, who was lying on the bed, growled and barked. The next day as he and his brother, Charles, were trying to catch a chicken which had strayed into the room, the same thing happened again. John was only a yard from the door, waiting to seize the chicken if it came his way, when once again the door slowly swung to.

There was evidence of an even more exciting pastime, for John Wesley may have been falling in love with Miss Kitty Hargreaves, who made so many appearances in his diary during the course of this summer. On 3rd June, 1726, his father, always suspicious of romance dawning in his children's lives and apt to try and frustrate it, sent Miss Kitty away, 'in suspicion of my courting her'. The situation which had arisen the previous year in relation to Varanese seemed to be coming about again.[1] Wesley was divided between attraction and the call of conscience. On Sunday, 3rd July, after talking with the Romleys, he wrote down a memorandum in his diary commending self-denial.

'As we would willingly suffer a little pain, or forgo some pleasure for others we really love, so if we sincerely love God we should readily do this for him. For this reason one act of self-denial is more grateful to our Master than the performance of many lesser duties. . . . Begin in small things first.'

And what was the small thing? Was it an association of ideas which made him write the next sentence in cipher: 'Never touch Kitty's hand again'? Whatever the inference, he walked with Kitty that evening and again the next day, and was frequently in her company during the days and weeks that followed. One Saturday evening, 13th August, he made a resolution that he would never touch any woman's breasts again. Once again the flame had been lit, and once again it burned faintly rather than brightly.

---

the company but this seems unlikely. Moreover he describes the expedition as occurring on 31st August, 1727; from the evidence of Wesley's diary it certainly took place on 25th and 27th August, 1726.

[1] See p. 208ff.

Pleasant as life seemed, there were undercurrents which sometimes upset its even flow. He could not help the constant feeling that he was wasting his time. 'Levity slays; intemperate sleep', he wrote down shortly after his arrival home, and the refrain was repeated time and time again concealed from prying eyes in Wesley's cipher. He was worried by the feeling that he ought to reprove others for the faults he detected in them and the realization that they might resent his advice.

'Whenever you speak anything sharp or by way of reproof,' he reminded himself on Sunday, 26th June, 'let your tone be peaceable, courteous and affable . . . never tell one in an ill-humour that he is so, but strive to deviate him. Don't sympathise with but sweeten one another.'

A fortnight or so later he talked with his mother about the virtue of prudence, 'the skill of adjusting all things the when, where, whom'. But was such prudence justified? Talking with his father and mother he compared and contrasted their advice. His father maintained stoutly that reproof was always right, even if the person reproved 'defend himself or perhaps fly in your face', but his mother advocated the use of persuasive arguments. 'God if he pleases to have him convinced will do it in his good time.' He was equally concerned with the extent to which anger was justified, and again consulted his mother, who told him that she thought that anger was completely unlawful if it took precedence of reason. 'Never', he noted as he began to write a sermon on Universal Charity, 'be angry but for God's sake.' This was on Sunday, 14th August, 1726. On 11th September he preached a sermon on deception and the next day after visiting the Rector of Lincoln, Dr. Morley, he danced at Will Attkins' home, only to note in his diary 'Levity-giving offence. Confirmed in my opinion that ye art of scandal is natural, not acquired—inasmuch as no place is free from it.' Then on the following day he began to write a sermon on rash judging, which he was to preach the next Sunday before he left for Oxford.

This ferment was not merely connected with his own introspective spiritual discontent, but was in part rooted in his family relationships. Well-meaning and religious people sometimes find it necessary to criticize others and to impose their own standards, especially their own moral standards, often causing ill-feeling and distress by their gratuitous but well-meant actions. Neither John nor Samuel, nor even Charles, was free from the temptations offered by this kind of interference, especially in the affairs of their own sisters; there was an inclination to moral dogmatism, sometimes founded on an inadequate judgement of the people concerned, which gave rise to embarrassment and trouble. The rector of Epworth was particularly at fault in this respect. In his treatment of his flock he occasionally acted as an arbitrary disciplinarian; he had once left his wife because she did not see fit to accept his politics. In his treatment of his daughters he showed a lack of insight, which sprang from the strong moral principles which motivated his actions. While Emily had been staying in London with her uncle, Matthew Wesley, she had met and fallen in love with a friend of John's, Robert Leybourne, a fellow of Brasenose. He was older than John and a contemporary and friend of Samuel's at Christ Church; indeed in 1725 Samuel and his wife had intended to stay in the Principal's lodgings, Dr. Shippen being away, at Leybourne's invitation if a misunderstanding had not arisen.[1] Emily's affair did not prosper, for though she held Leybourne to be a man of the 'highest understanding and the sweetest temper in England', his love was not as deep as hers.[2] It was, however, brought to an end principally through the interference of a member of the family, 'ill-fate in the shape of a near relation', possibly her mother, more likely her brother, Samuel, less likely the rector himself. The ending of the romance made her depressed and melancholy. 'For near half a year I never slept half a night.'

> Let Emma's hapless case be told
> By the rash young or the ill-natured old

she wrote to John. Even death itself was a 'consummation devoutly to be wished'.

If Emily's experience showed that the course of true love did not run

---

[1] Samuel had asked Leybourne to find him a lodging in Oxford. Leybourne had offered him rooms in Dr. Shippen's lodgings but as Leybourne did not reply to Samuel's acceptance of his offer (he said he did not receive the letter), Samuel took umbrage and took rooms elsewhere. They seem, however, to have been friendly with Leybourne during the visit: 'we were', John said, 'several times entertained by him, and I·thought very handsomely, nor was there the least show of dislike on either side. But what I heard my sister [presumably Mrs. Samuel Wesley] say once, on our parting with Mr. Leybourne, made the former proceedings a little clearer. "Thus should we have been troubled with that girl's attendance everywhere, if we had gone to lodge at Dr. Shippen's." ' What meaning are we to put on this sentence?

[2] In a letter to John, dated 7th February, 1733, she wrote 'when I loved L. he loved not me, though he was rogue enough to persuade me he did. Well so much for that!'

straight, Hetty's love was blighted from its very start.[1] She had grown up into a keen-minded, yet gay, young woman; at eight she was able to read the Greek Testament and throughout her life she indulged her skill in making pathetic if rather indifferent verses. But she was no bluestocking; indeed there was an unusual sparkle in her personality which spelled revolt against the disciplined life of the rectory. She fell in love with a young lawyer, Will Attkins; he may have seduced her. At any rate her absence from the rectory for a night roused the implacable wrath of her father. Whether he had already banned the marriage or whether the young man himself withdrew is not clear, but the elder Wesley bullied his daughter into a union with a plumber, William Wright, who later had a small works in Frith Street, Soho. 'I would have given at least one of my eyes for the liberty of throwing myself at your feet before I was married at all', she told her father after four years of married life; but the rector was unrelenting in his determination. The gaiety once so character-istic was crushed between the upper and nether millstones of parental severity and marital unhappiness. Wright was a wastrel, drunken and dissolute in his behaviour, having nothing in common with his cultured, sensitive wife. There can never have been affection, and there was soon 'cold neglect'. 'Those ears were ever free from matrimonial melody.' Her married life was horrifying.

'I had always such notions of wedlock as now; but thought that where there was a mutual affection and desire of pleasing, something near equality of mind and person; either earthly or heavenly wisdom, and anything to keep love warm between a young couple, there was a possibility of happiness in a married state: but where all, or most of these, were wanting, I ever thought people could not marry without sinning against God and themselves.'

And all were found wanting in Hetty's case. 'It was', she wrote patheti-cally, 'to say little of things quite past remedy.' But no sense of responsi-bility penetrated then or later the tough hide of her father: he spurned her overtures even when she confessed her penitence. He remained 'incon-ceivably exasperated' and would never see her or talk of her except with the utmost detestation. Even in 1729 he still spoke of her scandal and her wit as if the punishment for scandal had not served to eliminate all that remained of her wit.

[1] Cf. Quiller-Couch, *Hetty Wesley*; Maldwyn Edwards, *Family Circle*, 154–73.

Her fall from grace profoundly shocked her family and they found it difficult to believe that her penitence was genuine. Her crippled sister, Mary,[1] and her brother, John, were the exceptions to the chorus of self-righteous condemnation; John with his wider knowledge of the world and deep concern with Christian charity believed that there ought to be a reconciliation. His efforts only aroused his father's suspicion and animosity. After visiting the Ellisons, another unhappily married daughter, the elder Wesley told Charles that his brother had been disrespectful and deliberately defiant. Charles expressed his surprise and asked how John had given offence. The old man burst out, 'Every day, you hear how he contradicts me, and takes your sister's part before my face. Nay, he disputes with me, preach——' but failed to finish the sentence. The last word referred to a sermon on charity which John had preached at Wroot on 28th August, the day after his return from the second expedition to Lindholm. The theme of it had been in his mind for a long time. He had read the sermons on charity preached by Francis Atterbury and Samuel Clarke. He had told his mother that he intended to preach and had won her reluctant approval; she added shrewdly, 'You writ this sermon for Hetty; the rest was brought in for the sake of the last paragraph.' When he realized that he had given offence, he showed surprise in spite of the fact that he quite consciously intended to censure his father's conduct towards his sister; 'I had the same day the pleasure of observing that my father the same day, when one Will Attkins was mentioned, did not speak so warmly nor largely against him as usual.' He believed somewhat naïvely that what he had said had taken root in his father's mind. It had, but in a way other than that which he had hoped. When he went for a walk with Charles he learned how his father burst out against him, and on his return he went immediately and said how sorry he was for the offence he had given. He would never, he promised, contradict him again; he would transcribe for him whenever he wished (this seems to have been a further cause of offence). Father and son burst into tears; then they kissed. The old man said in his blunt way that he had always known

---

[1] In verses written to the memory of Mrs. Mary Whitelamb, Hetty later remembered how

> When deep immersed in griefs beyond redress,
> And *friends* and *kindred* heightened my distress:
> And by relentless efforts made me prove
> Pain, grief, despair, and wedlock without love;
> My soft Maria could alone dissent,
> O'erlooked the fatal vow, and mourned the punishment.

that 'John was good at bottom', and that he would give him some work to do for him the very next day.

John's diary confirms that he worked hard, transcribing Job, during the remaining ten days of his visit; but he decided to make 'rash judging' the subject of his final sermon. He said later that he preached with his father's approval and that his father never showed that he had again given offence. He was, however, deeply hurt and told Samuel that John had offended against the 53rd canon.[1] John, who surely showed a curious lack of imagination and insight in supposing that he could convert his father to a different attitude, remained impenitent. He believed that he had been poorly treated and reproached Samuel for the apparent support that he had given his father (though Samuel, like John, thought that the time had come for Hetty to be forgiven). The trouble passed, as such troubles do, but each conflict strained the sympathy and affection of those who were involved.

Oxford life afforded a pleasant change to Epworth and Wroot, more especially after the disagreements of the previous week. He was busy buying furniture for his rooms in Lincoln, including a grate (having the company of Mr. Ward on this errand).[2] He soon resumed his old routine, breakfasting with Sherman at Christ Church, with Isham at the coffee-house and with Potter, Shuckburgh and Burman, probably in his rooms. He noted that he had shared in a College fine, no more than 1s. 6d., but at least a testimony to his membership of a corporate body, owning property and enjoying responsibility. The Saturday after his return he read prayers in the College Chapel and on the Sunday rode over to take the service at Chislehampton. The ostensible reason for his return to Oxford was an appointment to preach the statutory sermon at St. Michael's on 29th September, when the College went in procession to the church. The following Sunday he rode out to the College chaplaincy at Combe where he read prayers twice. His reading seems to have been a little less serious than usual; Godfrey of Bouillon[3] (given to him by Sherman), the *History of Pyrates*,[4] and Lilly's life.[5] The uneasy pangs of conscience made

[1] 'If any Preacher shall, in the Pulpit particularly . . . of purpose, impugn, confute any doctrine delivered by any other Preacher in the same Church the churchwardens should signify the matter to the Bishop unless the preacher faithfully promise to forbear all such matter of contention in the Church.'

[2] The grate cost £1 10s.; tongs and shovel, 6s. 6d.

[3] Probably a translation of Tasso's *Jerusalem Delivered* (by Edward Fairfax).

[4] *A General History of the Pyrates* (by Charles Johnson), 1726.

[5] *The History of Lilly's Life and Times* (1715).

themselves felt and on the Saturday evening before he left with Hutchins
to visit his friends in the Cotswolds[1] he repeated the familiar phrase,
'idleness slays'.

Life went on during the autumn and early winter of 1726 in an uneventful, regular way. On his return he paid his respects to the Dean of
Christ Church, Sherman and Lord Dupplin. Dupplin was the son of the
Earl of Kinnoull and a nephew of Lord Oxford, who had contributed to
his expenses at Oxford. Canon William Stratford kept Lord Oxford informed of his nephew's progress. 'I take it', he wrote when arranging for
his set of rooms, 'Lord Dupplin must be upon a frugal foot.'[2] When
Kinnoull called on Stratford in June, 1726, he told Dupplin that the
greatest service that could be done him 'would be to prepare him to
resist the influence of the ill examples he would see in the world when he
left us. The father agreed with me entirely in morality and politics, and
talked like a Tory.'[3] It is difficult to know exactly how he became
acquainted with Wesley, but he may have taken over Wesley's rooms in
Christ Church since his accounts indicate payments made by Dupplin.[4]
The connection was kept up, for in May, 1737, John and Charles dined
with Lord and Lady Oxford, Lord Dupplin being of the company;[5] and
by coincidence a member of his family was a later rector of Epworth.[6]

Wesley was meanwhile engaged in preparing a theme for declamation
and a 'wall' lecture on friendship, part of the necessary if already somewhat moribund exercises for his master's degree.[7] The subject was,
however, appropriate, if friendship can be measured in terms of acquaintances, for he was still absorbed in a round of breakfasting and dining,
sometimes in the coffee house, sometimes in his own or in other Colleges.

[1] See p. 212ff.

[2] *Portland MSS.*, VII, 400. Cf. a later letter of 8th April, 1728. 'Young Murray
showed me a melancholy letter . . . from poor Dupplin, in which he owned that
he and his brother could not yet come down, because the father could not furnish
them with any [money].'

[3] *Op. cit.*, 438.

[4] A half-year's rent, £3 3s., on 3rd March, 1726; £5 on 20th January, 1727.

[5] *Journal of Charles Wesley*, i, 71.

[6] Hon. John Hay, rector from 1746. On 3rd July, 1748, Wesley noted that 'Mr.
Hay, the rector, reading prayers, I had once more the comfort of receiving the
Lord's Supper at Epworth' (which had been refused to him by Mr. Romley in
January, 1743).

[7] Six *Solennes Lectiones*, once dissertations in Natural and Moral Philosophy (A.
Clark, Introduction to the *Register of the University of Oxford*, ii, 76), but in the
process of becoming meaningless formalities, delivered to empty rooms.

III THE CHAPEL QUAD, LINCOLN COLLEGE, SHOWING WESLEY'S ROOMS

Thomas Photos, Oxford

Many of his friends dated from an earlier period: Sherman, Shuckburgh, Ward, Potter, Langford and Watkins, to mention a few, but there were also some new names: Paget,[1] Medley,[2] Howson,[3] Forrester,[4] Bull,[5] Nash[6] and Lysons.[7] He saw much of his brother's friend, Lushington, who was something of a 'smart' and with whom he played cards. He drank tea with Mr. Lawton, dined with Walker at Wadham and sat with Mr. Wilder. John Wilder was a much older man, a fellow of Pembroke since the beginning of the century and rector of St. Aldate's Church from 1724. Wesley was often in his company at this time, but he was later a severe critic of Methodism.[8] Other senior members with whom he had some acquaintance included a fellow of St. John's, Nathaniel Crynes, who was the esquire bedell of arts, and a fellow of Wadham, Philip Speke, who was one of the proctors in 1726. Many of these men were no doubt little more than passing acquaintances, but the list is evidence of the wide-ranging company in which Wesley was moving in 1726.

This is not to say that he did not pay attention to the more serious aspect of existence. He was engaged in a quantity of serious reading, including works by Leslie, Wallis, Norris and Zosimus; he consulted the books of Sir Walter Raleigh and Sir Kenelm Digby when preparing his lecture. On various Sundays he took services, for Hutchins in the College Chapel, and preached, as at St. Aldate's Church in the city. On 6th November, 1726, he breakfasted in College with Isham, heard Mr. Allen preach the University sermon on God's wisdom in the morning, dined with the Rector and later in the day read the College statutes[9] in preparation

---

[1] Probably Thomas Paget, matric., Queen's C., 1721, aged 15; B.A. 1725, M.A. 1728. Fellow of Corpus, proctor, 1737; later rector of St. Mawan, Cornwall, Clifton Maybank, Dorset, Bradford Abbas, Poyntington and Mells, 1751–83.

[2] John Medley of Lincoln, entered Lincoln C. as a gentleman commoner 20th October, 1724.

[3] Francis Howson, of Ulceby in Lincolnshire, entered Lincoln C. 6th May, 1724; took his B.A. in 1728, and M.A. in 1731; Lincolnshire fellow of Magdalen, 1732–7.

[4] Paul Forrester, matric., Ch. Ch., 1711, aged 18; B.A. 1715, M.A. 1718; vicar of Wootton Bassett, Wiltshire, 1724; d. 1761 (buried in Ch. Ch.).

[5] Edward Bull, matric., Ch. Ch., 1722; B.A. 1726.

[6] Possibly James Nash, who matric. Magd. H. in 1722 and took his B.A. in 1725.

[7] John Lysons, Demy of Magdalen C., 1725; fellow 1732–60, Senior Dean of Arts, Bursar and Vice-President.

[8] Cf. his printed sermon: *The Trial of the Spirits; or, a Caution against Enthusiasm, or Religious Delusion, in opposition to the Methodists* (1739).

[9] It is an illustration of his conscientiousness that he read the College statutes again a few days after the meeting.

I

for his first College meeting. This took place the next day, 7th November, and resulted in Wesley being elected by his colleagues as Greek lecturer, Moderator and Claviger. His relations with the resident fellows were particularly close during the winter of 1726. He was frequently having breakfast and dinner with them, and there were few days when he did not go to the Common Room. On 14th November, after fulfilling his duties as moderator, he read *Gulliver's Travels*, which had been published recently, and he found it so absorbing that he continued reading it in the Common Room, reproaching himself later with idleness; to make up for his lapse he concentrated the next day on studying the *Odyssey* and in translating Justin Martyr.

Such was the life of this young Oxford don during the winter of 1726–7. It is more than a pity that there was no Boswell to write down what Wesley and Tottenham said to each other when they returned from hearing Mr. Green preach on 'her ways are ways of peace', or to describe what went on at the breakfast party in Wesley's rooms on 17th November when he entertained Goodwin,[1] Watkins and Cox. The previous day he had engaged in vigorous discussion with Saunders about Aristotle's definition of motion, and with Paget he talked about the problems of gravity. On 22nd November he again declaimed in the schools and a few days later began to compose a 'wall lecture' on the souls of brutes, a subject which had earlier held his attention. He interspersed his reading of the *Odyssey* with the perusal of Beaumont and Fletcher's play *The Elder Brother*. On 4th December he preached at St. Aldate's, disputed in Hall three days later and divided the next day between preparation of his wall lecture (for which he was now reading Ditton's *Discourse*) and John Dennis' *Defence of Sir Foppling Flutter*. His zest for the Restoration stage continued; Southerne's play *Oroonoko* (based on Aphra Behn's novel), Taverner's *The Artful Husband*, as well as *Julius Caesar*, were all read by him in the course of a few wintry days. As he was reading Collier[2] at the same time he was by no means unaware that many frowned on the contemporary theatre and the plays performed there. It was now nearly Christmas and Wesley was preparing to spend it in the Cotswolds.

[1] Joseph Goodwin, Lincoln C., m. 1721, aged 17, B.A. 1724, M.A. 1727. His father was vicar of Shipton under Wychwood and died in 1726. His successor was only vicar for a year and seems to have been keeping the living warm for the younger Goodwin who became vicar in 1727 and remained until his resignation in 1773. John Wesley did considerable duty at Shipton, probably for Goodwin.

[2] *Short View of the Immorality and Profaneness of the English Stage* (1698). Wesley also read his *Essays on Moral Subjects*.

He did not return to Oxford until 16th January, 1727. The Christmas holidays had brought him both joy and sorrow;[1] Robin Griffiths' sudden death, though not unexpected, had given him something of a shock. Outwardly the rhythm of his life seemed unaltered. He reread Gulliver and embarked on Swift's *The Battle of the Books*, and Southerne's *The Fate of Capua*. He added Wycherly's *The Plaindealer* to the list of plays he had read and exercised his wit by answering the riddles in the *Ladies' Diary*. The interchange of visits was as frequent as ever; at New College with Taylor, tea with Lord Dupplin, breakfast with Potter, Wilder, Hammond, Medley, Yardley[2] (whom he had met in the Cotswolds), Lushington, Hutchinson, Bayliff and Saunders. But he was not wholly happy. He thought that he was making insufficient spiritual progress, and he could not help asking where this apparently useful, scholarly life was eventually going to take him.

He was especially concerned with the undisciplined character of his reading. Although he almost always finished a book, the wide range of his reading suggests lack of depth. When he was breakfasting with Potter on 20th January, 1727, they talked of a recent dispute between Bishops Hoadly and Atterbury over a sermon on charity which the latter had delivered.[3] Three days later he resolved to limit his use of time wisely. Two days later, on 25th January, Wesley confessed to his mother that in reading the works of Atterbury and Hoadly, 'I was so injudicious as to break off in the middle'.

'I could not conceive that the dignity of the end was at all proportioned to the difficulty of attaining it. And I thought the labour of twenty or thirty hours, if I was sure of succeeding, which I was not, would be but ill rewarded by that important piece of knowledge whether Bishop Hoadly had misunderstood Bishop Atterbury or no.'

He was curious for knowledge but time was too short to indulge such a passion: 'methinks it is great ill-husbandry to spend a considerable part of the small pittance now allowed us in what makes us neither a quick nor a

[1] See p. 214ff.
[2] The son of George Yardley of Notgrove, Gloucester; matric., Trin. C., aged 17, in March, 1723; B.A. 1726, M.A. 1729, B.D. 1741. Fellow of Trin., d. 29th April, 1756.
[3] In a funeral sermon on Thomas Bennett, Atterbury had argued that if there was no after life, men would be more miserable than beasts and the best men the most miserable. Hoadly criticized his interpretation of the text he had chosen (1 Cor., xv, 19). See T. Beeching, *Atterbury* (1909), 44–5; Hunt, *Religious Thought in England* iii, 78–9.

sure return'. 'I am perfectly come over to your opinion,' he told his mother, 'that there are many truths it is not worthwhile to know.' His intellectual efforts must henceforth be increasingly canalized.

With this object in mind he drew up a scheme of studies. He had written to his mother, after leaving his brother's room at Christ Church on Wednesday, 25th January, 1727. Next Friday he embarked on his scheme. He would now concentrate as far as possible on what seemed serious and important to him. Mondays and Tuesdays were to be for the study of Roman and Greek history and literature; Wednesdays for Logic and Ethics; Thursdays for studies in Hebrew and Arabic (probably from Mr. Gagnier, the College's instructor in these subjects); Fridays for Metaphysics and Natural Philosophy; Saturdays for the composition of poetry and oratory; Sundays for Divinity. He would not keep these resolutions,[1] but the anxiety to use his time to the best advantage was one of the factors which contributed to his decision that the secret of the right use of time was early rising in the morning. 'I am full of business,' he told his mother on 19th March, 1727, 'but have found a way to write without taking any time from that. 'Tis but rising an hour sooner in a morning and going into company an hour later in the evening; both of which may be done without any inconvenience.'[2] The habit of early rising, sometimes as early as four and rarely as late as six, was one which remained with him throughout life, and to which he contributed excessive importance.

He was not merely worried about his work. He was also concerned about his future career. He was engaged for some time on the lectures which he was due to give to qualify for his master's degree. He was examined on 7th February, 1727, and disputed for his degree the next day. After his first examination he found recreation in playing two games of billiards, and in spending the evening with his brother at his rooms in Christ Church.[3] His graduation as a full master made some difference to the

---

[1] A list in his diary particularizes: *Monday*-morning, the Greek poets, Homer, Historians, Xenophon; afternoon, Latin poets, Terence, Historians, Sallust, Cicero. *Tuesday*-morning, Terence, Sallust, Cicero; afternoon, Homer, Xenophon; *Wednesday*-morning, Logic, Aldrich, Wallis, Sanderson; afternoon, Langbaine's *Ethics*; *Thursday*-morning, Hebrew Grammar, Psalter; afternoon, Arabic Grammar; *Friday*-morning, Le Clerc, Locke, Clarke, Jackson; afternoon, Bartholine, Robinson, Rohault; *Saturday*—write sermon, letters, verses. Sunday was to be given up to Divinity and making notes on what he had read.

[2] *Letters*, i, 43; cf. *Works*, vii, 69, 'Redeeming the Time'.

[3] Sherman had tried to help the Wesleys by suggesting a financially satisfactory arrangement by which Charles Wesley should share a garret with another man

possible courses which his career might take. Although he was now in receipt of a fellow's stipend, he was still short of money. His income as a fellow had only just covered his expenditure, nor was he yet a tutor. 'As for pupils I am not qualified to take them till one of our tutors goes away; when that will be is very uncertain.'[1]

In his unsettled frame of mind he was attracted by the possibility of school teaching. The appointment to the headmastership of Skipton School in Yorkshire was subject to a number of conditions laid down by its sixteenth-century founder, William Erymsted. In the first instance it rested with the vicar and churchwardens of Skipton, but if they failed to find a man sufficiently learned (*habilis*) within a month of the vacancy, the appointment lapsed to the rector and fellows of Lincoln College. If they failed, the appointment lapsed to the Dean and Chapter of St. Paul's, London. As happened later in the century, giving rise to interminable litigation and riotous disputes,[2] it seemed likely that the appointment might lapse to the College. In 1751 Richard Bainbridge, a fellow of the College, who was approached with respect to the headmastership, described it as a 'charming piece of preferment especially to a person that is not averse to ye charges, attendance, and duty of a school; it is one of ye best endowed schools, not only in ye north but in England. Ye real estate brings in to ye Master £160 per. ann. He must indeed pay ye Usher. It is a pleasant market-town where provisions are cheap.' This seems to have been Wesley's impression in 1727: 'A good salary is annexed to it, so that in a year's time 'tis probable all my debts should be paid, and I should have money beforehand.' But he had been given a 'frightful description' of the place by some gentlemen who knew Skipton. Far from discouraging him, the very characteristics which his informant regarded as unpalatable, its inaccessibility and its lack of cultured companionship,

---

who wished to save money, and 'then, if he could but prevail upon someone else to give him seven pounds a year for his own room, he would gain almost six pounds year clear if his rent were well paid'. For some reason John Wesley thought the idea unsound and 'as I could not give him such an answer as he desired, I did not choose to give him any at all'. (*Letters*, i, 33.)

[1] *Letters*, i, 38; yet his letters to his father indicate that he certainly had a private pupil (L. Tyerman, *Samuel Wesley*, 402). His father wrote on 5th July, 1727, 'The reason why I was willing to delay my son John's coming was his pupil; but that is over.'

[2] V. H. H. Green, *Oxford Common Room*, 31–4, 74–7.

attracted him in his somewhat depressed condition. 'You can expect little company from without, and within there is none at all. I should therefore be entirely at liberty to converse with companions of my own choosing, whom for that reason I would bring with me; and company equally agreeable, wherever I fixed, could not put me to less expense.'[1] He was momentarily surfeited with society.

> 'I am so little at present in love with even company, the most elegant entertainment next books, that unless they have a peculiar turn of thought I am much better pleased without them. I think 'tis the settled temper of my soul that I should prefer, at least for some time such, a retirement as would seclude me from all the world to the station I am now in.'

But the churchwardens were able to make an appointment and the head-mastership of Skipton passed to William Banks, while he remained at Lincoln.

There was the alternative possibility of a College living, but John Wesley was as yet the junior fellow and had not been long in orders; he could hardly hope for an opening of that kind. Meanwhile he rode out from Oxford to take duty at parishes in the vicinity of Oxford. He was assiduous in his devotions. He was much affected by a sermon which Jonathan Colley, of Christ Church, preached in which he advised his hearers to avoid forwardness and to consider God under all the characters he assumes, as a good shepherd, a friend whom one can honour, and so imitate him in life. As always he felt a powerful sense of a directing providence. He was, he believed, physically small and weak for a purpose. 'I can readily trace the wisdom and mercy of Providence in allotting me these imperfections.' Under the merciful guidance of God, good would be extracted from evil. There followed a passage the detail of which may be difficult to interpret, but the broad meaning of which is clear: 'How can I skill of these thy ways'—he was referring to George Herbert's poem—'so well, that I am verily persuaded, had it not been for that sinful habit, I had scarce acquired any degree of any virtuous one?' Unsettled as he was, he could only believe that a directing purpose governed his existence. 'Is not this the finger of God? Surely none else could have extracted so much good from evil!' He was ordained to the priesthood in September, 1728, in the meantime satisfying the bishop's

[1] *Letters*, i, 43.

examining chaplain, Dr. Hayward, whom he knew well;[1] Hayward left an indelible impression on the young man's mind by saying to him, 'Do you know what you are about? You are bidding defiance to all mankind. He that would live a Christian priest ought to know that, whether his hand be against every man or no, he must expect every man's hand should be against him.'

Between 1727 and 1729 he was only in Oxford for comparatively short periods;[2] the feeling of dissatisfaction which he had lately experienced there, 'the inconvenience', as he phrased it in March, 1727, 'of being almost necessarily exposed to much impertinence and vanity', made him the more eager to undertake pastoral work elsewhere. It may well have been that his somewhat pedantic concern with drawing up a scheme of work, his over-scrupulous conscience, had provoked smiles in the Senior Common Room; his sense of humour was not highly developed. His father was increasingly infirm and had been long desirous that John should help him with his parish. He returned to Epworth in August, 1727, and was granted leave of absence by the College on 6th November, 1727 (and subsequently on 6th May, 1728, and 6th November, 1728). He was in Oxford for his ordination and then returned as a priest in September, 1728, to Wroot, where he remained except for journeys to Oxford and London until he came back to Lincoln as a College tutor in November, 1729.

[1] Thomas Hayward, D.D. of St. John's College, vicar of Byfield (1709–26) and of St. Giles', Oxford; vicar of Great Staughton, Hunts., 1721; of Canford, Dorset, 1721–3, and of Charlbury, Oxon., 1726–46. In his diary for 1st February, 1727, Wesley noted that he had had breakfast with Dr. Hayward. He was one of the subscribers to his father's book on Job, and to the funds of the Holy Club.

[2] The College accounts indicate that in 1726 he drew half Commons (8d.) for two weeks and full Commons (1s. 4d.) for four weeks in the fourth term. He drew 1s. for being resident on Dagville's obit day, 29th October. In 1727 he drew full Commons for the whole of the first term, except for three weeks when he was away, and for one week when he drew only half Commons. He was resident for the second and third terms, except for two weeks when he was away and four weeks when he drew half Commons, indicating that he was resident only a part of the time. He was away from Oxford for the whole of the fourth term, except for the tenth and eleventh weeks. In 1728 he was only resident for the twelfth and thirteenth weeks of the third term and for eight weeks of the fourth term. In 1729 he enjoyed full Commons for six weeks of the third term and half Commons for two weeks; he was in Oxford for the first week of the fourth term. He did not sign the Calculus, as fellows in residence were accustomed to do, on 22nd December in any year until 1729.

There is only a limited amount of evidence for Wesley's career between 1727 and 1729, but life went on at Epworth and Wroot much as it had done previously. For the most part he followed a fairly regular routine. He rose early and said his private prayers. He spent the morning in reading, helping his father in his work, sorting his papers, looking up references and drawing up a list of subscribers to the promised work on Job. He talked with his mother in the evening, once discussing Sally Kirkham and her friends, on another occasion his own faults, and often read out loud to her from his favourite books, sometimes from what he called novels,[1] sometimes from more serious works like the Bishop of Cork's book on *The Procedure, Extent and Limits of Human Understanding* (1728), which he admired so much that in spite of what he regarded as its imperfections he spent some time making an abridgement of it. On Sundays he usually took the service at Wroot, but he also preached at Flixborough and Burton. He often visited the neighbours, and danced in the afternoons and evenings. He read Rowe's tragedy, *Tamerlane*, with the Maws and later talked with them about the ingredients which created contentment, more especially decency and fine clothes; a fortnight earlier John had gone to Mr. Barnard's to be fitted for a new coat.

The monotony of his life on the island of Axholme was certainly broken during the last nine months of 1729 by a series of expeditions. In the summer he went to Gainsborough to visit the affectionate Miss Kitty Hargreaves, and was regaled by singing and playing, by quadrilles at Mrs. Lambert's, and by a happy intimacy. 'With Miss Kitty in her closet', he noted in his diary. He also made a number of visits to Lincoln where his sister Kezzy (and possibly Kitty Hargreaves as well) was a pupil teacher in a school belonging to a Mrs. Taylor, an experience which Kezzy certainly did not relish.[2] Here, too, he made good use of his time, visiting the Cathedral, reading *Eloise and Abelard*[3] in the library, and entertaining the ladies with various games, cross-questions and similes, songs and dancing.

At the end of October, 1729, he went to York, where he stayed with Mr. Patrick Gardon, visited the Minster and dined with the Precentor. He took the opportunity to pay a courtesy call on the son of his father's

---

[1] He was reading Fontenelle to his mother, probably the *New Dialogues of the Dead*, which had appeared in Vol. XII of *Modern Novels* (1692).

[2] See her letters of 26th January and 12th July, 1729.

[3] *Letters of Abelard and Heloise*, extracted from Mons. Bayle, tr. John Hughes (1729).

patron, the young Duke of Buckingham.[1] It may have been on this journey that he made the acquaintance of the philanthropic and pious Lady Betty Hastings, who lived at Ledstone Park, near Pontefract, and of whom Richard Steele had written in the *Tatler* that 'to love her is a liberal education'.

He had visited London twice in 1729, lodging with his brother Samuel, who was still teaching at Westminster School, visiting his uncles Timothy and Matthew Wesley, with whom his sister Hetty had been staying, and meeting old friends, Mr. Golburne, Mr. Iliff, Mr. Richardson, Mr. Le Hunte, his old tutor, Dr. Wigan, Mr. Lloyd, and Mr. Lewis. He saw a performance of *The Scornful Lad* at the Playhouse.

Although he had been living at home most of the time between 1726 and 1729, he had kept in contact with his College. His brother Charles was in residence at Christ Church. He kept up his friendship with some of his colleagues by correspondence, while Benjamin Mangey[2] seems to have visited him at Wroot, supping and playing cards with him there on 3rd and 5th November, 1729. He could hardly have met the valetudinarian William Lupton,[3] who died on 13th December, 1726, nor was he present at his successor, Lewis Fenton's, election in November, 1727.[4] Fenton, however, wrote to Wesley shortly after Christmas, 1727, to say how 'infinitely desirous' he was of making his acquaintance. 'And when', he added, 'I consider those shining qualities which I heard daily mentioned in your praise, I cannot but lament the great misfortune we all suffer, in the absence of so agreeable a person from the College. But I please myself with the thoughts of seeing you here on Chapter-day and

[1] Edward Sheffield, b. 1716, succeeded his father as duke 1721, d. 1735. His mother was the imperious lady who told Lady Huntingdon after hearing Whitefield preach that 'Their [Methodist] doctrines are most repulsive and strongly tinctured with impertinence, and disrespect towards their superiors. It is a monstrous thing to be told that you have a heart as sinful as the common wretches that crawl the earth. I cannot but wonder that your ladyship should relish any sentiments so much at variance with high rank and good breeding.'

[2] There is an earlier reference, 14th July, 1726, to being at B. Mangey's.

[3] Lupton had half Commons during one week when Wesley was resident in 1726 (*Calculus*, 1726, fol. 10).

[4] Moore suggested that Wesley returned to Oxford (in spite of ill-health) on horseback in October, 1727, 'probably to oblige Dr. Morley . . . on some election business' (*Life of Wesley*, i, 148), but Wesley was only nine days in Oxford, the Rector being ill at his Lincolnshire rectory with the result that the election which had been arranged for 16th October did not actually take place until 6th November. Wesley was not present at this meeting.

of the happiness we shall have in your company in the summer.'[1] Fenton
was himself given leave of absence in April, 1728, though he most certainly made Wesley's acquaintance later in the year.

Wesley realized that he might soon have to face the prospect of more
permanent residence in Oxford as a tutor of his College. On 20th January,
1728, Henry Sherman wrote to tell him that 'I believe the Gentlemen of
your College would be glad to see you too in Oxford, and I have lately
heard say that it would be much to your advantage to be here, for they
say Mr. Tottenham wants very much an opportunity of resigning his
Pupils to you.'[2]

He was at Oxford in the summer of 1729; but returned to Epworth in
the middle of August. He was not, however, to be at home as long as he
supposed. On 21st October, 1729, Dr. Morley wrote to tell Wesley that
the College had decided that the junior fellows who had been nominated
to the moderatorships should attend to their duties of their office in person. So far Wesley, although a moderator, had his duties performed by
one of the resident fellows; but the position had now changed. 'We all
thought it would be a great hardship', Morley told him, trans-
mitting the results of a College meeting, 'on Mr. Fenton, to call him from
a perpetual Curacy or Donative; yet this we must have done had not Mr.
Hutchins been so kind to him and us, as to free us from the uneasiness of
doing a hard thing, by engaging to supply his place in the Hall for the
present year. Mr. Robinson would as willingly supply yours, but the
serving of two Cures about fourteen miles distant from Oxford, and ten
at least as bad as the worst of your roads in the Isle, makes it, he says,
impossible to discharge the duty constantly.' In such circumstances the
Rector and his colleagues felt that it was desirable that John should return
into residence, though they had no objection to his taking pupils or a
curacy in the neighbourhood of Oxford. 'Your father may certainly
have another Curate, though not so much to his satisfaction; yet we
are persuaded that this will not move him to hinder your return to
College, since the interests of College, and obligation to statute require
it.'

John Wesley doubtless returned willingly. Devoted as he was to his
family, the social and intellectual resources of Epworth were limited; his

---

[1] Moore, *Life of Wesley*, i, 148–9.

[2] Sherman also referred to a design of Canon Stratford's to give some money to
some undergraduates; Charles Wesley had been recommended as a possible recipient.
Wesley F. Swift, *Proc. W.H.S.*, xxxii (1960), 126–7.

relations with his parents were occasionally strained.[1] Oxford would afford a greater opportunity for his pastoral as well as his scholarly work. The Holy Club was already in being through the activities of Charles and William Morgan at Christ Church; John had certainly identified himself with what they were doing during his recent residence at Oxford. He returned on 22nd November, 1729, and it was not for some time that he was again to receive leave of absence.

[1] E.g. the entry in his diary for 20th September, 1729: '6.30 p.m., supper, dispute with my father.'

CHAPTER VII

The Oxford Tutor, 1729–35

JOHN WESLEY returned as tutor to a College where he was well liked by his colleagues to take up a task which appealed to his pastoral and intellectual sympathies. If devoid of excitement, his life was in most respects congenial. He described his twenty-seventh birthday as the cheerfulest he had ever known. Residence at Epworth and Wroot may well have heightened by contrast the amenities of College life. He was an active member of the Senior Common Room, where the fellows, their guests and gentlemen commoners, foregathered after dinner and in the evening, talking, sipping wine and sometimes playing cards as the sea-coal glowed in the grate and candlelight softly illuminated the panelled walls and the decanters.

If there were later slight signs of strain in Wesley's relations with the other fellows, more immediately he was in close and friendly contact with those who were living in College, and often in their company. There were few evenings in 1730 when he did not sit in the Common Room, noting down in his diary the names of those who were present.[1] Richard Hutchins was probably his closest friend among the fellows.[2] They walked together, and discussed the problems of the day. Wesley went to the party that Hutchins gave for young graduates of the College on 13th February, 1730, and Hutchins made a point of going to St. Mary's whenever Wesley preached there. Wesley sought his advice over the difficult problem of Richard Morgan in 1734.[3] John Tottenham was another friend, but to Wesley's regret he resigned his fellowship on 25th May, 1730, and left Oxford for Somerset. He and his colleagues enjoyed what Wesley called Tottenham's Treat on 1st April, 1730, a festive

[1] He usually noted the presence of College guests and visitors, e.g. Mr. Whately, Mr. Whitehead, Mr. Salter, Mr. Berkeley, Dr. Hamilton, Dr. Cowper, Gibson the painter, Mr. Corsellis.

[2] Some historians (e.g. Luke Tyerman, *The Oxford Methodists*, 370-1) assumed that Richard Hutchins was himself an early Methodist. This is a mistake arising from a confusion with John Hutchings of Pembroke.

[3] See p. 194ff.

occasion to mark the end of his fellowship; and Wesley dined with him in 1733 when he revisited the College.

There were two senior fellows with whom his relations were also friendly, William Vesey and John Brereton. Vesey was a learned, widely read man, for whom he sometimes read prayers. He enjoyed his conversation as they took their post-prandial stroll in the College garden in the warm summer afternoons. After breakfasting with Vesey one autumn day Wesley picked mulberries in the College garden, preparatory to making mulberry wine in his rooms. Brereton was an older man who had charge of All Saints' Church at the end of the Turl where, for instance, Wesley preached on All Saints' Day, 1730, the day of the College Gaudy. On another occasion, 14th December, 1730, Brereton entertained John and his brother, Charles, to dinner before John took the service.

There were two other resident fellows, Euseby Isham and Michael Robinson. Isham, for whom Wesley had considerable respect,[1] resigned his fellowship on 24th June, 1730, though it was not very long before he returned to the College as its Rector. Wesley often accompanied Robinson to the coffee-house and after drinking tea with a number of his other colleagues, Hutchins, Vesey and Crew,[2] on 30th December, 1730, asked him to come with him to see the horse he had bought. Another wintry evening they sat talking about the existence of spirits. He went to Robinson's house-warming on 19th February, 1731, enjoying the music which followed. There is then every reason to believe that he played a full and sociable part in College life, if latterly there was a slight measure of withdrawal. On the evening following the College Gaudy in 1730 he accompanied his colleagues on a convivial outing to the Maidenhead Tavern opposite the College, and the next morning entertained Brereton, Vesey, Hutchins, Robinson, together with the Bible-clerk, Joseph Green, to breakfast. On 18th February, 1733, he noted that he and his colleagues had taken part in the annual Bursar's treat, and in the summer together with Thomas Vaughan, Matthew Horbery[3] and some of the fellows went up the river to Godstow.

He played a normal part in the business of the College and University,

[1] He heard Isham preach at St. Aldate's on 19th February, 1727, on the dependence of the understanding on the will, a theme which would have won his approval.

[2] Charles Crew was admitted servitor of the College on 26th February, 1730. This was most likely to have been his father, Isaac Crew, the vicar of Bitteswell, where Wesley sometimes stayed on his journey north.

[3] See p. 133.

attending Convocations and the Divinity disputations. He went to Convocation on 28th January, 1732, to vote for a new bedell, Mr. Park; he responded in the Divinity Schools on 12th December, 1731. He voted for the election of his colleague, Richard Hutchins, as proctor on 19th April, 1732. He attended the statutory College meetings when the scholars and exhibitioners were elected and other appointments to College office were made. On 6th November, 1730, Vesey was made Subrector, Hutchins Bursar; Wesley became the Moderator in Philosophy (with Peter Davis as Moderator in Logic) and Dymoke was appointed one of the Combe preachers. Shortly before Christmas the Bursar reported on the accounts to the fellows, a long meeting concluded by a College feast. It was an occasion in which every fellow had a proprietorial interest since the amount of his stipend depended on his share of the allowances and fines accruing from the renewal of College leases. Occasionally he took new pupils to be matriculated before the Vice-Chancellor.[1]

Much of this was simply routine but elections to College fellowships were more vital matters. The introduction of an uncongenial and tiresome fellow into a small society could then, as now, be socially disastrous; it will be recalled that nine months had elapsed before the fellows eventually decided to elect Wesley. They met at a quarter to nine on 10th June, 1730, to elect Peter Davis, a young graduate of Christ Church, as successor to Tottenham. Wesley walked with him round the College garden on Sunday morning, 21st June, the day before he was admitted to his fellowship in the College Chapel in the presence of Wesley and six of his colleagues. Isham's successor was a young Lincoln graduate, William Smith, of whom Wesley entertained great hopes. He had come from Leicester to the College as a servitor in 1726, a susceptible, pious young man whom Wesley cultivated. He may well have hoped that he would be his ally in the Senior Common Room in forwarding the purposes of his religious society, and his close association with Wesley and the Holy Club later earned him black looks from some of his older colleagues.[2] On his journeys northwards Wesley often stayed at Smith's parents' house at Leicester. A longish interval elapsed between Mangey's death in October, 1730, and the admission of his successor, Abraham Farrer, a young graduate of Balliol, on 2nd December, 1731.[3]

---

[1] Joseph Green on 22nd June, Thomas Greives on 13th August, and Joseph Leech on 8th December, 1730.

[2] See p. 141–2.

[3] *Vid.* the entries in Wesley's diary: 'Nov. 19, 1731, 4.30 p.m. at the Rector's; talk

The death of the Rector, John Morley, was an occasion of deep personal sorrow for Wesley,[1] and the election of his successor was a matter of moment. John Morley had a stroke in the winter of 1730 at his Lincolnshire rectory, but apart from a 'weakness in the fingers in his left hand', he appeared to be better. 'I am glad', John wrote to his father, who had kept him informed of the Rector's progress, 'the Rector is in so fair a way of recovery.' Morley, however, had a further stroke 'just after he had married a couple' at Scotton, and died the following day, 12th June, 1731. If not a profound scholar or a great head of a College, he had been a kindly and beneficent man and he remembered the College in his will.[2]

The election of the new Rector, unlike others in the next century,[3] passed off uneventfully. Wesley however played a discernible part in bringing about the victory of his friend, Euseby Isham. The fellows who were living in or near Oxford foregathered in the Senior Common Room on the evening of Tuesday, 15th June. The following morning Wesley had a long talk with Michael Robinson and in the evening he saw Vaughan. On Thursday he conversed at length with the most recently elected fellow, his friend, William Smith. On 21st June he had breakfast with Hutchins, though he was engaged during most of that and the following day in entertaining his friend from London, Mr. Iliff. All these meetings with the different fellows cannot have been accidental. They were concerned with the pre-eminent topic, who was to be the next Rector of Lincoln? Wesley had already become convinced that Euseby Isham was the most suitable candidate. There was a meeting of the fellows in the Common Room on 23rd June, 1731, evidently to make arrangements, and here, or perhaps earlier, Wesley, Smith and Peter

---

of Mr. Farrer. November 20, The Rector came, talk of the examination. In the Common Room, examined Mr. Farrer. November 23, Farrer elected.'

[1] See p. 88.

[2] Hearne said that 'he died worth about 5 or 6 thousand pounds. He hath left an hundred pounds to Linc. College, to be preserved till they have enough to buy a Living with.' A College order of 22nd December, 1731, asserted that the £110 bequeathed by Morley should be added to the £30 which he had given earlier, to be laid out towards the purchase of an advowson of a living which was to be annexed to the headship of the College, a project which never materialized. A later order of 18th January, 1733, ordered that Queen Anne's Medals in silver which Morley had also given to the College should be placed in the archives of the College library; but it does not appear what eventually happened to them.

[3] Green, *Oxford Common Room*, 146 ff.

Davis agreed to vote for Euseby Isham. The next morning he breakfasted with a number of the other fellows who were as yet uncommitted, Hutchins, Robinson, Brereton and the elderly senior fellow, Knightley Adams, who had come up from his country rectory on purpose to vote at the election. The next Saturday morning, 25th June, Wesley met Isham and engaged, he noted, in good talk with him. The fellows met in the Common Room on 29th June under the chairmanship of William Vesey, the Subrector, and at half-past five in the evening Wesley promised Isham personally that he would vote for him. On 9th July, 1731, Euseby Isham was elected Rector after prayers in the College chapel; the fellows dined together later in the day.

Isham was scholarly, courteous and well-born. Hearne called him an 'ingenious' man after hearing him preach a University sermon in 1728,[1] and to this epithet he added in 1731 the adjectives 'good-natured' and 'honest',[2] a judgement confirmed by the suave Wesley Hall, who commented later that he had always been kind and had accepted a copy of Raphael's cartoons from him. On the eve of the election Isham told Hearne that if he were the Head of a House and married subsequently, he would resign the headship since he did not believe that Heads of Houses ought to be married. If he were elected, he said that he would never allow influence or 'sollicitation whether by letter or otherwise' to affect the election of fellows in the College, but would be guided 'purely and wholly by merit'; 'in such cases even his nearest Relations should have no influence over him'.[3] His portrait reveals a pleasant, rosy-cheeked, well-preserved man. In 1731 he had no matrimonial projects in mind, but by the spring of 1732 he had had 'a fair offer' by a lady which he had declined 'in a very handsome manner (for he read his answer, having then just wrote it, and was going to send it by Post to the Gentleman who had wrote to him for the Lady, to me)'.[4] Yet, like other bachelors of mature age, he did not persist in celibacy, and marrying, became the father of a future Warden of All Souls.[5]

---

[1] Hearne, *Collectanea*, ix, 395.

[2] *Op. cit.*, x, 434. His relations with Hearne were friendly (*op. cit.*, ix, 235; x, 92; xi, 129, 140, 155), a tribute to his studious interests and an indication of his High-Tory, High-Anglican inclinations with which Wesley doubtless sympathized. His nephew, Edward Isham, was Tory M.P. for Northamptonshire.

[3] *Op. cit.*, x, 435.

[4] Hearne, *Collectanea*, xi, 44.

[5] Edmund Isham, Warden from 1793–1817. The Rector had married a Miss Wood, 'worth £3000 Fortune', on 24th February, 1735.

IV EUSEBY ISHAM, RECTOR OF LINCOLN, 1731–55
Thomas Photos, Oxford

The fellows who had elected Isham did not foresee the future. For the moment they were only concerned to fulfil the traditional protocol which required that the election should be confirmed by the Visitor of the College, the Bishop of Lincoln, and that the new Rector should be subsequently installed in the stall of All Saints' Church by the Subrector. On Thursday, 13th July, 1731, five of the fellows, Hutchins, Dymoke, Davis, Smith and Wesley, and the newly elected Rector dined together in the Common Room and later in the early afternoon set out for Buckingham where they stayed the night, engaging in such animated conversation that Wesley did not get to bed till midnight. They started off at seven the next morning, reached Bedford by half-past twelve and by the evening were at the Bishop's palace at Buckden. Dr. Reynolds received them graciously and confirmed Isham's election; it seems likely that he gave them lodging for the night. They did not immediately return to Oxford but took the opportunity to visit Cambridge, where they supped at the Mitre and were entertained by Mr. Russell of St. John's College. They beguiled the journey home by composing verses and looked over Lord Cobham's famous house and gardens at Stowe. It only remained for Isham to be formally installed as Rector, a ceremony carried out in All Saints' Church at a quarter past ten on Wednesday, 21st July, 1731.

Isham's election could have made some difference to Wesley's life. If Morley's successor had been hostile or even less sympathetic, Wesley's connection with the College would in all probability have ceased earlier. Although Isham may have been occasionally embarrassed by Wesley's religious activities,[1] he was generally good-tempered and courteous. 'The Rector', John told his brother Samuel on 17th November, 1731, 'is much at your service, I fancy I shall sometime or other have much to say to you about him.'

Dr. Euseby Isham was essentially a kindly, sympathetic man who was ready to talk with the tutor about his pupils or to advise him in other matters. Wesley often read his sermons to the Rector before delivery, probably to ensure that they were unlikely to give offence to other senior members of the University. On 24th March, 1733, Wesley read his Easter sermon; on 31st October the Rector read another of Wesley's sermons. In return he asked Wesley's opinion about a sermon that he himself was to deliver.[2] Isham was a serious, religious-minded man with

---

[1] See p. 142.
[2] 22nd November, 10.30 a.m. at the Rector's; he read his Sermon for Easter.

K

whom Wesley could talk about the sacraments and the Divinity disputa-tion,[1] and there were occasions, as on Ash Wednesday, 1733, when he asked Wesley to read prayers at his lodgings. Wesley often dined with him, sometimes with his other colleagues. The Rector's brother, Sir Justinian,[2] was an occasional guest whom Wesley met at dinner on Christmas Day, 1732. Three days later, all the fellows in residence had dinner and supper with the Rector and his brother and played cards. A year later when Wesley's father was staying in Oxford over Christmas, Isham invited John Wesley to read prayers and later entertained them both. Both Isham and his brother were among the subscribers to the pro-jected work on Job, as were also some of the fellows and former under-graduates.[3] At times the Rector was justifiably concerned at Wesley's indiscreet religious zeal, but realized his merits, and on 28th June, 1734, made a donation to the work of the Castle, a gesture by which Wesley was obviously touched.

Wesley had been recalled to act as tutor to the undergraduates, and it was as a teacher and preceptor that he had returned into residence in November, 1729. He was already well-read in the classics and in divinity. These, together with logic, were the principal subjects in which he had to guide his pupils. Like all his contemporaries, he regarded Aldrich's textbook on logic, *Compendium Artis Logicae*,[4] with profound reverence; he supplemented his teaching on logic and classics by reading Sanderson and Langbaine.[5] Long after he had left Oxford the imprint of the syllo-gistic reasoning which he had learned and taught remained. 'For several years', he wrote much later, 'I was Moderator in the disputations which

[1] E.g. 7th October, 1732, 5.50 p.m., at the Rector's talk of Sacrament; 24th October, 1732, 10.45 a.m., at the Rector's, talk of Divinity disputation.

[2] Born in 1687, succeeded to the baronetcy in 1730, died 1737. He had some reputation as an antiquary.

[3] In addition to the College library, Robinson, Fenton, Davis, Smith, Farrer, Hutchins, Tottenham, Vesey and Vaughan were subscribers; Brereton was men-tioned as a possible subscriber. Other Lincoln subscribers were William Cleaver, Pindar, Bulman, Hamilton, Westley, Horbery, Williams, Thorold and Morgan.

[4] Originally written to instruct a son of Lord Carlisle, it was published in 1691; but a fourth and revised edition by Dean Mansel was published as late as 1862. Wesley published a translation in 1750, *A Compendium of Logick*; cf. *Journal* for 25th March, 1750. The second edition contained an appendix 'Of the manner of using Logic, extracted from Bishop Sanderson.'

[5] Gerard Langbaine, *Ethices Compendium . . . ut fertur admotum et nunc demum recognitum et emendatum . . . accedit Methodus Argumentandi Aristotelica ad mathematicam redacta. Disposuit et limavit . . .* J. Hudsonus (1721).

were held six times a week at Lincoln College in Oxford. I could not help acquiring hereby some degree of expertness in arguing; and especially in discerning and pointing out well-covered and plausible fallacies.' He fulfilled his duty as Moderator by lecturing or presiding over disputations in the College Hall at ten or eleven on week-day mornings.

At first he seems not to have had a private pupil, though he certainly gave his brother, Charles, and their mutual friend, William Morgan, what could be called tutorials. With them he read Milton's poetry, Lucas' popular devotional work, Norris' sermons, lives of Bonnel and de Renty and the warning tract known as the *Second Spira*.[1] The character of these books suggests that this reading may have been part of that prescribed for the recently formed Holy Club.[2] In June, 1730, he noted proudly that he had his 'first pupil', in all probability Joseph Green, the Bible clerk whom he had introduced to the Rector on 10th June and whom he took to be matriculated two days later. Green's father lived at Shipton, where Wesley often took the service for his friend, the former Lincoln undergraduate, Joseph Goodwin. It was probably through Wesley's efforts that Green came to Lincoln. He was soon calling on Wesley, who lived in rooms just above him in College, at ten every morning, presumably for tuition.[3]

On 4th June, 1730, the Rector had allocated eleven men to Wesley, John Westley, Jonathan Black, from Harringworth in Northamptonshire, Thomas Waldegrave, a Lincolnshire boy from Londonthorpe, two northerners, Thomas Hylton from Monkwearmouth and Robert Davison from Durham, John Bartholomew from Dorchester, Dorset, John Sympson, almost a neighbour, from Gainsborough, Edward Browne, a merchant's son from St. Asaph, Richard Bainbridge from Leeds, and George Podmore from Edgmond in Shropshire. None of these ever achieved great distinction, but Bainbridge was later a fellow of Lincoln,[4] while Thomas Waldegrave was subsequently elected a fellow of Magdalen and was Edward Gibbon's first tutor.[5] It is one of the minor

---

[1] See p. 196n.

[2] See pp. 154–5.

[3] He helped Green in other ways, viz., 'Lent Mr. Green for oaths 6s. 0d.; for Castle (presumably Holy Club), 1s. 0d., for coals 4s. 3d., to make up caution money 8s. 0d.'

[4] 1736–52.

[5] Waldegrave, who served as proctor in 1745, resigned his fellowship on presentation to the vicarage of Washington, Sussex, in 1754. He bequeathed £1,500 in New South Sea Annuities 'to that generous, independent and honourable society

ironies of history that in going through the plays of Terence with the precocious young man Waldegrave was probably reproducing the notes which he had once learned from John Wesley; but Gibbon thought the tutorials so unrewarding that he resolved to absent himself from them.[1] There were few days when Wesley did not give up some hours, usually either at ten in the mornings or two or five in the afternoons, to his pupils; even on Sundays and holy days he noted in his diaries that he had seen his pupils, presumably to give them religious instruction.

It is not very clear what the College tutor in the eighteenth century was expected to teach outside the lectures in Hall where he presided over disputations or commented on the Greek Testament.[2] Fortunately John Wesley has himself left a list of the books which he read with his pupils. In 1730 he instructed them in Virgil's Aeneid, Terence's plays, Horace's poems, Juvenal's Satires, Phaedrus, and Anacreon. In English they studied Richard Lucas' *Enquiry after Happiness*, Norris' *Sermons*, Stephen's *Letters* and half of John Ellis' *Defence of the Thirty-nine Articles*. Next year he read *Gentleman Instructed*[3] and Charles Wheatley's *The Church of England Man's Companion* with one pupil. With another he perused Atterbury's sermons and Edward Welchman's *Articuli XXXIX Ecclesiae Anglicanae*. With another he ended Cicero's *De Natura Deorum* and read his Tusculan Disputations. With another he studied Aldrich's *Logic*, but

---

of Magdalen College in Oxford of whose bread . . . I have eaten these fifty years'. (W. D. Machray, *A Register of Magdalen College* (Oxford), v, 71–3.)

[1] 'The first tutor into whose hands I was resigned appears to have been one of the best of the tribe: Dr. Waldegrave was a learned and pious man, of a mild disposition, strict morals, and abstemious life, who seldom mingled in the politics or the jollity of the college. But his knowledge of the world was confined to the University: his learning was of the last, rather than of the present age; his temper was indolent . . . he proposed that we should read every morning from ten to eleven the comedies of Terence. The sum of my improvement in the University of Oxford is confined to three or four Latin plays. . . . During the first weeks I constantly attended these lessons in my tutor's room; but as they appeared equally devoid of profit and pleasure, I was once tempted to try the experiment of a formal apology. The apology was accepted with a smile.' Soon Gibbon ceased to turn up for his tutorials, though he enjoyed his tutor's society, preferring it to that of his contemporaries; 'in our evening walks to the top of Headington Hill, we freely conversed on a variety of subjects' (*Autobiography*, 47–8). Richard Woodesdon (see pp. 74, 75) had taught Gibbon at Kingston.

[2] He lectured on the Gospels in 1730, in 1731 he took classes in Hall on the Acts of the Apostles and St. Paul's Epistle to the Romans.

[3] *A Gentleman Instructed in the conduct of a Virtuous and Happy Life*, William Darrell, 6th ed. (1724).

to so little effect that when they had finished it they began all over again. Finally a fifth pupil read the plays of Terence as well as Aldrich with him. He had evidently acquired something of a reputation as a tutor in logic as three young graduates of the College, William Smith, George Bulman, and Frederick Williams were given tuition in the ubiquitous Aldrich.

He took his pupils' intellectual problems seriously, correcting declamations for Edward Browne on 22nd September, 1730, and for Joseph Leech on the afternoon of 28th February, 1733, and teaching Thomas Greives an hour later that same day; earlier he had spent some time thinking out syllogisms for an exercise in logic. On 26th June, 1732, he wrote out a logical problem for Smith. In the winter of 1733 he noted wearily that his pupils would not learn Hebrew and on the last day of the year he was angry because they had failed to turn up.

His relationship with these young men was much more than that of teacher and pupil. Hitherto his contacts at Lincoln had been with men of comparatively senior status like William Cleaver, Matthew Horbery, the son of a former vicar of Haxey, and a future fellow of Magdalen[1] and his neighbour, Robert Pindar, who matriculated as long ago as 1726. Now he was concerned with supervising younger men who had just entered the College, and he certainly set out to take an interest in them far beyond the obligations of a tutorial nature. He sat with young Joseph Green at the Bear. In August, 1732, after calling on Benjamin Holloway, son of the rector of Middleton Stoney, who was to enter the college in the following November, he accompanied Richard Bainbridge on an expedition to Cottisford and Rousham. He said later that he made no attempt to persuade his pupils to become members of the Holy Club, but he had too strong a personality to keep his religious views in the background. His diary shows that he regularly invited his pupils to breakfast and prayers, and those who showed any interest in the activities of the Holy Club were subsequently brought under close supervision and spiritual discipline. His first book, *A Collection of Forms of Prayer for Every Day in the Week*, with

[1] 25th April, 1731: '5.15 p.m. In talk with Mr. Horbery.' Born at Haxey, 1707; matric., Lincoln C., 1726; Lincolnshire fellow of Magdalen, 1733; later, B.D., D.D., Dean of Divinity, Vice-President, declined the suggestion that he should stand for the Presidentship being 'of such uncommon modesty and invincible diffidence that nothing could draw him out into public life'. He was successively vicar of Eccleshall and Standlake, where he was buried, and held a prebendal stall at Lichfield from 1736. Dr. Johnson told his widow that he considered his sermons to be 'excellent', and Garrick described him as 'one of the best deliverers of a sermon he had ever heard'. (Nichols, *Literary Anecdotes*, ix, 558–63.) Cf. pp. 236–7.

preface and questions for self-examination, was written for his pupils and published in 1733.[1]

It is possible that the Rector was increasingly and explicably unwilling to entrust Wesley with the care of pupils because of his close identification with the Holy Club. In August, 1733, Wesley told his mother that he had as many pupils as he required. 'If I have no more pupils after these are gone from me, I shall then be glad of a curacy near you: if I have, I shall take it as a signal that I am to remain here.' There were in fact only a small number of new entries at Lincoln every year.[2] Wesley seems to have been only on intimate terms with his earlier pupils and either because of lack of time or because the Rector was anxious about the recruitment of impressionable young men his later pupils were few. This view is supported by Richard Morgan's unfriendly picture of Wesley in a letter to his father. Indeed, he wanted to be transferred to the other tutor of the College, 'reckoned one of the best tutors in the University', and of whom Lord Lichfield had so high an opinion that he thought to send his eldest son to Lincoln.[3] 'He has', he wrote, 'what few are in college (except one Gentleman Commoner and two servitors who are Mr. Wesley's pupils) under his tuition.' If Morgan was correct, then at the beginning of 1734 Wesley had, presumably in addition to Morgan, only three other pupils, probably Westley Hall (who was a gentleman commoner), Matthew Robinson, and either Joseph Green or Joseph Leech, all of whom were servitors. We should, however, be careful about accepting Morgan's statement without qualification, and other evidence would suggest that Wesley was at least being consulted on tutorial matters by other members of the College.

[1] In 1734 he published *A Treatise on Christian Prudence*, extracted from John Norris, and in 1735 a translation of à Kempis' *Imitatio Christi*, *The Christian Pattern*, printed by his friend, Charles Rivington.

[2] Of the eight men admitted in 1732, only one, John Robson, became an intimate friend of Wesley and one other, Adamson, an acquaintance; of the eleven admitted in 1733, five, Richard Morgan, another gentleman commoner, Philip Craig, Henry Brown, Warner and Hutton, the brother of Thomas Hutton, another undergraduate at Lincoln and son of the Gainsborough attorney, made some contact with Wesley; of the eight admitted in 1734 (including Willis, who later treated George III for madness) only Charles Westley was in any way connected with Wesley.

[3] Actually, George Henry Lee, the third earl and future Chancellor of the University, matriculated at St. John's College in 1736. Morgan may have got this piece of gossip from John Warner, an undergraduate at Lincoln whose father, Richard Warner, lived at Ditchley, where Lord Lichfield's house was designed in all its splendour by Gibbs. For Wesley's relations with Richard Morgan, see p. 194.

His residence at Lincoln may have attracted a number of undergraduates to the College. John Sympson, who was admitted as a servitor in 1728, lived in Gainsborough; so did George and Thomas Hutton, whose father was a local lawyer. Joseph Green, from Shipton, probably entered the College as a Bible clerk partly through Wesley's support. He certainly played a part in the admission of two of his other protégés, Westley Hall and John Whitelamb. Westley Hall was admitted as a gentleman commoner on 22nd January, 1731, and John Whitelamb was admitted as a servitor on 10th April, 1731, and, much to Wesley's satisfaction, was later given a scholarship. Hall, who came from Salisbury, was related through his mother to John Westley, who was already an undergraduate at Lincoln. His mother, who was a daughter of a vicar of Imber, near Warminster, had married a clothier, Francis Hall; his brother, Robert, later Lord Mayor of London and knighted in 1744, was the father of the Lincoln undergraduate; 'My first cousin, John Westley being there . . . John Wesley my tutor', as Hall later commented.[1] John Whitelamb, 'poor starveling Johnny', was the son of humble parents (his father Robert, however, is described in the matriculation book as Robert, gentleman of the parish of Hatfield), who lived at Wroot, the dreary village where Wesley acted as curate; and he had been employed by the elder Wesley as his amanuensis. He was an intelligent young man, who entered the College at the unusually late age of twenty-two; Wesley had great hopes of Whitelamb, but as in the case of Westley Hall, they were steadily to evaporate. Of the twelve young men who entered the College in 1731, the one who was eventually to repay Wesley's tutorship most was in his first year practically unknown to him; James Hervey, the son of the curate of Collingtree.[2]

Although Wesley was as far as possible rationing time to serve the more serious pursuits of life, he neither withdrew from social life nor ceased to take part in the normal recreations of Oxford. Twice, on 10th March and 19th May, 1730, he went dancing. Genuinely fond as he was of music, he seized such opportunities as Oxford then presented, once attending a concert with Charles and William Morgan; and in the summer he himself studied the gavotte from *Otho*, 'Non e si vago e bello'. He occasionally went on the river; on 28th September, 1730, he gathered walnuts. Walking was his normal exercise, with Charles and Morgan, to Binsey, round the Meadows, or in Merton garden, once with Wilder and Dr. Grove.

[1] See *Proc. Wes. H.S.*, v, 146–51; cf. 1939–42, 28–31.
[2] See p. 188–9, 262ff.

He was now the proud possessor of a horse.[1] This was in effect a first necessity if he was to take services at the villages in the neighbourhood of Oxford.

'Yesterday', he told his mother on 28th February, 1730, 'I had the offer of another curacy to continue a quarter or half a year, which I accepted with all my heart. The salary is thirty pounds a year, the church eight miles from Oxford; seven of which are, winter and summer, the best road in the country. So now I needn't sell my horse, since it is at least as cheap to keep one as to hire one every week.'[2]

This curacy was almost certainly at Pyrton,[3] near Wallingford, where in addition to taking the service on Easter Day, 1730, he read prayers most often in the course of the year. During 1730 and subsequent years he took services in other churches in the vicinity of Oxford,[4] but the obligation of preaching to the prisoners gradually limited these more distant services. A horse enabled him to make other excursions. He and his brother often visited Mr. Woods at Abingdon, where they met the young Robert Kirkham, now ordained, and joined with their friends in songs, supper and cards. His Oxford friend, Gwynne, rode with him to Shipton and Ascot, where he stayed with Mr. and Mrs. Brooks; on his way there he met his old friend from Epworth, Miss Kitty Hargreaves, at Burford, and enjoyed 'tea and rhymes'. In the middle of September, 1730, he made an expedition with Cox and Watkins to Aynho and Astrop, and walked in the gardens of Lord Cobham's house at Stowe.

There were friendly occasions when he dined with senior acquaintances in the University, Dr. Tanner and Dr. Rye of Christ Church, for instance, or Emily's former suitor, Robert Leybourne of B.N.C., or entertained friends from outside. On 29th May, 1730, he conducted Lord

---

[1] Cf. the entry in his diary for 8th July, 1729: 'walk . . . to Yarnton . . . saw my horse'.

[2] *Letters*, i, 48.

[3] Pyrton was a parish in the gift of the Dean and Chapter of Christ Church. There would have been a vacancy following the incumbency of Antony Reed who was vicar from 1714 to 1729.

[4] He preached at Fleet Marston and Winchendon three Sundays in 1730, at Buckland (for Dr. Burton), three times, at Combe, Shipton, Ascot, Holwell, Stanesfield, Bampton, Black Bourton, Ferry Hinksey, and Stanton Harcourt, as well as in a number of Oxford churches, St. Aldate's (for John Wilder), St. Thomas', St. Ebbe's, St. Martin's, Carfax (where he preached before the Mayor on Sunday, 5th November, 1732), All Saints', and St. Mary's, between 1730 and 1735.

Oxford round the College library at Lincoln.[1] At the beginning of July, 1733, he entertained some visitors who had come to Oxford to attend the celebrations which marked the end of the Trinity term, Mrs. Boyse, Serena,[2] and possibly Mr. Tooker.

He took them to the Sheldonian Theatre, but as they could hear nothing of the proceedings there they came away. The next day, Saturday, 7th July, 1733, they walked in Trinity garden, saw the Picture Gallery, and watched the procession: in the afternoon Wesley listened to *Esther* with them. A few days later he accompanied Serena and Mrs. Boyse down the water to a meadow below Iffley, where they sang and danced and listened to the French horn in the warm summer evening. The day after, having risen at a quarter to four, he rode to the Bear at Blenheim and thence went with Serena to Stanton, for a short visit.

These excursions were a welcome break in the regular routine of Oxford life, whether they took Wesley to the familiar Lincolnshire countryside, to his friends in the neighbourhood of Gloucester and Stanton, or to London. It was his normal practice to visit London during the winter months, though in 1733 he was there in the summer. He usually left Oxford at an early hour; in January, 1730, he set out with his brother Charles and William Morgan at five. They travelled via Beaconsfield which they reached at mid-morning and arrived at Samuel's at Westminster by the late afternoon. It was a pleasant and successful visit, involving the renewal of old acquaintances, tea and cards with Mr. and Mrs. Rhodes, dinner with Dr. Burton, supper and songs with Mr. Lewis, and talk of his parents and sisters with Uncle Matthew. He took advantage of his stay at Westminster to visit the school and see the Latin play; the following Saturday he went in the afternoon to the House of Commons. On Sunday he preached and took communion at the Duke Street Chapel and in the afternoon he went to the Almoners Chapel, where he heard a sermon from Mr. Fitzgerald. Before he left for Oxford he went to the King's Head in Southwark with Mr. Horne and in the afternoon attended a performance of *Hamlet* at the theatre in Goodman's Fields.[3]

[1] Lord Oxford wrote to Dean Swift in 1730 (to whom Alexander Pope had also written with the same object) to urge him to get subscriptions to Samuel Wesley's book on Job; he added, 'Three sons he had bred up well at Westminster, and they are excellent scholars.'

[2] See p. 224.

[3] Situated on the north side of Ayliffe (now Alie) Street. Opened 31st October, 1729, and closed on 23rd May, 1732. It was demolished and its manager, Henry

The brothers' attendance at the London playhouse opens up a new, intriguing and obscure aspect of their lives. From a letter which Charles wrote his brother in January, 1729, it appears that he and possibly John had not been immune to the attraction of the actresses whose performances they witnessed on their occasional visits to London.

Charles referred to a flirtation with a young actress in which he had been involved. John had thought little of the young lady's talents, but his brother, disillusioned as to her character, yet affirmed her capacity. 'She's qualified for the Stage for being a Whore-sun! waster; an Eye-witness commends her capacity in spight of the villanous words that Barford had put into her mouth.' The young woman in question had a mother who had evidently hoped to further the affair, possibly to push Charles into marriage, certainly to entangle him beyond recall.

'To do the Old Lady Justice,' he told his brother, 'she *did* give us opportunities enough could I but have had the Grace to have laid hold on them and but for my strange College dullness Molly *might* have made something of me. . . . Hints were *lost* upon so dull stupid a Fellow as I was; and as such no doubt I have been since sufficiently laughed at.'

Had Lushington, his friend from Christ Church, been in his place, he would certainly have made a much better use of his opportunities. Charles had fortunately seen the danger in time, though whether as a result of his 'pretty creature's' own frailty or his realization of where the affair might lead him it is impossible to say. 'My eyes were partly opened by my last saving journey to London.' Henceforth he would see her no more save on the stage at the Playhouse with the 'Musical-box . . . between us and you on one side of me.' He had learned his lesson. Henceforth he would be less 'addicted to Gallantry and doing what Sister Hetty with less justice said you did—liking Woman merely for being woman'.

Is it possible to throw any additional light on this curious incident? The play was almost certainly Richard Barford's *The Virgin Queen*, performed at the Theatre Royal in Lincoln's Inn Fields in 1729. It is a poor play which earned Alexander Pope's scorn,[1] and was the solitary piece

---

Giffard, constructed a new theatre on the same site. Giffard (1699–1772) took the part of Hamlet and his wife acted as Ophelia in the play seen by Wesley (C. B. Hogan, *Shakespeare in the Theatre, 1701–1800* (1952), 119).

[1] 'Bless me! a packet—'tis a stranger ruse,
     A Virgin Tragedy, an Orphan Muse.'
                              (*An Epistle to Dr. Arbuthnot*, 155.)

from the pen of its author, who may have been the Richard Barford[1] whom Wesley met in Pitt's rooms at Exeter on 24th February, 1726. The part of the Queen, Olympia, was taken by one of the company, a Mrs. Buchanan.[2] Two years later John Wesley called on Mrs. Buchanan at the Lincoln's Inn Theatre at half-past three on Saturday afternoon, 6th February, 1731; John was with her again at five and at six 'Miss Molly' came.[3] He sat talking three-quarters of an hour and to his note of the meeting he added the revealing words, 'Hope still.' He attached the enigmatic comment, 'Perhaps Innocent!' to his account of the meeting with Mrs. Buchanan. He called on her again when he visited London in the summer, on 5th August, 1731.

The question must be faced as to whether John may not himself have been at least emotionally engaged in these youthful indiscretions. Charles told his brother that he had learned more about 'your dear creature' at Lincoln's Inn Fields Theatre. At thirteen years old the Duke of Richmond had taken a fancy to her[4] and set her up; from him she had passed through several other hands until she had come into 'happy Mr. Thompson's'.

> 'She had once set up for a Milliner, but it would not do; Nature and her stars (I think 'tis very gallant in me to lay the blame upon *them*) having designed her for the stage, but enough of her—I'll blot my brain and paper no longer with her.'

It is difficult to name the good lady to whom Charles was referring or to know whether it was the self-same Miss Molly to whose charms he had himself fallen victim temporarily. Whatever the truth of the matter, John was less deeply involved than Charles; but it is an episode in their careers of which we should dearly love to learn more.

His visits to London gave him an opportunity not merely to visit his Uncle Matthew and his Aunt Nancy, but to converse with friends, some of whom had been his contemporaries at Oxford: Mr. Golburne, Mr. Rhodes, Dr. Wigan, Mr. Wogan whose proposals for education he read

---

[1] Matric., Exeter C., 10th May, 1723, aged 16; B.A. 1727, M.A. 1729.

[2] Mrs. (Charles) Buchanan died in 1736. She played a number of Shakespearean parts: Lady Macbeth, Mrs. Page, Portia, the Duchess of York, Calpurnia, Andromache, Goneril.

[3] Miss Molly was evidently the name of Charles' lady friend: 'I'm much of your opinion as to Molly's Design upon me, but can't imagine the Mother would purvey no better for her Daughter', he told John.

[4] There is no mention of any such indiscretion in the Earl of March, *A Duke and his Friends, the Life and Letters of the Second Duke of Richmond*, 2 vols. (1911).

carefully, Mr. Laserre, Mr. Le Hunte, Mr. Spicer, Mr. Iliff, Mr. Robert Westley, the London merchant whose son was an undergraduate at Lincoln, and Dr. Burton. At his brother's house at Westminster he met Dr. Berriman, a friend of Burton's and a member of the S.P.C.K., who was the rector of St. Andrew Undershaft, and Burton's relative, Edward Bentham, a fellow of Oriel, who later became the Regius Professor of Divinity (from 1763–76). Another London acquaintance was the publisher, Charles Rivington, who had published many theological works of High-Church views and later issued some of Wesley's writings. He was often in the company of the wealthy churchman, Sir John Phillips,[1] who took him to St. Paul's and Westminster Abbey in his coach, and in 1733 went with him to visit Bishop Clavering, a former undergraduate of Lincoln and Regius Professor of Hebrew at Oxford.[2]

A visit in the summer of 1732 was significant for the conversation which he had with William Law in his garden at Putney. Law was a man whom he admired greatly and by whose writings he was especially influenced.[3] Immediately after their discussion he began reading the mystical medieval work, *Theologica Germanica*, on Law's advice. It was during the course of this stay in London that he visited Colonel Oglethorpe, the founder of the colony of Georgia, in company with his sisters, and was admitted a corresponding member of the S.P.C.K. In the winter of 1733 he spent three hours in close talk with Law, though he confessed that he had not clearly understood all that Law had said.

His sojourn in London must be associated with the works that he was doing in Oxford. Although he took the opportunity to visit the theatre, seeing Congreve's *The Old Bachelor* in company with Patty in 1732, to attend the coffee-house and to take part in cards and singing, his acquaintances were serious-minded men of views similar to his own, interested in missionary activity and the work of the S.P.C.K. and likely to be sympathetic towards the Holy Club. When, for instance, John Wesley was in London in April, 1733, he noted that he had talked with Phillips and Rivington of Communion and the Methodists, as they rode in Phillips' coach to Hackney. They probably took the Methodists more seriously than most of his Oxford contemporaries and some of them contributed their cash as well as their prayers to his venture. London must have awakened him to the fact that Oxford in the eighteenth century was still

[1] See pp. 166–7.
[2] See pp. 26, 38.
[3] See pp. 277–8.

profoundly provincial and may well have made him ask himself whether the University was a proper setting for the fulfilment of his vocation.

What in fact did Oxford make of John Wesley in these years? His impact on the University must not be exaggerated. Probably the majority of its senior and junior members had hardly heard of him or the Holy Club in spite of the way in which the controversy had sprung into print. It was a negligible force in the general life of the place; but where Wesley and his friends had influence, it was impossible to ignore it. Lincoln College was in many ways the society most likely to be affected. Christ Church was a larger institution, more variegated socially, and more able to absorb its enthusiastic few. Besides, John Wesley was a stronger and more forceful personality than Charles. His industry and his power of concentration revealed by the hour-to-hour diary of his daily activities were really amazing. Even on the occasions when he felt unwell (and he suffered much from bilious catarrh) he rarely permitted sickness to interfere with his daily routine. When he got up on 9th October, 1730, he was sick and laid down, but he said his private prayers at seven and was with Mr. Gerard for breakfast. On 14th May, 1731, he was ill and took a purge in the morning but was with William Morgan by eleven and did not go to bed specially early. He caught cold, so he tells us, on the evening of 18th June, 1732, but took prayers for Clayton at seven the following morning. A sore throat was soon countered by a posset and a sweat. The colic which afflicted him on 15th June, 1733, only drew the comment that he was 'enabled to bear pain without a murmur'. There is little doubt that he had imposed a regime upon himself which demanded self-discipline and strong will-power; if he rose, as he often did, between four and five, there is nothing to indicate that he went to bed at an abnormally early hour. There were times for prayer and times for work, times for pupils and times for visiting the Castle and Bocardo; and life went on with clockwork regularity.

If Wesley possessed the will-power to rule his own life in so masterful a way, he could hardly prevent himself from influencing those around him. The evidence, slight as it is, is sufficient to suggest that he may have played a prominent part in the life of the College. His association with the Holy Club and his religious development had inevitable repercussions on members of the Senior Common Room. The Rector and his colleagues, well-disposed as they were, watched the development of his religious society with justified anxiety. Young William Smith's adhesion aroused them to a measure of resentment; excessive enthusiasm of any kind, and religious enthusiasm in particular, can easily break up the harmony of a placid, peaceable and friendly society. Wesley himself told his mother that Mr. Smith had no sooner begun 'To husband his time, to retrench unnecessary expenses, and to avoid his irreligious acquaintances' than he became the target of venomous criticism, 'as if he had entered into a conspiracy to cut all their throats'.[1] In August, 1732, John Clayton told Wesley that he had visited Lincoln every day

> 'big with expectation, to hear of some mighty attack made upon Mr. Smith; but I thank God, I have always been disappointed; for not one of the Fellows has once so much as tried to shake him, or to convert him from the right way'.

On Sunday he had 'met with a rub' by Vesey who had refused to read prayers for him in the College Chapel to enable him to go to Christ Church; but he had gone to the Rector, who had immediately promised to perform his duty, 'and encouraged him to proceed in the way he was in, and, if possible, to make further progress in virtue and holiness'. Smith 'goes out of town to-morrow morning', he added, 'and so will be entirely out of danger from the Fellows of Lincoln'.[2] It is difficult to argue that the fellows had not behaved with perfect propriety and Christian tolerance towards their two enthusiastic colleagues.

Yet worried they must have been. When the Rector saw Richard Morgan shortly after his arrival, in early November, 1733, he 'cautioned me against Mr. Wesley's strict notions of religion' and told him that the College's known connection with the religious society had deterred several from entering. The Rector's advice was well-meant, and he was stating no more than the truth when he alleged that some had been discouraged from going to Lincoln because of the rumours circulating about the Holy Club. Morgan's earlier assertion that the other fellows of the College had a great aversion to Wesley was ill-founded; though there were occasions when they were not wholly displeased when Wesley left for the bleak Lincolnshire pastures. 'I am not satisfied (as I have told the Rector for this twelve month past) that the Wednesday fast is strictly obligatory; though I believe it very ancient, if not apostolical', he wrote to John Robson on 30th September, 1735, but he also remarked trenchantly that the dining in Hall on Friday was completely unjustified 'It is

[1] *Letters*, i, 137–8.
[2] *Journal*, viii, 276.

giving offence in the worst sense, giving men occasion to think that innocent which is grossly sinful.'[1] If Wesley took this sort of line at College
meetings and in the Senior Common Room, his colleagues may have
been occasionally and justifiably embarrassed and irritated. But there was
never any serious friction. John Wesley's genuine goodness and courtly
charm smoothed over any possibility of trouble. He continued to enjoy
Dr. Euseby Isham's esteem and to regard him with respect and affection.
Richard Hutchins remained a confidant; and to William Vesey he sent
later in 1740 a copy of his Georgia journal which the College library still
possesses.

The University authorities had less personal contact and might be
expected therefore to view his activities with a more objective and critical
eye. He wrote to and talked with the Bishop of Oxford on a number of
occasions during these years, and in 1734 visited him at his London house,
but Bishop Potter was for the most part sympathetic and encouraging.
The Vice-Chancellor was more wary. The recent pamphlets made him
anxious lest the University should be disturbed by controversy or heterodox teaching. Wesley went to see the Vice-Chancellor on Tuesday
morning, 13th March, 1733. What ensued does not appear but later in the
day he called on the Dean of Christ Church, but 'a gentleman stept in
before me'. However, he called on the Dean at nine-thirty the following
morning and then went at ten to the Vice-Chancellor with whom he
talked about methodism and the pamphlets; he discussed with the Dean
similar topics as well as the attendance at Communion. Wesley was due to
preach the University sermon at St. Mary's on 1st April, 1733, and
appeared to have submitted to the Vice-Chancellor's request that he
should go through his sermon on the Saturday evening before its delivery.
Whether he was asked to change any of its substance does not appear but
he got up very early and at half-past five on Sunday morning was reading
it to Hervey.[2] When he preached the sermon to which Hutchins came to
listen he 'did not look' round the church at the congregation. He went
immediately to take a service at the Castle, talked with two of the

---

[1] *Letters*, i, 183. A College order of earlier date (20th October, 1668) laid down
that Saturday was no longer to be observed as a fast day unless 'the succeeding day
be such an holy-day as shall require it according to the injunctions of the Church
of England, and that Commons shall be served up in the Hall as at all other nights
in the week'. (*College Register*, I, fol. 160.)

[2] The diary reads: ' 5.30 a.m. repeated Sns to H.' This is likely to be Hervey as he
usually signified Hutchins with the phrase 'Hu'.

prisoners and by three was Londonwards. The authorities were quietly anxious but no more. There was no question of a persecution or even of attempts at positive dissuasion. The real question facing John Wesley was whether the University was the field in which to work out his life and satisfactorily to fulfil his missionary vocation.

CHAPTER VIII

The Foundation of the Holy Club

In John Wesley's oft-quoted words,

> 'In November, 1729, four young gentlemen of Oxford, Mr. John Wesley, Fellow of Lincoln College; Mr. Charles Wesley, Student of Christ Church; Mr. Morgan, Commoner of Christ Church; and Mr. Kirkham of Merton College; began to spend some evenings in a week together, in reading chiefly the Greek Testament.'

Much must, however, be added to this bare summary if the significance of the foundation of the Holy Club is to be appreciated.

John's brother, Charles Wesley, was in the first instance responsible for bringing together a small group of young men who tried to implement their religious beliefs by further study and practical Christianity. Five years younger than John, Charles had been sent to school under his elder brother Samuel at Westminster, preparatory to his entry at Christ Church in the summer of 1726. Since John was away for much of the time in Lincolnshire, Charles at first placed greater reliance on Samuel, but he was drawn to an increasing extent to depend upon John.

> 'He pursued his studies diligently,' John wrote later, 'and led a regular, harmless life; but if I spoke to him about religion, he would warmly answer "What, would you have me to be a saint all at once" and would hear me no more.'

'My first year at College', Charles confessed, 'I lost in diversions: the next I set myself to study.'[1]

For various reasons he was in a confused state of mind throughout 1729. The flirtation with Miss Molly[2] may have helped to create inner tensions. John was sufficiently perturbed by his letters to put peremptory, enigmatic questions: 'How these Accidents shall be the last?'; 'What company was in the York coach?'; 'What said B. and I.?'; 'What were

---

[1] He was admitted as a reader to the Bodleian Library, Oxford, on 19th April, 1729 (W. D. Machray, *Annals of Bodleian Library*, 460 n.).

[2] See pp. 138–9.

the amazing particulars?' Charles, however, hedged in his reply. The answers to John's questions were 'fitter for a private conference'. Earlier he had described Christ Church as 'a cursed society', but the atmosphere of Dean's Yard, Westminster, was no better. What had given rise to trouble there remains mysterious, but his sister-in-law, Samuel's wife, was a determined and at times censorious woman who may conceivably have reacted unfavourably to Charles' emotional entanglements. At Christ Church he was at least able to breathe a 'free tho' sharp air'. Yet eager as he was to live a religious, strict life, he regretted that he was such a dull dog and lacked the quality of worldly perception. 'Want of money and clothes are great temptations to dullness', he explained to his brother.

The impoverished state of his finances made Charles the more depressed. Like John, he could hope for little from Epworth and could not see 'the Human means of getting clear of Debt which I must inevitably run farther into every day'. He wished that he could be in Epworth with John but where was the money to take him there and bring him back? As he sat by a fireless grate on a frosty January day in his rooms at Oxford, he soliloquized grimly,

> '. . . 'tis in the power of a few Epworth or Wroot guineas and clothes to give things the favourable turn and make a gentleman of me. Come money then and quickly to rescue me from my melancholy maxim "ex nihilo nihil fit".'

He called in his muse to explain his disconsolate position; but the muse evidently lacked inspiration.

> No longer now on Hinxy's Horrell's[1] airy Vane
> With thee shall I admire the subject plain
> Or where the sight in neighbouring shades, is lost
> Or where the lengthened Prospect widens most;
> While on the tunefull Poet's (something) song
> Or Truths Divine flowd easy from thy Tongue.

The only answer that he could give to his brother's questions was the refrain, 'I am turned out with some shillings.'

It is against this background that what Charles termed his 'reformation' has to be placed. He was evidently now working hard for his degree. 'I am very *desirous* of knowledge but can't *bear* the drudgery of it near so well as you could', he told John, but he was making progress even

[1] Hinxsey, in the neighbourhood of Oxford; Horrel, the hill near Stanton in the Cotswolds (see p. 203).

in the 'extraordinary Business of Thinking'. Having recently finished his Collections, he was now 'Head of the Third Class and shall be of the Table this term, and then there will be brave Living for me!' He asked John's advice about a suitable tutor, especially to coach him in prose composition, and he wondered whether John would consider Mr. H. suitable. This may have been Hutchins of Lincoln. In any case John's return at the end of 1729 changed this situation since he virtually became his brother's supervisor in classical learning as well as his moral and religious preceptor.

At what date Charles became aware of the need for a more disciplined religious life it is impossible to say, but a marked change came in 1729.

'I verily think', he wrote to John in January, 1729, 'I shall never quarrel with you again till I do with my Religion, and that I may never do *That* I am not ashamed to desire your prayers. 'Tis owing in great measure to somebody's (my Mother's most likely) that I am come to think as I do, for I can't tell myself How or When I first awoke out of my Lethargy,—only that twas not long after you went away.'

It would indeed have been difficult for two men of such sensitive conscience as John and Charles, coming from so pious a household, not to feel perturbed at the religious situation in Oxford. While religious life there inclined to be conventional in belief and practice, disbelief had increased in fashionable intellectual circles outside the University and through a minority of dons and a nucleus of undergraduates was infiltrating into the chosen fields of orthodoxy. In October, 1726, John Wesley had noted in his diary that he had been talking with his friends Harrison and Burman of 'despisers of religion' and a fortnight later with Harrison of Arianism and Deism. In all probability unorthodoxy had only a small following in the University where most of the official tutors were in Anglican orders, but it had attracted enough disciples to alarm the University authorities.[1] They were probably mainly perturbed by the way in which fashionable infidelity encouraged tepid Christians to be still more lukewarm in their beliefs and religious observances. Although the Heads of the Houses were not unanimous and the Dean of Christ Church in particular opposed the measure with 'might and main', a majority brought pressure to bear on the Vice-Chancellor, Dr. Butler, to issue a circular letter urging College tutors to inform their pupils of their Christian duty by 'explaining to them the articles of religion which they

[1] Cf. pp. 29–30.

professed, and are often called upon to subscribe', and by 'recommending to them the frequent and careful reading of the scriptures, and such other books as may serve more effectually to promote christianity, sound principles and orthodox faith'. The Vice-Chancellor recommended the prohibition of irreligious books 'to guard the youth of this place against the wicked advocates for pretended human reason against divine revelation.' This notice, a copy of which John Wesley had requested his brother to send him, had been posted in the majority of College halls, but there had been some opposition, notably from the Dean of Christ Church, who had refused to allow it to be put up in Christ Church Hall.[1]

Charles Wesley sympathized entirely with the Vice-Chancellor's request. It expressed precisely what he felt about those

> '. . . ill-designing persons . . . who . . . the more effectually to propagate their infidelity, have applied their poison to the unguarded inexperience of less informed minds',

and he was dismayed at the indifference of the Dean, of whom indeed he had a low opinion,[2] to the apparent danger in which true religion was placed. Charles Wesley would play his part in sustaining the faith in which he had been educated in his own way.

What did Charles' 'reformation' amount to?

> 'I went to the weekly sacrament,' he wrote later, 'and persuaded two or three young students to accompany me, and to observe the method of study prescribed by the statutes of the university. This gained me the harmless name of *Methodist*. In half a year [after this] my brother left his curacy at Epworth, and came to our assistance.'

It meant, then, a more disciplined life, harder study, a regular prayer life, regular reading of the Bible, regular attendances at the Holy Communion. It was *au fond* something profoundly personal and spiritual.

How then did this change of life on Charles Wesley's part arouse the attention of other members of his College and so attract comment, much

---

[1] This was probably less because the Dean was, in the words of Wesley's biographer, 'a friend to infidelity' than because, following a tradition of his society by no means dead, he resented direction from outside authority, even from the Vice-Chancellor himself.

[2] 'Our Dean', he remarks, 'has narrowly miss'd of Preferment of late and thro' his own refusal too; he had the Proffer of the Bishopric of Peterborough, but wd. not accept it without the Deanery of Windsor annext; however he *Will* be removed speedily, the Queen having promised to prefer him for the Good of Christ Church. *Amen!*'

of it distinctly unfavourable? As a result of his changed attitude Charles evidently took a less prominent part in the social life of his College. He did not give up these things, any more than he had given up Molly, without reluctance, but a stricter life entailed an element of withdrawal. This is best illustrated by Charles' criticism of his friend, Bob Kirkham. Kirkham, who was the brother of John's close friends in the Cotswolds, was an undergraduate of Merton.

'I am not uncharitable in my opinion; you can't imagine how wretchedly lazy he is and how small a share of either Piety or Learning will content him; Four hours a day he will spare for Study out his Diversions, not so many hours for Diversion out of his Studies.'

Because Kirkham only worked four hours a day (and the judgement throws an incidental light on the eighteenth-century undergraduate if a man working as much as four hours a day could be regarded as 'wretchedly lazy'), Charles was ready to condemn him. He had rid himself of unsuitable diversions; let Kirkham do so too.

There was what may be termed a negative side to the positive act of withdrawal. History shows clearly enough that pietism often carries with it an element of social intolerance and condemnation which tends to irritate the victims of this particular form of social ostracism. Charles was not a patient man by temperament.[1] He could not conceal from his friends his disapproval of their way of life. Bob Kirkham was a good-hearted man but not a natural scholar; he had spent some time with John at his home where John gave him extra tuition. Charles suspected that Kirkham would sooner or later 'hanker after Oxford', and wondered what the Epworth household would make of 'poor Bob'. John found him hang heavily on his hands—and so did Mrs. Wesley. Charles' sentence speaks volumes: 'There's Old Consultations in my Mother's Chamber "What's to Do" I dont question.' After Kirkham came back to Oxford, Charles' sister Patty wrote to him telling some of the 'Secrets of Epworth Economy' and probably giving an Epworth opinion on Kirkham, who was furious that Charles would not show him the letter. 'What is to be done with him think ye?' Charles wrote, 'he's past my Skill, I wish he mayn't be beyond yours too.' Charles may well have been justified in his assessment of Kirkham, but his criticism betrayed a feeling of self-righteousness which seems sometimes inseparable from a high moral tone.

[1] 'My Patience, which as you know is but a slight at best' (20th January, 1729).

A similar judgement may be passed on Charles' criticism of his friend Stephen Lushington.[1] Lushington had been unduly extravagant, had got into debt and had borrowed money from Charles and John, among others. Much to the irritation of the College authorities Lushington had returned late at the beginning of the Hilary term, 1729,[2] and he was soon involved in the financial tangles resulting from over-spending (according to Charles, his last half-year cost him £130). When he went down, Charles was confident that his mother would not allow him to return to Oxford. Charles had loaned him a shirt (which he had recovered) and half a guinea; even Bob Kirkham had contributed half a crown. All now depended 'upon his honour'. And then Charles made his comment:

> 'Exit Lushington. Will I ever trust a Friend again that has no religion? I *Did* think our Friendship would have lasted for *This* life but what Intimacy can I ever have hereafter with a Man of His Morals and His Gratitude? God be praised he had rob'd me of Nothing but my Money.'

This criticism may have been equally justified, but the tone in which it was uttered had that slightly unctuous flavour which would create criticism among his contemporaries. In fact Lushington paid his debts and was certainly in the company of the Wesleys at a later date.

Charles' attempts to proselytize may have evoked unfavourable response among some of his friends. He described one incident in a letter to John which is illuminating in a number of ways.

> 'I have a modest, humble well disposed youth lives next me, and have been, thank God, somewhat instrumental in keeping him so. He was got into vile hands, and is now broke loose. I assisted in setting him free, and will do my utmost to hinder him from getting in with them again. He was of opinion that passive goodness was sufficient; and would fain have kept in with his acquaintance and God at the same time. He durst not receive the sacrament, but at the usual times, for fear of being laughed at. By convincing him of the duty of frequent

---

[1] Lushington, the son of Sir Stephen Lushington, of Sittingbourne, Kent, had been a contemporary of Charles Wesley's at Westminster. He matriculated at Christ Church on 13th June, 1726, aged 17, took his B.A. in 1730 and M.A. in 1733. His brother, Henry, was vicar of Eastbourne from 1734 to 1779.

[2] 'Lushington is not come to College yet tho there has been a terrible uproar about his *not* coming.'

communicating, I have prevailed on both of us to receive once a week. He has got Nelson[1] upon my recommendation, is resolved to spare no pains in working out his salvation.'

Charles was, however, well aware that other people were critical of his attitude, placed 'hard constructions . . . upon our acquaintance', saying that 'He is a Cully—I a Sharper.' Moreover he himself confessed that he was personally averse to appearing in his friend's company in public, though directed to do so by his conscience. He was a young man, he told John, worthy of his charity and acquaintance. It is difficult to establish his identity. It looks as if Charles thought that he was his social inferior. If this were so, it would prevent identification with William Morgan, his most fervent supporter in the youthful religious society, for Morgan's father was a wealthy Dublin lawyer.

In 1729 the Holy Club was so insignificant that few in the University noticed it. Charles was associated with only two other members of the University. He could indeed point proudly to his own personal record. He was working harder and praying more regularly. But even this was not all plain sailing, and on occasion Charles experienced difficulties, the inevitable periods of coldness from which the spiritual life is never immune:

'I think I may truly esteem it as natural and just consequences of my past life. One who has for almost 13 years been utterly inattentive at public prayers can't expect to find there that warmth, he has never known, at his first seeking.'

But he reassured John,

'. . . that my falling short of my duty in one particular shan't discourage me from vigorously prosecuting it in the rest. I look upon this coldness as a trial. . . . I *must*, I *will* in spight of nature, ye devil, take pains: while my strength lasts I will put it to ye utmost stretch for a day's relaxing throws me back to my first setting-out; I won't give myself *Leizure* to relapse for I'm afraid if I have no Business of my own the Devil will soon find me some.'

The previous Saturday evening being out late 'upon a design to do Lushington a piece of service' on his return to his rooms, he found his

[1] Robert Nelson's *A Companion for the Festivals and Fasts of the Church of England*, a favourite book with members of the Holy Club. Nelson was a personal friend of Charles' father, and an ardent supporter of religious societies who contributed £5 towards the Free School at Epworth.

mind in too much of a whirl to say his prayers. As a result he spent a troubled and sleepless night and arose two hours later than usual, 'in utter despair of receiving the sacrament that day'. He went to Church and there it occurred to him that it was more sinful not to receive the sacrament than to receive it with inadequate preparation.

> 'I did find myself affected, stayed . . . not only received the Sacrament with greater warmth than usual but afterwards found my resolutions of persevering considerably strengthened.'

His growing spirituality cannot however have made very much impact on the placid, wealthy and socially distinguished society in which he lived.

Although Charles was responsible for initiating the work of the Holy Club what he did is itself only explicable in terms of Epworth parsonage and of his brother John's influence. Behind Charles can certainly be glimpsed, as he himself commented, the figure of his mother. His relations with John had deepened long before he returned to Oxford to take up his tutorship. Although little has survived of their correspondence, there is enough to prove that Charles relied greatly on John for advice, especially in spiritual matters;

> '. . . it is through your means,' he told John, 'I firmly believe, that God will establish what he has begun in me; and there is no one person I would so willingly have to be the instrument of good to me as you.'

Certainly, with the possible exception of his mother, there was now no one in his family whom he esteemed as much as John and to whom he was so ready to open his heart. His sister Hetty had been uncommonly kind to him during his recent stay in London, sympathetic to affairs of the heart as her unhappy experience had made her, but his sister-in-law, Samuel's wife, 'would willingly have me think you don't care a farthing for me'. He felt his separation from John and his own comparative loneliness.

> 'My standing *here* is so very slippery, no wonder I long to shift my ground [to Epworth]. Christ Church is certainly the worst place in the world to begin a reformation in; a man stands a very fair chance of being laughed out of his Religion at his first setting out, in a Place where tis scandalous to have any at all. Was the Damning others the only means of saving themselves they could scarcely labour more heartily.'

John's presence in Oxford during the summer gave him great pleasure, and in its turn it brought John face to face with the problem of practical Christianity which Charles was seeking to solve. No one can have been better pleased at his summons back to Oxford in November, even though neither he nor anyone else can have seen that John's return betokened a significant change in the future history of the infant religious society which he had started.

Although John had been kept fully informed of Charles' spiritual development, had aided, abetted and advised him in his spiritual struggles, he had not as yet been fully involved in the regime he was sponsoring; but John had his own spiritual problems, for which he had found no effective solution. His daily diary affords the fullest evidence of his constant striving after a standard of religious practice and behaviour below which, so he felt, he was as constantly falling. The diary is full of resolutions which were broken as soon as they were made. We should beware of accepting all that Wesley himself said about the matter at its face value; his over-scrupulous nature involved him in exaggeration and distortion where the spiritual life was concerned. He was himself genuinely convinced that he must repeatedly reaffirm the principles of Christian behaviour by which he lived. The self-examination to which he constantly subjected himself comprised his thoughts and his acts. Had he had frequent thoughts of God and made ejaculations to him? Had he been fervent in prayer when by himself in church? Had he maintained a warm and even purpose of obedience to God? Had he said Grace at breakfast and dinner and reflected over his tea? Was goodwill the spring of all that he did in relation to others? Had he conversed as usefully as he could? Had he been angry or indulged in proud, evil and uncharitable thoughts? Had he visited a rich or a poor man first? Had he been careful to distinguish God's motions from the Devil's? Had he laboured in all his words and actions to be sincere, courteous and elegant? Had he been rudely merry or morosely serious? These unexceptionable questions which he asked himself, usually on Saturday evenings, and as his spiritual life progressed on each evening of the week, revealed his scrupulous concern with the practice of his Christian faith. The Holy Club was to provide a satisfying and absorbing solution to some of the problems confronting Wesley, even if in his search for a final authority its activities did not prove ultimately complete. A religious society designed to cultivate the life of prayer and the sacrament and to sponsor serious reading provided him with an opportunity which parish work at Wroot could not. It fitted into the pattern

of his devotional and theological reading, with what he had learned from
à Kempis, Jeremy Taylor, Norris and others of his favourite writers. It
gave him the opportunity to show the mettle of which his Christian life
was composed and to prove to his mother that her early teaching had not
been in vain.

How did it progress in the early months of John's tutorship? John was
already aware of what his brother was engaged in doing and had certainly
associated himself with his activities earlier in the summer. He spent much
of the very evening of his return to Oxford on 22nd November, 1729,
with Morgan, and prayed with him in his rooms the next Sunday morning. In the weeks that followed there were few days in which he was not
at some time with his brother and Morgan. They did not merely breakfast and pray together but they went for walks, to Binsey, for instance,
attended concerts,[1] went to a dance at Mr. Colley's,[2] and rowed up the
river.[3] Furthermore, John's devotional life had already a pattern which
fitted in well with the objects of his brother's society. He regularly
attended the Communion service at Christ Church on Sunday morning
at quarter past seven, usually breakfasting with Charles afterwards. On
week-days he rose at an increasingly early hour, at any time between five
and six, engaged in private prayer, read some devotional work and the
Greek Testament; throughout the day he sought to remind himself of his
vocation. In later self-examination he asked of himself if he had used a
collect at nine in the morning, midday, and three in the afternoon, and if
he had ejaculated with fervour every hour. The diary was becoming
steadily more and more a record of religious activity, monotonous,
regular yet impressively consistent. The Holy Club stimulated such
activity.

Yet in the first instance its objective, secular as well as religious, was to
augment the habits of study which Charles had once found so difficult to
sustain and which Morgan may well have found unpalatable. Here John
as a more mature, intelligent, scholarly minded man, was a tremendous
asset. In effect he became his brother's and his brother's friend's tutor. On
1st January, 1730, he began Lucretius with Charles; on 22nd January he
read a book of Solomon with Morgan and in March studied Hebrew
with him. 'Our design', he told Morgan's father later, 'was to read over
the classics, which we had before read in private, on common nights, and

---

[1] 26th August, 1730.
[2] 20th March, 1730.
[3] 8th June, 1730.

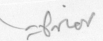

on Sunday some book in divinity.' In pursuit of this object Wesley read Phaedrus, Terence, Virgil's Aeneid, Horace and Juvenal, with Charles and Morgan in 1730 and for religious reading some Milton, a collection of Lucas' works, Norris, lives of Bonnel and de Renty, and the *Second Spira.*

The Holy Club slowly made headway, but those whose membership was continuous were few. 'Your son, my brother and myself, and one more agreed to spend three or four evenings in a week together', was Wesley's own account of the position to Richard Morgan in November, 1729. Towards the end of 1730 it consisted of 'five persons'; a few years later Morgan's second son spoke of a membership of seven. Who was the fourth member in November, 1729? Later Wesley said it was Kirkham, but his memory was almost certainly at fault. It was more likely to have been Francis Gore of Christ Church,[1] who was frequently in the company of John, Charles and Morgan in the winter of 1729–30. Bob Kirkham, of Merton College, joined them in February, 1730; he had taken a fancy, John informed his mother, 'into his head that he would lose no more time and waste no more money'. As a result Kirkham had decided to give up tea for breakfast[2] and to drink no more ale in the evening than was necessary to quench his thirst and he determined to study hard, 'to read Greek or Latin from prayers in the morning till noon and from dinner till five at night'. He had kept these resolutions, somewhat, one feels, to John's surprise:

'. . . he has left off tea, struck off his drinking acquaintance to a man, given the hours above specified to Greek Testament and Hugo Grotius,[3] and spent the evenings either by himself or with my brother and me'.[4]

Gore disappeared from the diary in the autumn of 1730 and the most likely fifth member of the Holy Club was another Christ Church man

---

[1] Matric. 1727, aged 17, B.A. 1732, later barrister-at-law of the Middle Temple. Francis Gore seems more likely to have been a member of the Holy Club than his brother Charles, who only matriculated in July, 1729. Francis was an old boy of Westminster School. Charles Gore became a member of Parliament and supported the Whig opposition against Walpole (J. B. Owen, *The Rise of the Pelhams,* 107, 596).

[2] Although he was frequently engaged in drinking tea, Wesley's suspicions of this liquid, and of green tea in particular, which later became obsessive, had already started. Cf. *A Letter to A Friend Concerning Tea* (1748) and *Letters,* ii, 159.

[3] The reference is to Grotius, *Annotations on the Old and New Testaments* (1641–6).

[4] *Letters,* i, 48–9.

and son of the Mayor of Oxford,[1] John Boyce, with whom Wesley was breakfasting after his Sunday communion on 6th and 13th September, 1730. On 10th January, 1731, he talked with Morgan at Sir John Boyce's house, dined with Sir John on 30th June, and supped with the family on 26th December, 1731.

It is, however, important to realize that there were a number of other men on the periphery of the Holy Club, who were at least interested in its activities. Bulman, Bingham, Graves, Cox, Watkins, Rhodes,[2] Spicer, Golburne,[2] and Horne, were all names that recur in connection with the Wesleys and Morgan; and it is easy to conjecture that they must have known of what was happening and probably sympathized with the objects of a religious society. This was even more likely to have been the case if Wesley was following the calculated procedure for selecting his friends which he later ascribed to this period.

'I narrowly observed the temper and behaviour', he said, 'of all that visited me. I saw no reason to think that the greater part of these truly loved or feared God; therefore when any of them came to see me, I behaved as courteously as I could; but to the question, "When will you come and see me?" I returned no answer. When they had come a few times, and found I still declined to return their visit, I saw them no more.'[3]

Wesley's return to Oxford may have seen a change in the type and number of his acquaintances, and his friends were likely to be sympathetically inclined towards his religious society. John's sporadic contacts with John Burton of Corpus were the more significant as Burton, who had been a friend of Wesley since 1725, enjoyed a considerable reputation as a tutor and classical scholar. He listened keenly to what Wesley had to tell him about the activities of the Holy Club and gave the venture his moral support. Dr. Burton, with whom Wesley had dined on Whit Sunday, later attended one of John's meetings and drank tea with him on 13th June, 1730. An indication of growing interest in missionary

---

[1] John Boyce, Mayor of Oxford, was knighted on the occasion of George II's Coronation. His son matriculated at Christ Church in 1727, aged 16; took his B.A. in 1731 and M.A. in 1735.

[2] William Golburne, son of Urian G., of St. Margaret's, Westminster, matriculated at Balliol College in 1728, and took his degree in 1732; a Christopher Rhodes, an old boy of Westminster School, matriculated at Christ Church in 1730.

[3] 'On Leaving the World', *Works*, vi, 447.

activity is shown by Wesley's reading the work of the Danish missionaries on Whit Sunday, 1730.[1]

Thus the news of what John and his confederates were doing slowly
began to percolate among their contemporaries in the different Colleges
where they had acquaintances. Wesley's presence and reputation gave
the society the leadership and fillip it required. This was more necessary
as it was soon to widen the area of its activity, to leave the pious, scholastic atmosphere of College rooms for the drearier lodgings of prisoners
and debtors in the Castle and in the Bocardo.

The activities which the Holy Club were to sponsor were very much
in line with the philanthropic spirit of the times. The accounts of Lincoln
College in the early eighteenth century tell of occasional gifts to prisoners,[2]
and Perceval referred to a collection of £19 5s. taken at a dinner at the
Rose Tavern on 11th March, 1735, after the anniversary meeting of the
S.P.C.K. for the relief of poor prisoners.[3] Many people were interested in
improving the prisoners' lot and in prison reform. With this work the
S.P.C.K., of which John Wesley became a member in 1732, had long
been concerned. In 1700 the treasurer of the society reported that he had
been engaged in discussing proposals for regulating the manners of
prisoners at Newgate. The agenda included the problems arising from
the 'personal lewdness' of the keepers and their liability to corruption, the
consumption of strong liquor, swearing and gambling, the corruption of
new prisoners by old lags and the neglect of religious worship. Two years
later the S.P.C.K. sent six copies of John Kettlewell's[4] *Office for Prisoners*
and a Bible, 'for the use of White Chappell Prison', and at its meeting in
February the Society decided that each county jail in England should
receive a package of religious literature published under its direction,
inclusive of Kettlewell's *Office*.

Soon the problem was brought before a more influential public, more
particularly as the result of the enthusiasm shown by Oglethorpe for

[1] These were the Danish missionaries in Trankebar in South India. The reports
of Ziegenbalg and Plütschau had been translated into English by Anton Boehme
(d. 1726), Chaplain to Queen Anne's husband, Prince George of Denmark.

[2] In addition to a number of other small charitable benefactions (e.g. 6d. to a poor
woman of Magdalen parish, 2s. 6d. to two shipwrecked families, 1s. to a sufferer by
fire, 6d. to Goody Jervis) the accounts for 1722 record payments of 1s. to the prisoners
in Bocardo, 1s. to a poor woman in the jail, and 4s. 6d. to prisoners in Bocardo, and
a poor clergyman and Abraham.

[3] Egmont's *Diary*, ii, 159.

[4] Fellow of Lincoln, 1675–83.

improving the lot of poor debtors.[1] On 25th February, 1729, a parliamentary committee was set up to 'inquire into the state of the gaols of this kingdom'. The committee, which included Oglethorpe and Thomas Winnington among its members, drew its material from conditions in the Fleet Prison, but revealed a horrid story of laxity and corruption. A second report, which Wesley read with great interest when he was at Epworth on Wednesday evening, 17th September, 1729, referred to conditions in the prisons of the Court of the Marshalsea and of the King's Palace Court of Westminster; presented in 1729 it exposed an equally unpleasing state of affairs. A later report, presented in May, 1730, dealt with conditions in the King's Bench Prison. The only result of these reports was a Bill for the relief of debtors which would have been extremely valuable if the proposals had been properly carried out. Yet all this activity served to bring the needs of the prisoners, and poor debtors in particular, before a comparatively well-informed and enlightened group of people. Wesley's brother Samuel, for instance, had been so stirred by the report of the 'late glorious Proceedings' of the parliamentary committee that he had plunged into verse, writing *The Prisons Open'd*:

> Yet Britain cease my Captives' Woes to mourn,
> To break their Chains, see Oglethorpe was born!

The Holy Club's activity was an aspect, a vivid practical aspect, of contemporary interest in prison improvement.

William Morgan, rather than John or Charles Wesley, had the actual responsibility for widening the scope of the Holy Club's activities. During the summer of 1730 Morgan called at the local prison in Oxford Castle to talk with a man who had murdered his wife. Later he made contact with some of those who were imprisoned for debt, and learned that they would appreciate visits from himself and his friends. John Wesley and his brother went with Morgan to Oxford Castle on 24th August and as a result of their experience decided that it was worth repeating. A week later, on 31st August, he accompanied Morgan to visit a sick woman in the town.

> 'In this employment, too, when we came to reflect upon it, we believed that it would be worth while to spend an hour or two in a week; provided the minister of the parish in which any such person was were not against it.'

[1] On Oglethorpe, see L. F. Church, *Oglethorpe* (1932); A. A. Ettinger, *Oglethorpe* (1936).

John was obviously concerned that the society should not trespass outside authorized terrain and in the autumn of 1730 he turned to a number of people for advice. His father gave him his warmest approval, incidentally revealing that as an undergraduate he had himself visited the prisoners in the Castle, 'and reflect on it with grave satisfaction to this day'. He rejoiced that his two sons had been given 'grace and courage to turn the war against the world and the devil', and he was particularly pleased that John had so

'. . . fast a friend as Mr. Morgan, who, I see, in the most difficult service, is ready to break the ice for you. You do not know of how much good that poor wretch who killed his wife had been the providential occasion. I think I must adopt Mr. Morgan to be my son. . . .'

He warned him, however, to get the approval of the governor of the prison and of his Bishop. Ten days later Wesley made contact with Mr. Gerard (who acted as chaplain to the men condemned to death), breakfasting with him on 7th October and again on 9th October (in spite of the fact that Wesley was feeling unwell that morning); at his first meeting Gerard told him that he was sure that the Bishop would approve, and later having spoken with the Bishop he reassured Wesley that Dr. Potter was pleased with Wesley's undertaking and wished it every success. Later, in 1731, Wesley also wrote to seek the advice of his friend, Joseph Hoole, the vicar of Haxey. Hoole, who was a graduate of Sidney Sussex College, Cambridge, was a friend of the Non-juror, John Byrom, who stayed with him at Haxey on 19th October, 1733, where he met young Matthew Horbery. He was later one of the little learned group which included Byrom, Thomas Deacon, John Clayton, and the librarian Robert Thyer, which used to meet in the reading-room at Cheetham's Library to engage in learned discussion about the patristic writings and other theological works.[1] He left Haxey in 1736 to become rector of St. Ann's, Salford.[2] He was therefore likely to have been very sympathetic towards the objects of the Oxford Holy Club. He gave the scheme his blessing, only qualifying it with the desirability of getting previous approval from the vicar of the parish in which they were acting.

Thus in the autumn of 1730 the Holy Club widened its activities, visiting the sick and the Oxford prisoners at the Castle and the Bocardo. At first Wesley confined his visits to the Castle to Saturday afternoons, but

[1] *John Byrom*, ed. H. Talon, 15.
[2] He was the author of *Sermons on Several Important Subjects*, 2 vols., 1741.

he soon went there more frequently; on Sunday, 8th November, 1730, he noted for the first time that he read prayers at the Castle. An increasing number of his friends began to show some interest; after visiting the Castle on 8th December, Wesley was round at Langford's where he talked with Martin, Watson and Bateman. Wesley and his friends were already taking an interest in the prisoners' concerns,[1] more especially in the debtors, seeking to secure their release where the sum of money for which they had been imprisoned was small; both John and Charles knew from their father's experience what a debtor prisoner felt like. 'We can't compass Thomas Burgess's liberty yet, though it seems to have a fairer show than formerly.' 'On Sunday they had prayers', he wrote to his father on 11th December, 1730, 'and a sermon at the Castle; on Christmas Day we hope they will have a dinner; and the Sunday after, a communion. . . .' A few days previously through William Morgan's efforts they were now permitted to visit the other prison, the debtors' prison above the north gate of the city known as the Bocardo. His father rejoiced in his son's activities.

> 'I hear my son John has the honour of being styled the "Father of the Holy Club"; if it be so, I am sure I must be the grandfather of it; and I need not say that I had rather any of my sons should be so dignified and distinguished than to have the title of His Holiness.'

The increase in activity had aroused some mockery and criticism.

> 'Almost as soon as we made our first attempts this way, some of the men of wit in Christ Church entered the lists against us; and, between mirth and anger, made a pretty many reflections upon the Sacramentarians, as they were pleased to call us. Soon after, their allies at Merton [probably reacting against Bob Kirkham's decision to join the Holy Club], changed our title, and did us the honour of styling us The Holy Club.'

This raillery, much of it in all probability good-humoured, was the first sign of incipient opposition. It was the not unnatural reaction of comparatively worldly young men to the regular devotional life and good works of other young men who took themselves seriously and whose actions were an implied criticism of the conventional Christianity of their fellows. There was evidently a feeling that so extreme a piety denoted an

---

[1] His accounts show the gift of small sums to the prisoners, e.g. 6*d.* to John Costar, Will Lardner, Thomas Waite, etc., and some expenditure on wood and candles for them.

admixture of hypocrisy. 'They pretended', in the words of a contemporary,

> '... to be more religious than their Neighbours ... they put a gloomy and melancholy face upon Religion, and affected greater Austerities and Exemplariness, than the Doctrines of the Gospel requir'd.'

It was rumoured that their activities had been discussed by the authorities of Christ Church and that 'Dr. Terry[1] and the censors[2] were going to blow up the Godly Club'. It is very possible that such criticism may have deterred undergraduates and senior members of the University from betraying a sympathetic interest in their proceedings.[3] Yet there is very little to substantiate the rumours that the authorities were going to take action against the Methodists; it was most likely the invention of their young critics. Wesley's own relations with the officials of College and University seemed amicable.[4] He had breakfast with Dr. Tanner, one of the Canons of Christ Church, on 16th May, 1730, and on 10th July talked with him after paying a visit to the Castle. He was with the Bishop's Chaplain to the prisoners, Mr. Gerard, on 12th August, later walking out with Charles and Morgan to Barton, presumably to visit the Boyces. Bishop Potter himself invited Wesley to preach at the Ordination service on 19th September, 1730, a pleasing gesture as it was on this very day five years earlier that Potter had ordained Wesley. Wesley would certainly have discussed his activities with the Bishop, either in talking to him before the service or at the dinner in the Audit Hall that followed it.

[1] Dr. Terry was Regius professor of Greek, canon of Christ Church, and rector of Chalfont St. Giles until his death in 1735. Wesley went to hear him preach on 21st March, 1730.

[2] The Censors were the senior tutorial and disciplinary officials of Christ Church.

[3] Wesley in the account which he gave Richard Morgan described how a 'gentleman, eminent for learning, and well esteemed for piety, ... told his nephew that if he dared to go to the weekly communion any longer he would immediately turn him out of doors. That argument, indeed, had no success ... upon which the uncle ... changed his method, and by mildness prevailed upon him to be absent from it the Sunday following; as he has done five Sundays in six ever since. This much delighted our gay opponents ... especially when, shortly after, one of the seniors of the College having been with the Doctor, upon his return from him, sent for two young gentlemen severally, who had communicated weekly for some time, and was so successful in his exhortations that for the future they proposed to do it only three times a year' (*Letters*, i, 130). It has been suggested, though without much basis, that this refers to Robert Kirkham of Merton and his uncle, Henry Kirkham, vicar of Stanway.

[4] See pp. 143–4.

M

Throughout 1731 the Holy Club made sound progress. John and his friends were regular in their religious devotions. In a typically outspoken letter Charles criticized the conduct of the Communion at Christ Church at Whitsun:

> 'On Whitsunday the whole College received the sacrament, except the servitors (for we are too well bred to communicate with them, though in the body and blood of Christ) to whom it was administered the next day; on which I was present at church, but with the Canons left the sacrament to those for whom alone it was prepared.'

He enquired of his father whether the scandal that his remaining with the servitors would give was justified or not. John was now so involved in the religious activities of the Castle that he conducted only a few services outside Oxford during the year. He was constantly visiting the Bocardo and the Castle, reading prayers and taking services at the latter.

> 'Before reading he asked', John Gambold recounted later, 'whether they had prayers yesterday? (for some serious men among the prisoners read family prayers with the rest), whether they had read over the heads of it to them, and afterwards went on in the same book for a quarter of an hour (the books they used were the *Christian Monitor*, the *Country Parsons' Advice to the Parishioners*, and such like);[1] and when he had done, he summed up the several particulars that had been insisted on, enforced the advice given, and reduced it at last to two or three sentences which they might easily remember.'

Morgan had started a school for the prisoners' children. From a few allusions it seems likely that these earnest young men may already have begun to carry their prayer meetings into the town; such would seem the interpretation to be put on the entries in Wesley's diary: 'Prayers at Mrs. Cox' and 'Prayers at Mrs. Eagles'.

The fortunes of the society fluctuated. When John and Charles came back from Epworth in the summer of 1731 John told his father despondently that 'our little company that used to meet us, is shrunk into almost none at all.' Robert Kirkham was soon to become his uncle's curate. John Boyce was at his father's house at Barton.[2] Morgan was ill at Holt. 'And a

---

[1] A note in Wesley's hand refers to the distribution of books to the prisoners, viz.: *The Whole Duty of Man* to Richard Bradley, K. J(ervas), Arthur J(ervas) and Richard Lardner, *The Christian Monitor* to Bradley and Jervas, and one copy to Bocardo, *The Companion to the Altar* to Bradley, Atkins, Will. Breeze, W. Green, K. Jervas, W. Biggs and Thomas March.

[2] Boyce married a wealthy heiress, a Miss Hudson, July 29, 1731 (Hearne, *Collectanea*, x, 443, 459).

young gentleman of Christ Church, who used to make a fourth, either afraid or ashamed or both, is returned to the ways of the world, and studiously shuns our company.' But there were still many sympathizers on the periphery; and in spite of all setbacks, the prisoners at the Castle at the close of 1731

'. . . have still the Gospel preached to them, and some of their temporal wants supplied, our little fund rather increasing than diminishing. Nor have we yet been forced to discharge any of the children which Mr. Morgan left to our care.'

As for John Wesley, the Holy Club had become more and more the centre of his interests. He was far too conscientious to neglect his tutorial work. He was much too balanced not to realize that it would be a mistake to use his position as a tutor to oblige his pupils to join the society; but it was inevitable that he should talk over its work with his young men. In reading prayers with them he opened the way to their positive co-operation if they wished it. At the same time, he was anxious that his religious life should not get out of balance. When he was staying at Stanton rectory with the Kirkhams in the summer of 1731 they had discussed the meaning of being 'righteous over much' and being 'too strict in religion'. They concluded that these phrases implied the 'carrying some particular virtue to so great a height as to make it clash with some others' or 'laying too much stress on the instituted means of grace' or

'the multiplying prudential means upon ourselves so far, and binding ourselves to the observances of them so strictly, as to obscure the end we aimed at by them, either by hindering our advance in heavenly affections in general, or by retarding our progress in some particular virtue'.

Wesley's critics thought that he was in fact guilty of this last charge; that his rule of life imposed too severe burdens and because too severe so useless. Wesley naturally enough was unwilling to accept this judgement and appealed to his mother.

'If you, who are a less prejudiced judge, have perceived us faulty in this matter, too superstitious or enthusiastic, . . . we earnestly desire to be speedily informed of our error. . . . Or whatever there may be . . . in which you have observed us to be too remiss, that likewise we desire to know as soon as possible.'

His mother's reply does not survive. Sensible and shrewd as that good lady was, she could hardly be called an unprejudiced judge in matters of this kind. There can be little doubt that she gave the regime of the members of the Holy Club her full approval.

Yet the evidence does suggest 'the multiplying prudential means'. John Wesley's company was changing, being confined more and more to those who thought as he did; he was beginning to appear less in the Senior Common Room of Lincoln, to take less part in the innocuous amusements of his earlier days. It was as yet a very slow withdrawal, so much so as to be very nearly imperceptible. The more serious he became the less he read light literature. He was already beginning to apportion his income, so that a balance could be used for charitable purposes, particularly to help the prisoners. Considering the economies to which he had been forced in earlier days, this was perhaps no very difficult thing for Wesley to do; but if he were not yet rich enough to buy John Whitelamb a College gown,[1] at least there is no sign of grave financial stringency.[2]

These were, perhaps, matters of major moment. The full meaning of his regime appears in the trifling detail of every-day existence. Always obsessed with minutiae, though seldom confused by it, he was already beginning to account for every minute of his day. He drew up, if not in 1731, a year or so afterwards, a series of questions which he was to ask himself daily. On Sunday he asked whether he had frequently conversed with God and spent his time in Church wholly in prayer. On Monday he questioned whether he had spoken unkindly or received the infirmities of others with pity or anger. On Thursday he asked whether he distinguished God's motions from the Devil's. On Friday had he submitted his will to the will of everyone who opposed it or indulged any sense? Had he born cheerfully any accidental inconveniences? Had he contrived

[1] 'John Whitelamb wants a gown much, and I am not rich enough to buy him one at present. If you are willing my twenty shillings . . . should go toward that', he wrote to his brother, Samuel, on 17th November, 1731 (*Letters*, i, 115).

[2] In a sermon on 'The More Excellent Way' (No. LXXXIX), John Wesley referred to his own experience in a passage often quoted: 'First, if you have no family, after you have provided for yourself, give away all that remains. This was the practice of the young men at Oxford who were called Methodists. For example. One of them gave away thirty pounds a year. He lived on twenty-eight, and gave away forty shillings. The next year receiving sixty pounds, he still lived on twenty-eight, and gave away two and thirty. The third year he received ninety pounds, and gave away sixty-two. The fourth year he received one hundred and twenty pounds. Still he lived as before on twenty-eight; and gave the poor ninety-two.' This was doubtless Wesley's procedure, but the figures can hardly be reliable indications of his actual income in these years.

pretences to avoid self-denial? Had he shown any heat? Some rough notes reveal further the care with which he planned his week. He would only drink one glass of wine or ale in Common Room or Hall. He would never taste of more than three dishes at any single meal. In Common Room he would try to help himself last and take only one slice of pudding. On fast days he would eat less at breakfast and dinner and while the bell rang on Fridays (probably for dinner in Hall) he would reflect on his resolutions. He planned existence with a military precision. 'Would I but employ a third of my money, and about half my time, as other folks do, small matters would be easily overlooked. But I think *nil tanti est*.' It was hardly surprising that he should be accused of 'singularity', or of wanting mirth. 'Mirth, I grant,' he told his brother Samuel, 'is fit for you; but does it follow that it is fit for me?' The advice that he later gave his Methodist preachers already summarized his attitude to life in 1730–1. 'Never be unemployed a moment. Never be triflingly employed. Never while away time.'

The will which could sponsor so regulated a regime and which had done so much in eighteen months to bring the activities of a few young men before the notice of the University and town was powerful indeed. Clothed in prayer and humility, charity and grace, it possessed a relentless and serious quality. On 1st March, 1731, Wesley confided that he would never 'give any one up till he disclaims my help *totidem verbis*, or I have tried him ten years'. The small frame encased a masterful personality. John Wesley was the evident leader of the Holy Club, as it confronted its first major crises through the death of one of its members, young William Morgan.

CHAPTER IX

The Progress of the Holy Club

THE last four years of Wesley's tutorship were a period of criticism and consolidation in the history of the Holy Club. It survived the first full-scale attack made on its activities; but the publicity which it received gave rise to suspicion of its activities in the University which was not easily stilled. If it had evoked opposition among the Colleges, it won support from some of the townspeople. Wesley also had sympathetic friends in London, like Sir John Phillips, who were ready to forward its purposes with charitable donations.

Sir John Phillips, of Picton Castle, who succeeded his father as fourth baronet in 1695, was a prototype of the eighteenth-century philanthropist.[1] He was 'the ornament and in a great measure the Support' of the S.P.C.K. as well as the patron and benefactor of the Society for the Propagation of the Gospel, which sprang from the S.P.C.K. in 1701, and the Society for the Reformation of Manners. It was a result of his interest that some ninety-five free schools were set up in Wales, largely under the aegis of the S.P.C.K. between 1699 and 1737. In March 1698, as an M.P. for Pembroke, he introduced a Bill for the suppression of blasphemy and profaneness which would have made adultery punishable by death.[2] His austere, puritanical moral code combined with a genuine goodness and loving affection—his letters to his wife are singularly attractive—obviously drew him to Wesley and his friends.[3] By 1729 he was blind and a widower but his zeal for good works was as great as ever. He was perhaps the greatest single supporter of the Holy Club's charities, and shortly before his death on 5th January, 1737, Phillips guaranteed Whitefield an annual allowance to enable him to stay at Oxford.

[1] In 1883 the Phillips estates consisted of 23,084 acres in Pembroke and Carmarthen, bringing in an annual revenue of £23,815.

[2] The act eventually made denial of the Trinity punishable by three years' imprisonment; the harsh clause was thrown out (Narcissus Luttrell, *A Brief Relation of State Affairs* (Oxford, 1857), iv, 354, 355).

[3] On 11th September, 1732, Wesley noted that he read his parents Sir John's letters. Wesley entertained Mr. Bernewitz, the tutor of his children, in Oxford in 1733.

V THE YOUNG MR. WESLEY
Thomas Photos, Oxford

The really active work had, however, to be done within the University, where the 'good society' as Anne Granville called it certainly had a few sympathizers among the senior members of the University. The Rector of Lincoln contributed a subscription and Wesley's accounts include five shillings given by the Bishop's chaplain, Mr. Hayward. Naturally the bulk of the financial support came from the members of the religious society themselves; Wesley noted that he had collected five shillings from Mr. Morgan, his brother, Mr. Boyce, and himself. Its effectiveness, however, came not from the charities it distributed but from the enthusiasm of its members, young graduates and undergraduates.

These years were a significant period in his own spiritual development. Occasionally he still went dancing and played cards; but he was more and more reluctant to take part in activities of this kind. When he dined at Mr. Wilmot's with the Rector and his brother, Sir Justinian Isham, on 30th December, 1732, he merely 'looked on' as they played cards.[1] On another occasion, 26th December, 1733, he was 'importuned to play' by his colleagues, and won! When he was staying with friends in October, 1733, courtesy demanded that he should go with them to the races, and he was much relieved that bad weather prevented his giving the function more than his token approval. He began to order his day so that he rose even earlier in the morning, often at four and rarely after six.[2] He added to his religious obligations fasting on Wednesdays and Fridays. All these absorbing activities allayed the daemon of spiritual dissatisfaction; but they did not wholly defeat it. There were moments when he confided to himself that he was extremely 'dispirited'.[3] He could not see clearly into his own future. He resisted almost brutally the suggestion that he should

---

[1] It should be added that 30th December was a Saturday evening and Wesley may have thought that this was an improper form of preparation for the next day's Communion. A few days previously, 28th December, he played cards at the Rector's, where Sir Justinian was obviously staying.

[2] In his sermon on 'Redeeming the Time', he wrote later: 'To be satisfied I procured an alarum, which waked me the next morning at seven . . . yet I lay awake again at night. The second morning I rose at six; but notwithstanding this, I lay awake the third night. The fourth morning I rose at four; as, by the Grace of God, I have done ever since, and I lay awake no more.' He added that 'lying in bed' is the 'chief real cause of all nervous diseases . . . why nervous diseases are so much more common among us than among our ancestors . . . by soaking so long between warm sheets, the flesh . . . is parboiled, and becomes soft and fleshy. The nerves . . . are quite unstrung.' It 'opens the way, and prepares the soul, for every other kind of intemperance'.

[3] E.g., entries for 11th and 12th December, 1733.

return to parochial life and succeed his father at Epworth by stressing the unique opportunity that Oxford offered him for fulfilling his vocation; yet in his heart of hearts he was not satisfied that his life as a fellow of Lincoln College fulfilled the divine commands under which he laboured.

He still sought an ultimate authority and he believed that he had found it in the traditions and teachings of the early Church. Fundamentally the members of the Holy Club tried to return to the 'ancient, if not apostolical' practices of the Church. This was where Wesley's own studies, his reading of the High Anglican writers, had persuaded him that the life commanded in the Scriptures was in practice carried out. He and his fellows felt that what contemporary Oxford lacked was practical primitive Christianity.

> 'They imagine', Richard Morgan wrote in his invaluable if hostile account of the Holy Club in 1734, 'they cannot be saved if they do not spend every hour, nay minute, of their lives in the service of God. And to that end they read prayers every day in the common jail, preach every Sunday, and administer the sacrament once every month. They almost starve themselves to be able to relieve the poor and buy books for their conversion. They endeavour to reform notorious whores and allay spirits in haunted houses.[1] They fast two days in the week, which has emaciated them to that degree that they are a fearful sight. . . . They rise every day at five of the clock, and till prayers, which begin at eight, they sing psalms, and read some piece of divinity. They meet at each other's rooms at six of the clock five nights in the week, and from seven to nine read a piece of some religious book.'

He added that from 'six to seven they read over the petitions of poor people and receive their wants, dispose of pious books and fix the duties of the ensuing day'. Making allowance for Morgan's unfriendly attitude, his is a convincing account of what the Holy Club was trying to do at the end of 1733 and 1734, showing that Wesley and his friends held practical Christianity as the most significant and apostolic expression of true religion.

Meanwhile the Holy Club had come under fire. It had no more zealous member than William Morgan, though his comparatively junior status and weaker intellectual capacity had given John Wesley the lead in his society. When the Wesleys returned from the Cotswolds to Oxford on

---

[1] E.g. in his diary for Saturday, 18th March, 1732, he went with Mr. Smith and another friend to Waddesdon and after supper noted that he was at 8.30 p.m. 'in the haunted house'.

31st May, 1731, Morgan was sick at Holt. He was, however, back in Oxford by the time of Wesley's own return from Lincolnshire in the middle of September,[1] and he was with him on many occasions until June, 1732. Morgan's health was already causing alarm. On 29th March, 1732, Wesley had had supper with him and talked of the letter that he had recently received from his father, expressing grave displeasure at the way in which he was behaving. When he had received it Morgan had not been well enough to read it himself and had asked Wesley to read it out to him. His father (who was Second Remembrancer of the Exchequer in Dublin) intimated that he was spending the money intended for his education at Oxford in an unsuitable way:

'. . . you shall no longer be tied to any fixed allowance; what sums are necessary for your health shall immediately be remitted. But then I must tell you, it is for these uses alone, your health and education, that I mean to supply you.

'You can't conceive', his father continued, 'what a noise that ridiculous Society which you are engaged in has made here. Besides the particulars of the great follies of it at Oxford . . . it gave me sensible trouble to hear that you were noted for your going into the villages about Holt, entering into poor people's houses, calling their children together, teaching them their prayers and catechism, and giving them a shilling at your departure.'

His allowance was intended to supplement his exhibition to 'afford you physic and a comfortable subsistence with reasonable and moderate recreations'.[2] The letter sounded a warning note to which both Morgan and Wesley might have been well advised to listen; but Wesley did not find it easy to understand the other man's point of view,[3] and Morgan was ill in body and in mind. Wesley was away from Oxford in the early part of May, 1732, but on his return made a point of immediately calling on his friend, breakfasting with him after Communion at Christ Church and drinking tea with him the same evening. At the end of February

---

[1] Wesley was back in Oxford on 17th September; he was with Morgan at 6.30 after preaching at the ordination on September 19th; he read prayers with Charles, Morgan and Cox on 22nd September.

[2] *Letters*, i, 121–2.

[3] In his later, lengthy letter to Morgan's father, Wesley interpreted the phrases 'comfortable subsistence . . . reasonable and moderate recreations' quite gratuitously and unjustifiably as 'gaming and the other fashionable expenses of the place' (*op. cit.*, i, 124).

Wesley had already told his mother that he thought that Morgan was dying.

> 'He can neither sleep, read, stand nor sit. . . . Surely now he is a burthen to himself and almost useless in the world; his discharge cannot be far off.'

Morgan himself, in the full flush of religious enthusiasm, had a year back been 'exceedingly well pleased' with the thought of dying shortly; but the actual experience had weakened his earlier enthusiasm. He would not talk of it; 'without hands, or feet, or head, or heart, he is very sure his illness is not increased'. It would hardly have been in Wesley's temperament to have kept silent on so vital an issue. 'The Wesleys', Richard Morgan wrote to Charles after his son's death, 'he raved of most of all in his sickness.'

Morgan left Oxford for Dublin in June, 1732, Wesley having helped in the packing, but his health did not improve in Ireland and on his doctor's advice he began a return to England, travelling in easy stages, accompanied by the servant who had been with him at Oxford. It was soon apparent that his mind was diseased. He talked wildly and incoherently and would shout out during his sleepless nights. On the second day of his journey he refused to use his bridle, insisting that God would guide him; but divine guidance proved somewhat unreliable as the horse went to drink in a disused quarry and threw its rider With great difficulty the servant brought him back to Dublin, where he rapidly became worse.

> 'He was raving mad, and three men set over him to watch him and hold, and by the direction of the physicians he was threatened with ropes and chains, which were produced to him and rattled.'

There were strong indications of religious mania. He spoke constantly of the Wesleys and

> '. . . used frequently to say that enthusiasm was his madness, repeated often "Oh religious madness!" that they had hindered him from throwing himself out at the window, and named some other persons and things that I shan't mention; but in his greatest rage never cursed or swore or used any profane expressions.'

Perhaps fortunately on 26th August, 1732, William Morgan died. Naturally his father believed that his association with the Wesleys must in part be held accountable. Rumour in Oxford also asserted that Morgan's illness had been made worse and his death hastened by the regime to which he had submitted as a member of the Holy Club; his emaciated appearance was plainly a result of religious fasting. On Sunday, 15th October, John Wesley heard of this unpleasant charge, possibly at the Rector's where he dined with Hutchins and Farrer, possibly from his pupils with whom he spent an hour that evening, possibly from Charles. His immediate reaction was to write the long oft-quoted letter to Morgan's father, explaining in great detail the origin, growth and development of the Holy Club, and showing that its activities could have had nothing to do with the illness of his son.

This explanation convinced Richard Morgan and indeed stilled his fears to such an extent that he decided to entrust his younger son, Richard, to Wesley's care at Lincoln. The members of the Holy Club cannot be blamed for the impact which religious enthusiasm had made on a peculiarly sensitive and emotional man, but Morgan's subsequent madness was in part a result of his excessive concern about religion. Recent experience at universities has shown that too-abundant religious zeal, more especially in its extreme Evangelical forms, can create a lack of balance which may precipitate a mental crisis. John Wesley was himself so very far from being a neurotic that he often failed to see where the relentless pressure of religious zeal could lead young men. In later life he deprecated the hysteria to which his preaching sometimes gave rise, without realizing that the mainspring in causing the psychological unbalance may well have been his insistence on personal salvation and justification by faith. Contemporaries assumed that fasting was the principal reason for Morgan's illness but Wesley was able to show that fasting had only recently become a feature of his teaching. They might have been more alarmed had they been equipped with a knowledge of modern psychology.

If Wesley had been able to overcome Richard Morgan's misgivings, his opponents in the University cannot have been as easily satisfied. The increase in the activities of the Holy Club had brought it more prominently to the notice of the authorities. His efforts on behalf of one of the prisoners, Irwin, at the Castle brought him into contact with the Bishop of Oxford, and he was with the Vice-Chancellor on a number of occasions during the year. He visited Cuddesdon on Monday, 2nd October, 1732, and discussed with the Bishop the administration of the Communion at Christ Church and St. Mary's, the disuse of fasting and the penal laws. The Bishop proved a sympathetic listener, but the Vice-Chancellor seems to have temporized. He also talked with the Vice-Chancellor (to whose

lodgings he was accompanied by Clayton and Clements) about the celebration of the Holy Communion at St. Mary's, putting forward various
objections, which he had previously discussed with Thorold and Hutchins.
The Vice-Chancellor saw Wesley on Tuesday, 17th October, 1732, talking with him about his protégé, Irwin, and 'of the Methodists'. It is
worth noting that the accusation relating to Morgan's death had been
brought to Wesley's notice a few days previously, and it may well have
been this charge which he was anxious to discuss with the Vice-Chancellor, and to refute. There is nothing to show that the authorities in
Church and University were anything but courteous and sympathetic in
their treatment of Wesley and the Holy Club at this stage; but they must
have been made much more conscious of its existence. On 9th December,
1732, hostile criticism found vent in a letter in *Fog's Weekly Journal*.

Wesley and his friends were obviously alarmed by this new display of
opposition and its possible effects on authority at the University. On 11th
December, 1732, the talk in Lincoln Common Room had turned on the
Methodists, though what was said Wesley does not recount. On Thursday, 14th December, Wesley again called on the Vice-Chancellor and
discussed another of his protégés at the Bocardo, Mr. Blair, and talked of the
Methodists in general. Five days later, Tuesday, 19th December, he called
on the Vice-Chancellor, where he also found the Master of Balliol, Dr.
Leigh, and began reading to them the letter which he had recently received
from William Morgan's father accepting Wesley's explanation and in
practice exonerating him and his brother from responsibility for Morgan's
death. Later, after Leigh had gone, they talked together about William Law.
On 22nd December, 1732, Wesley asked the Rector of Lincoln to read
his sermon, which he was to preach before the University on 1st January,
and which contained his view of Christian salvation. After the Rector
had finished reading and presumably expressed his approval, Wesley
raised with him the question of his pupils who went regularly to the
Communion at Christ Church. On this point the Rector was, at first, less
ready to support his colleague, but when the following Saturday, 30th
December, 1732, two Lincoln men, John Robson and Matthew Robinson, asked permission to attend the Communion there, Isham relented,
and the next day Wesley had the satisfaction of accompanying both of
them to Christ Church at 7 a.m. Meanwhile on 27th December, Wesley
called on the Provost of Queen's presumably to explain the work of the
Holy Club and silence the exaggerated rumours that were still circulating as a result of the article in *Fog's Weekly Journal* and the publicity

which the Holy Club had received in the course of 1732, partly as a result of the circumstances of young Morgan's death and partly as a result of the publicity given to the doings of the Holy Club.

The year 1732 had seen a welcome access of strength to the Holy Club in the number of young graduates and undergraduates associated to a greater or lesser extent with its activities. John Clayton of Brasenose was the most important recruit. When Wesley and his brother were in London during the winter they had called on Charles Rivington, the bookseller in St. Paul's Churchyard, a very good friend to Wesley. Rivington suggested that they should make the acquaintance of his Oxford friend, John Clayton, a tutor and fellow of Brasenose and himself the son of a Manchester bookseller. Wesley did not in fact follow up this suggestion, but Clayton stopped him in the street one day in April and gave him Rivington's good wishes. Wesley at once invited him back to his rooms in Lincoln where he explained the purpose of his religious society, which Clayton 'immediately and heartily closed with'. Soon after this meeting, which took place on 20th April, 1732, Clayton became a member of the Holy Club. He went to Communion at Christ Church with Wesley the following Sunday, 23rd April, and was one of the first people on whom Wesley called when he came back from Lincolnshire at the end of May. 'We fixed two evenings in a week to meet on, partly to talk upon that subject, and partly to read something in practical divinity.'

Clayton was a scholarly, high-minded man, twenty-three years of age in 1732. He was to be in Oxford only for another twelve months before returning to Manchester to become chaplain of the collegiate church.

His influence on the Holy Club and indeed on John Wesley himself was decisive, though their ways were later to part. A High-Churchman and Tory, who had been educated in the Non-juring tradition, the Holy Club appealed to Clayton because it seemed to him a return to apostolic tradition. His orthodoxy was unimpeachable. Whatever charge could be levelled at the Methodists at this stage of their history, it could not be one of heterodoxy. A student of early Church history and a fervent if somewhat uncritical patristic student Clayton was as eager as the Wesleys that the Church should follow without compromise in the footsteps of the apostles.

'Observing the Stations and weekly communion are duties which stand upon a much higher footing than a rule of a Society,' he told Wesley later, 'and they, who can set aside the command and the authority of His Church, will hardly, I doubt, be tied by the rules of a private Society.'[1]

Under his guidance the obligation to partake of the sacrament of Communion was even more significantly stressed; the group was for this reason sometimes called the Sacramentarians. Clayton was responsible for persuading Wesley and the other members of the Holy Club to observe the Wednesdays and Fridays as fast days.

'Fasting', Wesley told John Robson in 1735, 'is not a means of chastity only, but of deadness to pleasure and heavenly-mindedness, and consequently necessary . . . to all persons in all times of life.'

On 11th October, 1732, Wesley talked with his pupil Joseph Green about the keeping of the Wednesday fast. His contemporaries may well have found this feature of the Holy Club more surprising and unattractive than the attendance at the Sunday Communion and the works of charity. Young Richard Morgan told his father twelve months later that

'. . . though some of them are remarkable for eating very hearty on gaudy days, they stint themselves to twopence meat and a farthing bread, and a draught of water when they eat at their own expense; and as for supper, they never eat any.'

Throughout 1732 Clayton was in constant contact with John and his brother, both at the Castle and in their rooms. Wesley talked with him in the College garden about his pupils and showed his friends round the chapel at Lincoln. Through his initiative the Holy Club gained a footing in Brasenose.

John Gambold was another senior man who was brought into the orbit of the Wesley's influence in 1732. He had entered Christ Church as a servitor the same year as Charles Wesley, but he led an isolated, lonely existence for his first two years: 'I had no friend to whom I could open my mind, to any purpose.' His father, himself a graduate of Oxford and the author of a Welsh grammar,[2] was rector of Puncheston in Wales, where he died at the age of fifty-three in September, 1728. His declining health and eventual death fostered his son's temperamental melancholy. He later recalled his early life in lines of monotonous infelicity:[3]

[1] Tyerman, *Oxford Methodists*, 34.
[2] *A Compendious Welsh Grammar, or a short and easy introduction to the Welsh Language*, 3rd edn. (1833).
[3] *Works*, 2nd edn. (1823), 186–7.

In nature's ebbs, which lay the soul in chains,
Beneath weak nerves and ill-sufficing veins,
Who can support bare being, unendow'd
With gust voluptuous, or reflection proud?
No more bright images the brain commands,—
No great design the glowing heart expands—
No longer shines the animated face,—
Motion and speech forget their conscious grace.
How can the brave, the witty, and the gay
Survive when mirth, wit, courage die away?
None but the Christian's all-comprising power
Subdues each chance, and lives through every hour.
Watchful, he suffers all, and feels within
All smart proportion'd to some root of sin;
He strikes each error with his Maker's rod,
And by self-knowledge, penetrates to God.

If anything, his natural melancholy grew greater and was subsequently attributed by him to the heavy burden of sin.

'So God was pleased to order it, to disappoint and break a poor spirit, and to embitter the world to me; as I was declining to relish its vanities. . . . No man did care for my soul; or none, at least, understood its paths. They, that were at ease, could not guess what my sorrow was for. The learned endeavour to give me right motions, and the friendly to divert me. But I had a weight upon my heart, which only prayer could in some degree remove.'

This over-sensitive and introspective youth was just the sort of person who was likely to be attracted by the firm faith of the Wesleys and the absorbing activity of the Holy Club.

A friend happened to talk about the 'whimsical Mr. Wesley, his preciseness and pious extravagance', and Gambold, who had known him by sight for four years, plucked up courage to call at Charles Wesley's room and make his acquaintance. This was in March, 1730. Some time later Charles introduced Gambold to John, 'for', he told him, 'he is somewhat older than I, and can resolve your doubts better'. Gambold was with John, Charles and Mr. Smith on Saturday and Sunday, 24th and 25th June, talking later with John about his life in the country. He was ordained by Bishop Potter in September, 1733, and was subsequently appointed to a country living just outside Oxford, Stanton Harcourt, in the gift of Lord Harcourt.

While the full members of the Holy Club were few, many young graduates and undergraduates were interested in its activities:

'There is a society of gentlemen, consisting of seven members, whom the world calls Methodists', so wrote Richard Morgan in 1734, 'of whom my Tutor is President.'

Wesley vehemently denied that he was president but he was certainly the moving spirit and principal authority in the little society.

'I hope to God', John Clayton wrote to John Wesley in 1732, 'we shall get at least an advocate for us, if not a brother and a fellow-labourer in every College in town.'[1]

Some were friends of old standing, Nash, Graves,[2] Cox, Langford and Potter, most of them perhaps on the fringe of the society rather than deeply involved in it; Tom Horne of Christ Church was an old friend of Charles Wesley's who had matriculated in 1725 and taken his degree in 1728.

'I met and accompanied my friend Horne to the Convocation', Charles wrote on 9th February, 1737.

Others were more closely associated with the devotional and other activities of the Holy Club. They had won a foothold in Corpus Christi through a Mr. Patten,[3] 'who was chosen thither from our College' (B.N.C.). He had aroused the interest of his contemporaries by his fasting which had staggered many and made one 'perfect convert'. As a result Clayton himself had been asked by two undergraduates, hitherto unknown to him, to tell them 'my reasons for fasting and constant communion'. Patten had been greatly impressed by reading the University sermon which Wesley had preached the previous January on the Circumcision of the Heart; 'He was more affected with it than with anything I had either read or said to him about the necessity of being active.' Another of Clayton's pupils had promised to bring pressure to bear on a cousin

[1] *Journal*, viii, 281.

[2] Morgan Graves, son of Richard Graves of Mickleton; matriculated University College 1727; later barrister-at-law.

[3] Thomas Patten, son of a Manchester grocer, matriculated at B.N.C., aged 16, in 1730; took his B.A. from Corpus in 1733 and D.D. in 1754. He was a fellow of Corpus and rector of Childrey, Berkshire, where he is said to have been an exemplary parish priest. He was much esteemed by Dr. Johnson (*Boswell's Johnson*, ed. Hill, iv, 162). He died in 1790. Cf. entry in Wesley's diary for Sunday, 11th November, 1732: '7.15 am. Sn. Patten not there.'

of his at Queen's, a College which was soon to house a number of sympathizers. Brasenose was thus a small nucleus of activity, though apart from Matthew Salmon[1] and William Nowell,[2] it is not easy to recall the names of Clayton's 'little flock'. Salmon had matriculated at the age of sixteen in 1730. Wesley first met him at Clayton's rooms on 8th August and he was soon engaged in teaching the prisoners to read.

It is difficult to identify some of the other members. Mr. Martin was often in the company of the brothers during the year and helped with the services at the Castle; if he was already in orders he was probably Hudson Martin of Jesus College.[3] George Watson, who also read prayers at the Castle, impressed Clayton as a 'sober man in the main'.[4] Mr. Watkins, a fellow of Wadham, was an earlier friend of Wesley; he had been 'abroad for some time' with the result that during Wesley's absence in the summer the services at the Castle had been interrupted. John Spicer of Christ Church[5] was keeping to his resolution of early rising and had promised to 'shake off his idle acquaintances by proposing some useful subject of conversation to them'. William Haward[6] and Doyle were two others who showed an interest in the work at the Castle; so did Nowell, Clements and Nicholls, to whom Wesley read the letter that he had sent Morgan's father on 18th November; two days later he read it to Doyle in Haward's rooms in Magdalen.

If John Clayton whipped up enough enthusiasm among the undergraduates of Brasenose to attract a small following there, John Wesley

[1] Salmon later became hostile. 'When I happened to be in Oxford in 1742, Mr. [Charles] Wesley . . . entertained his audience two hours, and, having insulted and abused all degrees from the highest to the lowest, was in a manner hissed out of the pulpit by the lads' (M. Salmon, *Foreigner's Companion through the Universities of Oxford and Cambridge* (1748)), a charge which Charles Wesley vehemently repudiated.

[2] Matriculated B.N.C. 12th June, 1730, aged 16; B.A. 1734, M.A. (Oriel), 1738.

[3] Martin matriculated in 1728, took his B.A. in 1731, and his M.A. in 1734. There was also a slightly younger man called Martin, John Martin of Pembroke, who matriculated in 1729, took his B.A. in 1732 and his M.A. in 1735. A James Martin matriculated at B.N.C. in 1732.

[4] Watson matriculated Ch. Ch. 1725, aged 17; B.A. 1729, M.A. 1732; was ordained by the Bishop of Oxford, deacon in 1730, priest in 1731.

[5] John Spicer matriculated 20th May, 1729, aged 15, and took his B.A. on 12th March, 1733.

[6] William Haward, of Merton College, elected to a Yorkshire fellowship at Magdalen in 1730, later Dean of Divinity and Vice-President; later rector of Brandeston, Norfolk (1742), Upper Beeding, and Standlake, where he died in 1756, and where he was succeeded by Wesley's former friend, his colleague, Matthew Horbery.

N

might well have tried to do the same at Lincoln. He certainly had a number of supporters there, including William Clements,[1] who had matriculated at Lincoln at the early age of fourteen in 1726, and was subsequently elected a fellow of Magdalen. His father was a bookseller in St. Paul's Churchyard, who published Sacheverell's sermons, and his uncle was the well-known Oxford bookseller. When therefore Wesley's friend, the publisher Rivington, came to Oxford in July, 1732, he invited young William and his uncle to meet him; Clements was soon seeing much of Wesley and becoming more and more intimately associated with the activities of the Holy Club. A week after the meeting of the two publishers Wesley was reading Norris on 'Half-Christians' to Clayton, Rivington and Clements. The latter was as yet unsettled in his ideas, open to persuasion but reluctant to commit himself. 'Poor Mr. Clements', Clayton told Wesley on 1st August, 1732, 'is still wavering. He was with me last night two hours, but I doubt to no purpose.' 'I hope', he added at the close of his letter, 'I have made him a proselyte to early rising, though I cannot to constant communion.' Clements proved amenable to the influence which Clayton and John Wesley brought to bear. He had a long talk with Wesley on 25th October as a result of which he asked his President's permission to attend the Communion at Christ Church.[2] On 7th November, 1732, Wesley noted happily that Clements was 'engaged with us'.

His only follower among the fellows of Lincoln was William Smith, who aroused the irritation of his colleagues by becoming a member of the Holy Club.[3] In August, 1732, Clayton told Wesley that Smith had asked to be sent the clerical bands and poems that Wesley had promised to give him. Smith, who eventually became curate of Combe, did not find it easy to persevere. 'Alas! how lukewarm is piety become with me at the best; and fasting neglected, which I never looked for; not entirely dropped, I

---

[1] Clements eventually became vicar of South Brent, Devon, Lecturer of St. Stephen's, Walbrook, and St. Benet, Sherehog, London; Librarian of Sion College. He died in 1799 and bequeathed the College a portrait of Sacheverell and £100. He published *Eight Sermons* (1757), which included a Latin Oration spoken in the Hall of Magdalen on 22nd July, Founder's Day, 1733.

[2] The emphasis placed on the service of Holy Communion at Christ Church raises the question as to the attitude taken by the Cathedral clergy, to which there is no complete answer; but one of the chaplains, Jonathan Colley, was friendlily disposed to Wesley (see pp. 61–2). In 1732 Wesley wrote a sermon for his pupils on 'The Duty of Constant Communion' (No. C1).

[3] See pp. 141–2.

hope, but for a week or two, to be taken up and practised again incessantly.'[1]

It was Wesley's custom to invite his pupils to breakfast and prayers, but he did not wish consciously to obtrude or push the work of the Holy Club. On the other hand, he felt himself in some sense responsible for their spiritual health; underneath his gentle grace there was an iron will which did not readily stand opposition and which could not resist the temptation to bend others to his will, though he sincerely believed this to to be the will of God. John Gambold, writing somewhat later, explained that 'They took great pains with the younger members of the University, to rescue them from bad company, and encourage them in a sober, studious life. If they had some interest with any such, they would get them to breakfast, and over a dish of tea endeavour to fasten some good hint upon them; they would bring them acquainted with other well-disposed young men; they would help them in those parts of learning which they stuck at; they would close with their best sentiments, drive on their convictions, give them rules of piety, when they would receive them, and watch over them with great tenderness.'[2] Wesley used such an opportunity to talk with the Bible clerk of his College, Joseph Green, about fasting. Thomas Greives was another such pupil whom Wesley seems to have brought occasionally within the scope of the Holy Club's influence;[3] James Hervey was already feeling his way but had not yet come to a final decision. Robert Davison, another of his pupils at Lincoln, was associated with its activities in 1730–1.

Wesley had, however, four more convinced allies among the junior members of the College, though he was not without his anxieties about all of them. He was perhaps least worried about the egregious Westley Hall, who was already winning the confidence of the Wesleys as well as of the other members of the Holy Club. John Whitelamb was a special protégé of whom he had great hopes.

'He reads one English, one Latin, and one Greek book alternately', he wrote enthusiastically to his father on 11th June, 1731, 'and never meddles with a new one in any of the languages till he has ended the

---

[1] L. Tyerman, *The Oxford Methodists*, 27. He was ordained by the Bishop of Oxford in June, 1732.

[2] *Journal*, viii, 266.

[3] Wesley seems to have been entrusted with supervision of his allowance, viz., the entry in his accounts: 'Recd. of Mr. Greives for his use 11 guineas. Pd. to him for Mr. Combs 2 guineas &c.'

old one. If he goes on as he has begun, I dare take upon me to say that, by the time he has been here four or five years, there will not be such an one of his standing in Lincoln College, perhaps not in the University of Oxford.'[1]

It would have been difficult for Whitelamb to resist his tutor's advice, even if that tutor had not been John Wesley, but John was the son of his patron and a gentleman. Whitelamb was a humble Lincolnshire boy; no less than three times in 1732 Wesley had to see the Bursar about him, presumably because of his inability to pay his battels. When he was 'in talk' with Wesley or when Wesley talked about him with his friends, he could hardly do otherwise than conform to his tutor's views. He did his turn by taking care of the children from the school and the workhouse.

There remained Matthew Robinson and John Robson. The final struggle for their souls had not begun in earnest; but they were already involved to some extent in their tutor's good works. Matthew Robinson was a servitor and a Lincolnshire boy, the son of the vicar of Blyborough; he was seventeen when he matriculated in 1730.[2] Wesley tells us that he talked with him about the sacraments on 7th October and he obviously came more and more under his influence. John Robson, another north-country boy from County Durham, had only entered the College in May, 1732, but he too was often in talk with his tutor.

It is fair indeed to say that many of these young men were not in any way fully committed. Some indeed must have been like 'poor Mr. Brown' who had tasted 'too deeply of the pleasure of living in a gentleman's house for this fortnight to think of either rising in a morning or of fasting'.[3] Yet the number was sufficient, at least in a few Colleges, Christ Church, Lincoln and Brasenose, to raise queries in the minds of the senior members of their Colleges. Moreover, Wesley's connections included a few who had been once associated with his work but who had now gone down; he continued to see something of Boyce[4] and at least once Bob

---

[1] *Letters*, i, 85.

[2] He was later a fellow of B.N.C. (5th July, 1735), resigning in 1739. Later he was Master of Boston Grammar School, dying in 1745. He was ordained by the Bishop of Oxford in June, 1736.

[3] Brown is too common a name to allow correct identification, but this may have been Charles Brown, son of William Brown, of Stretton-in-the-Fields, in Leicestershire, who entered Lincoln on 10th April, 1731.

[4] Mr. and Mrs. Boyse were with him in Charles Wesley's rooms on the afternoon of 16th December when he read the elder Morgan's letter to them; but this was probably his friends from Berkswell.

Kirkham called on him in Oxford.[1] What he was doing had gained the interest and support of friends who lived in London—Rivington, Wogan and Laserre, all three of whom also visited him in Oxford, and the wealthy Sir John Phillips.

These were now much needed, for the work had been greatly extended in 1732. The two prisons, the Castle and the Bocardo, took up most of their time. The members of the Holy Club held services there regularly, prayers most Wednesdays and Fridays, a sermon on Sunday, and the Holy Communion once a month. 'Don't forget', Clayton reminded John Wesley, who was in London, 'a few Common Prayer Books for the Castle.' They also raised a fund to which they all contributed a tithe of their income to help pay the debts of those who were confined for relatively trivial sums and to provide medicines, books and the necessities of life. John Stephens, for instance, was to stay in the Bocardo to the next court leet,

> '. . . at which time he will put in a life of a cousin of his who lives in Cumner, who bargains to give him eight pounds. The rest of the money we may easily afford to advance from good Sir John's benefaction.'

And, Clayton added, Stephens would stay in the Bocardo for another three weeks more willingly as he had heard that John Wesley was returning to Oxford.

The young men did what they could to instruct the prisoners in the rudiments of reading:

> '. . . there are only two in the jail', Clayton told Wesley, 'who want this accomplishment,—John Clanville, who reads but moderately, and the horse-stealer, who cannot yet read at all. He knows all his letters, and can spell most of the common monosyllables.'

There were also the debtors' children whom the members of the Holy Club made some effort to instruct. They secured legal advice for the prisoners, advanced them money and tried to get them released. Not all of them were grateful for their intervention. The Bocardo was much disturbed by internal quarrels, so much so that one prisoner, Tomlyns, had had to be fettered and put in the dungeon, and another, Wisdom, had promised to hear Clayton read prayers, and yet had failed to do so.

[1] E.g. on Saturday, 3rd June, 1732.

'I sent for him yesterday, but he would not come down; and when I had done reading, I went upstairs to him, and upbraided him with breaking his promise, upon which he very surlily replied, that he had thought better of it since he had seen me.'

Some resented the religious exhortations and the call to repentance, which they associated with these fervent young men.

The majority, however, undoubtedly appreciated the kindness and humanity which lay behind the efforts of Wesley and his friends. Wesley was particularly interested in a prisoner called Irwin; he consulted Stewart, Bateman, the vicar of Thame, and his friends. On 15th June, 1732, he rode out to Cuddesdon to see the Bishop of Oxford and evidently secured from him permission to baptize Irwin; though the Bishop was reluctant to give Wesley a general commission.[1] Irwin was christened the next morning and subsequently prepared for confirmation. Once again, on 2nd October, 1732, following, he and Clayton rode out from Oxford and in spite of losing themselves *en route* arrived at the Bishop's palace shortly before midday. The purpose of the visit was to discuss Irwin's confirmation, but they stayed to dinner, where they were joined by Dr. Hammond; Wesley raised many pertinent issues with the Bishop including the celebration of the Communion at Christ Church and the University Church, and found him in gracious agreement with all that he said. They partook of tea and started off for home shortly after half-past three. Twelve days later he again set off with Clayton, this time taking Irwin with them; Wesley reminded them both of the rules of the Society before they set out. On their arrival at Cuddesdon the Bishop performed the rite of confirmation and invited them to dine with him; once more they discussed the Communion at St. Mary's and the possibility of infant confirmation.[2]

The interest and care which Wesley showed in Irwin's case can be paralleled in that of others. He went to immense trouble in the case of a Mrs. Topping; for weeks hardly a day passed without his discussing her problem with his friends.[3] It is not easy to unravel the details of the case, but on 1st August, 1732, John Clayton told Wesley that he had secured Mrs. Topping a copy of her son's indictment at the Assizes, and that she was trying to 'bring her mind into a due frame for the devout participa-

---

[1] The phrase in Wesley's diary reads simply: 'He ō giv an Commission.'

[2] Again the meaning is not absolutely clear; the phrase is 't. of Infant Com^n.'

[3] Cf. the entries in Wesley's diary for 12th, 19th, 20th, 21st, 22nd, 25th, 26th August and 7th November, 1732.

tion of the Holy Communion on Sunday next'. In the coming weeks
Wesley discussed the case with Clayton and Topping's lawyer and he
went out to see Topping at Cotmore on 21st August, riding out with
Richard Bainbridge, one of his pupils and taking advantage of the trip to
look at the house at Cottisford (but he could not get in) and at Rousham,
where he found Mr. Dormer at dinner. The next day he rose early and
by half-past five was going over Topping's accounts before visiting a Mr.
Sheldon, who may have initiated proceedings against him.[1] At any rate
Wesley persuaded Sheldon to re-examine his accounts. A few days later
he consulted with two others of those involved, Mr. Lord and Mr. Short,
before leaving for Lincolnshire. Clayton kept a careful eye on things while
he was away. In addition to getting advice from a London lawyer, he had
consulted with the Toppings' legal adviser:

'. . . he tells me that the sheep might be recovered for about two and
twenty shillings, which I promised to advance out of Sir John's money,
and he will engage to make better than forty pounds of them, which
he says will be more than sufficient for carrying on the suit. he since
informs me that Mr. Short did a very unlawful action in seizing the
sheep, and therefore we are obliged, I think, to recover them if possible.
They properly belonged to John Topping, and they now fall to his
mother as being her son's administrator. . . .'[2]

Undoubtedly Wesley and Clayton were able to identify themselves with
the interests of the prisoners whose causes aroused their sympathy. Clayton expressed his pleasure with all the felons with the exception of the
sheep-stealer,[3] who had been acquitted, and Salmon, who was to be tried
at the Warwick Assizes. He believed that Salmon was 'a suffering innocent man' and was going to help him to pay the expenses of having
witnesses subpoenaed at Warwick. John Wesley made a point of visiting
him in the prison at Warwick, both on his way north and on his return in
the autumn of 1732.

[1] 'You must know', Clayton wrote to John Wesley on 4th September, 1732,
'then that last week I writ out a state of her case and sent it up to London to one
Mr. Waddilove, an eminent attorney, who sent me down his opinion . . . informing me that the whole of Mr. Sheldon's proceedings were null and invalid, and that
if we had but a small sum of money we might sue him for a trespasser, and recover
very considerable damages.'
[2] *Journal*, viii, 278–9.
[3] He had been branded in the hand but was a 'great penitent'.

The story of their activities at Bocardo was similar; here the unpopularity of one Mr. Blair with his fellow-prisoners and the 'unjust persecution' under which he laboured aroused Wesley's sympathy. Again Blair's case engaged much of his attention during the autumn and winter of 1732.[1] He visited him and read to him, made contact with the lawyer Mr. Austin and wrote out his case. On 14th November he rose at four, went through his notes at five and breakfasted with Crotchley, who with Charles then made for Thame where they met at the local inn a number of others interested in Blair's problems. The Sheriff arrived at midday accompanied by Mr. Whitehead, the case was tried at two, and the charge was proved, though, added Wesley, no costs were given.

The activities of the Holy Club had now been enlarged to include St. Thomas's workhouse, which he visited with Clayton and Salmon on 11th August, 1732. Here again they interested themselves in teaching the inmates to read and in helping them generally. Clayton was concerned with an attempt to separate two of them, Goody Bossum and her husband, and gave a crown towards Goody's clothing, and was disappointed to learn later that she had 'made an elopement ... and God knows where she is gone'.

Finally Morgan appears to have brought together a number of poor children in a school where the members of the Holy Club tried to give them the rudiments of education.

> 'The school was', Gambold thought, 'of Mr. Wesley's own setting up; however, he paid the mistress, and clothed some, if not all, of the children. When they went thither, they inquired how each child behaved, saw their work (for some could knit or spin), heard them read, heard them their prayers or their catechism, and explained part of it.'[2]

When Clayton wrote to Wesley his long account of the activities of the Holy Club in August, 1732, he told him that he had been recently at the school and thought the children were going on pretty well, except

---

[1] See the entries in Wesley's diary for 12th, 13th, 16th, 17th, 27th, 31st October, 4th, 7th, 9th, 11th, 13th, 14th, 15th, 16th November, etc., 1732.

[2] Of instruction in the prison Clayton commented: 'One of my college scholars has left me, but the others go on mighty well. The woman, who was a perfect novice, spells tolerably, and so does one of the boys, and the other makes shift with spelling every word that is longer than ordinary. The boys can both say their Catechism so far as to the end of the Commandments, and can likewise repeat the morning and evening prayers for children in Ken's *Manual*. (*Journal*, viii, 277.)

'Jervaise's boy, who, I find, truants till eleven o'clock in a morning'. He had threatened the boy and the mother had said that she would see that he went. Clayton had obtained a shilling from the Vice-Principal of B.N.C. and had contributed a sixpence himself

'. . . to preserve the gown that is in pawn from being sold; and the woman who has it has promised not to sell it, provided Jervaise will bring her sixpence a week towards redeeming it'.

Thus, in spite of setbacks and hostile criticism, the Holy Club had made considerable progress during 1732. Indeed, throughout the next three years the pattern of its activities, the devotional readings, the visits to the prisons and to the workhouse, were not to change much. Wesley and his friends continued to offer sympathy, charity and religious guidance as well as occasional legal assistance to the poor and afflicted. Blair's case, for instance, continued to be much in his mind during 1733.[1] He talked of confirmation with Andrew Etty and baptized young John Stewart, perhaps the child of the Roman Catholic prisoner over whose future he was concerned early in 1734. Wesley continued to preach regularly at the Castle; on Sunday, 9th December, 1733, he spoke fervently about faith to the prisoners but there was no immediate response. In the spring, on 11th March, 1734, some of the prisoners began laughing when Wesley started to preach, but he stilled his insubordinate congregation with a look. There was nothing new or significant in the story of the Holy Club's activities between 1732 and 1735.

The interest shifts decisively to Wesley's relationships with the other members of the Holy Club and its sympathizers, and possibly to the growing interest shown in its activities by a group of townspeople who formed the nucleus of a new religious society. In all this there was, as one would expect, a debit as well as a credit side. Clayton's departure to Manchester must have been a serious loss, for he was an extremely energetic and conscientious man. Wesley visited him in the summer on his way to and from Lincolnshire. His stay was full, agreeable and enlightening. He arrived at the Bull's Head at Manchester at half-past six and was immediately taken by Clayton to have coffee at his house where he also met Joseph Hoole, whom he accompanied to the College. At nine they called on Dr. Byrom[2] and talked with him and Mr. Leaver about self-denial.

[1] See the entries in Wesley's diary for 16th, 19th February, 1st, 29th March, 16th, 17th April, 1st May, 17th June, 1733.
[2] Byrom was a friend of Clayton's and visited him at Oxford in June, 1731.

He was up early the next day joining Clayton and Salmon; soon after breakfast he renewed his acquaintance with Hoole and Leaver, and met the distinguished Non-juror scholar, Dr. Deacon.[1] Clayton showed him round the library, and in the afternoon, accompanied part of the way by Clayton, Dr. Deacon, Byrom and Salmon, he set out for Buxton and Chatsworth. He returned to Manchester on 2nd June, preached at the College at a service at six in the morning, then at Salford at nine, and again at the College at eleven, where, to Wesley's amazement, there were some five hundred communicants.[2] In the afternoon after dinner he preached at St. Ann's and spent the evening talking of religion with Hoole, Dr. Byrom and Mr. Bands. In February, 1734, Clayton revisited Oxford and Wesley was glad to have an opportunity to consult him over the problem of William Morgan's younger brother, and to have his opinion over the University sermon which he was shortly to preach and the text of which he gave him to read.[3] Sooner or later their ways were to part, for Clayton remained faithful to the conservative orthodoxy of his earlier life and felt that Wesley's theological position had gone astray; but his removal from the company of the Holy Club must have been a grievous blow. Quite apart from the loss of an intelligent and shrewd judgement, there was the inevitable reaction in Brasenose among his pupils; 'the day before', Wesley commented sadly, 'the last of Mr. Clayton's pupils who continued with us, informed me that he did not design to meet us any more', a statement which cannot be wholly true since Matthew Salmon was still an enthusiastic supporter of the Holy Club.

There were, however, important accessions during the last three years of Wesley's tutorship. On 11th February, 1733, Wesley noted that Thomas Broughton was present at his sermon. Broughton had entered University College in December, 1731, and was elected to a fellowship at Exeter College two years later. A week after hearing Wesley he went to the Communion at Christ Church, and was ardent to join the religious society; but in the intervening weeks his enthusiasm dwindled. When Wesley walked with him in the street on the 22nd he was 'much cooled' and by the end of the month was 'quite cold'. On the following Saturday and Sunday, 3rd and 4th March, Wesley had long talks with him and at their second conversation on Sunday evening read Norris on Temptation.

[1] See T. Broxap, *Thomas Deacon*.

[2] It should be added that Wesley's figures are often untrustworthy.

[3] This was probably the so-called Jacobite sermon, preached in June, 1734, the text of which does not survive. See p. 78.

Next evening Broughton affirmed his resolution to join with the Methodists and thenceforward was a fervent supporter of the Holy Club. Studious-minded, orthodox in his theological views, Broughton helped to make up for the loss of Clayton. 'Mr. Broughton', Benjamin Ingham commented, 'is really a holy man.'

Benjamin Ingham was an equally important asset. His first significant contact with Wesley occurred on 18th April, 1733, and he was soon involved in the Holy Club's activities. A young Yorkshireman from Batley, he entered Queen's College in 1730. Spiritually unsettled, he had been attracted by stories of the Methodists but had at first done no more than defend them against their adversaries. Once he had committed himself he proved a loyal and worthy supporter. In February, 1734, he was arranging meetings in his mother's house at Ossett, near Wakefield, along the lines of the Oxford society.[1]

'I have methodized my time according to the following scheme', he told John Wesley. 'Suppose I rise at five or sooner, I spend till six in devotion,—in repeating a hymn, and chanting a psalm, then praying and reading the Holy Scriptures. At six, Christian treatises. At seven we breakfast. I then get a lesson out of the New Testament, then a Collect, and most of the Common Prayer. Then forty-two poor children came to me to read. I propose to observe the three ancient hours of prayer when at home. From nine to eleven, I read in the Greek Testament, according to Frank's. At eleven, I go to teach the rug-maker's children to read. Twelve, dine; read Morris's Shorthand. Two, Greek Testament. Four, walk. Five, devotion. Six, Reading, I choose the subject beforehand. Seven, supper; and read Milton and other religious books with the family. Nine, prayer for myself and friends. On Wednesday and Friday, from eight to nine, meditate on my sins; twelve to one, on Christ's sufferings; two to three, read Morris. On Sunday, spend two hours in reading with the family of some poor neighbours.'

Eager and active, he asked Wesley to act as his spiritual director; but he was sometimes in indifferent health and easily depressed. Returning to Oxford in February, 1735, he was ordained deacon by Bishop Potter on 1st June and became 'reader of public prayers' at Christ Church, and at St. Sepulchre's, Newgate Street. On 17th June, 1735, he wrote to reassure Wesley that the rumours of coolness which had grown up between the brothers and himself had no foundation in fact:

[1] For information about Ingham taken from the *Batty MS.*, I am indebted to Mr. John Walsh, Fellow of Jesus College, Oxford.

'I have reason to believe you have met with a variety of trials at Epworth, and I have heard you evil spoken of abroad; and, for these reasons, I do assure you I love you the more.'[1]

He mentioned that the condition of some of the Oxford men was 'fluctuating'; but Salmon 'is a sincere friend'. 'All friends at Queen's College I left in a hopeful condition.' He, Gambold and Hall had been to visit William Law. 'We asked him some questions; but he talked only about man's fall, and the one thing necessary. He is a divine man.' Ingham was to be the only Oxford Methodist to accompany the Wesleys to Georgia in a few months' time.

It was during 1733 that James Hervey became more closely associated with Wesley and his group. John Wesley talked with him on the morning of 8th August, 1733, and the next day he attended an early morning meeting of the religious society. In September he had another long talk with him and convinced him of the obligation of the Friday fast. On Ash Wednesday, 1734, he urged on Hervey the necessity for keeping Lent and he went away much affected by what Wesley had said; the next day he enlarged on what he had previously said to Hervey and another Lincoln man, Greives. Hervey's progress was gradual but seemingly certain. On 13th April he sought the Rector's permission to take Communion at Christ Church, only to lower Wesley's spirits ten days later by missing the Communion at St. Mary's; '*ex illo fluere*'. The new recruit was a gentle, sentimental creature, whose willowy and delicate frame housed a stronger will and shrewder intelligence than his appearance and his lush prose style would suggest. He had matriculated at Lincoln on 8th April, 1731. The son of a respectable country clergyman, according to his own account he was lazy during his first two years in the College, when he had as tutor the conscientious Richard Hutchins. But in 1733 he came under Wesley's influence; when Wesley was in Georgia he wrote, on 2nd September, 1736, to thank him, 'as for all other favours, so especially for teaching me Hebrew'.[2] Eleven years later, when their intimacy had been long broken by religious differences, Hervey reassured him that

'I can never forget the tender-hearted and generous Fellow of Lincoln, who condescended to take such compassionate notice of a poor under-graduate, whom almost everybody condemned; and when no man cared for my soul.'

[1] Tyerman, *Oxford Methodists*, 61.
[2] Coke and Moore, *Life of Wesley*, 51.

Hervey, like Gambold, had been a lonely, rather unpopular figure before he was able to sublimate his frustration in the busy activity of the Holy Club.

His spiritual progress was rapid, though his account was in the fulsome rhetoric which marks his style and which presumably explains why Charles Wesley used to call him Isocrates.[1] In the first flush of pietism, Hervey wrote on 16th September, 1733, a long letter to his sister, profuse with metaphor and adjective, recalling the beauties of nature and the seriousness of religion.

'Though we are in the very prime and spring of our years, strongly disposed to admire, and perfectly capacitated to relish the gaieties of youth, yet we have been inured to moderate the warmth of our appetites, accustomed to anticipate in our minds the days of darkness, and incessantly disciplined with a remembrance of our Creator.'

He noted in typically ornate prose the fading beauties of the outward scene, the transitory nature of man's existence—

'No pleasing expectations refresh his mind; not the least dawnings of hope glimmer in to qualify the darksome looking-for of Death'

—redeemed by the fruit of unsullied virtue:

'To walk humbly with our God, dutifully with our parents, and, charitably with all, will be an inexhaustible source of never-ceasing comforts.'

'All will be soothed by this precious, this invaluable thought, that, by reason of the meekness, the innocence, the purity, and other Christian graces which adorned the several stages of our progress through the world, our names and our ashes will be embalmed; the chambers of our tomb consecrated into a paradise of rest; and our souls, white as our locks, by an easy transition, become angels of light.'

This effusion, typical of other letters written to his sister during his days at Lincoln, discloses not merely the conventional character of Hervey's piety but that his chief concern was with practical Christianity. Yet the morbidity[2] from which he was never long free and which formed such congenial soil for incipient Calvinism was already deeply rooted in his nature. This gentle, kindly man was fascinated by death. It was perhaps a

[1] Charles Wesley's *Journal*, ii, 393.

[2] Cf. his 'Meditations among the Tombs' in his excessively popular and widely read *Meditations and Contemplations* (1745-7), which had reached a twenty-fifth edition by 1791.

product of that ill-balance which brought him to a comparatively early grave. He told his sister, herself often ill, to rejoice in the afflictions which may soon carry her from the world of sense.

> 'There is', he wrote from College on 28th March, 1734, 'great reason for congratulation, on account of your being so choice a favourite of heaven, as your frequent sicknesses and often infirmities speak you to be . . . suffer yourself by this loving correction, to be made great— great in humility, holiness, and happiness. . . . Humble yourself under the mighty hand of God.'

When she asked him to write poems, Hervey sent her Edward Young's 'The Last Day': 'this almost Divine piece of poetry', as he described it in a letter of 2nd May, 1734, would 'improve and edify' as much as it would 'divert and delight'.[1] This rather unctuous and gentle creature was obviously, in Walter Chapman's words, 'a great champion of the Lord of Hosts' among the early Methodists, giving weekly readings to a religious society in St. Ebbe's. John Gambold recalled that he was a man of surprising greatness of soul.

> 'If you look for his virtues, you will not be able to discover them one by one, but you will see that he walks before God with a reverence and alacrity which includes them all.'[2]

Two other names made their first appearance in Wesley's diary in 1733–4, Charles Kinchin and George Whitefield. On 12th June, 1733, he noted that Kinchin, a young fellow of Corpus and rector of Dummer in Hampshire, had called, and on 4th September he sat with Mr. Lloyd, Mr. Lucas and Mr. Whitefield at the King's Head. Since their contribution to the work of the Holy Club was made somewhat later and most effectively after John Wesley's departure for Georgia, a consideration of their significance can be left till later.[3]

Many of these men had only joined their fortunes to the Wesleys after giving the matter very serious thought, and there were many others, especially Wesley's pupils, who wavered in their determination. There can be no doubt of Wesley's piety or of his serious concern for others, but his determination was equally plain. If a pupil of his showed a serious interest in religious matters, he would find himself in the constant, per-

---

[1] Quoted in Tyerman, *Oxford Methodists*, 205–6.
[2] *Arminian Magazine* (1798), 171.
[3] See pp. 260–2.

haps too constant, companionship of his well-meaning tutor. Joseph
Green and Tom Greives were Lincoln men often invited to meet Wesley
and eventually persuaded to his way of thinking. On 20th December,
1733, he could write that 'Green seemed affected'. In the summer he had
talked to Greives and Robson about the Communion and to help their
faith read Wynne's commentary on Locke's *Essay on Human Understand-*
ing to them; on 9th February, 1734, he could say of Greives that he too
appeared 'affected'. Another friend, Tom Horne, of long standing, was
resolute and a 'changed man'. On 8th November, 1733, Wesley met a
Mr. Greenaway[1] and found him a man of 'right' mind to whom he read
two days later Wogan's letter on the Communion; John Prince[2] was
another recruit who at first 'wavered', but with whom Wesley was reading prayers a week later and describing himself as 'not angry'. The next
day he quietly warned him against the taking of snuff. Prince was obviously somewhat uneasy as to his decision and Wesley feared that he
might secede. He was pleased to note on 4th September that he had not
left Communion; but soon he is no longer mentioned in the diary.
Prideaux Selby, the son of a merchant from Holy Island in Northumberland, had become a member of Lincoln as a servitor on 25th November,
1731, and was elected to a scholarship on 22nd February, 1733; Wesley
talked to him about Communion and by October he was one of the little
company who made their Communion at Christ Church on Sunday
mornings.

All was not plain sailing. Wesley was much perturbed about Clements
and anxious in a different sort of way about John Whitelamb; his colleague
William Smith too seemed for a time to be wavering but eventually
renewed his decision. After Communion at Christ Church, Clements and
his friend Nowell talked of leaving the society and two days later reaffirmed this resolution. There followed a series of meetings with Wesley.
Clements, John observed, 'was piqued at me', but two days later he
talked with him in company with Langlois and had breakfast with him
the following Sunday. Nowell was persuaded to give up his decision,
was introduced to Benjamin Ingham, and on 1st July, 1733, in company
with Hervey, Clements and Rivington the publisher, foregathered in
Wesley's room before going to the Castle. Johnny Whitelamb's problems
were probably different. He was a serious-minded youth on the eve of
ordination: indeed, he was so earnest that he provoked Charles Wesley

---

[1] See p. 238.
[2] Matric., Merton College, 29th March, 1729, aged 17; B.A. 1732.

to smile. 'You little thought', he wrote sadly some ten years later, 'when you laughed at me, for being shocked at your gay discourse, that you yourself should come to maintain the very notions which I had then.'[1] Yet the very fact that John Wesley was constantly consulting other people about him suggests that he was worried, if not by his religious views, by his manner of life; on 2nd August he had convinced Whitelamb of 'vanity' and persuaded him to give up his unsuitable friends. He may well have been involved in an affair of the heart which had its own complications.[2]

The spiritual rise and fall of two other Lincoln undergraduates, Matthew Robinson and John Robson, with whom Wesley was closely concerned, has an element of comedy and the entries in the abridged diary dealing with them suggest a kind of a spiritual temperature chart. They were constantly avowing their resolution, only to fall; they became, in Wesley's words, spiritually alive only to become spiritually dead. Their tutor proved an effective revivalist. Wesley talked with Robinson on 1st May, 1733, about the significance of grace and convinced him of its efficacy; a week later they strolled in the Grove[3] one summer evening. But, on Sunday, 24th June, Robinson talked of no longer communicating at Christ Church; Wesley, in a calm frame of mind, had several talks with him during the next few days, reading to him the letter which Wogan had written on the Holy Communion; but he failed to attend the Communion at the Castle a few Sundays later, and on 29th July Wesley felt very gloomy about his prospects. On Saturday, 11st August, Wesley had his pupils develop themes and was horrified when Robinson's was directed against the Methodists. He said nothing at the time, but called Robinson to him later in the day and was relieved when his pupil told him that he was only developing an argument. On 11th September he had another heart-to-heart talk with the young man. On 18th December, 1733, he invited Hutchins and Robinson to prayers and breakfast and was much concerned to find that the fire in his room was not lighted, a task which should have been carried out by Robinson;[4] Wesley was pained but not angry. The eventual outcome of the spiritual pupillage does not appear, save for a talk which Wesley had with him on Good Friday, 1734,

---

[1] L. Tyerman, *Oxford Methodists*, 384; cf. 'Do not, as you have formerly done, ridicule me for being too religious.'

[2] See p. 234.

[3] The College garden at Lincoln was so named.

[4] As a servitor of the College.

in which Robinson 'opened his [heart?]' and revealed to Wesley that he had been much influenced by Richard Morgan and the crisis which arose out of the letter that he had written to his father.[1] 'O accursed Letter' was Wesley's final comment.

John Robson's spiritual history followed a similar pattern. John Wesley was constantly seeking to guide him along the paths which he thought he ought to go, and particularly desirous of ensuring that he communicated regularly; he talked with him about this obligation on 16th July, and a fortnight later, having been made uneasy by Robson's conduct, found after a talk that he had 'not fallen'. He was much perturbed by his absence from Communion but found that he had only been kept from attending, as had Tom Greives, by heavy rain. On 4th November, Ingham told Wesley that morning that he would take Communion regularly at St. Mary's, and in the afternoon Wesley persuaded Robson to show greater resolution in the future. A week later he was still 'zealous', but on 22nd November he had 'not risen'; on 8th December he was 're-convinced' but by the 26th he 'failed to rise again'. Wesley had him in for a long talk at seven the next morning. On 17th January, 1734, Wesley rose at four, and zealously concerned that his pupil should keep to his resolution of rising early in the morning, went over at five to his rooms to ensure it; but an altercation resulted, and it was not until half-past six that Robson rose from his bed. The next day Wesley again called him at five, but again he failed to rise. That afternoon at four the older man brought pressure to bear on his recalcitrant pupil, and 'prevailed'. On the morrow of Ash Wednesday he reminded Robson of the need for abstinence during Lent (and later spoke also with Hervey and Greives of its meaning). Next day on his return from the Sheldonian Theatre, where he had seen the Prince of Orange being given an honorary degree and had been much impressed by his serious and unaffected bearing, he talked again with Robson of the virtue of giving up secular reading, presumably for Lent. It is an indication of the extent to which Wesley, once the ardent reader of Restoration plays, had himself changed in the last few years. In the early summer of 1734 the story started all over again. On 25th May Robson failed to rise, the next day he was in tears in Wesley's room and promised to do better. On 27th May he rose early, but two days later he missed Communion at St. Mary's, and on Monday failed to rise; sadly his tutor put a query against the words 'no more'. But the unfortunate youth was rising early on 5th June, failed to rise on

[1] See pp. 198ff.

O

the 18th June, was convinced of its necessity again the day after and over-slept the following day. He stumbled from his bed the next day, but as Wesley sternly commented, seemed 'quite dead'. By 7th August, 1734, he was happily in Wesley's view 'alive', and was still persevering on the eve of Wesley's departure from Georgia; in a letter that he wrote to him on 30th September, 1735, urging the obligation of the fasts on Wednes-day and Friday, and recommending the reading of Tilly's sermons on Free-Will, there was still a hint of Robson's failure to live a fully disci-plined life. 'I charge Mr. Robson in the name of the Lord Jesus that he no longer halt between two opinions.'[1] In the summer of 1733 Wesley was in a despondent mood. He spoke of a diminished number of pupils and of losses from the Holy Club. 'One of my young noblemen' told him on his return from Epworth that he was 'more and more afraid of singularity'. Another had been persuaded to differ from Wesley through reading his views on Authority. Both had come to believe that the Wednesday fast was not obligatory. 'A third . . . had been convinced by a fever and Dr. Frewin.' The number of those who communicated regularly at St. Mary's on Monday was shrinking; from twenty-seven they had shrunk to five. 'My ill success, as they call it,' he told his father, 'seems to be what has frightened every one away from a falling house.'[2]

Then, early in 1734, Wesley was confronted with a personal crisis arising out of his relationship with William Morgan's younger brother, Richard Morgan, whom his father had decided to send to Lincoln as a pupil of John Wesley's as a mark of confidence, but not without indicat-ing a certain apprehension and by asking John Wesley to discourage excessive religious zeal. The elder Morgan knew very little of the Wesleys personally, and if this was what he wanted he was placing Wesley in a difficult, if not impossible, situation. It would have been better to have entrusted Richard to a different tutor. It might have been wiser for Wes-ley to have refused his offer, though it is easy to see that he would have found it difficult to do so, remembering his close association with the elder son. Wesley, kind and forewarned by what had happened to William, decided that it was important to take his duties as a moral tutor very seriously; and even if he purposely refrained from propagating his particular religious views, his judgements on conduct were attached to

[1] *Letters*, i, 183–4.

[2] *Op. cit.*, i, 136. It was suggestive of this trend that Mr. Clements should have withdrawn his subscription towards the children's fund on the grounds that he was no longer able to afford it (6th November, 1733).

standards which, by ordinary conventions, made men more 'pure and holy' than the majority of their contemporaries.

Richard Morgan was himself unlikely to be the most responsible of Wesley's pupils. He aspired to be something of a young buck and had persuaded his father to let him go to Lincoln as a gentleman-commoner. 'He goes as well-rigged', his father told his tutor, 'and with as great a quantity of all sorts of apparel as I believe a Gentleman Commoner need to be furnished with.' In spite of a College rule passed shortly after Wesley's election to the effect that no dogs were to be kept in College, young Morgan followed contemporary undergraduate fashion by buying a grey-hound.[1] He knew too of his brother's fate and was anxious to avoid association with the Holy Club, of which indeed he must have had an unfortunate impression. He was soon conscious that in the eyes of the 'bloods' of the College and University he was compromised by the religiously minded company which he found himself obliged to keep. The problem of the young man who feels that sober company lowers his standing with his worldly minded friends was then, as now, a familiar feature of University life.

There is enough evidence to corroborate the impression that Wesley's kindly intentions overwhelmed young Morgan and seemed to him to be forcing him into a pattern of piety for which he had no natural leanings. Morgan had arrived at Lincoln on Tuesday, 30th October, 1733, and had breakfast with Wesley the next morning. After entering him on the College books, he introduced him to the Bursar and then spent the remainder of the morning talking with him, presumably about his brother. He stressed that William Morgan had not weakened his constitution by his 'great abstinence and strictness in religion', but young Morgan heard later through a brazier's wife that the Oxford physician, Dr. Frewin, had other views about the matter. The following day Wesley went for a walk with him and introduced him to James Hervey and his brother. It is evident that Wesley was intent on seeing that he moved in what he regarded as the right circles; he saw him at least three times on Friday, 2nd November, and may have called him from the Senior Common Room (of which as a gentleman commoner he was a member) that evening.[2] Next day, a Saturday, he took him and Hervey to the White Hart at

[1] Cf. the entry in John Wesley's diary for 14th November, 1733: 'talk to Morgan about his dog'.

[2] The entry in the diary reads simply: '7. Went to C.R. for Mo. None contradicted. V.F.'

Woodstock, and walked round Blenheim Park; they could not get in the house, but inspected the bridge and the monument. On Sunday evening he read some passages from Dr. Lucas on the temptation of riches at Morgan's room. Thus, willy-nilly, Richard Morgan found himself moving in the socially restricted circle of the Holy Club, even though no pressure was put on him to become a member. His tutor was constant in his supervision of his activities. No wonder that after dinner on Saturday, 10th November, only eleven days after his arrival in Oxford, Hutchins told Wesley that Morgan had complained to him of 'being confined'.

In spite of Hutchins' warning, Wesley did not relax his solicitude. There followed some weeks in which Wesley became increasingly anxious about Morgan's activities while Morgan felt obliged to conform to a mode of existence which he did not like. He obviously found it impossible to talk frankly to his tutor nor would Wesley have understood his position. The day after Hutchins had spoken to him, Morgan did indeed send word from the Senior Common Room that he was not going to join Wesley and his friends that Sunday evening, 'would not come to us!' in Wesley's words. On the other hand he had no wish to alienate his tutor. He went to Wesley's room that evening and apologized and 'all was well'. One has a slightly uncomfortable feeling that Wesley rather enjoyed these emotional scenes with their fervent reconciliations. He talked to Richard twice in the next few days and confided to his diary on the Saturday evening that there was 'more hope' for him. As a result, when he and Broughton and Morgan were walking in the College garden the next day, Sunday, 18th November, he found that Morgan responded when he 'opened religion' to him, so much so that he read the *Second Spira*[1] to Morgan in his rooms that evening and felt convinced that his pupil went away 'warmed' and 'affected'. On Tuesday he found him 'attentive'. Meanwhile Morgan had been writing to his father and as a result the elder Morgan sent Wesley a warning note. He was eager that

[1] This tract, of which the full title was *The Second Spira, being a fearful example of an Atheist, who had apostasised from the Christian religion, and died in despair at Westminster, Dec. 8, 1692*, was a piece of favourite reading with John Wesley. The victim bewails his previous faithlessness as he tosses restlessly on his death-bed. 'Oh that I was to broil upon that fire for a thousand years, to purchase the favour of God, and be reconciled to Him again! But it is a fruitless wish! Millions of millions of years will bring me no nearer to the end of my tortures than one poor hour.' His last words were, 'Oh the insufferable pangs of hell and damnation.' He evidently thought that it was suitable material for a young man like Richard Morgan. Cf. L. Tyerman, *Samuel Wesley*, 135–6.

his son should not fall into 'those over-zealous ways which . . . contributed to this great misfortune which finished my other son'. He wanted Richard brought up

'. . . a sober, virtuous and religious life, and to go to Church and sacrament according to the statutes and customs of his College; but for young people to pretend to be more pure and holy than the rest of mankind', he added sagely, 'is a dangerous experiment'.

He preferred that Richard should not make any charitable subscriptions since all that he had came from his father's allowance and was intended for 'his maintenance, education, and moderate and inoffensive recreation and pleasures'.[1]

Wesley replied to this letter on 17th December, 1733, giving a good report of Morgan,[2] and stressing that he had no intention of persuading him to join the Holy Club.

'All those gentlemen whom I have the happiness to converse with two or three times a week upon a religious account would oppose me to the utmost should I attempt to introduce among them one of whose prudence I had so short a trial and who was so little experienced in piety and charity.'

But Wesley did not realize the extent to which Morgan was reacting against the regime for which his tutor had commended him in his letter to his father. Although he was expected, he did not join John and Charles when they met together on the evening of 7th December. Four days later Wesley was reading Terence's plays with him and later corrected his declamation but showed some consternation when after talking with Morgan that evening, the young man strode off to the Senior Common Room. On Saturday, 15th December, Wesley finished reading Norris' discourses with him and the following evening was among the small company which included Charles and Broughton, which listened to a reading from Dr. Lucas, *On Happiness*. Wesley thought that he seemed 'affected' by this. Certainly he accompanied him to Communion at Christ Church the following Sunday. On the early morning of Christmas

---

[1] *Letters*, i, 143.

[2] 'Mr. Morgan usually rises about six, and has not yet been wanting in diligence. He seldom goes out of college unless upon business or to walk for his health, which I would willingly persuade him to do every day. He loses no time at taverns or coffeehouses, and avoids as much as possible idle company. . . . Some evenings every week he spends in the common-room, and others with my brother and me.'

Day, he read some passages from William Law and 'warned' him, presumably of the temptations afforded by the holiday season; in spite of this, he sat up to half-past four either on Christmas Day or the day following. Wesley at once reproached him and he acknowledged his fault. Subsequently he was introduced to Wesley's father, who had been staying in Oxford, and accompanied John and Charles to the coach to see him off on his return journey. Again, however, he made John angry by staying up to half-past five in the morning with his fellow gentleman commoner, William Thorold. Wesley told him that he must be careful of the company he kept, and that the Rector was against the kind of man with whom he had been recently associating. He again apologized but when they talked that evening, the atmosphere was 'heavy', in spite of which Morgan accompanied the brothers to Abingdon the next day and may have been cheered by some backgammon and cards and a reading of *The Mourner*. Wesley was, however, still uneasy, talked to the Rector about him on Saturday, 5th January, 1734, and again rebuked him that evening. He went to bed 'angry' and 'dejected', and felt that the best panacea for his erring pupil was a reading of Beveridge's sermon on the Straight Gate. Next Sunday he prescribed to a seemingly contrite youth a reading from Scougal's *Life of God in the Soul of Man* and it is hardly surprising to learn that he was 'warped again'. Wesley had certainly read out his father's letter to him[1] and he may well have considered that his tutor had given his father quite the wrong impression. Depressed by the atmosphere in which he was obliged to live and the continuous pressure which his tutor was bringing to bear upon him, he decided to pour out all his woes in a long letter to his father, describing the Holy Club and the life which he was obliged to lead.

He avowed his troubles frankly and fully. He told his father that the Wesleys sought to regulate his reading and to censor his friends.

'I am as much laughed at and despised by the whole town as any of them, and always shall be so while I am his pupil. The whole College makes a jest of me, and the Fellows themselves do not show me common civility, so great is their aversion to my tutor. . . .

'He has lectured me', Richard told his father, 'scarce in anything but books of devotion. He has given me a book of Mr. Nelson to abridge this Christmas. By becoming his pupil I am stigmatized with the name of a Methodist, the misfortune of which I cannot describe. . . . I think

[1] The entry for Wednesday, 5th December: '8.45 p.m. Morgan came . . . read Mr. Morgan's letter against strictness.'

it incumbent upon me to inform you that it is my opinion that if I am continued with Mr. Wesley I shall be ruined.'

The younger Morgan's feelings are easily understandable. The 'practical' Christianity of the Holy Club impinged upon soft consciences and made uncomfortable the more negligent conformity with Christian principle which has always been, and probably always will be, the characteristic of the majority of those who call themselves Christian. When to this demand for a higher standard is added the essential Puritanism of their conduct, we can understand why public opinion became somewhat inimical. Even Samuel Wesley felt its rigorism might be unduly excessive.

Before the letter was despatched, fate intervened in a curious way. At half-past three on the afternoon of 14th January, 1734, Wesley went to Morgan's room, had his attention drawn by the sight of the letter, read a few lines, the sense of which was sufficient to make him read the remainder, though this was in fact only half of the complete letter. He was naturally incensed and that evening confided to his diary that 'there was little prospect of Morgan because no sincerity in him'. At once he sat down to put straight what he regarded as the distortions in his pupil's letter, ascribing his hostility to the influence of evil companions,

'. . . men who retain something of outward decency, and nothing else; who seriously idle away the whole day, and reputedly revel till midnight'.

Morgan's father must have been greatly distressed by these events. He had already lost one son through religious enthusiasm, and was now made fearful that the other might be driven either to the extremes of religiosity or to dissipation. He comes out of the correspondence singularly well. He continued to give Wesley his support, but urged him to ensure that his son should not become a member of 'that strict society', a point upon which Wesley was very ready to reassure him. He enclosed a letter to his son, which he purposely left open for Wesley to read first, urging moderation and closer attention to his studies.

'What, Dick, did you so soon forget our stipulations and conditions on your going to the University, as to carry a greyhound with you to Oxford, and to attempt keeping him in your college, contrary to the rules of it? Did you not promise to stick to your studies and be as subservient to your tutor as if you were a Servitor? Go to bed by times; rise early. Omit no one College duty. Squander not away the morning in tea and chat.'

It is impossible not to feel that the elder Morgan was eminently sane and sensible. He had handled the crisis with great skill. Wesley had naturally felt aggrieved, the more so when he read the whole letter and heard from a Mr. Steer of a special plan that Morgan had had for annoying his tutor; but he, too, did not wish to lose the young's man's friendship. He lacked the imagination to see how he could have treated Morgan otherwise, and had Morgan been more mature and independent-minded Wesley might have alienated him for life. He talked with him and by Sunday, 20th January, 1734, only five days after the despatch of the letter, had convinced him that only 'few can be saved'. Although Morgan seems to have been but 'little affected' by reading Spenser with him, he was 'quite melted' by 4th February. On 26th February there was a heart-to-heart explanation and on 17th March Wesley felt that he had 'overborne' him. By the end of the month they were reading Law's *Serious Call*. The young Irishman was much more impressionable than his attempt at sophistication might suggest. His effort to win independence even at the cost of company of which Wesley disapproved had been effectively frustrated. He came more and more under the influence of Wesley's devoted pupil, James Hervey, and so joined the religious society of which he had at first been so suspicious. 'Mr. Morgan', Charles told John on 31st July, 1734, 'is in a fairer way of becoming a Christian than we ever yet knew him.' He was among the little company that saw the Wesleys off at Gravesend when they sailed for Georgia, and later wrote from Oxford where he continued to sponsor their work that he would himself very much like to join them in America. But ultimately he returned to Ireland where in due course he succeeded his father as Second Remembrancer to the Court of Exchequer at Dublin; and there, prosperous and respected, he was once more to entertain his old tutor on 15th July, 1769.

Thus, in spite of all the vicissitudes which attended its birth and growth, the Holy Club prospered. The attack in *Fog's Journal* had elicited a trenchant and compelling reply, reputed by some to have been written by William Law in *The Oxford Methodists, being some account of a Society of Young Gentlemen in that city, so denominated*, published at London in 1733. The author had gone to some trouble to make sure of his facts and used letters which Wesley had received from his father and from Mr. Hoole to substantiate his arguments. His informant, evidently Wesley himself, had stressed that

'Religion is a cheerful Thing, and the Satisfactions they reaped from the Sense of having perform'd what they took to be their Duty, however imperfectly, were greater and of a higher Nature, than any they had ever before experienc'd.'[1]

'It looks', commented the author, 'as if the strict Rule of primitive Christianity were remov'd a great way out of sight, that we are not able to behold the Attempt to revise them, without wonder and offence.'[2]

He ventured on a prophecy:

'. . . if it shall please God to give these Gentlemen the grace to persevere, and the Blessing of so long a Life, they may be the Means of reforming a vicious world: and may rejoice in the Good they have done, perhaps *Half a Century* after most of their *Social* Opponents, the gay Scoffers of the present Generation, are laid low, and forgotten, as if they had never been'.[3]

Whether it was indeed to be anything more than one of the many transitory religious societies to which the University gives birth history alone would show. Whatever John Wesley's own spiritual discontent, the story of the Holy Club was integral to his personal development as indeed it was also to the evolution of Methodism itself.

[1] *The Oxford Methodists*, 8.
[2] *Op. cit.*, 18.
[3] *Op. cit.*, 20.

CHAPTER X

The Cotswold Scene

FOR ten susceptible years John Wesley found solace and companionship among friends that he made in the three Cotswold villages of Buckland, Broadway, and 'dear, delightful' Stanton. Situated in the green vale of Evesham, quietly beautiful with their stone-built cottages and wooded glens, they provided a contrast with the windy, watery plain on which Epworth's miniature hillock rose, and there was an even sharper contrast in the cultivated and pleasant life of the clergy and gentry of the Cotswolds. The atmosphere of high endeavour and moral earnestness so characteristic of Epworth rectory was less obtrusive. There was no lack of religious conversation and of genuine piety but the sense of strain, rarely absent there, was happily lacking. There was, too, culture and refinement in the wider sense, not merely theological learning, but a general acquaintance with English literature, infused with something of the manners and customs of high society. The Granvilles were exceedingly well-connected; indeed their original presence at Buckland was more an accident of politics than anything else. The Winningtons were politically significant; Thomas Winnington was later to hold ministerial office and would have risen further had not he been cut off in the prime of life by the folly of his doctor. It was a pleasant, gay society, rural and yet not rustic, sociable and yet serious, into which John Wesley and his brother at first fitted happily.

There were five families among whom Wesley moved with domestic familiarity in the three villages, Buckland, Broadway and Stanton, which housed them. There were other acquaintances in the neighbourhood, the Allens of Guiting, the Freemans, the Smarts, the Deans, the Bradleys, the Fletchers, and Mr. Izod; but the names which recur time and again were the Tookers, the Granvilles, the Griffiths, the Kirkhams and to a less extent the Winningtons. The Rev. Trethewy Tooker, rector of Buckland from March 1714 until his death in January 1747, was a man of fifty in 1725; he had been educated at Christ Church, Oxford, and had been previously rector of Wheathill, Somerset. He was undoubtedly a clerical 'character', untidy, jovial and something of a buffoon.

> 'He never appeared to so little advantage as in the pulpit', Mrs. Pendarves wrote, 'and as companion a grazier's coat would have become him better than the clergyman's habit. He had a sort of droll wit and repartee that was diverting, but would have been more so, had it not been somewhat out of character and unbecoming the dignity of his profession. . . . He said he had a familiar that attended him; that he often appeared to him at home and abroad; warned him against danger, and advised him how to conduct himself in all exigencies. As much as I remember of Tranio's[1] conduct, I think did not do much honour to his familiar.'[2]

Tooker's Jacobite political views must have evoked a sympathetic response from young Wesley.

After the death of Anne and the accession of George I in 1714, a house in Buckland known as the Farm became the temporary home of the Granvilles. It was a comfortable, roomy place, 'neat furnished with home spun stuff, adorned with fine china and prints', looking on the Vale of Evesham, and backed by a high hill, Horrel.

> 'Nothing could be more fragrant and rural; the sheep and cows came bleating and lowing to the pales of the garden. At some distance on the left hand was a rookery; on the right a little clear brook runs winding through a copse of young elms . . . and fell with a cascade into the garden.'

The Granvilles were not, however, country gentry; in some sense they were political refugees.

> 'We were of the discontented party, and not without reason; not only my father, but all my relations that were in public employments, suffered greatly by this change. My father being a younger brother, his chief dependence was on the favour of the court and his brother's friendship, the first being withdrawn, he had recourse to the latter, and was offered by him a retreat in the country, and an addition to the small

---

[1] This was a nickname given to Tooker, following a fashionable habit of the time that was to make John Wesley Cyrus, his brother, Araspes, Mrs. Pendarves, Aspasia, her sister, Anne Granville, Selima, and others of their friends, Varanese, Sappho, and Serena.

[2] Lady Llanover, *The Autobiography and Correspondence of Mrs. Delany* (1861), i, 13–14.

remains of his fortune, he retired with my mother, my brother, my sister and myself.'

So wrote Mary Granville at a later date. Her father was a grandson of the Royalist general, Sir Bevil Granville, and a nephew of the Earl of Bath. He was the youngest son and married a daughter of Sir Martin West-comb, consul at Cadiz; his brother George, whom Queen Anne had created Lord Lansdowne, was a minor dramatist and litterateur. His sister Anne married Sir John Stanley, who was then secretary to Queen Anne's chamberlain, the Duke of Shrewsbury; as a little girl Mary Granville lived with them in Whitehall. Now with her mother and father, her brother Bernard and her sister Anne, she moved to the unfamiliar and at first unloved countryside. Fortunately they found the Tookers ready to wel-come them. They played whist with the rector and Mary, young, intelli-gent and beautiful, found a congenial companion in a Jacobite gentleman, a Mr. Twyford, a follower of Sir William Wyndham, who had taken shelter with the Tookers after Wyndham had come to terms with the government. She also made friends with the daughter of the neighbouring rectory, Sally Kirkham.

'We wrote to one another every day, and met in the fields between our fathers' houses as often as we had an opportunity, thought that day tedious that we did not meet, and had many stolen interviews.'

Mary Granville's life had, however, undergone many changes before she met John Wesley. Her father died in 1723 and her mother and her sister moved from Buckland to Gloucester. When she was staying with her uncle, Lord Lansdowne, she met a Cornish gentleman, a Mr. Alex-ander Pendarves, of Roscrow, and was pressed into marriage with him. She was seventeen and he was near sixty. It turned out most unfortunately.

'As to his person he was excessively fat, of a brown complexion, negligent in his dress, and took a vast quantity of snuff, which gave him a dirty look; his eyes were black, small, lively and sensible; he had an honest countenance, but altogether a person rather disgusting than engaging.'

Gromio, as she nicknamed him, was kindly and did not ill treat his wife; but he began to drink more than was good for him, and when he was sober, he was gloomy and sullen, 'which was infinitely worse to me than his drinking; for I did not know how to please or entertain him'. She found him dead beside her in bed in 1724, leaving her with only a medi-ocre fortune, 'but it was at my own command'. In the next few years she lived principally with her aunt, Lady Stanley, at Somerset House and Northend, moving once more in the first society; but she visited her mother and her sister at Gloucester, and her friends, the Kirkhams, at Stanton. It was here that John Wesley was to make her acquaintance.

The Kirkhams were the chief family in Stanton. The Rev. Lionel Kirkham had succeeded his father as rector in 1701, and his son Robert, who entered Merton College, Oxford, in 1729, probably succeeded him when he died in 1736.[1] There was also a younger son, Bernard, born in 1708, who matriculated at Corpus Christi College, Oxford, in 1735. Kirkham had three daughters, Sarah or Sally, born in 1699, Mary Elizabeth or Betty and Damaris, so named after her mother,[2] born 26th October, 1701. The Kirkhams were lively and hospitable. Sarah in particular was a young woman of good sense and fine sensibility. As a young girl she had been so much of a tomboy that Mary Granville's father had at first thought her an unsuitable companion for his daughter. She had the 'appearance of being too free and masculine', but he was soon won over by her 'extraordinary understanding, lively imagination and humane disposition'. Sally Kirkham was a gay, witty and sensible young woman to whom Wesley was immediately attracted.

The Winningtons were a county family who lived at Broadway. The best known member of the family was Thomas, the grandson of Sir Francis, and the second son of Salwey Winnington. He had been educated at Christ Church, where his stinginess earned him the name of 'Penny', but he had subscribed to the publication of Bishop Smalridge's sermons for which Wesley had a high regard. He was brought up a Tory, but saw where his bread was most likely to be buttered, and supported Walpole. His new allegiance won him the cherished reward of ministerial office. A nephew, Edward, was a contemporary of Wesley's at Trinity College, and his nieces, the daughters of his elder brother, Francis, who lived at Broadway, were friends of the Kirkhams. 'Who should I see at Court last night, nodding her head, but Molly Winnington?' Mary Pendarves wrote to her sister in February, 1734.[3]

The vicar of Broadway was John Griffiths, another Christ Church man who had been resident in Oxford as a chaplain at Magdalen. He

---

[1] The registers contain no mention of a rector's name until 1750, when Robert Kirkham signed as rector but he was signing the Overseers' books as chairman from 1745 and may have been rector from 1736. He died in March, 1767.

[2] It was also the name of an elder sister who died in infancy in 1698.

[3] Lady Llanover, *Autobiography and Correspondence of Mrs. Delany*, i, 428.

would seem to have been a bachelor of medicine as well as a master of arts and had been vicar of Broadway since June, 1703, when he was just under thirty years of age. His son John, better known as Robin, was a friend and contemporary of Wesley's, and a New College man; and his daughter Nancy soon became a close if inconstant acquaintance.[1] It seems very probable that it was through John Griffiths that Wesley was originally introduced to this Cotswold circle.

Although there can be little doubt that the friendships he made there only took second place in his development to those of his home and University, it is not easy to define exactly the content of this influence, which is far from unimportant. They offered him an opportunity to relax enjoyably; to pass the time in riding and walking, in cards and quadrilles, in singing and dancing and they provided a freer and more refined social atmosphere than that which Oxford or in certain respects Epworth could supply. Wesley was still in some ways a country boy when he came to Christ Church in spite of his education at Charterhouse and the contacts he made through his brother Samuel at Westminster. There may have remained a certain gaucherie which only slowly disappeared; 'those improprieties of behaviour', as he commented to Mrs. Pendarves in the autumn of 1730, 'in which my inexperience in the world so frequently betrays me'.

The social milieu there was however powerfully infused with an interest in spiritual matters. It has been surmised that Sally Kirkham was the 'religious' friend who introduced him to Thomas à Kempis; Wesley returned to Oxford from Stanton on 28th May, 1725, and the following day wrote to Epworth: 'I was lately advised to read Thomas à Kempis over, which I had frequently seen, but never much looked into before.' She may also have advised him to read Jeremy Taylor's *Holy Living and Dying*:

> 'I have heard one I take to be a person of good judgement say, that she would advise no one very young to read Dr. Taylor of *Living and Dying*; she added, that he almost put her out of her senses, when she was fifteen or sixteen years old, because he seemed to exclude all from being in a way of salvation who did not come up to his rules, some of which are altogether impracticable.'

Whether Sally was his spiritual guide or not, and the circumstantial evidence all points in this direction, the household at Stanton provided

[1] Mr. Swift tells me that the Broadway Registers record the baptism of Ann, the daughter of John and Elizabeth Griffiths, on 3rd June, 1708. John Griffiths died on 11th September, 1736.

ample opportunity for religious conversation. When he was there at Christmas, 1726, he talked of episcopal order and of mortification with Sally. On Christmas Day they discussed Vane's reasons for becoming a Roman Catholic and the state of the Church in the Indies, a dispute which roused Sally to unusual warmth; election and reprobation were some of the other topics which they talked about that Christmas vacation. All the young ladies, with the possible exception of Betty Kirkham, were genuinely desirous of self-improvement. The young, learned and attractive Oxford don, so eager to instruct others in the wisdom with which he fortified himself, found willing disciples. Mary Pendarves commented on the 'delight you take in not only entertaining but improving all those you converse with'. These lively young women formed a more responsive audience than the bored young men who later gathered to hear him discourse on the Greek New Testament in Lincoln College hall, or scanned Aldrich's compendium of logic in his rooms in the Chapel quad. It was pleasant to sit under the beech trees on Horrel's turf and look over to Stanton's spire and grey roofs while the young don spoke gravely on serious topics to his eager audience.

'I hope', he wrote to Anne Granville on 14th August, 1731, 'to retain some of the reflections which the smooth turf on which we sat, the trees overshadowing and surrounding us, the fields and meadows beneath, and the opposite hills, with the setting sun just glimmering over their brows, assisted Aspasia [Mary Pendarves] and Selima [Anne Granville] in inspiring.'[1]

These connections with the Cotswold families are also important for the part they played in Wesley's emotional development. He mixed freely with these young ladies of much the same age as his own,[2] flirted with them innocently, and indulged in intimate conversations and exchanged confidences. It is rarely of the young men of the district, Bob Kirkham, Harry Yardley, or young Winnington, that we read in the diary. It was the young women, and especially Sally Kirkham, or Varanese[3] as she

[1] *Letters*, i, 105.

[2] Sally Kirkham was twenty-six in 1725; Damaris was twenty-four; Mary Pendarves twenty-five; Nancy Griffiths was seventeen; John Wesley was twenty-two.

[3] M. Augustin Léger challenged the identification of Varanese with Betty Kirkham in his *La Jeunesse de Wesley* (1910), p. 97; but authors have continued to identify Betty with Varanese (e.g. J. M. Todd, *John Wesley and the Catholic Church* (1958), 36, 42), in spite of the conclusive argument put forward by Mrs. Harrison in her *Son to Susanna* (1937, Penguin edn., pp. 40–1). Cf. *W.H.S. Proceedings*, viii, 147–8. *It can now be stated categorically that Varanese was Sarah Kirkham.*

was christened by her particular friends, to whom he was attracted. Such attraction bordered on and could easily grow into love. When he visited Stanton in April, 1725, he had but recently heard from his sister Emily, a passionate, despairing letter of a woman whose love had been frustrated:[1]

'. . . whether you will be engaged before thirty or not I cannot determine; but if my advice is worth listening to, never engage your affections before your worldly affairs are in such a posture that you may marry very soon . . . were I to live my time over again and had the same experience I have now, were it for the best man in England I would not wait one year. I know you are a young man encompassed with difficulties that has passed through many hardships already . . . but believe me if ever you come to suffer the torment of a hopeless love all other afflictions will seem small in comparison of it.'

The letter was written from Epworth on 7th April, 1725; less than a fortnight later he noted in his diary 'first saw Varanese. May it not be in vain.'

John Wesley was in love with Sally Kirkham. He may for a moment have considered the possibility of marriage; he discussed the question of marriage with Robin Griffiths the day after his ordination. But he must have realized the basic good sense of his sister's remarks. As a recently ordained priest, expectant of a College fellowship, who was still in debt, who came from an impoverished family which lacked patronage, Wesley had nothing whatever to offer a wife. Sally's marriage to the local schoolmaster, John Chapone, had been already arranged, and took place on Wednesday, 28th December, 1725. Wesley, who had ridden from Oxford the previous day, was in the church and afterwards wrote in his diary, 'May God give her the happiness she deserves.' There is every evidence that Sally, who had five children, was in love with her husband. 'Sally', Mary told Anne Granville, 'is grown a conjugal creature and so fond of her husband, that it is full of nothing but "caro sposo".' Yet Wesley remained in love with Sally and Sally perhaps a little in love with him.

'I would certainly tell you', she told him in the autumn of 1726, 'if my husband should ever resent our freedom, which I am satisfied he never will; such an accident as this would make it necessary to restrain in some measure the appearance of the esteem I have to you, but the esteem as it is grounded on reason and virtue and entirely agreeable to us both, no circumstance of life will ever make me alter.'

[1] Stevenson, *Memorials of the Wesley Family.*

Later that evening as he sat with Sally and her sister, he leaned on her breast and clasped both her hands in his, and while her sister looked on tenderly, she said many 'obliging things'.

Was Wesley, then, to suffer, in the words of his sister Emily, 'the torments of a hopeless love'? There must have been regrets as he sat talking with Sally in the arbour or on Horrel, but the full consummation of marriage was something of which he felt and fought shy. There were tender words and soft sentiments but the flame burned low and was easily dimmed. He felt himself emotionally engaged but the engagement was inhibited by religious and psychological factors. His treatment of moral questions was at this time increasingly affected by his knowledge of early Church history and patristic teaching; he knew very well the grave suspicion with which the Fathers had regarded not merely irregular sexual relations, but anything which encouraged carnal feeling. When he was in London he sought to persuade his sister Hetty of the virtue of celibacy; he noted in his diary on Sunday, 26th August, 1733, that he had written a prayer for celibacy. It is interesting that Sally Chapone drew his attention to Mrs. Astell's proposal for establishing a Protestant nunnery, revealing perhaps her own one-time attitude to the problem of marriage,[1] and he was greatly impressed by Mrs. Astell's arguments. Sally, he told Anne Granville,

'. . . showed us her proposal to the ladies, which gave us several agreeable conversations. Surely her plan of female life must have pleased all the thinking part of her sex, had she not prescribed so much of the two dull things, reading and religion.'[2]

The lighthearted tone, adopted no doubt to please his correspondent, veiled his underlying suspicion, and perhaps fear, of a love that involved physical contact. He warned his followers at a later date of the dangers and temptations involved in meetings with women:

[1] Mary Astell (1668–1731) settled in London where she was a neighbour and acquaintance of Dean Atterbury. She was a close friend of Lady Elizabeth Hastings and had been a correspondent of John Norris of Bemerton. In her *Serious Proposal to Ladies* (1694) she proposed the establishment of a Protestant nunnery or rather a religious retirement, 'being not only a retreat from the world . . . but likewise an institution and previous discipline to fit us to do the greatest good in it'. There were to be no permanent vows or irrevocable obligations. It was to be conducted on Anglican lines with services 'after the Cathedral manner'; the Communion was to be celebrated every Sunday and holy day.

[2] *Letters*, i, 88–9.

P

'. . . on this and every occasion', he told them, 'avoid all familiarity with women. This is a deadly poison both to them and to you. You cannot be too wary in this respect.'

Whenever therefore the possibility of marriage loomed near, as it did in later years with Sophia Hopkey and with Grace Murray,[1] he fought shy of the final overture which would lead to the altar: his eventual marriage with Molly Vazeille on all accounts turned out disastrously. The relationship with Varanese, already married to John Chapone, was deeply happy, tender, sentimental, but void of passion. It was in part a marriage of minds and in part a marriage of souls, even if its foundation was physical attraction. His sister, Hetty, may have hit the nail on the head when she said that her brother liked a woman 'merely for being woman'. Later in March, 1731, his sister Martha, writing to him about her own involved relations with a Mr. Johnson, who was courting her, and John's suggestion that his own pupil, Matthew Horbery, might prove a likely suitor, stated that their sister Mary commented that she, Martha,

'. . . was just going after Mrs. Chapone and you, and she has mistaken charity as to wish to see me buried alive rather than I should love Mr. Horbery as well as Mrs. Chapone does you'.

Wesley would doubtless have at one time liked Sally to be his wife, but it was not to be nor in his heart of hearts did he really regret it. It was again Martha who said bluntly,

'Had you not lost your dear Mrs. C——n, where had your love been fixed? On heaven, I hope, principally: but a large share, too, had been hers: you would not have been so spiritualized, but something of this lower world would have had its part in your heart, wise as you are; but being deprived of her there went all hope of worldly happiness: and now the mind, which is an active principle, losing its aim here, has fixed on its Maker for happiness.'

It is, however, legitimate to ask whether the religious factor was the only one at work and whether it in its turn may not have veiled a psychological impediment to full sexual integration. Psychologically there are two profoundly significant aspects of his personality. The first is his basic reticence about himself. He wrote millions of words about his life. He did not merely write a day-to-day diary but he spent hours transcribing it and writing an abridgement of the transcription, and in his early years

---

[1] See A. Léger, *John Wesley's Last Love*.

sometimes wrote an annual abridgement of the abridged diary. These millions of words give an hour-to-hour, sometimes a minute-to-minute account of his daily activities, so that it is possible to say, except for the two or three years for which no diary is known to exist, what Wesley was doing on any day in any year between 1725 and 1791, and in the detailed earlier diaries (which ended in August, 1741) what he was doing at any time of the day on any day. Yet although there is much that reveals his thoughts about religion and the state of his soul, the personal conflicts, the genuine inner tensions, are buried, so much so that in some respects the great *Journal* is a singularly colourless document. He did not really bare the depths of his personality. With this reticence there must be associated an immaturity of outlook which persisted to old age. In many matters he remained astonishingly naïve for so intelligent and observant a man; he was also emotionally immature.[1] Moreover it has been long recognized that he compared his female friends with the figure of his mother, and found them wanting. They could be his confidantes but they would not provide the support he wanted. His religion allowed him less and less time for love, and paradoxically, because of the way in which he tried to spread the love of God abroad among his fellow-men, the real intimacy of love, whether of man for man or of man for woman, passed him by.

It is against this background that Wesley's relations with his friends in the Cotswolds have to be placed. It must have been at the instance of his friend, John Griffiths, of New College, the son of the vicar of Broadway, that he was first invited to Buckland and Stanton. There were indeed other Oxford connections; Edward Winnington, with whom he sat at the Greyhound on 25th October, 1725, was at Trinity; Harry Yardley, who had recently taken his degree at Trinity (of which he became a fellow), came from nearby Notgrove; but it was at Griffiths' invitation that he stayed in the Cotswolds and saw his beloved Varanese and met the Tookers. Tooker was with him for two days in Oxford in June and he had begun a regular correspondence with Nancy Griffiths and Sally Kirkham. He hired a horse to visit Broadway on Monday, 29th August, 1725, and was back at Oxford by 8th September; the entry which he put in his diary that evening, 'lying, detraction, sin in thought', suggests that

[1] In 1767 he published a tract on masturbation, *Thoughts on the Sin of Onan*. This was adapted from the work of Dr. Tissot, which he described as a 'most fulsome and shocking performance', and a French tract lately translated into English, much of which 'most of the London street-walkers would be ashamed to read aloud'.

he was indulging in self-recrimination evoked by what he felt he had said and thought during his visit. After sitting gloomily with Watkins of Wadham on his return from the Cotswolds on 30th October, 1725, Wesley confided that he had been guilty of 'lying, rash judgment, idleness, sins'. These self-accusations, though by no means abnormal on Saturday evenings, must have had something to do with his feelings for Sally, the realization that there was no prospect or possibility of marriage and the depression to which this must have given rise.

Although he continued to correspond with his friends, he did not stay with them until October 1726. His election to a fellowship at Lincoln may have given him additional social reassurance and he rode down to Buckland with his colleague, Richard Hutchins, who had a brother in the neighbourhood. His first morning he went out hunting with Winnington but in the afternoon he rode over to Stanton where he found only Damaris at home. The next day, after reading Lewis' poems to Miss Fanny Tooker in the morning, he walked over to Stanton and found a gay company assembled, including Mr. Chapone and his wife and Mary Pendarves. It was a pleasant and a carefree holiday, what with hunting and riding on the hills with Robin Griffiths and his father, supping at Buckland with the Tookers, and walking home to Broadway, lighted by the glow of the aurora borealis.[1] He played quoits and cards (and lost), dined with Mr. Dean, chatted with the Miss Winningtons, read a life of General Monk, Congreve's *The Way of the World* and one of his favourites, *The Song of the Three Children*, probably in his brother's poetic paraphrase. On his two Sundays he took the services and preached at Buckland and Stanton.

Yet it was a visit infused for Wesley with strong emotion. His feeling for Sally Chapone had grown rather than diminished. There is reason to think that her unmarried sister, and possibly Nancy Griffiths, may on their part have been attracted to the little man, so neat and precise, yet romanticized by the dark locks falling on his shoulder. Damaris asked him to come to Stanton without 'M', whose bad temper irritated her; she told Wesley that she was afraid that 'M' thought she, Damaris, loved Wesley

[1] Saturday, 8th October, 1726: 'Walked with Nancy to Buckland. Supper there. Aurora Borealis appearing by turns of all colours, chief red or brick colour. At ye height at 8, and very visible at 12, lighted home by it.' Cf. Hearne's entry in *Collectanea* for 10th October (ix, 202): 'On Saturday night last was a very great and remarkable Aurora Borealis, it having that day, and a day or two before, wonderfull fine Weather. It began about six Clock, & lasted a great part of the night. . . . The sky was very red, and flashes & Darts of Lightning were very frequent and frightfull from all Quarters.'

more than she did him. On another evening after Sally had gone to bed Damaris came and sat by him, professing her friendship; two days later as they sat together, Wesley told her that he wanted exactly the same freedom with her as with his sisters. She replied that he had it and on leaving for bed said to him, 'Good night, brother.' It is possible that Damaris would have wished for more, especially if the anonymous 'M', who appeared to Wesley to be 'jealous and ill-humoured', was her suitor. But Wesley sought to assure them both that his friendship was that of a brother for his sisters. He walked with them up Horrel Hill, and talked with Sally of his deep feeling for her.

'I were reflecting as we came hither, whether if we were to die immediately, the action we were upon would give us any pain; and we both agreed, in such a circumstance, this design would give us much more pleasure than travail.

'You know,' Wesley went on, 'you make me a little uncomfortable and I think it is almost sinful to use the expressions of tenderness which I use in relation to you in relation to other people. It isn't expedient or right to break off our friendship. It is one of my main incentives to virtue.'

'I never read over your last letter without tears,' Sally said feelingly, 'it animates my soul anew and gives it fresh vigour in any good design I have in view.'

Two days later, sitting on Horrel again, Wesley told both the sisters that 'in spite of the wise maxims of our sex I am not ashamed to say that I love you sincerely'. Sally replied that they hoped they were not 'behindhand' with Nancy, a reference which suggests that Nancy Griffiths resented the way Wesley was paying court to the Kirkham sisters rather than to her. The previous evening Wesley had noted that he believed Nancy to be false because she spoke against him behind his back. Sally went on to reassure Wesley that she loved him more than all mankind, except her father and her husband, and believed that Damaris did so too, though a maid must not say so much. Perhaps Damaris loved more than she could readily reveal. Just before Wesley left for Oxford she told him that she did not really love 'L' and besought Wesley to come over to Stanton in 'L's' company because she feared that 'L' might be angry.

Damaris' sister Betty was sooner or later also drawn within the companionable circle. 'Ask, I pray you,' his sister Mary had written on 30th January, 1726, 'Miss Betsy to buy me a little silk to knit you another pair of gloves, and I am sure the colour will doubly please you because of the

buyer.' Betsy's brother Bob wrote to Wesley on 2nd February, 1727, to tell him that 'you have often been in the thoughts of Miss Betsey, which I have curiously observed, when with her alone, by inward smiles and sighs and abrupt expressions concerning *you*. Shall this suffice? I caught her this morning in an humble and devout posture on her knees.' Wesley was already enmeshed in the toils. 'Had he', he had asked himself some weeks earlier, 'loved woman or company more than God?'

He was back with his friends in the Cotswolds for Christmas. He slept the first night at Broadway and then rode over next day to visit his friends at Stanton and Buckland; one of the first things he had to do was to clear up the misunderstanding that had developed with Nancy Griffiths. He may have done so to his own satisfaction, although he had a nightmare that night, and the next day talked with Varanese of his friendship with Nancy, but a later reference suggests that the two sisters remained at loggerheads with their neighbour from Broadway.

During his visit Wesley set out deliberately to be entertaining, thinking of topics which might be the subject of conversation. Indeed his friends' conversation covered a wide field over the Christmas holidays; they discussed reason in brutes and the breathing of flowers and fishes, a theme much in his mind as he was making it the subject of one of his exercises for his master's degree, the price of corn and the isle of Axholme, spirits and nightmares (at Mr. Cheshire's on Christmas Eve), law and juries (with Mr. Kirkham), horses and excisemen, the cases tried before Judge Price at the Exchequer, astronomy and comets, and the reason why physicians tend to be commonly atheists (with Mrs. Chapone), the use of languages, especially Arabic, and the current ode of Barreux in the *Spectator*. Conversation was free, polished and informed, and if from time to time as became countrymen it turned to talk of sheep, horses and corn, it was easily shifted to other matters. There was plenty of opportunity for reading aloud the long dark Christmas evenings, *Gulliver's Travels*[1] (which had so seized Wesley's imagination that having read it through at Oxford he read it aloud at Stanton), Nicholas Rowe's tragedies, *The Ambitious Stepmother*, *Lady Jane Grey* and *The Royal Convert*, Thomas Otway's *Venice Preserved*, Somerville's poems,[2] Shakespeare's *Othello*. Each evening saw some form of entertainment, generally cards, ombre,

[1] Dean Swift's *Travels into Several Remote Nations of the World by Lemuel Gulliver* was published in 1726.

[2] William Somerville's *The Two Springs* was published in 1725; his *Occasional Poems* in 1727.

loo, Pope Joan, and sometimes dancing; on the evening of Thursday, 5th January, 1727, they danced from dinner till seven and from supper to eleven. The merriment was such that Miss Fanny Tooker was kissed 'as timely by Mr. Smart as could be wished'. She blushed and excused herself but the incident was amusing. 'She was noted for good humours', Mrs. Kirkham told him, 'ever since she was a year old', and 'shy only to those she disliked'.[1] Before Wesley tumbled into bed at midnight he confided to his diary that Mrs. Freeman was a 'wonderful lovely woman'.

There were such frequent gaieties during the cold winter days that Wesley had less time than usual for serious reading; but on Christmas Day, 1726, he preached on the nature of the sacrament, affirming that its antiquity should not be stressed and that it should be regarded as an object of love rather than of fear. Amid the laughter and games he found time to read some Horace, Scheibler's *Metaphysica*, Lowth's *Directions for the Profitable Study of the Scriptures* and the *Count de Gabalis or the Extravagant Mysteries of the Cabalists*. Yet there must have been moments when his conscience demanded whether life was not too enjoyable and insufficiently strenuous.

His dalliance with the ladies continued. Hearing of a former suitor of Sally's, a Mr. Radcliff, he resolved to get to know him instantly, a resolution which curiously followed an earlier vow to give up no more time to trifles. His relations with the Kirkham sisters were, however, in his view no trifling matter. Nancy Griffiths was still in the picture, albeit viewed perhaps with some disfavour by Sally and Damaris. Damaris, 'the most artful in the family', and Betty still lingered in his presence. Indeed the latter was so affected by his reading of *Gulliver's Travels* that at the words 'Take care of this, gentle Yahoo', she burst into tears and rushed from the room. They talked gaily and seriously in the kitchen—Mary Pendarves was staying with them and was often one of the company—as the wind and the rain lashed the house.[2] Damaris cried out that she wished she had been a man for Wesley's sake. Varanese talked of her previous love affairs and of how she had once sworn she would only marry a wit. After finishing a game of ombre he followed Aspasia (Mrs. Pendarves) into the kitchen and on his saying 'how prettily shall we reflect on our past lives thirty or forty years hence?' she burst into tears and said that she should

[1] Cf. Wesley's other comments on M.T. in his diary: 'Not ungrateful but not grateful to the Granville's' (30th December, 1726); 'a little out of humor; irreverent to her father' (31st December, 1726).

[2] 'Very stormy' (8th January, 1727).

tell him then why she would never marry. Wesley raised the name of a possible suitor, L. She was taken aback and said that he had artfully wormed a secret from her. The conversation turned to sleeping and presumably the difficulty Aspasia found in early rising. Obsessed by the importance of the topic Wesley offered to wake her but she told him she could not say whether she would rise even if he did call her. He called in vain and she came down at ten, saying that she could not bear getting up when it was snowing. When he walked part of the way home with Betty a few days later, the talk was appropriately enough of loving husbands. Yet it was the incomparable Varanese who still undoubtedly held the chief place in his affections, while she still held him in loving esteem.

'When I first saw you', she told him, 'the utmost I desired was to take my hand round your neck. . . . This, this only a desire now. I was afraid then; it was only the improbability of attaining them that made me so moderate in my wishes. I could hardly presume that you would ever condescend so far. . . . The greatest pleasures of my life, I freely own, have been owing to friendship; in the number of my friends there is no one, I see, and always shall, in a stronger view than you.'

It was love, but love shorn of passion and suffused by sentiment.

The day after this conversation tragedy suddenly shattered the winter scene. On Thursday, 5th January, 1727, he had walked over to see Robin Griffiths and his father; on the 10th he heard that Robin was dead. At once he rode over to see the parents and found them bearing their bereavement nobly 'with regular, solemn sadness'. He offered to preach at the funeral and returning began to write his sermon; his heart can hardly have been in the game of cards he played that evening and little wonder that he lost. He had known that Robin was ill,[1] but the sense of loss was no less poignant. Only eighteen months earlier they had attended the funeral service of a young lady in Oxford with whom they had been friendly. While they waited Wesley had asked Robin in a whisper if he really thought he was his friend and if he did, why he did not show him all the good he could. Robin protested but Wesley intervened, besought him to be a whole Christian, 'to which I knew he was at least half persuaded already'. As a result he had 'turned exceedingly serious and kept something of that disposition ever since'. And now he had gone, and Wesley was preparing at Robin's own desire his funeral sermon. Robin had been,

[1] 'Yesterday was a fortnight, he died of a consumption. I saw him three days before he died.' (*Letters*, i, 40–1.) The sermon on 2 Samuel xii, 23, was printed in the *Arminian Magazine* (1797), 422–6.

Wesley remarked, 'to his parents an affectionate, dutiful son; to his acquaintances, an ingenious, cheerful, good-natured companion; and to me, a well-tried, serious friend'.

It was an upsetting close to his visit to the Cotswolds, made perhaps the more so for Wesley by Damaris telling him that she believed Mr. Chapone to be jealous. He went back to his life at Oxford but he could not forget easily the shock of Robin's death. His faith would not allow him to mourn. He disposed of the gown which the Griffiths sent to him, perhaps to his brother. He worked at the transcription of Fenelon's *Discourse on Simplicity* for Varanese, but another milestone in his life had been passed.

The lack of a diary from February, 1727, to May, 1729, makes the task of the historian of Wesley's relations with his Cotswold friends most difficult. He must indeed have visited them, but his relationship with Sally Chapone had become more formal as her devotion to her husband and to her children strengthened. If Bob Kirkham is to be trusted, Betty seemed to have her eye still on Wesley, but she was married in 1730 to a Mr. Wilson, possibly from Birmingham. The sturdy, jovial Bob, preparing for entry at Merton, Oxford, made an indifferent correspondent,[1] but at least he justified the brevity of his letter by the graphic excuse he offered:

> 'I am just going down to a dinner of calves' head and bacon, with some of the best green cabbages in the town. I wish I could send you a plate of our entertainment while it is hot. We just tapped a barrel of admirable cider.'[2]

He emerged from dinner 'with a belly-full' to remind his correspondent of Betty's ardour and with the frankness of a sixteen-year-old revealed that 'Your most deserving, queer character—your worthy personal accomplishments,—your noble endowments of mind,—your little and handsome person, and your obliging and desirable conversation, have been the pleasing subject of our discourse for some pleasant hours.' The

---

[1] 'I am condemned for brevity before I could put forth my defence. My plea is, I writ yours, as likewise one to Harry Yardley, of equal importance in the space of three hours. My letter was really longer than yours by Scripture proof; for you writ scarce much out of your abundance of thoughts; whereas I writ all that I thought of, and thought of all I could write . . .

> 'For when you write, smooth elocution flows:
> But when Bob scrawls, rough ignorance he shows.'

[2] Letter of 2nd February, 1727 (L. Tyerman, *Wesley*, i, 49).

Kirkhams must have found it difficult to know exactly how to take the little Oxford don, but they were kindly and hospitable folk who recognized his true worth.

In his years as a resident tutor at Lincoln College he visited them with fair frequency, though he did not make many long stays. He was there in June and again in August, 1729. The pattern of these and of later visits remained similar. He engaged in serious talk and religious discussion with Sally and her friends on walks up Horrel Hill or sitting in the garden arbour in the rectory or at Mr. Izod's, and he took his part in dancing and quadrilles, singing and cards. He read to his young friends the *Art of Thinking* and his brother Samuel's poem, *The Pig and the Mastiff*. A discussion with Sally over Locke's ideas generated some heat. Another day he was introduced to Betty's future husband, Mr. Wilson, of Birmingham.

He was there again for a few days in May, 1730, when he visited the Winningtons, where there were tea, music and dancing, and for a rather longer period in August when he preached and read prayers in Stanton Church. He was also employed in rather more domestic tasks, gathering fruit with Mrs. Fletcher, and helping Mrs. Kirkham make sillabub; later he entertained the ladies with a reading of Lewis' poems. Mary Pendarves and her sister, Anne Granville, were staying there at the time, and Mary's request for a copy of a sermon she had heard him preach led to a regular correspondence, and, on Wesley's side at least, to another of those relationships which verged on love.

Neither Mary Pendarves, whom he had christened Aspasia, nor her sister Anne (or Selima) lived any longer at Buckland. Mary Pendarves spent most of her time with Sir John and Lady Stanley in Whitehall and in close proximity to the court and high society, while her sister, Anne Granville, who was as yet unmarried, made her home with her mother at Gloucester, where Wesley visited them in October, 1730, and May, 1732. John Wesley was never in love with Mary Pendarves in the sense that he was in love with Sally Chapone, but the occasional glimpses that he caught of her at Stanton or on a short visit to Oxford as well as her thoughtful letters greatly touched him. He acknowledged that in the first instance he enjoyed writing because she evoked the image of their mutual friend, dear inimitable Varanese. It aroused that 'soft emotion with which I glow even at the moment, while I consider myself as conversing with a kindred soul of my Varanese'. But slowly the stronger personality of Aspasia seemed to replace the softer sway of Sally. He did not indeed differentiate between his friends—

'I often pour out my heart by myself, when it is full of Selima and Aspasia and Varanese. Thus I endeavour to steal into their protection . . .'

but the picture of Aspasia grew more luminous. He was full of praise. 'If your understanding could not appear in a stronger light than when it brightened the dear hill [he meant Horrel], the field, the arbour, I am now forced to confess your temper could; you even then showed but half your goodness.' He imagined her and her sister lighting up the garden at Stanton like the sun. She and her sister

'. . . would have appeared even in that faint light which the moon glimmering through the trees poured on that part of our garden where I was walking! how little would the eye of the mind that surveyed them have missed the absent sun!'

Gradually the compliments became less stilted and more genuine. He tells her he feels similar emotions to those 'with which my heart frequently overflowed, in the beginning of my intercourse with our dear Varanese'. He felt too the same instinctive feeling that it was an affection which because of its unavailing outcome would be similarly tinged with melancholy.

'I perceive that I am making another avenue for grief, that I am laying open another part of my soul, at which the arrows of fortune may enter. . . . Should one to whom I was united by the tenderest tie, who was as my own soul, be torn from me, it would be best for me. . . . Surely if you were called first mine ought not to overflow because all tears were wiped from your eyes. . . . Tell me, Aspasia; tell me, Selima, if it be a fault that my heart burns within me when I reflect on the many marks of regard you have already shown.'

In spite of the inclusion of Selima's name, this sounded very like a declaration of love; if John Wesley had had a little more encouragement from Mary Pendarves he would have been more forward still, though doubtless he would have hesitated before crossing the Rubicon into the unexplored territory of married life.

Mary Pendarves was not, however, in love with John Wesley. She was a woman of intelligence and charm who discovered in him much to admire. For a time at least she found the correspondence a spiritually exciting experience. She was often genuinely bored with the trivialities and irreligion of the social circles in which she moved. Both she and her sister regarded Wesley as a preceptor in religious matters as 'two pupils who are desirous of improving their understanding and friendship'. They admired him for his rectitude and devotion to principle, and consulted him as to what they should do and what they should believe. Mary Pendarves had been to two operas: 'I hope it is not a fault to be transported by music.' What of music on Sundays? What advice should be given to a young friend who found the fulfilment of her religious obligations unrewarding?

To all these and other questions Wesley replied gravely and conscientiously. He told Anne Granville that in addition to her studies in divinity, she should undertake work in history and poetry. He seems in part at least to have undertaken an abridgement of the Bishop of Cork's work for their benefit.[1] And all the time he reiterated his indebtedness to their friendship. 'How gladly do I fly to you, how earnestly do I hope for your assistance?' 'You have kept yourself unspotted from the world; I am sullied with many stains.' 'While I read your letters I find myself carried above the world.' The religious advice and the sententious morality were intertwined with tenderness; 'I have a thousand things to say', he told Mary Pendarves. 'I cannot say half of what I feel.'

The ultimate outcome could be foreseen. Mary Pendarves was an admirable, cultured woman, refined and sensitive but she was a woman of the world. She liked its vivid life. Her letters to her sister are full of accounts of balls and operas, with graphic descriptions of fashion and society. She would not knowingly have hurt his feelings, and she was flattered by his attentions; but she must have been puzzled by his intense earnestness. She valued his advice but she would have found his presence in her London home just a little embarrassing. She did not wish to be too involved. It seems likely that the Bishop of Cork's abridgement remained unread,[2] and that some of the sentiments in her letters were included rather because she thought they would please her correspondent than because she was genuinely concerned with the questions she was raising. When the pressure of social activities forbade a response to his letters, she wrote in a pleasantly contrite fashion, but the time might come when even John Wesley would perceive its underlying note of insincerity.

This was, however, not the case in 1730 nor in 1731. Sally Chapone had

---

[1] *The Procedure, Extent and Limits of the Understanding*, 103 pp., dated Christmas Eve, 1730, consisted of two books, 'The Ideas of Sensation', and 'Pure Intellect, Knowledge and Evidence'.

[2] Both she and her sister commented on the difficulty of reading Wesley's abbreviations, an objection with which the writer sympathizes; cf. *Letters*, i, 78, 83.

a daughter, Sarah, to whom Mary Pendarves and her sister acted as god-mothers. In October Wesley stayed with Mrs. Granville at Gloucester, his arrival delayed by the fact that his horse ran away from him, and was entertained with music and a visit to the College. He talked with another of her guests, a Mr. Castleman, quite possibly the fellow of All Souls of that name, and read Edward Young's poem on the *Last Days*. At the beginning of November Mrs. Pendarves and her sister visited Wesley on their way to London from Gloucester. 'When we go to town we shall call at Oxford. We don't know at what college to inquire after our agreeable friends.' John and his brother rode out to accompany the coach in which their sisters and their mother were travelling from Burford.[1] He entertained them with tea, and next morning joined their brother and uncle, Lord Lansdowne, at the Bear, before the sisters set off for London.

> 'Our journey ended with as good success, though not altogether so much satisfaction, as it begun. The company in the coach were tolerably entertaining and very complaisant. . . . The life of noise and vanity that is commonly led here cannot possibly afford any entertainment for you. When we have an opportunity of conversing with a reasonable friend, we wish that Cyrus [John Wesley] and Araspes [Charles] were added to the company.'

John was at Stanton three times in 1731. In May, 1731, he took services in Stanton Church, walked to Horrel and sat in Varanese's arbour before breakfast. He breakfasted with the Winningtons, and read Prior's poems to Damaris. He spent some time at Broadway with Nancy but was caught in the heavy rain returning to Stanton where the evening ended with cards. He read Lewis' poems and David Mallet's play, *Eurydice*, to the company, but kept de Renty's life to read aloud to Varanese in the garden arbour. It must have been at this time that Sally introduced Mrs. Astell's *Proposal* to him, a work which at once attracted him and which he mentioned to the Granvilles. They had a picnic tea on a haystack one Saturday afternoon and on Sunday evening, having preached and taken prayers earlier, he was 'much tempted' to play cards in the evening. He

---

[1] On 3rd November, 1730, he wrote: 'For the sake of those less experienced travellers who have the cold hills beyond Burford to go over, I shall greatly wish that these sharp winds may either stay with us or be quite gone before Monday.' Mrs. Pendarves wrote to him on 19th November: 'The pleasure you and your brother gave us of your conversation at Burford, the entertainment we had upon the road to Oxford, which neither the dirty way nor rattling wheels could entirely deprive us of . . .' (*Letters*, i, 60, 61).

rose at a quarter to three (having gone to bed at half-past twelve the same morning) and after Damaris had given him breakfast, he set out for Oxford at four. The only regret he felt was the absence of Aspasia. On his walks with Varanese, in the 'almost uninterrupted conversation' with her, they had pointed to where she sat or walked, 'reflections which, though extremely obvious, yet could not but be equally pleasing, but give a new degree of beauty to the charming arbour, the fields, the meadows and Horrel itself'.[1]

He was again in the Cotswolds in September, 1731. On his arrival he was disappointed to find only Damaris at the rectory, but the next day he talked with Varanese and met her future protégé, Elizabeth Elstob, the Anglo-Saxon scholar who was acting as a schoolmistress in the neighbourhood to eke out the livelihood which enabled her to follow her unusual studies.[2]

The summer of 1732 saw the friends together again. Wesley had written regularly to Aspasia and to Selima in the preceding months. He was as eager as ever, avid for her letters, urging her to write oftener and seeking her opinions on whether he was guilty of being too strict in religion. Mrs. Pendarves replied cautiously to this last question.[3] She was perhaps getting just a little bored with the correspondence as preparations for her trip to Ireland where she was to stay with the Wesleys of Dangan went forward. He observed he had told her at the beginning of 1731 that he had noticed 'strange intimations you have sometimes given of being afraid to converse with me'. Her correspondence with Wesley (and indeed with Sally Chapone also) got behind hand; 'Is it utterly impossible that I should hear a little oftener from dear Aspasia?' Already she had to find excuses to justify her failure to reply to his importunate letters.

[1] Cf. letter of 17th June, 1731: 'We had so much pleasure in the late hours we spent at Stanton, that nothing could have added to it but Selima or Aspasia' (*Letters*, i, 88).

[2] 'September 12, 4.45 p.m. Mrs. Elstob; 13th, 2 p.m. Mrs. Elstob.' Later he read her *Anglo-Saxon Homilies*. Cf. her letter of 17th August, 1735, to George Ballard. She told him that she was kept busy at school 'till six at night when I have the duty of the day and am then frequently so fatigu'd that I am obliged to lye down for an hour or two to rest myself and recover my Spirits' (*Ballard MSS.*, xliii, 5–6).

[3] 'The imputation thrown upon you is a most extraordinary one; but such is the temper of the world, where you have no vice to feed their spleen with they will condemn the highest virtue. O Cyrus, how noble a defence you make, and how you are adorned with the beauty of holiness! You really are in a state to be envied; but you deserve the happiness you possess . . . I may aspire after some part of it.' (*Letters*, i, 95.)

'I have not heard from Sally a good while', she wrote to her sister in July, 1731, 'I am indebted to Cyrus, but I will write as soon as I can. If you write to him soon, you may say I am in some hurry for my intended journey.'

She wrote contritely and at length before she sailed for Ireland on the *Pretty Betty* in September. While she was away Anne wrote to John of self-improvement, of Burkitt's *Notes on the New Testament* which she had been reading, of a charming hymn composed by Charles, which she had read, and of a letter from Aspasia saying that she was much concerned that she had not written to John. But in May, 1732, Wesley journeyed down to Stanton and after a short visit to the Kirkhams set out in the pouring rain for Gloucester, where he was entertained by Mrs. Granville and Selima. They showed him the sights and introduced him to their friends, the scholarly Mr. Newton,[1] Mrs. Viney and Mrs. Ironside; he preached at the College and St. Nicholas's Church on the Sunday. When he returned to Stanton, life followed its normal round of walks and discussions. He saw something of Mrs. Griffiths and Nancy, read some plays, *Macbeth* and *Julius Caesar*, and one evening after supper, when Mr. Griffiths came round, they 'romped'. His good spirits were not affected by the absence of Mary Pendarves, but he was hurt at her continued silence.

His friends may well have noticed his increasing seriousness. When he was at Stanton in September and early December, and again for a night in January, 1733, he still played cards and joined in singing; in the winter, he read the *Phaedra* and *Hippolytus* with Mr. Kirkham. Yet there was perhaps a growing note of earnestness. In the early summer Sally's sister Betty had died, no great loss if Mary Pendarves is to be believed; 'Poor Mrs. Wilson!' she wrote on 28th June, 1732,

'I am sorry for the shock her death must have given Sally, . . . but I hope when she considers the great advantage her sister in all probability will receive by the exchange she has lately made, that she will be reconciled to the loss of a sister that has given her more woe than happiness.'

Wesley did not mention the death in his diary, but he may have visited her husband in Birmingham in May, 1733.

[1] 'If you can get a tolerably neat frame and glass at Gloucester, put Swift's picture-frame in one before you give it to Mr. Newton' (Mary Pendarves to her sister, 2nd March, 1734); 'The Rev. John Newton lives in the lower College Yard at Gloucester . . . well-worthy the most ingenious man's friendship and acquaintance' (Sally Chapone, 30th March, 1745).

Another female friend had made her appearance, Serena, probably Susan Boyse,[1] the daughter of Mrs. Robert Boyse,[2] who lived at Berkswell and with whom Wesley sometimes stayed as he journeyed north. Serena was often at Stanton where on 22nd September, 1732, John read to her the highly moral tale, *The Second Spira*, and walked with her until Bob Kirkham arrived. In December, 1732, he was with her in the parlour at Stanton, talking with her and Varanese of self-denial. In May of the following year he accompanied the Boyse family to Birmingham, where they met Mrs. Beale and Serena, who later set out with Mrs. Boyse for Stanton. In July, 1733, he entertained them during the festivities which marked the end of the Oxford summer term. A year later he noted down in his abridged diary that he had explained the prayers to Serena. There were few signs of a romantic attachment but the development of a regular correspondence indicates a close friendship.

There were signs that his contacts with Stanton and Buckland were beginning to grow weaker. Sally's interest was in her husband and children; she continued to read widely and her correspondence with George Ballard reflects her interest in literature. Elizabeth Elstob never forgot how Mrs. Chapone helped her, collecting money for her and moving the Queen, Caroline, to grant her an annuity of a hundred pounds a year. She certainly did not lose sight of Anne Granville or of Mary Pendarves; but the time would come when John Wesley would be on the periphery of her acquaintances. His 'singularity', the extent to which he excluded secular literature from his field of reading, his obsessive concern with salvation, must have made him an increasingly embarrassing guest. He was at Stanton four times during 1733 and at least twice during 1734, but his stays were short. His visits followed the same routine; he busied himself in domestic duties, helping Damaris to shell peas in June, 1733, talking in the garden, reading Varanese's papers—for she engaged in writing—and playing cards in the evening; in January, 1734, he seems to have been accompanied by Richard Morgan and went for a walk with young

[1] On Monday, 3rd October, 1737, Charles Wesley stayed with the Boyse family at Berkswell and commented 'The family showed me all possible civility, especially dear Susan, for whose sake I had come' (C. Wesley, *Journal*, i, 77).

[2] Mr. and Mrs. Robert Boyse or Boyce of Berkswell are not to be confused with Mr. John (later Sir) John Boyce of Oxford, whose son was a member of the Holy Club, though they may have been related. An entry in Wesley's diary for 3rd January, 1727, reveals the presence of both Mrs. Boyse and Mrs. Beale at Stanton. They are later found together with Serena, especially at Birmingham (cf. the entries in Wesley's diary for 14th and 15th May, 1733, and 6th June, 1733).

Bernard Kirkham. On 15th November, 1734, Damaris married Edward Palmer of Berkswell. It cannot have been only on the Kirkhams' side there was a slight air of constraint. He and his friends had given themselves so completely to that 'good society' which Anne Granville commended in her letter that the pleasant company and comfortable life of Stanton rectory may well have seemed to him unresponsive to the challenge of the Gospel.

There was too no news from Ireland. The promised letter from Mary Pendarves did not arrive. She had had qualms about her failure to write as early as the spring of 1732:

'Cyrus', she wrote to her sister, 'by this time has blotted me out of his memory; or if he does remember me, it can only be to reproach me. What can I say *for* myself? What can I indeed say *to myself*, that have neglected so extraordinary a correspondent? I only am the sufferer, but I should be very sorry to have him think my silence proceeded from negligence; I declare 'tis want of time.'[1]

She returned to England in the spring of 1733 and after visiting Lady Weymouth at Longleat went to her mother and sister at Gloucester; but it was not until July 1734 that she eventually wrote to John Wesley.

'The more I consider the obligations I had to continue my correspondence with one who hath showed me so many marks of an unfeigned desire to assist and promote my eternal happiness, the deeper is my concern for having forfeited so great an advantage. I am so sincerely sorry for the ill impression I have given you of myself, that I shall shun you as a criminal would a judge.'

Wesley's reply effectively cut off any hope of further correspondence. 'Alas, Aspasia! are you, indeed, convinced that I can be of any service to you?' He must doubt her words since for so long and resolutely she has thrust his advice from her. 'Doubtless you acted upon cool reflection; you declined the trouble of writing, not because it was a trouble, but because it was a needless one.' 'I sincerely thank you for what is past.' So a cold wind blew over the memories of past correspondence. 'It may be said with equal justice of every sort of conversation with Aspasia or you', he had once written to her sister, 'that it brings to its sweetness no satiety.'

---

[1] 'Then there's poor Sally too, who I think of every day, but cannot find a moment to tell her so, though soon I will endeavour to acquit myself in a proper manner to them both.' (*Autobiography and Correspondence*, i, 343.)

Q

For once, Mary Pendarves had protested too much.[1] Wesley, who had perhaps flattered himself that he was so much more than one among her many friends, one who was more to her than 'the honest-hearted man who earnestly desires the salvation of his fellow-creatures', felt the humiliation, and coolly if courteously brought the friendship to a close.

There can be little doubt that the friendships which had sustained him for so long meant much to him and greatly influenced the development of his personality; but the cool passion to which they gave rise faded as the high endeavour of a holy life shaped his will. It is perhaps fanciful to assume that unrequited love helped to create the mental state which made him ready to leave England and Oxford for what he fondly if inaccurately believed to be the primitive innocence of America. There, as he told Dr. Burton, he might be able to 'attain such a purity of thought as suits a candidate for that state wherein they neither marry nor are given in marriage, but are as the angels of God in heaven'.

[1] Cf. Aspasia's letter to Dean Swift in 1733: 'If I were writing to a common correspondent I should now make a fine flourish to excuse myself for not sooner answering the favour of your letter . . .'

CHAPTER XI

The Family at Epworth

THE lifeline which attached Wesley to his home in Lincolnshire was founded on affection and the extent to which his early environment had already moulded his character and fastened him to his family. Every year, sometimes twice, in 1733 three times, he went back to Epworth to see his parents, sisters and friends in the neighbourhood.

'Were it not that we desire to have as much as we can of yours and my father's company while we are yet alive', John told his mother in February, 1732, 'we should scarce be induced to go an hundred and twenty miles to see Epworth steeple.'[1]

Even at Oxford there was much to remind him of his home, the presence of his brother at Christ Church, and of Rector Morley at Lincoln (until his death in 1731), and of others who had or were to have connections with his home ground. His predecessor, John Thorold, and his brother William, a gentleman commoner of the College, and his colleagues, Michael Robinson and Charles Dymoke, were Lincolnshire men. Two sons of one of the most important landowners in the island of Axholme, Mr. Pindar, John and Robert, were undergraduates at his College; John Sympson, and the two sons of the local lawyer, Thomas Hutton, came to the College from nearby Gainsborough. Matthew Robinson was the son of the vicar of Blyborough, and John Whitelamb, who had lived in the district all his life, was soon to return to marry Wesley's sister Mary, and to become the rector of Wroot. Dr. Leybourne, a fellow of Brasenose, and another friend of Wesley's who usually called on him when he came to Oxford,[2] had been for a time the suitor of his sister Emily. Three young graduates, two from Lincoln, Westley Hall and Matthew Horbery, who

[1] *Letters*, i, 118.
[2] E.g. 'June 3, 1730, at Leborn's, tea; March 10 and June 27, 1732, at Dr. Leyb.; July 28, 1733, breakfast with Mr. & Mrs. Leybourne; September 13, 1733, at Mr. Leybourne, much company.'

helped Wesley's father in preparing his book on Job,[1] and one from Queen's, Benjamin Ingham, fell at various times in love with his sister Patty; and Hall eventually married her, to her lifelong disadvantage.

He spent several months at different times at Epworth between 1729 and 1735, usually travelling by the same route, but often making a deviation to Stanton, and in 1733 and 1734 to Manchester, where he visited his friend John Clayton. He stayed with friends and acquaintances on the way, frequently with William Smith, who lived at Leicester, sometimes with Charles Crew, an undergraduate of the College, whose father was vicar of Bitteswell, occasionally with his Christ Church contemporary Burman, at Warwick. In February, 1733, he arrived at Warwick to find Burman ill; by the advice of the apothecary, Mr. Hall, he was blooded and he persuaded Wesley to stay the following day and take his services at Coventry. On his journey from Manchester to Epworth in 1733 he called on Mr. Rivington at Chesterfield, and took the opportunity to look over Chatsworth on a summer's evening and to investigate Pool's Hole at Buxton, which led to the enigmatic comment 'at the end of it, strange, no answer'.

The journeying entailed in visiting Epworth was sometimes strenuous. In the summer of 1731 he and his brother walked home. John Wesley had gone to Communion on Easter Day, read prayers at the Castle at half-past ten, went round to his brother Charles at half-past twelve and set off for Stanton an hour later. After leaving Stanton they breakfasted at Mickleton and dined at Snitterfield, reaching Berkswell where they stayed that evening. The following day they set off at a quarter past five, breakfasted at Coventry, dined at High Cross and reached Leicester, where they stayed the night. On the Thursday, 22nd April, they set off at the usual time, made for Sedghill, where they had breakfast, and supped with Mr. Cash. They spent the Friday at Lincoln and part of the Saturday morning with sister Kezzy and Miss Kitty Hargreaves, reaching Epworth that evening.

'Our walk', John told his father in respect of his return journey to Oxford, 'was not so pleasant to Oxford as from it, though in one respect it was more useful; for it let us see that four- or five- and twenty miles is an easy and safe day's journey in hot weather as well as cold.

[1] 'As for the "Testimonia Arianorum" . . . it happens well that I have a pretty good copy, though not so perfect as that which is lost, and will get Mr. Horberry to transcribe it as soon as he returns from Oxford.' (18th June, 1731, L. Tyerman, *Samuel Wesley*, 411.)

We have made another discovery, too, which may be of some service; that it is easy to read as we walk ten or twelve miles; and that it neither makes us faint, nor gives us any other symptom of weariness, more than the mere walking without reading at all.'[1]

From this time forward Wesley rarely went a journey without a book to read. Even when he rode home on horseback, the journey was made singularly unpleasant by the weather or other circumstances. He mentions riding in pouring rain and along flooded roads. Returning from Warwick to Banbury in February, 1733, the roadway became so bad that he rode in the fields, where he was stopped roughly by a countryman, to whom he gave twopence. In the autumn of 1733 his horse became so tired that by the time he reached Newark he had to walk, and at Thurmaston near Leicester he decided to leave it. He stayed at Lutterworth with the Powells, who entertained him at the races and at a dance, but the following day his horse fell in a ditch and it required six men to drag the horse out. He continued his journey but his horse fell again the next morning. These journeys must have provided an invaluable experience and preparation for the long travels throughout the length and breadth of the British Isles which engaged so much of his future life.

When he arrived home life followed a pattern with which he had been long familiar. There were the usual rounds of visits to the neighbours, to the Maws and the Pindars, the Barnards[2] and the Hooles, the Clarks and the Popplewells. Indeed the only exceptional event of any significance in the five years was the fire in his brother-in-law, Richard Ellison's malt-kiln, in September 1732, which burned for three days. There were ample recreations, songs and dancing, games of cards and outings. Occasionally he went on longer expeditions to Gainsborough to visit his sister Emily, who kept a school there, and other friends, Hutton the attorney, and Mr. Dixon. On his way home he often spent a day or so at Lincoln, where his sister Kezzy was for a time a pupil teacher at a boarding-school kept by a Mrs. Taylor; it seems possible that Miss Kitty Hargreaves was also employed there.[3]

[1] *Letters*, i, 84. Compare the comment in a letter of similar date to his mother: 'The motion and sun together, in our last hundred-and-fifty miles' walk, so thoroughly carried off our superfluous humours, that we continue perfectly in health, though it is here [i.e. Oxford] a very sickly season.' (*Op. cit.*, i, 85.)

[2] A member of the Barnard family is said to have been the man who rescued John Wesley from the fire at Epworth rectory in 1709 (*N. and Q.*, 280; *W.H.S. Proc.*, iv, 216; 1939–42, 8–12.)

[3] In his diary Wesley refers to S.K., evidently his sister Kezzy, and to M.K., who

The excursions to Lincoln, where he stayed at the Angel, were pleasant occasions for Wesley. His sister Emily had been a teacher at the same school but the conditions were such that in spite of dissuasion from her brothers, Samuel and John, she had decided to leave and set up her own school at Gainsborough.

> 'Never was such a Teacher', she told John, '. . . so foolishly lost so unnecessarily disobliged. Had she paid my last year's wages but the day before Martinmas, I still had staid: instead of that, she has received *one-hundred and twenty pounds* within these three months, and yet never would spare one *six or seven pounds* for me, which I am sure no Teacher will ever bear. The jest is, she fancies, I never knew of any money she received; when, alas, she can never have one *five pounds* but I know of it.'[1]

Kezzy seems to have been little happier at Lincoln. Her brother advised her about suitable and serious reading such as Norris' *Reflections on the Conduct of the Human Understanding*, but although she had time to read, she had no books nor the money to buy them. 'I have Nelson's *Method of Devotion*, and *The Whole Duty of Man*, which is all my stock. As to *History* and *Poetry*, I have not so much as *one book*.' Kezzy and Kitty Hargreaves, to whom Wesley had for long been attracted, looked forward to John's visits. 'I must not expect any thing', she wrote in January, 1731, 'that will give me so much pleasure as the having your company so long.' When he was at Lincoln in July, 1730, he amused them by reading *Gulliver's Travels* and apparently saw some Indian warriors. On his way back to Oxford in May, 1731, he went to prayers with Kezzy and Miss Kitty, read Law's *Serious Call* to Miss Kitty, with whom he had dinner, and passed the evening cheerfully with music and cards. He was back at Lincoln on 21st August, 1731, finding much company at Mrs. Taylor's, and he called on and may have dined with the Dean; on his return he spent some time with the two girls and read with them Hatchett's play *The Fall of Mortimer*. Sister Kezzy was at home when he was next at Epworth in

---

seems her constant companion. This is obviously Miss Kitty Hargreaves (cf. references in Emily's letter—Mrs. Taylor and Kitty give their service—and Kezzy's letter—'Miss Kitty went to 6 o'clock Prayers till she got the fever; and I never miss except sickness prevent me'). Kezzy's letter is dated 3rd July, 1731. In her letter Emily wrote: 'Kez is gone home for good and all.'

[1] Adam Clarke, *Memoirs of the Wesley Family*, i, 539–41. Cf. the letters of 26th January and 12th July, 1729.

April, 1732; but on his way back to Oxford he visited Mrs. Taylor at Lincoln and spent a little time with Kitty Hargreaves. Again in January, 1733, he was at Mrs. Taylor's but found to his regret that Kitty was in Hull. In May he made a special trip from Epworth to Lincoln to visit Mrs. Taylor's, where Miss Kitty was still working; Kezzy was also there, but the fact that she was at Gainsborough the next day, when he returned via Manchester and Stanton to Oxford, would suggest this may simply have been a visit to Lincoln. Yet when he was at Lincoln in September, 1733, he talked with her about John Whitelamb, a talk which left her 'calm'. Whether she left the boarding-house at Lincoln in 1732 or later, her father's failing health soon made it desirable that she return home.

For the most part then, life continued an uneventful course. Once, on 13th April, 1732, he had tea with Lady Betty Hastings at Ledstone Park; she asked him to translate or transcribe some verses for her, a task he conscientiously carried out. It was a visit which later provided food for conversation at Epworth. In the main Wesley's chief occupation was to help in the usual services; when his father was ill in early 1734 he took burials and christenings as well. As his father's health declined he relied more and more on him to correct his great work on Job and to transcribe and write for him, while his mother appreciated the opportunity to talk with him and to hear him read, now the Bishop of Cork's book on *Human Understanding*, now the *Theologica Germanica*. There were indeed more down-to-earth tasks, gathering mulberries and picking plums from the rectory garden and bargaining over the sale of walnut trees with a 'supposed' Mr. Lee from Hull, whom Wesley discovered to be an impostor.

The interest of his time at Epworth arises chiefly from the personal relationships in which he was involved. He had been brought up, it has been stressed earlier, in a predominantly feminine setting without much contact with the children of the district until he went to Charterhouse. His mother was still his chief confidante. He could discuss with her the problems of his relationship with Varanese and the Kirkhams, the difficulties confronting William Morgan,[1] or, more generally still, the character of women. On 7th November, 1729, her reading matter and his faults provided food for conversation. He maintained his intimacy with his sisters who rejoiced in his success, fluttered dove-like around him and

[1] 25th September and 14th October, 1729.

sought his advice over the problems of their lives. He was their counsellor, guide and friend. The advice that he gave them, especially in their love affairs, was not always the best; but Wesley was here handicapped by his own poor judgement. There were too many factors, too many psychological issues, involved in the tangled relationship which was so often a feature of these affairs. It must, moreover, be remembered that the elder Wesley was always suspicious of his daughters' intentions, especially since Hetty's affair. Hetty was now in London, where John was from time to time to see her, endeavouring to come to terms with her coarse and drunken husband. The Ellisons were in Lincolnshire and often visited by John and his brother; but the fire which ruined his property led to a separation from his wife. It had perhaps been long in coming; 'under his unkindness she well-nigh sank into the grave'. Nancy Lambert and Charles alone of Samuel Wesley's children made a success of their marriages, though Mr. Lambert was from time to time less abstemious than he might have been.

John Wesley had always been the confidant of Emily and cherished her friendship with Leybourne. 'Let me have one relation I can trust,' she had written in 1725, 'never give any hint to anyone of aught I write to you.' Her sensitive spirits were depressed by the break-up of this friendship and the underpaid drudgery which she had endured in 'licentious' Lincoln. Yet she seems to have made a success of the school she had opened at Gainsborough. 'I shall furnish my School with canvas, worsteds, silks . . . and am much afraid of being dipt in debt at first.' This, as she said, was no unfamiliar experience and John lent her three pounds at the start. When he called on her at Gainsborough on 8th May he found a great deal of company. Then romance began to flower again. He was a Quaker doctor, possibly the Dr. Huntingdon mentioned in Wesley's diary, a man whom she described as 'a faithful friend, a delightful companion, and a most passionate lover'.[1] It is true that his enthusiasm for the Whig government offended her Tory opinions and resulted in a heated argument which lasted for two hours, and that she objected to the way in which he showed jealousy when she talked to another man; but the ultimate barrier to a happy outcome was John's inexorable objection to a Quaker as a husband. 'So farewell George Fox, and all thy tribe, for Rockwood and Ringwood and Towler and Tray.'

So she continued to teach her girls at Gainsborough and to seek her brother's counsel.

[1] Maldwyn Edwards, *Family Circle*, 139–40.

'Full well you know that even from our childhood you have been selected from all our numerous family for my intimate companion, my counsellor in difficulties, the dear partner of my joys and griefs.'

She was distressed then when 'hardly for no offence' he showed his disapproval.

'Whatever faults I have been guilty of in respect of God, to you I have been blameless, except loving you too well has been one; and considering you are a man I do too well love, that is the very thing which has disobliged you.'

An intelligent woman, the best reader of Milton that he knew, as Wesley once said, Emily was demanding and jealous. In middle age she was married by John on the eve of his departure to Georgia to Robert Harper, one of the family in the district with whom he had been long acquainted. Harper was an apothecary by profession but so poor at his business that he relied on the profits of the school which she continued to run at least for a time at Gainsborough. He took the money that she had earned, and 'thought himself very kind if once in six months he gave her ten shillings'. She was forced to sell her personal belongings to live. 'I have yet a bed to lie on but Christmas will soon be here, and if Bob Harper will do nothing to raise a half-year's rent I cannot get it myself, though I could somewhat towards it: and 'tis a cold time of year to be turned out of doors.' 'Forsake her not in the day of her distress', she wrote to John. It were better, she thought, that he should come to comfort her at Gainsborough rather than visit Count Zinzendorf in Germany. 'Had my soul been lost by self murder, my damnation would justly have been laid at your door.' Harper was probably a feckless man, but the middle-aged, disappointed schoolmistress, fretful, caustic, possessive, was an unsuitable bride. Whether Harper had died we do not know, but in 1740 she came to the Foundry and at the Preacher's House in West Street she lived a virtual pensioner of her brother's, no doubt given to good works and immersed in genuine if unofficious piety until she died in 1771.

Emily Wesley's fate has taken us beyond the period of Wesley's departure for Georgia. In 1735 she was still divided between school-teaching and romance. On 19th May, 1733, he was walking in the rectory garden with his brother, Samuel, and discussing the 'quarrel' with Emily, unconscious of where the fates were leading her. He was besides concerned about the future of his protégé, 'poor starveling Johnny' Whitelamb, who must already have been paying court to his sister Mary, 'patient grizzle Moll', as Charles once described her. Mary was deformed, but of pleasing countenance. She helped to run the household, and, shrewd and kindly as she was, her crippled state made it unlikely she would have many suitors. Whitelamb, for all his outward religiosity, had given Wesley much anxiety in his last terms at Oxford, which he eventually left without taking a degree. He had not always conformed to the disciplined life which Wesley expected the members of the Holy Club to follow; he had moved occasionally in doubtful company and developed questionable views. Yet the poor scholar had eventually submitted, and in 1733 he had been accepted for ordination.

John Wesley cannot therefore have been best pleased when he learned in September from his colleague, William Smith, that Whitelamb had been courting a certain Miss Betty. This young lady cannot be identified, but that Wesley was discussing the problem with a Mrs. Etty, who may have been one of the inmates of Bocardo, makes it likely that 'Miss Betty' was socially ineligible for the wife of an intended cleric, however humble his own origins. On 15th September, the very day after he had been told about the affair, he talked of it with his pupil (and Whitelamb's friend), Matthew Robinson, and later went out to Medley Lock to discuss it with a certain Mr. Hawkins. Another young lady, Sally Lumley, with whom he talked about Whitelamb the following morning, was also involved; Sally was probably Betty's sister, for when Wesley went out to Medley after a meeting of the Holy Club the following Monday afternoon, low in spirits, he found that Betty was not at home and when Sally saw him she ran away. If she supposed that she was preventing the evil day of an interview with the determined little don, she was mistaken. John Whitelamb was called to his rooms and next day Wesley went out to Medley to confront Mr. Hawkins and Betty; they confirmed the worst, or perhaps it would be better to leave Wesley's own word 'all'.[1] Fortunately he had already arranged to leave for Epworth and John Whitelamb was in his company when they set out at half-past one on Tuesday afternoon, 19th September, 1733.

What was he to do about it? He at once talked it over with Kezzy, who took it calmly and presumably suggested that Mary should be told. Two days later—he had been ill the day before—he told her everything of Whitelamb's doings. She took it well; 'was resigned' were the words he used; and Whitelamb was brought to see the error of his ways. He

---

[1] Cf. a later entry in his diary for 9th November, 1733: '[Matthew] Robinson came. Talk of J[ohn] W[hitelamb]. At his room. Betty there. Ego in portu.'

subsequently married Mary, was ordained and found a small reward of his labours in preferment to the poorly paid and dreary rectory of Wroot, which Samuel had held in plurality with Epworth since 1725. In the letter which he sent to the Lord Chancellor, in whose gift it was, asking for Whitelamb's appointment, Samuel Wesley stressed its drawbacks.

'It lies in our low levels, and is often overflowed. During the time I have had it, the people have lost the fruits of the earth to that degree, that it has hardly brought me £50 per annum, omnibus annis; and, some years, not enough to pay my curate there his salary of £30 a year. . . . I gave my consent to his marrying one of my seven daughters, and they are married accordingly; and, though I can spare little more with her, yet I would gladly give them a little glebe land at Wroot, where, I am sure, they will not want springs of water. But *they* love the place, though I can get nobody else to reside on it.'[1]

It was to this melancholy, waterlogged parish whose people Whitelamb's sister-in-law Hetty described

> As asses dull, on dunghills born;
> Impervious as the stones, their heads are found,
> Their rage and hatred, steadfast as the ground,[2]

that Johnny Whitelamb was consigned for the remaining thirty-five years of his life.

On 1st November, 1734, Mary died in childbirth and Whitelamb, of whose career Wesley had once had such high hopes, stagnated at Wroot. Old Mr. Wesley, who also had always a high regard for his protégé,[3] suggested to James Oglethorpe that he should get the disconsolate young man to go to Georgia. But it was John Wesley and not John Whitelamb who crossed the Atlantic. Whitelamb remained at Wroot living on a faith which was steadily eaten away by doubts of one kind and another. Sometimes he moved towards deism; sometimes he was attracted by the thoughts of conversion to Rome. 'I cannot see', he wrote to Mrs. Hall in

[1] L. Tyerman, *Oxford Methodists*, 377.

[2] *Op. cit.*, 378. Hetty also wrote a long and glowing poem *To the Memory of Mrs. Whitelamb*, who had been the only one of her sisters to sympathize with her in her own unhappy love affair (see p. 110).

[3] 'He is indeed a valuable person,' Wesley told the Lord Chancellor on 14th January, 1734, 'of uncommon brightness, learning, piety, and indefatigable industry; always loyal to the King, zealous for the Church, and friendly to our Dissenting brethren, and for the truth of his character I will be answerable to God and man.'

1755, 'how Christianity can possibly support itself under the wing of Mother Church.' In 1742 Whitelamb heard Wesley preach at Epworth, standing by his father's tombstone, but he went away without attempting to converse with him. 'God grant you and your followers', he wrote after hearing him preach, 'may always have entire liberty of conscience! Will you not allow others the same?' The question was well put for 'poor starveling Johnny' had taken a line of his own, and Wesley's final comment expresses an unusual bitterness, a measure of the extent to which he realized that his early promise had come to nothing and the exhortations at Oxford had in the end proved barren. 'Oh, why did he not die forty years ago, while he knew in whom he believed?' he commented harshly and yet pitifully when he learned that Whitelamb had died on 4th October, 1769.

Martha or Patty Wesley, as she was called, was much more of a problem than Emily or Mary. She had acted like Hetty as governess to the children of Mr. and Mrs. Grantham at Kelstern, but neither she nor Hetty stayed long. Patty came back to Wroot but far from settling down; she complained of her lot. 'A grumbletonian like Pat' was an expression Charles had used. Subsequently, in 1729, she went to live with her Uncle Matthew in London, where she remained, apart from longish visits to Epworth, nearly six years, and where John Wesley was to visit her from time to time. Her disturbed condition had in part been caused by an unsatisfactory love affair with the local curate and schoolmaster, Mr. Romley, which her father had brought to an abrupt end.[1] In the autumn of 1730 she was being courted by a Mr. Johnson, but she had responded to his passionate avowals with letters of 'quite extraordinary coldness'. At the end of the year his lack of prospects and his relations' disapproval of his intended bride brought the affair to a close. So, at least, Patty had hoped, for she did not really love him. Then, after three months' interval, he had written as passionately as ever, offering marriage and stating that his brother who was in Orders had married a lady with a fortune of £2,000 and that he had promised to set him up in business. Patty wrote frantically to ask John's advice. John had pressed the claims of a young Lincoln

---

[1] John Romley was certainly in love with Hetty and this was the match of which the elder Wesley disapproved. In addition to acting as schoolmaster he was also the curate and did some work as an amanuensis for Wesley's book on Job. He was later hostile to John Wesley, and was said to have been too fond of his liquor, but he was sometimes in Wesley's company at this time, e.g. on 1st June, 1729, he rode with Mr. Romley to Flixborough. Adam Clarke stated wrongly that he was a graduate of Lincoln College (*Memoirs*, i, 472). He was the son of William Romley (see pp. 68, 106).

graduate, Matthew Horbery, but while she liked his conversation he was she said no more a lover than 'a Grand Turk',[1] an expression that seems indeed strangely inappropriate. She could not conscientiously consider marriage with him. Should she marry Johnson who, through his intermediary, John White,[2] announced his imminent arrival in Epworth? It was true that she did not love him, but she had no hope that she would ever be allowed to marry the man she loved; 'that happiness tis likely would ruin me'. She did not wish to make a fool of Johnson. Besides, when her father died, there was no prospect of any money; marriage was the only guarantee of security. 'I may as well be contented with one I am not very fond of now as stay till I am destitute and may be marry a man that neither loves me nor I him.'

What John Wesley advised we do not know, but he must have been pleased at this evidence of Patty's confidence in him as also in the slightly pathetic attempts she was making to further his projects at Epworth.[3] 'I had some talk not long since with Nancy Dixon and N. Taylor about the Sacrament. Nancy Dixon promised me as before that she would receive it as soon as she was sixteen, but the other, tho past sixteen, said she was too young. I would gladly persuade both her and her sister to communicate this Easter, but I fear I shan't be able.' At any rate, both Mr. Johnson and Mr. Horbery disappeared from the scene, though the latter continued on visiting terms.[4] In November, 1733, John found Patty in a much distressed state at her uncle's house in London and managed to persuade her, not merely of the love of God, but of the virtue of a life of celibacy. In August, 1732, he had been sufficiently concerned to read her letters to his mother, whose advice he sought. Sister Patty returned to London on 22nd July, 1734, and on 6th September John Wesley was able to note

[1] 'Our good people take it for granted that every time I see and talk with Mr. Harberry I love Mr. Johnson so much the less.' She engaged Horbery in talk when he called at the rectory because he was the best conversationalist she knew.

[2] Or, possibly, John Whitelamb.

[3] Patty was not devoid of a sense of humour. In a postscript to her letter she wrote, 'I once knew a pretty sort of youth in Oxford called Mr. Charles Wesley. I should be glad to hear if he is in the land of the living.' In later years her conversation was much esteemed by Dr. Samuel Johnson.

[4] Visiting Gainsborough on 21st May, 1733, Wesley saw the Huttons and the two other Lincoln men, Sympson and Horbery. Horbery's parents died when he was young, leaving £400 which enabled him to be educated at the local schools at Epworth and Gainsborough. He married Sarah Taylor, the daughter of the vicar of Chebsey in 1757 and so resigned his fellowship at Magdalen. See p. 133.

down the beginning of yet another unfruitful romance, for his friend Benjamin Ingham had now fallen in love with her.[1]

At this time Wesley had reason to believe that his other sister, Kezzy, was in love with another of his pupils, Westley Hall; indeed he had written down as much in his diary for 1st May, 1734. He was unaware of the complications implicit in the situation or how unfortunate he had been in originally entering Hall at his College or introducing him to the household at Epworth. Hall, who had matriculated at Lincoln in January, 1731, was plausible, shrewd and religious in a somewhat sanctimonious sort of way; he quickly made himself useful to Wesley in the Holy Club and won his esteem. He was, as his tutor put it, 'holy and unblameable in all manner of conversation'. Wesley took him to Epworth where he created an equally favourable impression; Mrs. Wesley described him in March, 1734, as a man of 'extraordinary piety and love to souls'. Later Wesley visited Hall's home at Salisbury. Wesley arrived at Salisbury wearied by the journey, for it had rained continuously since he had left Oxford, and if he had been edified, he could hardly have been stimulated by reading Ludolf's *Remains* on his way. But, fortified by a diet of gruel and water, he soon revived and engaged in earnest conversation with the rector of St. Martin's, Mr. Greenaway, whom he had previously met at Oxford and described as a 'man of a right mind'. He visited Bemerton, a place which interested him particularly because of its associations with John Norris and George Herbert, and he preached there. He was impressed by Wilton House, but thought that the statues and pictures (Vandyk's piece! Alas!) suggestive of human vanity. He was pleased by the religious tone of the conversation with his friends. Mrs. Periam, an acquaintance of Hall's, 'opened her heart' to him and even his landlady appeared 'contrite' and 'affected'. He returned to Oxford 'dirty' as a result of another wet journey, and smiled a little grimly as he noted down that 'Hall said it would rain no more.'

There is little doubt that the expedition had done much to confirm Wesley's good opinion of Westley Hall and that he viewed his approach to Kezzy as did the remainder of the family at Epworth with a good heart. Hall was, however, the type of man who can combine a genuine interest in religion, a plausible tongue, a rather meretricious charm with a ruthless pursuit of his own interests. He was a smooth rascal who was soon courting both Patty in London and Kezzy in Epworth. Hall met Patty at the

[1] Ingham eventually married Lady Margaret Hastings, the sister of Lady Betty Hastings.

London house of John's uncle, Matthew, and made a secret proposal of marriage, which she accepted. Later in the year he accompanied John and Charles to Epworth, where he set about wooing Martha's sister, Kezzy, with great ardour; the servants and neighbours began to ask 'When Miss Kezzy was to be married?' On Wesley's way back to Oxford he visited Clayton at Manchester, who was amazed by what John told him of Hall's conduct. With his High-Church views, Clayton was a strong upholder of clerical celibacy, and, ignorant of Hall's previous understanding with Martha (or Patty) Wesley, he deplored his conduct:

'He [Clayton] asked whether he had made any promise of marriage. And on his answering "No", told him to pray earnestly, and then to consider whether he was at liberty to marry any one, being so fully convinced as he was that celibacy was the more perfect way.'[1]

The situation was further complicated by the inveterate hatred which Whitelamb had conceived for Kezzy because of her virulent opposition to his own marriage to her sister, Mary, 'believing him not to be a good man'. Accordingly Whitelamb wrote to Hall painting a black picture of Kezzy, insisting, however, that he should keep the matter secret.

This situation continued until the spring of 1735, when John Wesley, taking matters in his own hands as was so often his custom, tried to make Hall come to a decision. In March, John learned that his father was dangerously ill at Epworth and calling on Hall, who had been sick, suggested that he should ride with the brothers to Lincolnshire. Hall, who had seemed in pain, insisted that he should accompany Wesley to Communion at Christ Church, but at first refused to go to Epworth. 'I could not sit upon a horse a hundred yards, if you would give me the world.' In spite of this, only a few hours after, he told Charles that he was going to walk to Epworth, which he did, 'through wet and deep roads, for above a hundred miles'.[2] At first all went well, since Hall's arrival seemed to revive the elder Wesley, and obviously pleased both his inamorata, Kezzy and Patty (who had returned from London to Epworth); but shortly after Easter he began to cool in his relations with Kezzy, though it was still very far from clear what his real intentions were. It soon became

[1] The details which follow come from a fragment of Wesley's journal (*Journal*, viii, 147–55).

[2] This must have been good going! The brothers left on Sunday, 30th March, which was the Sunday before Easter, and presumably the day on which Hall must also have left Oxford. They were all at Epworth by Good Friday following.

plain that Hall was determined to marry Patty and, in spite of remonstrances from John Wesley,[1] he eventually did so. In so doing Hall effectually ruined the lives of both Wesley's sisters, for while Kezzy seems willingly to have given him up, she never fully recovered from the experience she had been obliged to undergo, while Martha was to live out a most unhappy marriage.[2] Charles and Samuel Wesley were extremely incensed at Hall's action and were later to write poems and letters denouncing him as a smooth-tongued hypocrite. 'Smooth-tongued' he certainly was, for after the marriage he thought to go with Wesley to Georgia.

'I found all my relations labouring to dissuade my sister, and all his importuning him day and night, not to go to Georgia', John Wesley wrote on 22nd September, 1735. 'She heartily repented of her purpose, and joined with them to bring over him. He stood steadfast against them all. Good and bad words were equally lost upon him. He received both Deacon's and Priest's Orders of the Bishop of London for that purpose, and was appointed minister of Savannah in the room of Mr. Quincy.'

He bought clothes and furniture and had actually hired a coach to take his wife and himself to Gravesend when he suddenly changed his mind.

[1] Wednesday, 6th August, 1735: 'Talked with my sister P. and endeavoured to convince her Mr. H. and she could not marry with innocence; but with no success.' Over a week later, the 14th, he remonstrated with Hall, 'but without effect'. It was now that Wesley learned what Whitelamb had written to Hall about Kezzy. Later, in August, Hall showed Wesley Whitelamb's letters, 'which did indeed give such a character of poor Kezzy and that supported with so many matters of fact, that I myself could scarce tell what to say or think'. Yet since the letters contained facts which Wesley himself was in a position to disprove he persuaded Hall once again to reconsider the matter. Indeed it appears that Hall once more turned towards Kezzy. 'I asked my sister K. how he behaved, and what he said. She told me he behaved toward her with as much tenderness as ever. That he said he found she had been unjustly aspersed, and came to give her an opportunity of clearing herself. . . . He appeared much grieved for what he had done with regard to my sister P., and at parting (with K.) took off one of his rings, which he desired her to wear, till he came again and exchanged it for a wedding ring.' This incident took place on 2nd September, 1735; by 15th September Westley Hall was married to Patty Wesley.

[2] The marriage, treated as the epitome of conjugal virtue, was celebrated in verses in *The Gentleman's Magazine* for September, 1735, p. 551:

> Such are *Hall* and *Westley* joining
> Kindred souls with plighting hands,
> Each to each entire resigning,
> *One become* by nuptial bands.

He told Oglethorpe that his uncle and mother had promised him a living, 'and so he resolved to stay in England'. It is impossible to say how far his intention had been frustrated by his relatives' pressure; there was an element of neurotic calculation in most of the things that he did. He was very far from having lost the confidence of John Wesley or others of his relatives; but Samuel, more perceptive than his brothers in analysing character, did not hesitate to tell John in a letter of 29th September, 1736, that

'Brother Hall's is a black story. There was no great likelihood of his being a favourite with me; his tongue is too smooth for my roughness, and rather inclines me to suspect than believe.'

The full irony of Westley Hall's position had not yet been revealed.

As his father's health declined, Wesley was faced with another problem, the future of the parish of Epworth, where the rector hoped that one of his sons might succeed him. The old man had had a serious accident in June, 1731, when he and his wife, Patty and the maid, were going in the wagon to see the ground he leased of Mrs. Knight at Low Millwood. The rector was sitting in a chair at one end of the wagon when the horses took fright, throwing him headlong on the track. He evidently suffered a severe concussion. His wife offered him some ale, 'he looked prodigiously wild, but began to speak and told me he ailed nothing. I informed him of his fall. He said he knew nothing of any fall, he was as well as ever he was in his life.' They called for Mr. Harper, the apothecary, who blooded him. As he became increasingly infirm, he relied on John and Whitelamb to transcribe his work on Job, which was now nearing completion. In October, 1732, Susanna reported that her husband was 'in a very Bad State of Health. He sleeps little and eats less. He seems not to have any apprehension of his approaching exit, but I fear he has but a short time to live. . . . Everybody observes his decay but himself, and people really seem much concerned both for him, and his family.' Once again the old man rallied; but when John Wesley returned home in January, 1733, he found his father seriously ill, and Dr. Mason in constant attendance, so much so that at four on Sunday, 21st January, he wrote that his father was 'given over' and he said prayers with him as he had been doing the past few days; but he took a turn for the better and by 29th January he was out of danger. On 15th February, 1733, he told his mother that he was glad that his father was recovering, 'though it can be but very slowly, considering how his strength is exhausted', and he

R

trusted that he would not be tempted out by the finer weather in the spring until his health had fully recovered. In fact he was sufficiently well to travel to Oxford for the Christmas of 1733, spent an enjoyable few days with his son, playing cards at the Rector's, meeting John's friends, Richard Morgan, Hervey, Broughton, and preaching to the prisoners at the Castle on Sunday, 30th December.

The ageing rector was eager that the future of the living should be decided before his death. When he had been ill in January, 1733, the question had been discussed with John and his mother. Samuel had only recently become headmaster of Blundell's School, Tiverton, and would be in no position to accept the offer of the living. Charles was not yet ordained. John was therefore the man whom Samuel intended to succeed him. When the question was mooted, he showed himself at first indifferent. As he explained to his mother, he did not feel sure that he was strong enough to carry out the work that the care of the parish entailed.

'I knew if I could stand my ground here and approve myself a faithful minister of our blessed Jesus . . . then there was not a place under heaven like this for improvement in every good work.'[1]

He remained undecided. In November his father wrote to him, urging him to accept the living to preserve the work which he had been trying to do for the past forty years and 'on account of the dear love and longing which the poor people has for you'.[2] It must also have been in the rector's mind that John's appointment would provide a home for his widow and his unmarried daughters.[3]

John Wesley replied in a very lengthy letter[4] in December, 1734, concluding that 'I am not likely to do that good anywhere, not even at Epworth, which I may do at Oxford', and so rejecting his father's suggestion. The reasons which he gave are so revealing and interesting that they require further analysis. He began by saying that his decision as to whether he preferred a College life to 'that of a rector of a parish' should depend upon a paramount consideration, as to which course of life

[1] *Letters*, i, 134.

[2] Priestley, *Letters of Samuel Wesley*, 48–50.

[3] In her letter of 25th October, 1732, Mrs. Wesley had commented that 'The two girls, being uneasy in the present situation, do not apprehend the sad consequences wch (in all appearance) must attend his Death so much as I think they ought to do; for as Bad as they think their condition now, I doubt it will be far worse when his head is laid.' (*W.H.S.*, 18–19, 169–72.)

[4] *Letters*, i, 166–78.

tended more to the glory of God. He was convinced that Oxford provided the best opportunities for the cultivation of personal holiness and his own salvation, and that these things could not be separated from the good of others and of the Church in general. 'It is every physician's concern to heal himself first . . . because it seems we may judge with more ease, and perhaps certainty too, in which state we can most promote holiness in ourselves' in order that 'we can promote it in others'. Oxford provided the right environment in which 'I can most promote this holiness in myself'.[1]

What were the ingredients which Wesley so opportunely found at Oxford? He put first the conversation and example of his friends.

'I know no other place under heaven where I can have always at hand half a dozen persons nearly of my own judgment and engaged in the same studies: persons who are awakened into a full and lively conviction that they have only one work to do upon earth . . . who . . . have according to their power renounced themselves, and wholly and absolutely devoted themselves to God.'

This is a blessing which he would find nowhere else in England. At Oxford he was free from 'trifling acquaintance'.

'I have no such thing as a trifling visitant, except about an hour in a month, when I invite some of the Fellows to breakfast. Unless at that one time, no one ever takes it into his head to set foot within my door, except he has some business of importance to communicate to me or I to him.'

Whenever he was away from Oxford, even for a week, he found that the company and conversation of the outside world made him eager to return.

'The far greatest part of the conversation I meet with abroad . . . turns on points that are absolutely wide of my purpose, that no way forward me in the business of life.'

He wrote scathingly of half-Christians who insensibly undermined his resolutions. At Oxford he was able to

'. . . avoid that bane of piety, the company of good sort of men,

[1] 'By holiness I mean not fasting (as you seem to suppose), or bodily austerity, or any other external means of improvement, but the inward temper, to which all these are subservient, a renewal of the soul in the image of God.' (*Op. cit.*, 168.)

lukewarm Christians (as they are called), persons that have a great concern for but no sense of religion. I say, "God deliver me from an half-Christian".'

At Oxford Wesley enjoyed a freedom from financial worry which would, he implied, surely not be the case at Epworth. 'My income is ready for me on so many stated days, and all I have to do is to count and carry it home. The grand article of my expense is food, and this too is provided without any care of mine. I have nothing to do but at such an hour to take and eat what is prepared for me. My laundress, barber, &c, are always ready at quarter-day; so I have no trouble on account of these expenses.'

His life provided him with the opportunities he required to cultivate personal holiness. 'I have the opportunity of public prayer twice a day and of weekly communicating. . . .' Outside Oxford he might well find it difficult to stand his ground against temptations to self-indulgence and intemperance in sleeping, eating and drinking, in irregularity of study. He admitted that there were many who abused College life,[1] but he did not believe because the abuse existed, that the life of a College don could not be spiritually useful.

Indeed, in more ways than one, Oxford provided many opportunities for useful service.

> 'There is scarce any way of doing good to our fellow creatures for which here is not daily occasion . . . here are poor families to be relieved;[2] here are children to be educated; here are workhouses wherein both young and old want, and gladly receive, the word of exhortation; here are prisons to be visited, wherein alone is a complication of all human wants; and lastly, here are the schools of the prophets—here are tender minds to be formed and strengthened, and babes in Christ to be instructed and perfected in all useful learning.'

If mistakes were made, then there were friends to encourage and advise; 'the good Bishop and Vice-Chancellor are at hand to supply (as need is)

---

[1] 'Yet, granting the superlative degree of contempt to be on all accounts due to a college drone; a wretch that hath received ten talents, and yet employs none; that is not only promised a reward by his gracious master, but is paid beforehand for all work by his generous founder, and yet works not at all;—allowing all this . . . I do not apprehend it will conclude against a college life in general.' (*Op. cit.*, 172.)

[2] 'We have here a constant fund (which I believe this year will amount to near eighty pounds) to supply the bodily wants of the poor, and thereby prepare their souls to receive instruction.' (*Op. cit.*, 174.)

their want of experience'. If there were also contempt and opposition these were the inevitable concomitants of practical Christianity; 'until he be thus contemned, no man is in a state of salvation'.

Epworth could provide nothing like this. His father had argued that he would have the care of two thousand souls.

'Two thousand souls! I see now how any man living can take care of an hundred. At least I could not; I know too well *quid valeant humeri.*'

His father had said that his people were eager for John to be their pastor, but of this he was rightly sceptical.

'How long will it last? Only till I come to tell them plainly that their deeds are evil. Alas, sir, do I not know they used you since? Why, just as every one will be used whose business it is to bring light to them that love to sit in darkness.'

John Wesley was doubtless sincere in asserting that he believed that Oxford provided more opportunities for fulfilling his vocation than Epworth, but in other ways the letter is an appalling piece of self-indictment. Its tone of conscious superiority combined with a genuine but somewhat repellent humility showed that the cultivation of personal holiness could produce a peculiarly unpleasant priggishness. It says much for the toleration of the fellows of Lincoln and the real charm of Wesley's personality, which the letter serves to conceal, that his colleagues treated him so graciously. The unreadiness to step outside the circle of the select and self-appointed Christian group, the general air of smugness and even of self-satisfaction for all the self-criticism the letter contains, leave an unpleasing taste. Had John Wesley said frankly that he preferred the life of an Oxford don to that of a country rector because it suited him better and gave him more opportunities for carrying out his life's work, no objection could be raised. He had himself told his father how often he had been dispirited and depressed. If Wesley wanted the life of self-denial and contempt, the bearing of the cross, all the things which he stressed so much, then the parish of Epworth provided them as richly as did Oxford. He had in fact to justify his refusal of the living to himself rather than to his father. The letter revealed, lucid and carefully argued as it was, a mind in a considerable state of confusion. Yet within two years of writing this letter, Wesley, though still a fellow of Lincoln, was working as a missionary in Georgia.

Wesley himself felt that his arguments had not been wholly satisfac-

tory. His brother Samuel obviously thought that they were insincere·
When he urged on Wesley that it was a breach of his ordination vow to
refuse the cure of souls, he was in no position to set himself up as a critic,
though John parried his criticism with an equally evasive answer. He
might, he said, take a College living at Michaelmas, an odd answer from
a man who had a month ago written a letter twelve printed pages
long to justify his belief that his life's work lay in Oxford. Made anxious
by his brother's reproaches, he wrote to the Bishop of Oxford, who was
reassuring; there was, he said, no obligation at ordination to take the cure
of any parish, 'provided you can as a clergyman better serve God and His
Church in your present or some other station'. It seems ultimately that
John Wesley intimated that he would be willing to take the living (which
was in the gift of the Lord Chancellor), but by that time it had been
offered to and accepted by Samuel Hurst.

The old rector was ill again in the spring of 1735, and died on 25th
April of that year. John and Charles were present at his death-bed, and
the latter described it in a moving letter to his brother Samuel. The dying
man received Communion. 'The fear of death he had entirely conquered;
and at last gave up his latest human desires, of finishing Job, paying his
debts, and seeing you.' He spoke lovingly to his children, saying to
Charles, 'Be steady. The Christian Faith will surely revive in this kingdom; you shall see it, though I shall not.'

His death marked the end of a stage in John's life. For all his latent
defects of character, Samuel Wesley in the main had been an affectionate
father, a good husband and a conscientious pastor whose life had been
passed in waters that were rarely untroubled. It seemed almost fitting
that as the old rector was 'buried very frugally, yet decently' in the
churchyard, Mrs. Knight 'seized all her quick stock, valued at above
£40 for £15 my father owed her'. His debts were computed at about
£100. John completed his *Dissertationes in Librum Jobi*, which was published in time for him to present a copy to Queen Caroline, to whom it
was dedicated, on Sunday, 12th October, 1735, shortly before he sailed
for Georgia. His mother went to stay for a time with her daughter at her
school at Gainsborough, then in September, 1736, moved to Samuel at
Tiverton before retiring to live with the Westley Halls. She told Samuel's
mother-in-law that both of them treated her well; 'Mr. Hall behaves like
a gentleman and a Christian.' She went back to Tiverton for the latter
part of 1738 and ultimately joined John Wesley at the Foundry. His
father's death brought the lifelong connection with Epworth and Wroot,

with its many significant associations, to a close. Although John Wesley would from time to time return to his childhood home and take up the broken threads of earlier friendships, in fact life at Epworth became in April, 1735, a matter of past history. A few weeks earlier he had declared almost vehemently that Oxford was the only place in the world where he could serve God as he felt he was called to serve him; and within six months the good ship *Simmonds*, with Wesley on board, was ploughing the Atlantic on her way to Georgia.

CHAPTER XII

The Departure from Oxford

AT the end of December, 1734, John Wesley had vigorously reaffirmed to his father his decision to stay at Oxford and on that ground had rejected the suggestion that he should succeed him at Epworth. While it seems probable that he may have had second thoughts on this score, they came too late for a reconsideration of his position. His father was dead and the family were now dispersed. In the autumn of 1735 John and his brother Charles sailed on their great adventure for Georgia in the *Simmonds*. This was not as much a reversal of his earlier decision as it may seem. If Wesley had been appointed rector of Epworth, he would have been obliged to resign his fellowship at Lincoln.

'If this way of life [he meant his life as an Oxford fellow] should ever prove less advantageous, I have almost continual opportunities of quitting it; but whatever difficulties occur in that [viz. as rector of Epworth] . . . there is no returning, any more than from the grave. When I have once launched out into that unknown sea, there is no recovering my harbour.'

To accept a living meant therefore, like marriage, a point of no return; but John Wesley could easily obtain leave of absence as most of his colleagues did from time to time from his College and visit America. There was nothing in any way unusual about a fellow who was largely non-resident. His College still gave him a home and a small stipend; it was a refuge, and indeed fulfilled that function until his unfortunate marriage in 1751. There was no reason in 1735 to suppose that John Wesley's departure for Georgia meant that he was leaving Oxford permanently.

Still his decision to go to America represented a degree of dissatisfaction with his life in Oxford. His letter to his father was a piece of special pleading, and to some extent, if quite unconsciously, a dishonest piece of special pleading. He may well have not wished to cut himself off from Oxford life or to take a decision which would imperil his fellowship; but he was

248

talking to his brother Samuel on 15th January, 1735, of the possibility of taking a College living:

> 'There are four cures belonging to our College, and consistent with a fellowship. I do not know but I may take one of them at Michaelmas. Not that I am clearly assured that I should be false to my engagement were I only to instruct and exhort the pupils committed to my charge.'

Subsequently he reviewed the suggestion that he should succeed his father at Epworth. What then had created this inner dissatisfaction? He must have found the attitude of his colleagues at least perplexing, just as they must on occasion have found his austerity of life and attitude irritating. There were indications that he was getting fewer pupils to teach. In August, 1733, he had told his mother that if he had no more pupils 'after these have gone, I shall then be glad of a curacy near you'. There was an element of spiritual *accedia* in his life in 1735 which Oxford developed rather than discouraged.

Even at the close of 1733 and the beginning of 1734 there were signs of depression and dejection, from which indeed Wesley was never fully free. Once in a moment of despair he had thought of becoming headmaster of Skipton School. Now another possibility loomed which provided the two things which he required, an escape and a challenge. He had evidently not been happy about the refusal to take a parish, and he may well have thought that in some sort of way he had failed to maintain in practice the high principles to which he had appealed. The missionary journey to Georgia would show the reality of those principles and provide an escape from the Oxford scene which he badly needed. It was in some ways simply an extension of the practical Christianity which was the basis of the Holy Club. Neither he nor Charles seems to have given very much thought to the future of the Holy Club, the importance of whose activities he had so vigorously stressed in his letter to his father. This was possibly because he realized that the generations passed so quickly that it might in any case be an evanescent institution, possibly because he was content to let others take the responsibility in his absence, principally because his work in America could be an extension of the work of the Holy Club in Oxford. The trip to Georgia might also be seen as an escape from the humdrum responsibilities of Christian work at Oxford. In his letter to his father he had stressed the need for self-improvement and the cultivation of personal holiness, at the same time adding that these could not be separated from the improvement of others and the growth of their personal holiness; America would, he believed, provide opportunities for the cultivation of all of these.

His statements in this respect must be placed side by side with what he wrote to Dr. Burton in October, 1735. The striving for personal sanctification, which contributed to his mental and spiritual tension in these years, drove him to Georgia as it had kept him in Oxford.

'My chief motive, to which all the rest are subordinate, is the hope of saving my own soul. I hope to learn the true sense of the gospel of Christ by preaching it to the heathen. . . . A right faith will . . . open the way for a right practice . . . you will perhaps ask: Cannot you save your own soul in England as well as in Georgia? I answer, No; neither can I hope to attain the same degree of holiness here which I may there; neither, if I stay here, knowing this, can I reasonably hope to attain any degree of holiness at all.'

Besides America might seem to provide an escape from the temptations which elsewhere barred the way to personal holiness. A comparison of the arguments in his letters to his father and to Dr. Burton are instructive. In both he stressed the vocation to personal holiness. In the first he justified his stay at Oxford and his refusal to accept the living of Epworth on the grounds that conditions at Oxford were propitious for the cultivation of the holy life. In the other he argues similarly that America would provide an even better soil for personal sanctification.

'Toward mortifying the desire of the flesh, the desire of sensual pleasures, it will be no small thing to be able, without fear of giving offence, to live on water and the fruits of the earth. This simplicity of food will, I trust, be a blessed means, both of preventing my seeking that happiness in meats and drinks which God designed should be found only in faith and love and joy in the Holy Ghost; and will assist me—especially where I see no woman but those which are almost of a different species from me—to attain such a purity of thought as suits a candidate for that state wherein they neither marry nor are given in marriage. . . . Neither is it a small thing to be delivered from so many occasions, as now surround me, of indulging the desire of the eye. They here compass me in on every side; but an Indian hut affords no food for curiosity, no gratification of the desire of grand or new or pretty things.'[1]

[1] *Letters*, i, 188–91.

'The stressing of his own personal salvation', it has been said recently,[1] 'was only the subjective side of his entire inner development, the primitive Christian attitude and its inner core'; but the decision was something very personal. He compared what he believed to be the worldly society of Oxford with the primitive simplicity of the people to whom he was going.

> 'They [i.e. the Indians] have no comments to construe away the text; no vain philosophy to corrupt it, no luxurious, sensual, covetous, ambitious expounders to soften its unpleasing truths, to reconcile earthly-mindedness and faith, the Spirit of Christ and the spirit of the world. They have no party, no interest to serve, and are therefore fit to receive the gospel in its simplicity.'

It was an idealized and highly romanticized picture, in line with the cult of the noble savage characteristic of the eighteenth century, and no wonder that Wesley returned a sadder and wiser man, no wonder that the colonists found their pastor bewildering and irritating. Yet the primary note is one of escape rather than of fulfilment. In another age and another church Wesley must surely have been a monk at least for a time. The comparison with Luther in more ways than one is inescapable. Luther sought the authority which he fundamentally needed in the ascetic practices of an Augustinian house; if a man could have reached heaven by monkhood Luther would have done so. Wesley similarly sought salvation through the work of the Holy Club and the conversion of American Indians.

At the same time it would be ludicrous to leave the matter there. Wesley was genuinely a good and great man. The call to mission work in Georgia was a challenge as well as an escape, a challenge to a life of self-denial and of preaching the Gospel to the heathen. At Oxford, he had been concerned with the manifestation of practical Christianity, and by that he understood the Christianity of the apostolic age, which must include preaching the Gospel to all the world. Wesley had an understanding of the missionary duty of the Church, indeed a theoretically surer one than most Christians of his time.[2] The preaching of the Word of God to

---

[1] Schmidt, *The Young Wesley, Missionary and Theologian of Missions*, 21.

[2] Cf. Dr. Martin Schmidt's articles, 'The Young Wesley, Missionary and Theologian of Missions' (1958) and 'Der Missionsgedanke des jungen Wesley auf dem Hintergrunde seines Zeitalters', *Theol. Viat.*, I (1948–9); but I believe Dr. Schmidt claims too much (e.g., 'He was possessed by the missionary idea in a manner rare in the whole history of the Church').

native peoples was a scriptural and an apostolic obligation. Wesley believed that the American mission field would present him with more effective opportunities for carrying into practice the teaching and discipline of the early Church by which he was so disturbingly drawn. He was to take two or three comrades, members of the Holy Club if possible, with him; the conditions, as Burton stressed, would give him full opportunity for evangelistic work on the voyage, as well as at Savannah, where he was to be Anglican chaplain to the colonists and to work among the Indians.

The idea of the missionary task of the Church had been long familiar to him.[1] His father had talked more than once of becoming a missionary, while his mother delighted to read of the exploits of the Danish missionaries off the coast of Tranquebar, in India, about whom he was again reading, presumably in Boehme's translation, in 1730. He became a corresponding member of the Society for Promoting Christian Knowledge when he was in London on 3rd August, 1732. The Society was closely associated with projects for alleviating the condition of those in prison and with Oglethorpe's plans for starting a colony to settle debtors in America. The people with whom he was associated in London, more especially Sir John Phillips, were strong supporters of its work. Oglethorpe had long been a familiar name in the Wesley family, and the subject of Samuel's poems;[2] the work which he had already done in relation to prison reform would certainly have won him Wesley's esteem. A few days before he was admitted a member of the S.P.C.K., he had been in talk at Oglethorpes' house in London. He had probably read of the arrival in 1730 of the Cherokee chieftains whom Sir Alexander Coming had brought to England and presented at court,[3] and on 11th July, with his sister Kezzy, he had gone to see the 'Indian kings' at Lincoln. Moreover, his own interest in debtors' prisons made him particularly sympathetic towards Oglethorpe's schemes; in 1732 he read an account of Georgia.[4] The persecution to which the Protestants at Salzburg had been subjected by Archbishop

[1] See Martin Schmidt, *The Young Wesley, Missionary and Theologian of Missions* (1958).

[2] 'An Ode to James Oglethorpe Esq., Written soon after the Death of Lady Oglethorpe, His Mother', Wesley, *Poems*, 370–6.

[3] Coming arrived at Dover on 5th June, 1730. 'He brought with him the Crown of the Cherokees, and let the Secretary immediately know he had power to lay it at his Majesty's feet, and had brought with him seven of the chief Indian warriors or generals.' (J. Oldmixon, *History of the British Empire* (1741), i, 500–1.)

[4] Presumably *An accurate account of the province of South Carolina and Georgia* (London, 1732).

Firmian and the schemes for settling them in Georgia would have equally won his approval.[1] The elder Wesley had suggested that John Whitelamb should offer his services after the death of his wife, Mary, and one of his parishioners John Lyndal accompanied Oglethorpe on his first voyage to Georgia.[2]

The colony was in fact only three years old in 1735. A petition asking the King to grant a charter had been drafted in 1730, but the charter was not actually signed until 21st April, 1732. Oglethorpe[3] himself sailed with a group of pioneer settlers on 17th November, 1732, and reached Charleston on 13th January, 1733. At a meeting of the trustees, among them Wesley's friend, Dr. John Burton, on 27th July, 1732, the possibility of sending some of the twenty-three thousand refugees from Archbishop Firmian's domains was discussed sympathetically, and in January, 1734, the first group of Salzburghers set out for the new colony. Oglethorpe returned to England in April, 1734, bringing with him Tomochici, the chief of the Lower Creeks, his wife Senauki, and his nephew and heir, Tooanahouis; he wrote to Sir John Phillips of his arrival. 'I shall leave the Indians at my estate [at Westbrook] till I go to the City, where I shall have the happiness to wait upon you.' The native chiefs were interviewed by the trustees, presented to the King and Queen at Kensington Palace and later to Archbishop Wake at Lambeth. 'They had apprehensions that he was a conjurer, but the kind reception he gave them altered that imagination.'[4] On his first voyage Oglethorpe had taken out as chaplain Henry Herbert, a son of Lord Herbert of Cherbury, but he died shortly after his arrival. His successor was the Rev. Samuel Quincey, but his ministry was unsuccessful, partly because of his own ill-health, and the trustees, exasperated by his failure to send in any reports, decided to terminate his contract.

They had now to decide the question of his successor. Since the death of his father in April, John Wesley had been in a disturbed state of mind. For some time he and his brother had been the guests of James Hutton, a

[1] Cf. *An Account of the sufferings of the Persecuted Protestants in the Archbishopric of Salzburg* (London, 1732), which he was reading on 15th July, 1732, after writing to Sir John Phillips. One of the sponsors of the relief fund, which reached £33,000, was Sir John Phillips.

[2] L. Tyerman, *Samuel Wesley*, 425–30.

[3] On Oglethorpe, see L. F. Church, *Oglethorpe* (1932); A. A. Ettinger, *Oglethorpe* (1936).

[4] Egmont's *Diary*, ii, 121–2.

young Oxford graduate, and his father, a Non-juring clergyman, who kept a boarding-school next door to Samuel's former house in Westminster. Wesley had to see his father's work on Job through the press. It was at this juncture that Burton met him and pressed on him the possibility of accompanying Oglethorpe to Georgia. But before he came to a decision he consulted a number of his friends, his brother Samuel, William Law, Byrom and Clayton, whom he travelled to see at Manchester. His mother signified her approval: 'Had I twenty sons I should rejoice if they were all so employed.' Burton too wrote urgently, stressing that what was wanted was not 'plausible and popular doctors of divinity . . . for the ease, luxury and levity in which they were accustomed to indulge disqualified them for such a work', but men 'inured to contempt of the ornaments and conveniences of life, to bodily austerities and to serious thoughts'. Ten days later Wesley told him that he was prepared to accept the trustees' offer.

The question now remained as to who should compose the company.

'I take', Lord Egmont wrote, 'the sudden resolution of the four gentlemen now mentioned of going over to help the cause of religion as a particular providence and mark of God's favour to our designs.'[1]

John was himself to be the pastor for Savannah as well as the principal missionary, while his brother Charles, hastily ordained,[2] was to travel as Oglethorpe's secretary. Wesley hoped that other members of the Holy Club would follow his example, and the exuberant Westley Hall firmly announced his intention of travelling to Georgia, in spite of persuasive entreaties from his friends and relatives to abandon the project. At the last moment he decided otherwise. He 'had got all things ready for his departure, having hired a coach to carry himself and his wife down to Gravesend', but then he told Oglethorpe that he had been promised a living and was not going. Matthew Salmon of Brasenose had been dissuaded by his father and mother from joining the expedition. Thus the only other member of the Holy Club to accompany the Wesleys was the faithful Benjamin Ingham. They were, however, joined by a London friend, Charles Delamotte, the son of a Middlesex magistrate and very devoted to John Wesley. They were seen off by Burton, James Hutton and Richard Morgan.

[1] Egmont's *Diary*, ii, 196.

[2] Bishop Potter made him deacon on 5th October, 1735; Bishop Gibson of London ordained him priest the following Sunday, 12th October.

'We had two cabins allotted us in the forecastle; I and Mr. Dela-motte having the first and Messrs. Wesley the other. Theirs was made pretty large, so that we could meet together to read or pray in it.'

They had embarked at Gravesend on 14th October, 1735, but it was not until 10th December that the *Simmonds* actually sailed from Cowes Roads for the New World.

On the eve of what he believed to be his departure John wrote a letter to his brother Samuel, to tell him that on the previous Sunday he had presented his father's book on Job to the Queen; but he used the opportunity to make a scathing criticism of classical learning. Too many classical authors (besides Ovid, Virgil's Aeneid, and Terence's *Eunuch*) 'inflame the lusts of the flesh' and 'feed the lust of the eye and the pride of life'. He assured his brother that his chief task as an educator was not to instruct his pupils in the 'beggarly elements of Greek and Latin' but 'in the Gospel'. The letter revealed the great change that had taken place in Wesley since he returned a tutor to Lincoln in 1729. He had shed slowly but surely his many humane interests and activities to become a man of one idea; the academic was transformed into the evangelist. The field of vision had narrowed but was illumined by a glowing sense of vocation.

CHAPTER XIII

The Early Methodists at Oxford

DEPRIVED of the leadership of the Wesleys, the religious society at Oxford was bound to fall on evil days, for John provided it not merely with spiritual guidance, but a sense of direction. Its future, even its every existence, now depended largely upon the zeal of the graduates, undergraduates and townspeople who had so far been involved in the work. The University population shifted quickly. Undergraduates were only in residence for a limited number of years. The young dons, who were most attracted by the kind of activity which the Wesleys had promoted, were the more likely for that very reason to seek a cure of souls outside the University rather than to remain as resident fellows. It is difficult to gauge the support that the Holy Club had won in the town. It had its definite supporters like Charles' friend, Mr. Sarney, but principally it was represented by a group of pious women who could hardly be expected to carry on the work in the Oxford prisons. Indeed the religious society was almost imperceptibly beginning to change its character, being less an impulse to practical and charitable activity than a meeting for mutual spiritual help, prayers, hymns and Bible-reading. It was not surprising that the work lost impetus while the Wesleys were in Georgia, but was given renewed life by Charles Wesley's return.

A list of contemporary date[1] gives the names of some twenty members of the Holy Club on the eve of the departure of the Wesleys and Ingham. It includes the two Wesleys, Gambold and Whitefield as well as a number of less well-known names, Horne, Smith and Evans of Christ Church,[2] Hervey, Robson, Gridsley and Hall of Lincoln, Salmon of Brasenose, Broughton of Exeter, Chapman and Kitchen of Pembroke, Ingham, Atkinson, Watson, Washington, Bell, Wilson and Smith of Queen's College. Some of these had already left Oxford before 1735. Thomas

[1] I owe information about this list to the kindness of Mr. John Walsh, of Jesus College.

[2] He is not to be identified with William Evans who entertained John Wesley many times in Oxford in the coming years and collected his stipend for him. In 1739, Byrom called at the Brays in London and found with the Wesleys and Hall, 'Evans of Oxford, a tradesman'.

Horne of Christ Church was a friend of Charles Wesley's, who had been associated with the Holy Club for many years. Henry Evans was still an undergraduate; he was the son of a Welsh clergyman from Machynlleth and graduated in 1736. Matthew Salmon of Brasenose graduated in 1733 and had seriously considered joining the Wesleys on their Georgian expedition. Walter Chapman took his B.A. in 1732 but remained in Oxford studying for his M.A. He became a member of the Holy Club at the end of 1733 or the beginning of 1734.[1] He wrote to Wesley in September 1736 stressing his indebtedness for 'your kind concern and repeated endeavours for my spiritual good', but a little saddened that 'you have given me no testimony of your affection since your leaving England'. It was in accordance with what must strike the modern reader as the somewhat naïve attitude of these youthful Methodists that Chapman held Wesley's silence to be 'a providential punishment and scourge, for my slow and slender proficiency under the blessed means I enjoyed of your's, and your dear brother's conversation' rather than an indication of Wesley's absorption in other things or comparative neglect of the Holy Club. Chapman was, however, engaged in reading five times a week to a religious society in St. Ebbe's parish.[2]

Thomas Broughton had already left Oxford, but was still visiting the Bocardo in November, 1735. Kitchen must be a misprint for Kinchin of Corpus. The Smiths are not very easy to identify, and it is surprising that William Smith of Lincoln should not have been included in the group. Richard Smith of Christ Church matriculated in 1732 and took his degree in 1736, but he was not an enthusiastic follower and is to be identified with the 'poor languid Smith' whom Charles sought to persuade 'to resume all the rules of holy living' in February, 1737.[3]

Smith of Queen's is most likely to have been John Smith from Durham,

[1] Wesley received a letter from Chapman on 26th January, 1734. Next day, a Sunday, Chapman called on Wesley and talked of reading at the Castle. 'He afraid of doing less', was Wesley's comment. On 26th February they again talked, mainly about the Communion at Christ Church, and the need for courage. 'He seemed affected'. On 20th March he was convinced of the stationary fasts.

[2] L. Tyerman, *Oxford Methodists*, 362–3. Chapman was a close friend of Hervey and later had a church in Bath, of which Hervey took charge in the summer of 1743 while he was away in Devon (*op. cit.*, 208, 215, 230). It was possibly to his mother that John Wesley was writing from Savannah in March, 1737 (*Letters*, i, 218–20).

[3] *Journal of Charles Wesley*, i, 68. Cf. Ingham's comment in October, 1737: 'Dick Smith is weak, but not utterly gone.' The common identification with William Smith, fellow of Lincoln, is groundless.

who matriculated at the age of seventeen on 30th May, 1734. There was a strong Methodist coterie in the Queen's College, some of the members of which were to keep the religious society in existence in the University in the years of the Wesleys' absence. Ingham, its moving spirit, was already in Georgia with Wesley, but Christopher Atkinson did not take his degree until February, 1736. Henry Washington had matriculated on 5th July, 1733, aged sixteen, and did not take his B.A. until 1737. His friend, Robert Watson, was more senior; he had matriculated at the age of eighteen on 18th March, 1730, and had already taken his B.A. in 1735. Wilson was most probably Roger Wilson who matriculated on 22nd March, 1734, and took his B.A. in February, 1738. John Bell also matriculated in 1734 and graduated in 1738. It is worth observing that all the members of this little group in Queen's were northerners, of comparatively humble origin; Atkinson came from Windermere, Washington from Penrith, Watson from Cumberland, Wilson from Wallsend (Northumberland) and Bell from Dovenby in Cumberland.

This leaves the small Lincoln group, whose members had already been closely associated with their one-time tutor. John Robson, to whom Wesley had written so straightly on the eve of his departure from Georgia, was as spiritually diffident as he had been for some years past. Richard Morgan, writing with unconscious irony in view of his own earlier spiritual history, told Wesley that Robson was in a 'dangerous way', being 'convinced of the necessity of being a Christian, but cannot leave the world', a state in which he appeared to continue. 'Mr. Robson and Greives', Ingham told Wesley in October, 1737, 'are but indifferent: the latter is married to a widow, and teaching school at Northampton.'[1] It may be that Greives is to be identified with Gridsley since no one of that name matriculated at Lincoln or any other College during this period.[2] The list which is incomplete does not include Richard Morgan, who was still a zealous member of the society. Indeed, shortly after Wesley's departure Morgan was summoned by the Rector, Dr. Isham, who remonstrated with him for his 'strict way of life'.[3] He told Morgan that he looked thin and feared it was due to fasting. 'I told him', Morgan

[1] L. Tyerman, *John Wesley*, i, 137. Robson maintained his contacts with the Wesleys for some time, and was sometimes in the company of John Wesley, but by 1743 Charles noted that he was 'quite removed from the hope of the Gospel; denying both justification and sanctification.' (C. Wesley, *Journal*, i, 124.)

[2] There was a Thomas Greasley of Lincoln who matriculated 31st March, 1726, and took his B.A. in 1730.

[3] Letter of 25th September, 1735, quoted in Tyerman, *Oxford Methodists*, 21-2.

replied, 'I dined in the hall on Wednesdays, and that I eat bread and butter on Friday mornings.' Isham advised him to drink something instead of tea after fasting, advice which he agreed to follow. The Rector then raised the question of his not coming to the Senior Common Room, a privilege which he enjoyed as a gentleman commoner. 'I said I intended to sit there three nights every week' and he promised to dine on the Hall even on Fridays, a proposal of which Isham very much approved. Morgan was eager to prevent the Rector or his tutor, Richard Hutchins, from writing to his father, while the Rector was simply interesting himself in what he considered the young man's welfare. Just as Morgan had once suspected Wesley of insincerity, so Morgan now in similar fashion spoke insidiously and unjustly of Isham.[1] For the moment he was carrying on the Wesleys' work at the Bocardo, visiting there three days a week. He went to the religious society at the house of Mr. and Mrs. Fox to read every Sunday night 'to a cheerful number of Christians', and every day to read with the Foxes and the landlord and landlady of a certain Mr. Dickison, 'who is an Israelite in whom is no guile', extracts from Bishop Wilson's *Catechism*.[2] Morgan's father had, however, heard of his son's renewed attachment to the Methodists and mindful of what happened to his elder son had written to Hutchins and wisely taken the precaution of controlling the expenditure of his allowance for fear that he should give it to charity.[3] His time at Oxford was indeed drawing to a close. He settled his battels on 27th March, 1736.[4] and by September was in Leyden studying Physic by his father's orders.[5] William Smith, though still friendly towards Wesley, was

[1] 'You cannot sufficiently arm me against the Rector. I suspect him of insincerity to you. I want to know whether you ever did. I believe, and Mr. Horn is of the same opinion, that my going to Ireland [to his home] depends on my going into the hall on fast days. The Rector said as much as if you frightened others from religion by your example; and that you might have done a great deal of good, if you had been less strict. . . .' This is surely a testimony to Isham's good sense.

[2] Letter of 27th November, 1735, quoted in *Journal*, viii, 264–5.

[3] Wesley's diary shows that Richard Morgan had disobeyed his father in respect of this matter and by June, 1734, was beginning to subscribe to the friends of the Holy Club.

[4] He received £25 18s. from the man who took over his rooms, Mr. Walwyn, for the furniture of his chamber and cellar; £6 10s. for his pictures and the remainder of the coal, and £7 0s. 6d. for a third of what he had expended in improving his rooms. His account, which included twelve guineas for tuition, does not suggest he had been unduly parsimonious; he had to pay Mr. Brown, his tailor, £26, no small sum.

[5] Letter of 3rd September, 1736, from James Hutton: 'Mr. Morgan is obliged by

insufficiently enthusiastic to draw the ill-will of his colleagues on him and was in any case carrying out pastoral work as chaplain at Combe.[1] James Hervey alone among the Lincoln men remained a devoted disciple.[2]

There was, therefore, a nucleus of young men, some of them more experienced than others, who were carrying on the work that had been done by the Wesleys within the Colleges, in the prisons and workhouses, in the school, and in the religious society in the town. George Whitefield was the most distinguished, though he was a comparatively late-comer to the Holy Club. He had entered Pembroke College as a servitor in 1732, already aware of their activities; 'I had heard of and loved them before I came to the University; and so strenuously defended them when I heard them reviled by the students, that they began to think that I also in time should be one of them.'[3] But it was some little time before he made contact with the Wesleys; in his own words:

> 'For about a twelvemonth my soul longed to be acquainted with some of them, and I was strongly pressed to follow their good example, when I saw them go through a ridiculing crowd to receive the Holy Eucharist at St. Mary's. At length God was pleased to open a door. It happened that a poor woman in one of the workhouses had attempted to cut her throat, but was happily prevented. Upon hearing of this and knowing that both the Mr. Wesleys were ready to every good work, I sent a poor aged apple-woman of our college to inform Mr. Charles Wesley of it, charging not to discover who sent her. She went, but, contrary to my orders, told my name. He, having heard of my coming to the castle, and a parish church sacrament, and having met me frequently walking by myself, followed the woman when she was gone away, and sent an invitation borne by her to come to breakfast with him the next morning.'

Whitefield went on:

> 'And, blessed be God, it was one of the most profitable visits I ever made in my life. My soul, at that time, was athirst for some spiritual friends to lift up my hands when they hung down, and to strengthen my feeble knees. He soon discovered it, and, like a wise winner of

---

his father's orders to study physic at Leyden, where the name of Wesley stinks as well as at Oxford.' (L. Tyerman, *John Wesley*, i, 132.)

[1] In 1741 Wesley visited Smith and his wife at Combe, and Smith consulted him about sermon writing: 'Smith came,' he noted on 10th July, 'corrected his sermon.'

[2] See pp. 262–3.

[3] Whitefield, *Journal*, ed. W. Wales, 36.

souls, made all his discoveries tend that way. And when he had put in my hand professor Frank's treatise *Against the Fear of Man* and a book entitled *The Country Parsons advice to his Parishioners*, the last of which was wonderfully blessed to my soul, I took my leave.'[1]

He was also much influenced by another work which Wesley lent him, Henry Scougal's *The Life of God in the Soul of Man*.

At Gloucester, where he was for the latter part of 1735, he got together a small group which he conducted along the lines of the Holy Club, and on his return to Oxford naturally took over the superintendence of the small society there while the Wesleys were journeying to Georgia. Youthful, magnificently eloquent, commanding, he was at the same time a splendid and superficial figure. He lacked the slow and steady application which might have given him advancement in academic society, and there was an element of rhetoric and rhodomontade that made him a less stable and more typical evangelist than Wesley. He was ordained by the kindly Bishop Benson of Gloucester on 20th June, 1736, and started to help the studious Kinchin at his country rectory at Dummer, near Basingstoke. While Whitefield continued to be interested in the progress of the Oxford society he did not believe that he was responsible for fostering it. He began to think that it was right for him to undertake missionary work in Georgia, and actually sailed for America shortly after Wesley's return. He spent the greater part of the intervening period away from Oxford, preaching in London and the West Country.

In default of Whitefield, the lead fell to two other ordained men, Kinchin and Gambold. Kinchin was still young—he had matriculated at the early age of fourteen in 1725—but he was a fellow of Corpus Christi and held the country living of Dummer, where first Whitefield and later James Hervey acted as his curates. When Whitefield took duty at Dummer in 1736, he found that Kinchin was well-loved by his people,[2] and he followed his example of dividing the day into three parts, eight hours for sleep and meals, eight for study and retirement, eight for reading, catechizing and visiting the parish; but during his period of residence at Corpus he was assiduous in helping the religious society.

John Gambold at Stanton Harcourt was much nearer, but less capable of

[1] *Journal*, 36–7.

[2] At this time he was a High Churchman, but he was later attracted to Moravian teaching.

Kinchin was one of those who was willing to sign receipts recommending Byrom's shorthand, which John and Charles Wesley also used (*Byromiana* (1954), 50).

taking a lead. Although he was closely associated with the Wesleys until he was drawn into the orbit of the Moravians,[1] and so separated from them, he remained a dreamy, sensitive and unworldly man. Indeed the lack of religious assurance so characteristic of the man in his earlier years never really deserted him. He was a religious seeker, living a sequestered, secluded and introspective life; he read widely in religious mysticism.

> 'He gave way to desponding thoughts; neglected his person and apparel, confined himself as much as possible to his room; and applied, in search of information and comfort, to the works of such authors as he supposed would satisfy his inquiries, namely the fathers of the first ages of the Christian Church . . . he adopted their sentiments, went the same lengths with them in the scenes of imagination, and, by degrees, became so much like one of them, that his cast of mind bore a nearer resemblance to that which was peculiar in them, than to any that appeared among the moderns.'

This scholarly recluse bore little resemblance to the neat and businesslike brothers.

The religious society at Oxford was therefore practically left to its own resources. John Thorold, the previous holder of Wesley's fellowship at Lincoln, writing to him on 24th May, 1736, gave him news of his friends. Broughton was curate at the Tower and was about to preach to the prisoners in Ludgate. Whitefield and Hervey were shortly to be ordained. Sir John Phillips had been unable to attend the meetings of the societies recently because of illness, but was allowing Whitefield twenty pounds a year.

> 'Several of Mr Broughton's late parishioners at Cowley forget not the assembling of themselves together, notwithstanding the manifold discouragements from the world. Your friends at Oxford continue to exhort and edify one another.'[2]

Among such friends Hervey was probably the most distinguished, 'that great champion of the Lord of Hosts', as Walter Chapman called him.

While he was in residence Hervey must certainly have been the leading spirit among the Oxford society; but he was himself soon to move away from Oxford. He had been elected to one of Lord Crewe's exhibitions, and in order to retain the emolument of £20 a year attached to it, his

---

[1] See C. W. Towlson, *Moravian and Methodist*, 1957.

[2] *Evangelical Magazine* (1744), 295. Broughton and Henry Washington later became 'estranged', denying salvation by Christ's imputed righteousness. (C. Wesley, *Journal*, i, 119–20, 124, 126.)

father urged him to get a curacy at Oxford (he had been ordained by the Bishop of Oxford on 17th September, 1736). As he believed that this course of action might prevent someone more deserving from holding the exhibition, he left Oxford to become Kinchin's curate at Dummer. In 1738 he went as chaplain to Paul Orchard at Stoke Abbey, in Devon, and two years later as curate to Bideford. Latterly he held his father's living at Weston Favell. Hervey's theological position was already tinged with the Calvinist ideas which led eventually to the controversy with John Wesley.[1] Writing to George Whitefield on 29th July, 1735, he spoke of the desirability of a weekly celebration of the Holy Communion.

'The holy eucharist is a communion of the body and blood of Christ; —a participation of all the benefits procured for us by His most meritorious passion. In this most comfortable sacrament, pardon is freely offered to us all.'

But he added that no reliance must be placed on good works as a means of salvation:

'All your own righteousness are as filthy rags and will be utterly unable to gain your acceptance. . . . There is nothing else under heaven whereby you can be saved, but His meritorious passion. Unless His body pleads in your behalf, you are covered with shame, and everlasting confusion.'

The religious society, deprived of the energetic leadership of John Wesley, was thus experiencing some difficulties. There was an undoubted element of insecurity and frustration which inhibited progress. This was in part a sequel to the prominence which the Georgian venture had acquired, not merely in the mind of Wesley himself, but of his friends. Morgan expressed his urgent desire to join Wesley in Georgia. Mrs. Fox was also set on going: 'Mrs. Fox', Morgan told Wesley, 'just now came to me to let me know that she is desirous to go to Georgia, and that her husband and she have agreed to go there, if accepted of. By the return of the ships', he added a little unkindly, 'we shall be able to judge of their sincerity.' James Hervey compared Wesley and Ingham to Noah and his family as they disembarked from the Ark.[2] John Wesley himself, too,

---

[1] These were put forward in *Dialogues between Theron and Aspasia*, 3 vols. (1755). Wesley wrote *Remarks on Theron and Aspasia*, in which he sought to correct Hervey's reliance on the doctrine of imputed righteousness.

[2] *Arminian Magazine* (1778), i, 130–2.

felt that the missionary call should awaken response in those who had been his friends at Oxford.

> 'Where are ye who are very zealous for the Lord of hosts? Who will rise up with me against the wicked? Who will take God's part against the evil-doers? Whose spirit is moved within him to prepare himself for publishing the glad tidings to those on whom the Sun of Righteousness never yet arose, by labouring first for those his countrymen who are else without hope as well as without God in the world?'[1]

Six months later he pressed his former associate, John Hutchings, to join him,[2] and when this request appeared vain, he despatched Ingham to make a personal appeal. But Ingham became absorbed with the Moravians, and this too came to nothing.[3] Wesley could not repress his feeling of disappointment as he told Dr. Humphreys, the secretary of the S.P.G., on 22nd July, 1737, that primitive Christian enthusiasm seemed dead.[4] It seems very likely that Wesley was himself experiencing a sense of disillusion, as he found his white congregations difficult and the Indians less responsive than he had supposed they might have been. It was against a darkening cloud and a growing crisis that the Georgian venture began to close.

Charles Wesley, disappointed by his own experience, had already returned to England, landing at Deal on 3rd December, 1736. He found many critical of his activities. When he dined with his uncle, Matthew Wesley, shortly before Christmas, the old man 'bestowed abundance of wit on my brother, and his apostolical project' and said laughingly that the French, if they had any 'remarkably dull fellow among them', sent him to convert the Indians; but Wesley soon checked his sneers.[5] Neither of the brothers had much sense of humour. Late in January, 1737, he called on Mary Pendarves just as she was reading a letter which reported his own death; but he does not state what welcome he received, merely adding rather bitterly, 'Happy for me, had the news been true! What a world of misery would it save me.'[6] Ten days later he was with the Bishop of Oxford at his London house to tell him that the Bishop of London

---

[1] *Letters* of John Wesley, i, 204–6.
[2] *Op. cit.*, i, 211 ff. [No = *Rich. Morgan*]
[3] *Op. cit.*, i, 320 ff.
[4] *Op. cit.*, i, 225.
[5] C. Wesley, *Journal*, i, 59.
[6] *Op. cit.*, i, 66.

would have nothing to do with Georgia, a view that Dr. Potter refuted, encouraging Wesley to 'acknowledge the Moravians as our brethren'.[1] The visit to the Bishop came shortly after his first journey to Oxford. Undoubtedly from the point of view of the remaining members of the Oxford society Charles' return meant a reinvigoration. He arrived back at Oxford on Tuesday, 8th February, 1737, lodging with his old friend, Mr. Sarney, in order to vote at the parliamentary election. That very evening he talked to the religious society, where he was pleased to find Kinchin 'changed into a courageous soldier of Christ'. He encouraged the society by telling its members about Zinzendorf and the Moravians and by reading portions of his brother's journal to them. The next day he accompanied his friend, Horne, to Convocation to vote in the election for a burgess for the University; Charles Wesley cast his vote for the independent Tory, William Bromley, who was returned.[2] Later he visited the Castle and renewed acquaintance with some of the inmates. 'Honest' Thomas Waite was still in prison but Mrs. Topping, with whose troubles John Clayton had been so concerned five years earlier,[3] was dead. In the evening he spent some time with 'my old pupil, Robert Kirkham, as before, in mutual exhortation' and met his younger brother, Bernard, an undergraduate at Corpus. Later in his stay he talked with Gambold and Kinchin and tried to persuade Richard Smith and Carter to keep to their old ideals. He also dined with his old friend, Mr. Woods of Abingdon, 'the same kind friendly man'.

He made a courtesy call on the Dean of Christ Church, Dr. Conybeare, who had as a ministerial Whig been strongly in favour of Bromley's opponent, Robert Trevor. The Dean expostulated with Wesley on his action, 'for voting against him (as he called it)', but after an hour's discussion they parted good friends. The next day Charles called on the Rector of Lincoln, who was eager to hear news of John Wesley. The Rector received Charles 'very affectionately'.[4]

It was obvious that he could not accomplish much in so short a visit, but he renewed some of the contacts with his friends and was back again at the end of April, 1737. Before this, visiting at Mrs. Pendarves, he had been pressed to accompany her sister, Anne, whom he was very pleased

[1] C. Wesley, *Journal*, i, 67.

[2] W. R. Ward, *Georgian Oxford*, 153–4. Bromley was elected by 329 to 126 votes. He died, however, five weeks later.

[3] *Journal*, viii, 278–9.

[4] C. Wesley, *Journal*, i, 68.

to see again, her brother, Bernard, and her future husband, Mr. Dewes, to Mickleton. They set out on the 22nd March, breaking their journey at Oxford, where Charles met Gambold and was 'much moved by hearing' the history of his brother, John. Naturally he took advantage of his stay at Mickleton to ride over to Stanton, 'where they were all overjoyed to see me; especially my first of friends, Varanese'. He could not resist introducing religious topics into the conversation, seeking to persuade Anne Granville of the 'fewness of those that are saved', and remarking sadly, if a trifle pompously, 'How little is she advanced in the school of Christ, who is not convinced of this truth!' Her brother proved more amenable, and was much affected by a chapter that Charles read from William Law's *Serious Call*; but whether from courtesy or conviction does not appear. From Mickleton he made his way to Oxford, where he stayed as usual with Sarney, though not it would seem in great comfort, for he had to sleep on the floor. He breakfasted with a young undergraduate from Magdalen, Charles Graves,[1] the brother of the poet, Richard Graves, of Pembroke, who tearfully revealed to him that he had 'never felt any true joy in religion'. As with Granville, he told him to go and read William Law. He visited Gambold at Stanton Harcourt and found him more cheerful, and the Dean of Christ Church, upon whom he called subsequently, was 'very kind and friendly'. He spoke to the prisoners and found them attentive.

He was again in Oxford during the course of the summer, partly because his sister Kezzy was staying with the Gambolds, and partly to hearten the society. Charles Graves called on him the day of his arrival 'in an excellent temper. I encouraged him to go on in the narrow way, and strongly recommended stated hours of retirement.' Graves' adherence suggests that there was a reawakening of interest among the undergraduates. This is also the impression given by a letter from Ingham to John Wesley, written in October, 1737, for while Ingham deplored Charles' reticence—'he neither writes to me, nor comes to see me'—he reported that things at Oxford were relatively prosperous.

'All friends at Oxford go on well. Mr. Kinchin, Mr. Hutchins,[2] Mr.

---

[1] Matric. 14th October, 1736, aged 19; demy 1736. B.A. 1740. Vicar of Tissington from 1759 to his death in 1787. In a letter to the fellows of Magdalen, Charles Graves recanted his views in 1740, but two years later wrote to retract 'that scandalous paper, so unchristianly imposed upon me'. (*Journal*, iii, 40–2.)

[2] Not Richard Hutchins of Lincoln but John Hutchings of Pembroke.

Washington, Bell, Turner,[1] Hervey, Watson, are all zealous. Mr. Atkinson labours under severe trials in Westmoreland; but is steady, and sincere and an excellent Christian. . . . Mr. Thompson, of Queen's, has declared his resolution of following Christ.'[2]

On 7th July, after dinner with another sympathizer and friend, Lady Cox,[3] he had another talk with Graves, who appeared overjoyed at the change in his life. He was the more horrified to learn three weeks later that he had been carried away as 'stark mad'. Charles Wesley believed that he had been put away purposely by his friends and was very relieved to find him recovered in the autumn. 'At night he came in [to Sarney's], fell upon my neck and burst into tears. It is hard to say, whether his friends' hatred, or his love, of me, exceeds.'[4] There were indeed disconcerting if not unexpected signs of opposition. In the Long Walk he came across two acquaintances, Battely of Christ Church, and Matthew Robinson, his brother's pupil at Lincoln, and now a don at B.N.C., but they were very distant. They urged him to export more of the 'Cowley saints' to Georgia and charged the Methodists with 'intrusion, schism and bringing neglect upon the ministry'. Charles Wesley left them with the dogmatic warning: 'Remember, you will be of my mind when you come to die', and the next day departed for London with Richard Morgan and Charles Kinchin.

In spite of such opposition, headway had been made at the University. Even Charles Graves' brother, Richard, seemed favourably impressed by Charles Wesley's adjurations.[5] He could not indeed stir Richard Smith to any enthusiasm, even by suggesting that he should go to bed at regular hours (presumably to facilitate the early rising by which the Wesleys set

[1] Thomas Turner of Webley, Herefordshire, was admitted servitor of Lincoln College on 13th May, 1736.

[2] L. Tyerman, *Wesley*, i, 137.

[3] Ann Foulkes, the daughter of Dr. Peter Foulkes, Canon of Christchurch, whom Wesley had known earlier (Diary, 8th August, 1729, '4.0 p.m. Miss Foulks'). Cf. *Letters*, i, 233. She married Sir Robert Cox.

[4] C. Wesley, *Journal*, i, 76.

[5] On 10th October, Charles called on Richard Graves. 'I went to his rooms, talked the whole matter over, and were both entirely satisfied. Then I spoke of my making his brother Charles mad; hoped he himself would be one of those whose life fools count madness, explained the nature of true religion. . . . He was greatly moved; complained that he could not pray. I appealed to him, whether he had not formerly felt more solid pleasure in religion than in all the caresses of the world. He confessed it, and resolved to return. I earnestly recommended Law, the daily retirement, as my last legacy. . . . We then kissed, and parted. . . . ' (*Journal*, i, 77.)

such store), and poor Mr. Carter was dying but there were hopeful signs elsewhere. A young fellow of Jesus College, Christopher Wells,[1] was hovering on the brink of conversion. Charles read William Law on the Redemption to him.

> 'In the afternoon I met Mr. Wells alone', Charles Wesley wrote in his diary for 29th September, 1737, 'and had some close talk with him upon the new birth, self-renunciation, &c. He confirmed reputation was his idol; rejected his own righteousness: convinced but fearful: longing to break loose. I went with him to the Chapel; and afterwards resumed the subject. He seemed on the brink of the new birth.'

Wells remained irresolute, but was eventually 'convinced of the truth'. In August, 1738, Wells was present at John Hutchings' rooms when Charles Wesley told him of an experience which Kinchin had recently had and which did much to confirm Wells' faith.[2] In November, 1738, Charles preached the faith of the Gospel at Wells' rooms to Wells and a Mr. Hoare; later in the day he rode with Wells and Kinchin to Coggs, 'where we spent the evening in prayer and the Scriptures'.[3] Although Kinchin was still at Dummer, he remained in close contact with Charles, who indeed described him as his 'inseparable companion', and with the Oxford society. On Saturday, 8th October, Charles tried to arrange a meeting of this society 'as my brother &c used formerly', at which Kinchin, Henry Washington of Queen's, Hutchings and Sarney were present. That evening, after visiting Tom Horne at Spilsbury (where he was now vicar), he returned 'to read *Nicodemus*' at Queen's. Kinchin and Hutchings were also present at Mr. Fox's when Charles came to Oxford in August, 1738, to take his turn at preaching. Later Seward spoke of Kinchin expounding to a group which included forty gownsmen; in February, 1738, Charles prayed at Mr. Sarney's 'with some scholars'. After he preached to the poor prisoners in the Castle on 29th August, Watson was among the members of the society present at their meeting.[4] It thus seems very likely that the revival of interest in the University antedated John Wesley's return to England.

[1] Matric. 15th July, 1721, aged 15; B.A. 1724, M.A. 1727, B.D. 1735. In Wales Wells later asked Charles Wesley to preach in his churches. Cf. C. Wesley, *Journal*, i, 254, 255, 257, 259, 287, 288, 299.

[2] Charles Wesley's *Journal*, i, 129.

[3] Charles Wesley's *Journal*, i, 137. This was Joseph Hoare, matric. 14th March, 1727, aged 18; B.A. 1730, M.A. 1733, B.D. 1741, D.D. 1768. Fellow of Jesus and Principal from 1768 until 1802.

[4] *Op. cit.*, i, 77.

This was also true of the townspeople, as the gatherings at Mr. Fox's and Mr. Sarney's suggest. At the meeting to which allusion has been made which took place on 29th August, 1738, all those present were 'earnestly seeking Christ'. 'I read the Homilies, and continued instant in prayer. A woman cried out, "Where have I been so long? I have been in darkness: I never shall be delivered out of it"—and burst into tears.'[1] The meetings were beginning to assume the emotional tinge which often gave rise to this religious exhibitionism. Mrs. Cleminger, 'too, appeared in the pangs of the new birth'. Fox, who had been rescued by the Wesleys from the debtors' prison, had been for some time a pillar of the society. Combes, who may also have been in the debtors' prison, accompanied Charles Wesley to Oxford in September, 1738. Combes expressed religious doubts.

> 'I was moved', Charles wrote, 'to sing "Salvation by faith", then "Faith in Christ". I told him, if the Spirit had convinced him of unbelief, he could of righteousness also, even before we reached Oxford. I stopped and prayed that he might believe. Immediately he told me, he was such in a blessed temper, as he never before experienced. We halted, and went to prayers. He testified the great delight he felt, saying, it was heaven, if it would but continue. . . . We sang and shouted all the way to Oxford.'

Mrs. Platt[2] was another who was brought to the light of genuine belief. Charles Wesley read out his sermon to the society, ending with 'my usual question, "Do you deserve to be damned?" Mrs. Platt at once shouted out, "Yes, I do, I do!"' Charles Wesley then prayed that God would send his Holy Spirit to promise salvation if there was any genuinely contrite soul there. 'Again she broke into strong cries, but of joy, not sorrow, being quite overpowered, with the love of Christ.' Wesley asked her if she believed in Jesus. She answered 'Yes' and while she continued kneeling, all the members of the society joined in thanksgiving. It was at the climax of this emotional scene that Kinchin added, 'Have you forgiveness of sins?' She replied 'I am perfectly assured I have.' 'Have you', he then asked, 'the earnest of the Spirit in your heart?' 'I have; I know I have; I feel it now within.' It was this experience of Mrs. Platt's which

---

[1] *Op. cit.*, i, 128.

[2] She had been connected with the religious society for some time as entries in Wesley's diary indicate, e.g. on 15th October, 1733, he noted that she had been 'blooded'; on 31st January, 1734, he talked with John Platt of early rising.

had done so much to confirm the faith of Mr. Wells. There is then little doubt that in spite of a breach with John Sarney, which marred his stay at Oxford in the early autumn of 1738,[1] and the friendly but critical attitude of the Dean,[2] the society had made marked progress during the period which immediately preceded John Wesley's return to England.

Obscure as the story of the Holy Club at Oxford may appear to be during the Wesleys' absence in Georgia, there are certain indications that it was changing shape. It was attracting an increasing number of townspeople, and had a diminishing following among the young dons. While it still sponsored work among the prisoners, it was much more occupied with mutual self-exhortation, with pious practices, readings, prayers and meditations, and more dominated by the search for personal salvation and sanctification than for Christian righteousness and brotherhood.

[1] 'I called on my friend that *was*, John Sarney, now entirely estranged by the offence of the cross.' (Thursday, 28th September, 1738.)

[2] 'I waited upon the Dean; but we could not quite agree in our notions of faith. . . . We wondered we had not hit upon the Homilies sooner; treated me with great candour and friendliness.' (Thursday, 31st August, 1738.)

CHAPTER XIV

John Wesley's Conversion

SO much has been written about Wesley's experience in Aldersgate Street on 24th May, 1738, that any further discussion might seem needless. Yet because it brought one effective period of his life, the Oxford period, with which this book is primarily concerned, towards its close, a few comments may be allowed, though no final or dogmatic statement can be made on what was ultimately a personal, subjective experience. Psychologically it provided Wesley with a feeling of reassurance about his faith which, in spite of continuing doubts and recurring depression, created an inner spiritual dynamism which had been lacking. It was a crisis of a major order from which Wesley emerged in some sense a changed man, though the characteristic features of his personality were the same as they had previously been. It added to rather than subtracted from the personal faith which he had acquired in long years of religious experience. It did not in any significant way change his character but it underlined and confirmed his conviction of the truth of the message which he was seeking to give his fellow-men and women. It supplied him with that which he had sought in vain since he ceased to be dependent on his mother, a feeling of confidence in and dependence on an uncontrovertible authority.

Yet it was less the beginning of a new phase than a vital and critical stage in a development which had started at Epworth and continued at Oxford. The Roman Catholic writer, Maximin Piette, held that his 'conversion' was to be dated from his ordination in 1725; but as later critics have shown this is an over-simplification founded on a meaningless phrase in Tyerman's learned biography. If there was a precise moment which crystallized Wesley's spiritual development, then it occurred in May, 1738, but the moment may not be detached from what had gone before nor should it be seen as a final and irrevocable experience.

John Wesley's conversion was the climax of a spiritual development, itself the product of various influences. The predominant religious ethos in early eighteenth-century Oxford was a High-Churchmanship rooted in patristic writings and traditions broadly represented by Hooker and

Laud, and fashioned since the Restoration by the course of events. The policy and fate of James II had placed the High Churchmen in an unacceptable quandary. In an effort to produce a stable front against the aggressive papalism of the foolish Stuart monarch, they had sponsored overtures to dissenters which implied greater theological comprehension and a possible revision of the existing prayer book. Against such potential latitude one High-Church group, the altitudinarians as they were sometimes called, reacted strongly. The more rigid, headed by the Non-juring bishops, refused to countenance the monarchy of William III and looked to a Stuart restoration. They continued to hope that the future James III might be guided towards the Church of England. One of the Non-jurors consulted the deposed king as to the appointment of George Hickes as a suffragan to the Non-juring Bishop of Norwich. The Non-juror, Charles Leslie, actually went to the Court of St. Germain to act as Anglican Chaplain there. Indeed, the interest in fostering relations with Gallican Catholicism shown at the end of the seventeenth century may have been founded partly on the belief in the possibility of a reconciliation with what some believed to be potential non-papalist Catholicism. Non-juring Catholicism was clearly associated with what the Orange or Hanoverian monarchy believed to be treasonable activity. Yet the Non-jurors, if possessed of learned, fervent and saintly advocates,[1] were comparatively few in number, and separated from their High-Church brethren by their unreadiness to compromise with an elective monarchy.

Theologically they had much in common with the other High Churchmen of late seventeenth- and early eighteenth-century Oxford. The phrase 'High Church' has a somewhat wider connotation than is generally supposed, since it was broad enough to embrace the Whig John Potter (whose *Discourse of Church Government* betrayed the influence of Dodwell) and the heretical Cambridge mathematician, William Whiston, whose eccentric if learned advocacy of the Apostolic Constitutions led him into trouble.[2] Certain basic assumptions stood out clearly. Bishop Talbot, of Oxford, deploring them in 1712, summarized them as 'the independency of the Church upon the State', 'A Proper Sacrifice in the Sacrament of the Lord's Supper', 'the necessity of sacerdotal absolution' and 'the invalidity of baptism administered by persons not epis-

[1] Two of the principal Non-jurors, George Hickes and John Kettlewell, had been fellows of Lincoln College. The Manchester Non-jurors, Thomas Deacon and John Byrom, were both acquainted with the Wesleys.

[2] George Every, *The High Church Party, 1688–1715*, 125, 133.

copally ordained'. These implied a view of the authority of the Church and its sacraments out of sympathy with Latitudinarian theology and Low-Church attempts at comprehension. This attitude was founded on what its advocates held to be the practice and principles of the primitive and apostolic Church, in themselves the measure of orthodoxy. Such High-Churchmanship, with its powerful political feelings reflected in current controversy relating to such topics as occasional conformity, the imposition of the Church's penitential discipline and the powers and policy of Convocation, tapered off into unexpected points. It harbingered, for instance, an interest in mystical theology and the possibility of reconciliation with non-papalist but essentially Catholic churches, like the Gallican Church, and also with German Lutheranism.

One of the most interesting of contemporary Oxford figures was the patristic scholar, John Grabe. A Prussian by birth, his study of the Fathers had brought him in 1695 to the verge of entering the Roman Church, but he was encouraged by the German pietist, Philip Spener, to visit Oxford before taking this step. He found that the Church of England, not Roman, yet Catholic and apostolic, met his intellectual and spiritual requirements. Bishop Lloyd of Worcester made him a deacon in 1700 and he continued to press on with his learned patristic studies and with schemes for a union of the Church of England with the reformed Lutheran Churches of Prussia and Hanover which could be based upon a revised liturgy, Catholic and apostolic in its set-up. Grabe himself preferred to communicate after the order of the Scottish Prayer Book of 1637 or the English liturgy of 1549. In so far as he epitomized the High-Church tradition of Oxford at the time of Wesley's entry at the University, he showed that founded as it might be on patristic theology, it had yet components which brought it into touch with German pietism and post-Reformation Catholic devotional literature.

The political and intellectual developments currently associated with Oxford's religious life quickened the separation from the establishment in Church and State, for the slight resurgence of High-Churchmanship at the end of Anne's reign was soon countered by the universal preferments of Latitudinarian Whigs to the episcopal bench under the first two Hanoverian kings.[1] The Church was confronted by growing infidelity. 'There seems', as the author of the *Letter to a Convocation Man*

---

[1] Queen Caroline certainly favoured High Churchmen, and was responsible for the preferment of Thomas Sherlock to the bishopric of Bangor in 1728, but the Whig Latitudinarian churchmen remained in the ascendant.

T

commented, 'to be universal conspiracy . . . to undermine and overthrow the Catholick faith'.

It was in such an atmosphere that John Wesley and his brother moved from adolescence to manhood. The moral theology of Epworth may have been harsher and more demanding than that of contemporary Oxford but the rector of Epworth's views were theologically sympathetic towards those currently taught at Oxford. He had himself been involved in more than one theological controversy on the High-Church side.[1] John Wesley was a voracious reader,[2] but the range of his theological study on close investigation appears somewhat limited. He certainly read books by Samuel Clarke, William Wollaston and John Locke with which he fundamentally disagreed, but by and large his theological study falls into certain definite compartments.

The basic emphasis in his reading was on patristic learning and the teaching of the Fathers. Like the dons of whom Amhurst wrote so contemptuously, Wesley read the writings of the Fathers of the early Church in Grabe's *Spicelegium*; he also studied Wake's *Apostolic Epistles* and *Fathers*, Reeves' *Apologies of Christian Martyrs*, St. Augustine's *Confessions*, Lactantius, Vincent of Lerins' *Commonitorium*, and more recent works on the early Church like William Cave's *Primitive Christianity* and Marshall's *Penitential Discipline of the Primitive Church*.[3] His reading led him to fasten particularly on certain features of the apostolic age, that the Church was the body of the elect, that in the *communio sanctorum*, in Dodwell's words, none were admitted 'to this profession of Christianity but they who had first given some evidence of their sincerity', that it was sustained by the sacrament of the Holy Communion and by a penitential discipline, in which fasting had an important part, designed to cultivate the personal holiness of the individual Christian.

The majority of contemporary works on theology that came his way were by writers in the tradition of the Non-jurors and High Churchmen. His favourite authors in his Oxford period, some of whose books were later reprinted in his *Christian Library*, were men like John Norris,[4]

---

[1] Viz. in his attack on dissenting academies and championship of Sacheverell.

[2] See Appendix 1, 'Wesley's Reading', 1725–34.

[3] In September, 1733, Clayton replied to Wesley, who had asked his advice about reading in a letter which contained allusions to the Epistles of St. Clement, St. Ignatius and St. Barnabas, the Shepherd of Hermas and the Apostolical Constitutions.

[4] On Norris, see F. J. Powicke, *John Norris* (1898). Norris was much indebted to Malebranche, whose works Wesley also read. Cf. 'I have followed Mr. Norris's

Bishop Bull (whom he later criticized), Beveridge, Sprat, Atterbury, Sharp, Smalridge, George Hickes, John Kettlewell, Charles Leslie, Richard Fiddes, Robert Nelson, Bishop Ken and John Rogers. He read the tract on toleration written by Edward Synge, the Archbishop of Tuam, who had opposed the Toleration Act of 1719 because he feared that it would promote the spread of Popery. His awareness of current theological controversy is shown by his perusal of Henry Stebbing's tracts against Bishop Hoadly, and Wall's important book on Infant Baptism. His concern with the Holy Communion led to his reading in Eucharistic Theology, John Johnson's *The Propitiatory Oblation in the Holy Eucharist*, Bishop Wilson's *Instruction for the Lord's Supper*, Scanderet's *Sacrifice the Divine Service*, and Brevint's *The Christian Sacrament the Lord's Supper*,[1] as well as a number of tracts designed to prepare the worshipper for a worthy reception of the Sacrament.

John Wesley was not a profound or creative thinker. While his theological reading was within certain limits relatively wide, it was apt to be somewhat superficial. Many of the books that he perused were relatively elementary introductions or companions to the subjects of which they treated, reminding the reader of what Wesley himself tried to do in the *Christian Library* at a later date. Such were, for instance, William Lowth's *Direction for the Profitable Study of the Scriptures*, Charles Wheatley's *The Church of England Man's Companion*, and Thomas Bennet's *Directions for Studying*.

The final group of theological literature which he read was different in scope. It was pre-eminently concerned with the life of devotion and with practical Christianity. He read the lives of pious Christians; of the seventeenth-century soldier and missionary, de Renty, whom he described as one of the 'brightest patterns of heavenly wisdom', of James Bonnel, of Ambrose Bonwick, a young Cambridge student who died in his study at College with his books of devotion beside him,[2] of the Christian soldier, Mr. Illidge; and works of moral exhortation like the

---

advice these thirty years, and so must every man that is well in his senses.' (*Letters*, iii, 175, 16th April, 1756.)

[1] John and his brother published extracts from Dr. Brevint's work, interpreting his ideas in a more definitely Catholic way than he had done himself, as a preface to *Hymns on the Lord's Supper* (1745).

[2] Bonwick's father, Ambrose (1652–1722), was a schoolmaster and Non-juror. His son (d. 1729), a scholar of St. John's College, Cambridge, was likewise a Non-juror and a man of sensitive and scrupulous conscience.

Second Spira and Josiah Woodward's *Fair Warning to a Careless World*. If the emphasis in his own life was more and more on personal sanctity, so his reading became inevitably devoted to that end; St. Augustine's *Confessions*, Ephrem Syrus' *On Repentance*, Heylin's *Devotional Tracts*, Spurstow's *Meditations*, Richard Lucas' *Enquiry*, John Scott's *The Christian Life*, Spinckes' *Meditations and Devotions*,[1] and some of the better-known works of post-Tridentine Catholicism, Sales' *Introduction to a Devout and Holy Life*, and Rodriguez' *On Humility*, Castiniza's *Spiritual Conflict*, and the writings of Fénelon, the Archbishop of Cambrai, as well as sundry other works of a similar character. There were three writers whom Wesley regarded as epochal in his development—Thomas à Kempis, Jeremy Taylor and William Law. A passing fascination with mystical theology brought him to a study of A. H. Francke's *Nicodemus* and some of the German pietists.

All this reading should have had the effect of making him into a conventional, scholarly High Churchman, and this in a sense is what John Wesley was in his Oxford years; he was interested in talking with John Clayton about the minutiae of ceremonial[2] as well as about the major issues of Christian faith.

In his appreciation of the early Church, its scriptural and apostolic traditions, John Wesley was primarily concerned with the sanctification of the individual Christian. He has described this development in an autobiographical statement which was certainly coloured by his later experience but may be broadly accepted as correct. In 1725 he read

[1] Cf. Clayton's letter to Wesley (September, 1733): 'On Wednesday and Friday I have for some time used the Office for Passion week out of Spinckes' "Devotions" and bless God for it. . . .'

[2] He discussed with him such questions as the keeping of Saturday ('I do not look upon it as preparation for Sunday, but as a festival itself', Clayton told Wesley on July, 1733; 'and therefore I have continued festival prayer for the three primitive hours, and for morning and evening, from the Apostolical Constitutions. . . . I look upon Friday as my preparation for the celebration of both the Sabbath and the Lord's Day; the first of which I observe much like a common saint's day, or as one of the inferior holidays of the Church. I bless God I have generally contrived to have the Eucharist celebrated on Saturdays as well as other holidays, for the use of myself and the sick people whom I visit'), prayers for the faithful departed, the observance of the Stations, and the Mixed Chalice ('As to the mixture Mr. Colly told me he would assure me it was constantly used at Christ Church. However, if you have reason to doubt it, I would have you to inquire; but I cannot think the want of it a reason for not communicating. If I could receive when the mixture was used I would; and therefore I used to prefer the Castle to Christ Church . . .').

Jeremy Taylor's *Rule and Exercise of Holy Living and Dying* and was especially affected by that part of it which dealt with 'purity of intention'.

> 'Instantly I resolved to dedicate all my life to God, all my thoughts, and words and actions, being thoroughly convinced, there was no medium: but that every part of my life (not some only) must either be a sacrifice to God, or myself, that is, in effect to the devil.'[1]

Next year, in fact his memory here played him false,[2] he read à Kempis' *Christian Pattern* in Dean Stanhope's translation. 'I saw that giving even all my life to God (supposing it possible to do this, and go no further) would profit me nothing, unless I gave my heart, yea, all my heart to him.' He realized that the 'simplicity of intention and purity of affection' of which à Kempis wrote were the 'wings of the soul' without which it can never ascend to the mount of God. Finally, a year or two after, he read William Law's *Christian Perfection* and *Serious Call*. 'These convinced me, more than ever, of the absolute impossibility of being half a Christian, and I determined, through his grace (the absolute necessity of which I was deeply sensible of) to be all-devoted to God, to give him all my soul, my body, and my substance.' Law, who had been a fellow of Emmanuel, Cambridge, was ordained in 1711 but refused the oath of allegiance to George I. 'I expected to have had a greater share of worldly advantages than what I am now likely to enjoy.' He turned to writing, defending what he considered the Christian faith against Hoadly and Mandeville and demonstrating the absolute unlawfulness of stage entertainments. Wesley was greatly attracted by Law's ethical idealism, and momentarily by the mystical detachment with which it was associated.[3] He visited Law on a number of occasions at Putney,[4] talking with him on 28th November, 1734, for no less than three hours, and as a result was persuaded to read the *Theologica Germanica* and other mystical works.

[1] From Taylor he learned especially the virtue of humility, the assurance of the forgiveness of sins and the practice of making rules of life and resolutions; cf. H. Trevor Hughes, 'John Wesley and Jeremy Taylor' in the *London Quarterly* (October, 1949), 581–601.

[2] He was certainly reading à Kempis in 1725, in all probability before he began reading Jeremy Taylor.

[3] Cf. J. Brazier Green, *John Wesley and William Law* (1945).

[4] 'Monday, 31st July, 1732, at Putney [where Law was acting as tutor to the young Edward Gibbon] in the garden in talk—began *Theologica Germanica*.' 'November 28, 1733, 9.15 a.m. with Mr. Law, not understood all he said.' Cf. *Letters*, i, 161–3, 238–44; iii, 332–70.

Wesley was himself incorrect in supposing that à Kempis, Taylor and Law were the only significant writers who influenced his spiritual development at this period, but they more than the many others whom he read were primarily responsible in cultivating his search for personal salvation and personal holiness, which he believed to be a prerequisite before he could bring others to this end.

Yet the emphasis he placed on this and on the example of the primitive Church, its discipline, its fasts, its sacraments and its order, led him, as it has led others since his day, to stress detachment from the world rather than redemption through it. His was then primarily the gospel of ascetic aloofness rather than of affirmation, and it necessarily set up tensions which his environment, whether at Oxford, at Epworth, or at Stanton, served to foster. A detailed examination would demand an entire book. He had a strong and vital faith in the Christian Gospel. There was never a hint of doubt in his mind. He was a natural believer. He had carried this faith into practice in the life of Oxford and Epworth by frequent and regular reading of the Bible and constant prayer and communion; he took his part in acts of continuing charity and goodwill. What more could he demand of himself? He had to an increasing extent overcome the temptations involved in trifling company and worldly amusement. There were three features of his life which prevented a complete spiritual harmony.

In the first place there was the turbulent emotion which friendship with his feminine friends aroused. In the second place, there was a feeling that in spite of his high pretensions there was an element of disillusioning failure. He cannot have been entirely happy about his relations with Richard Morgan; or about the calmer criticisms voiced in Oxford. His refusal to follow his father at Epworth, which among other consequences turned his mother and his sisters from their home, was neither a happy nor an easy one. Finally, he had become so obsessed with the notion of 'half-Christians' that he may have begun to wonder whether he was himself in danger of becoming one of those whom he condemned.[1] The mission to Georgia thus offered an escape and a challenge. He sailed for America in a state of considerable emotional and spiritual perturbation.

The Georgian experience, though of vital significance, did nothing whatever to solve the confused problems in Wesley's mind. Indeed, in

---

[1] Cf. his comment in 1741: 'I did go thus far [i.e. being almost a Christian] for many years as many of this place [Oxford] can testify . . . yet my own conscience beareth me witness in the Holy Ghost, that all this time I was but almost a Christian.'

some ways it had been a disillusioning process. Instead of spending his time preaching to the Indians, he had found himself coping with disagreeable and difficult colonists who resented his high-handed attempts to apply to their moral lapses the penitential discipline of the early Church. His own and his brother's lack of experience and their limited knowledge of human nature were a disservice and they were at once made the stalking-horse of intriguers who sought to vilify Oglethorpe. There seemed no escape from growing unpopularity which reached its climax when Wesley, at the close of an incredibly indiscreet relationship with Sophy Hopkey, used ecclesiastical discipline, as it appeared to the colonists, to forward his personal ends. He had courted Sophy Hopkey, but Sophy was no Kitty Hargreaves or Sally Chapone, or Mary Pendarves. The repercussions of the unfortunate affair between the high-minded young don and the sensitive Sophy re-echoed through the colony and reached the Mother Country.

The occasional missionary journeys to the Indians were not particularly successful, for the Indians, simple-minded in their acceptance of religious faith, were often treacherous and beastly; they preferred, so far as its ethics were concerned, other and stronger things than the pure milk of the Gospel. Discouraged by his experience, Charles Wesley had already left for England, and his brother was not long in following him. In some ways his departure was more of a flight from rough colonial justice than the decent and decorous ending of a colonial chaplaincy.

The Georgian visit was none the less extremely noteworthy. It may not have taught John Wesley very much about human nature but it made him realize that the life of the Holy Club, austere and self-sacrificing as it undoubtedly was, yet lacked a certain dynamic quality when it came to dealing with a group of hard-bitten worldly men and women. Moreover conditions in the colony instead of making the life of personal holiness more possible made it more difficult to achieve. Wesley himself felt a deep sense of personal failure, more so than at any time in his career. He felt that he lacked the self-assurance and conviction which came from a divinely given faith, and he compared his own lack of faith and courage, the depression to which he was subject, with the abundance of these qualities displayed by the Moravian missionaries.

The role of the Moravians in Wesley's spiritual development has been repeatedly stressed.[1] He had been tremendously impressed by the courage

---

[1] Cf. C. W. Towlson, *Moravian and Methodist* (1957).

they had shown in the stormy Atlantic weather, and later they had raised with him in blunt fashion the question of a saving faith.

'I asked Mr. Spangenberg's advice', he wrote in his *Journal*, 'with regard to myself—to my own conduct. He told me he could say nothing till he had asked me two or three questions: "Do you know yourself? Have you the witness within yourself? Does the Spirit of God bear witness with your spirit that you are a child of God?" I was surprised and knew not what to answer. He observed it, and asked "Do you know Jesus Christ?" I paused and said, "I know he is the Saviour of the world." "True," replied he, "but do you know He has saved you?" I answered, "I hope He has died to save me." He only added "Do you know yourself?" I said, "I do." But I fear they were vain words.'

In his comparatively confused state of mind, Spangenberg's question only raised further the fear that he was 'almost a Christian' but 'not a whole Christian', and the emphasis his Moravian friends placed on justification suggested a possible way out from the spiritual crisis through which he was living.

He returned to England and Oxford uncertain of the future. He was still a fellow of Lincoln[1] and it was open to him to return into residence. Indeed the possibility of doing this recurred to his mind more than once during the next few years. John Hutchings stressed the Holy Club's need of a resident leader in Oxford. 'God formerly set His seal to your labours of love in this place, and I hope He will be pleased to bless your endeavours yet more.' He had landed at Deal on 1st February, 1738, and on the 17th returned to Oxford, making for the house of his brother's friend, John Sarney, a prominent mercer in the city, whose name appears frequently in the Council records between 1739, the year in which he paid fees for admission to the Mercers' Company, and 1751.[2] Both Charles and the Moravian, Peter Böhler, were with him. 'All this time', he wrote of his visit to Oxford, 'I conversed much with Peter Böhler; but I understood him not, and least of all when he said *Mi frater, mi frater excoquenda est ista*

---

[1] Tom Horne received Wesley's stipend on his behalf on 23rd May, 1737.

[2] *Council Acts*, 221, cf. 222, 227 (when he became a freeman, 1740), 232 (named a cloth searcher, 1741), 234 (a chamberlain, 1741), 238 (mayor's chamberlain), 243, 244, 246 (junior bailiff, 1744), 250, 251, 261, 271, 280. 1742. Sarney was the 'only one now remaining here of many who, at our embarking for America, were used to "take sweet counsel together" and rejoice in "bearing the reproach of Christ".' (*Journal*, i, 439.)

tua philosophia.' The undergraduates laughed at Böhler and Wesley as they walked in the College quads, understandably enough if Böhler were bearded and shabbily dressed, habits now more normally associated with undergraduates themselves, though no less to be deprecated. Böhler disregarded the episode; 'My brother, it does not even stick to our clothes.' He was the more troubled by the brothers' failure to win what he regarded as the assurance of a true faith. John, he wrote to the Moravian leader Zinzendorf, 'knew he did not properly believe on the Saviour, and was willing to be taught'. Charles[1] 'is at present very much distressed in his mind, but does not know how he shall begin to be acquainted with the Saviour'. The day after their arrival John Wesley and Böhler went to visit the vicar of Stanton Harcourt, John Gambold, at whose house John's sister Kezzy was staying. Wesley had been perturbed by the influence which pietistic and mystical writings had over his old friend and he was pleased to find him 'recovered from his *mystic* delusion, and convinced that St. Paul was a better writer than either Tauler or Jacob Boehme'. Before they left, they (Charles had joined them) 'prayed and sang together'; returning to Sarney's house there was a prayer meeting 'with some scholars and a Moravian'.[2] The next day, which was a Sunday, John preached at the Castle 'to a numerous and serious congregation' before returning to London on the Monday.

John had not expected to return shortly, but soon after leaving Oxford he learned that his brother Charles had fallen seriously ill of pleurisy. Just about to leave to visit his elder brother Samuel at Tiverton, he was informed on Thursday, 2nd March, that 'Charles was dying at Oxford', and set off for that city at once. Fortunately Charles was in fact already recovering, though he was later to suffer a further attack (his illness and the enfeebled state in which it left him must be regarded as an important psychological preparation for his conversion), and significantly Böhler was with him. It seems likely that he had remained in Oxford where he was carrying out a small preaching mission, attended, it would seem, by among others Watson, Washington and Combes.

The following Sunday, 5th March, Wesley had a long, serious conversation with Böhler which was to be a turning-point in his religious history. Böhler convinced him that he lacked that faith 'whereby alone we are saved'. He enquired of the Moravian whether he ought not to leave off preaching if he lacked the final assurance of salvation. Böhler told him

[1] J. Wesley, *Journal*, i, 440.
[2] C. Wesley, *Journal*, i, 82.

that this was unnecessary and in answer to Wesley's query as to what should be the content of his sermons he replied confidently: 'Preach faith *till* you have it; and then, *because* you have it, you *will* preach faith.' This sound piece of psychological advice made a powerful impact on the spiritually sensitive Wesley. The very next day, Monday, 6th March, he endeavoured to put it into practice during a visit to Oxford prison. He preached 'salvation by faith alone' to a prisoner under sentence of death, Clifford.

> 'Peter Böhler had many times desired me to speak to him before. But I could not prevail on myself to do so, being still (as I had been many years) a zealous asserter of the impossibility of a death-bed repentance.'

It must be remembered that Wesley was still very much under the influence of his Georgian experiences, and now began to write out his account of 'An Affair with Miss Sophy Hopkey', which he completed on 14th March.

Before Whit Sunday, 1738, Wesley made a number of further short visits to Oxford, all of them contributing in a small way to our understanding of his later experience. He had left Oxford in company with Charles Kinchin, who had been acting as a general overseer of the religious society there in addition to looking after his parish of Dummer, near Basingstoke, and with Fox, the man from the debtors' prison whom the Wesleys had befriended. Their purpose was to visit another of the former senior members of the society, John Clayton, at Manchester;[1] but they were back by Thursday, 21st March. During their journey they had ridden part of the way with an 'elderly gentleman' who was going to Oxford to enter his son at a College. In the course of conversation they discussed the providence of God in such a way as to evoke their companion's gratitude. A week after their arrival Peter Böhler again told Wesley that he needed faith and assurances above everything else; as a result 'The next morning I began the Greek Testament again, resolving to abide by the "law and the testimony"; and being confident that God would hereby show me whether this doctrine was of God.' The next

---

[1] Wesley, accompanied by Kinchin and Fox, visited Clayton on 17th March, 1738. 'Mr. Hoole, the rector of St. Ann's church, being taken ill the next day, on Sunday, 19th, Mr. Kinchin and I officiated at Salford Chapel in the morning, by which means Mr. Clayton was at liberty to perform the service of St. Ann's; and, in the afternoon I preached there on the words of St. Paul, "If any man be in Christ, he is a new creature".' (*Journal*, i, 445–6.)

Sunday his sermon at the little village of Wytham, near Oxford, was on the 'new creature'. That evening he attended a religious society where he expounded a chapter from the New Testament. On Saturday, 1st April, he attended the religious society at Fox's, where, his heart being 'so full', he appeared to have indulged for the first time in extempore prayer.

He had been much moved the previous Monday by a visit which he and Kinchin paid to a condemned man, possibly Clifford again, at the Castle prison. Kinchin had spoken on the text, 'It is appointed unto men once to die', and then they had prayed together in 'such words as were given'. The effect of the prisoner was to Wesley extremely gratifying. He 'kneeled down in much heaviness and confusion' having 'no rest' in his bones by reason of 'his sins'. After a space he got up and said eagerly, 'I am now ready to die. I know that Christ has taken away my sins; and there is no more condemnation for me.' He continued to show the same composed cheerfulness when he was taken to execution; and in his last moments he was the same, enjoying a perfect peace, in confidence that he was 'accepted in the Beloved'.[1] These emotional scenes, the preaching of a reassurance to others which he did not himself wholly share, must have intensified Wesley's desire for complete confidence in his own faith.

He had spent the greater part of the day before the meeting at Fox's in writing a sermon for the Sunday. He had risen at half-past four, was at Fox's at one in the afternoon and later in the evening went to a religious meeting in Washington's rooms. The next day was Easter Sunday. He rose rather later than usual, robed at eight and at nine preached in the College Chapel on the text 'The hour cometh, and now is when the dead shall hear the voice of the Son of God, and they that hear shall live'; the theme is again obviously closely linked with his spiritual mood. The service ended with the Holy Communion,[2] and he noted in his diary of the congregation 'all serious, all stayed'. After the service he called on the Rector, Dr. Isham, at his lodgings; he was 'kind'. He preached twice later in the day on the same text, at the Castle and at Carfax (though whether at the church or at a religious society is not clear). He was twice at Fox's during the day and later called on one of his colleagues, William Vesey.

[1] J. Wesley, *Journal*, i, 448.
[2] The College accounts for 1738 note the payment of wine for the Chapel on Easter Day, 3s. 6d.; later for washing the Communion linen and surplice, 1s. 6d. The last payment for wine for this purpose had been on the first Sunday in Lent, when presumably the Sacrament was also celebrated. (*C. Bk.* (1738), fol. 21.)

On Easter Monday he left Oxford for Kinchin's rectory at Dummer. The journal certainly suggests that he was in a state of spiritual expectancy which recent experience had helped to stimulate. 'I see the promise; but it is afar off', he had concluded his entry for 2nd April, adding that he had left for Dummer, 'believing it would be better for me to wait for the accomplishment of it in silence and retirement.' He was at Dummer until 17th April, following his usual routine of prayer and meditation, Bible-reading, conversing, writing and helping with the services, though the household was somewhat perturbed by the illness of Kinchin's sister Molly. He returned to London via Oxford, finding his brother still with Mr. Sarney; 'at home', he notes on the Tuesday morning, 'sang with Charles'. Since Wesley seemed to use the phrase 'at home' to describe his rooms in College, this may indicate that he stayed in the College where he began reading the life of the seventeenth-century Quaker, Anna Maria Schurmann.

He was in London for about a week, still inwardly perturbed and in close touch with Böhler; his continuous harping on the subject of faith during the course of a visit to Blendon distressed his brother and another old Oxford friend, Thomas Broughton, still a fellow of Exeter College. The latter could not understand Wesley's lack of confidence; 'he could never think that I had not faith, who had done and suffered such things'. The next day he went to a meeting of the Trustees for Georgia, but before it had ended he left to start his journey for Oxford, where he arrived once more on Thursday, 27th April. The further heightening of his mood may be noted in his insistence during the journey to some fellow-travellers whom he met at Gerrard's Cross, 'to a young man whom I overtook on the road', and later to his friends at Oxford of 'the faith as it is in Jesus'.

He was only in Oxford until 1st May, when hearing that his brother was again ill he made for London, and the routine of his visit followed the same pattern as on earlier occasions. He stayed with Mr. Sarney and spent his time in reading, writing and at meetings of the religious societies. Among those with whom he was in contact were Evans,[1] Kinchin, Hutchings (of Pembroke, not his colleague at Lincoln),[2] and the Foxes. He was more than gratified by the way in which Hutchings and the Foxes bore witness to the effectiveness of instantaneous conversion, the subject

[1] In later years of his fellowship at Lincoln either Timothy or William Evans was entrusted with collecting his College stipend.

[2] Son of Richard H., of Woolmiston, Somerset, he matriculated at Pembroke on 30th May, 1734, aged 18, and took his B.A. in 1738.

which now absorbed his attention more than any other: 'two living witnesses that God *can* (at least, if He *does* not always) give that faith whereof
cometh salvation in a moment, as lightning falling from heaven'. On
Sunday he preached at the Castle and celebrated Communion.

He was not to visit Oxford again until after the momentous experience
of the Aldersgate Street meeting, returning to preach the University
sermon on 11th June, 1738. This sermon may not have been freshly
written,[1] but in it Wesley strongly stressed the necessity for justification
by faith and the impossibility of good works before justification. Man, he
told his listeners, cannot be saved by his own works, 'were they ever so
many or holy, they are not his own, but God's. But indeed they are all
unholy and sinful themselves, so that everyone of them needs a fresh
atonement.' He stressed his belief that the believer is free from the power
of sin.

> 'Ye are saved from *sin*—saved both from the guilt of all past sin—
> from fear of the wrath of God . . . both often expressed in the word
> justification, which, taken in the legal sense, implies a deliverance from
> guilt and punishment, by the atonement of Christ actually applied to
> the soul of the sinner now believing on him, and a deliverance from the
> (wholy body) of sin, through Christ formed in his heart.'

Faith was the pressing necessity of the age.

> 'At this time, more especially, will we speak, that "by grace are ye
> saved through faith" because, never was the maintaining this doctrine
> more seasonable than it is at this day. Nothing but this can effectually
> prevent the increase of the Roman delusion among us. . . . Nothing
> but this can give a check to that immorality which hath "overspread
> the land as a flood". . . . Nothing but this can stop the mouths of those
> who glory in their shame, and openly defy the Lord that bought them.'

What significance is to be attached to Wesley's conversion? It certainly
did not establish or crystallize his theological standpoint. In later years he
would modify his views on justification by faith, as in 1765 he modified
the wording of this sermon.[2] Throughout his life he remained a fervent

---

[1] *Sermons of John Wesley*, ed. E. H. Sugden, i, 35 ff. Probably preached at St.
Ann's, Aldersgate, on 14th May and at the Savoy Chapel; and on the morning of
11th June at Stanton Harcourt.

[2] In the newly written sermon salvation was taken to include prevenient grace,
justification and sanctification, which is spoken of as identical with regeneration in its
beginning but as going on gradually to entire sanctification. He admits that good
works could be done before conversion.

opponent of Calvinist predestinarianism and Zwinglian anti-sacramentarian views.[1] Indeed, apart from the new stress on justification by faith for which there were ample precedents in Anglican formularies, there was no major difference between what Wesley believed before and after 1738. He had never for instance adhered to a belief in justification by works nor, as has been sometimes asserted, did he ever suppose that he would be saved by a form of Christian ethical idealism. He wrote later of the sermon that he had preached before the University in January, 1733, that

> 'I know not that I can write a better. . . . Perhaps, indeed, I may have read five or six hundred books more than I did; but I am not sensible that this made any essential addition to my knowledge in divinity. Forty years ago I knew and preached every Christian doctrine which I preached now.'[2]

He came to reject much of the Moravian teaching as he had also discarded the Mystics,[3] but his life bore witness to the effective influence of both. His theology was neither perfectly consistent nor coherent. He was not a creative thinker and his theological ideas were in the main a pastiche of orthodox doctrine supported by his own spiritual experience. Yet these beliefs, their rigidity mellowed by age and spiritual insight and rid of certain non-essential features, were essentially the same as those that he had held as a young fellow of Lincoln before he went to Georgia. Christian perfectionism was implicit in his thought and action long before 1738.[4] The ideal of an apostolic, primitive Church, which he sought to bring back to the contemporary Church of England, continued to be the basic foundation of his activity. If, on the one hand, it was a body of the elect bound together by the realization that they were justified by the saving faith of Christ, on the other it was characterized by a peripatetic

---

[1] 'I fell among some Lutheran and Calvinist authors, whose confused and undigested accounts magnified faith to such an amazing size, that it quite hid all the rest of the commandments.'

[2] Cf. writing to Lord Dartmouth about the American colonists he affirmed, 'I am a High Churchman, the son of a High Churchman, bred from my childhood in the highest notions of passive obedience and non-resistance' (14th June, 1775).

[3] 'Of Calvinism, Mysticism, and Antinomianism have a care,' he wrote in 1783, 'for they are the bane of true religion; and one or other of them has been the great hindrance of the work of God wherever it has broke out.' (*Letters*, vii, 169.)

[4] Cf. his comment: 'In the same year (1733) I printed (the first time I ventured to print anything) for the use of my pupils *A Collection of Forms of Prayer*, and in this I spoke explicitly of giving "the whole heart and the whole life to God". This was then, as it is now, my idea of perfection, though I should have started at the word.'

ministry rather than a parochial organization (for which Wesley had scant regard), and by an episcopal and presbyteral order. He remained a loyal member of the Church in which he had been ordained. In 1788 he advised 'all their people in his name to keep close to the Church and Sacrament'.[1] Two years later he told Bishop Tomline of Lincoln, 'the Methodists in general are members of the Church of England, they hold all her doctrines, attend her services, and partake of her Sacraments'. His belief in the authority of presbyters to ordain priests was no novelty, for many churchmen, high and low, at the end of the seventeenth century had assumed that there were precedents in the history of the early Church for presbyterian ordination.[2] 'I believe', he wrote in 1784, 'I shall not separate from the Church of England till my soul separates from my body.'[3] 'I still think', he said three years later, 'that when the Methodists leave the Church, God will leave them.'[4]

If his conversion made little apparent difference to his theological thinking or to his manner of life, what was its true significance? It is not the function of this book to enter into the long debates contingent on this question.[5] Yet his 'conversion' made some difference to John Wesley. His new-found confidence in the saving merits of Christ cannot be identified simply with a turning towards God.

'After', he wrote in June, 1740, 'we had wandered for many years in the *new path* of Salvation by faith and works, about two years ago it pleased God to show us the *old way* of Salvation by faith only.'

[1] He published his early sermon, 'The Duty of Constant Communion', in 1788, adding in the preface 'The following discourse was written above five and fifty years ago, for the use of my pupils at Oxford. I have added very little, but retrenched much; as I then used more words than I do now. But, I thank God, I have not yet seen cause to alter my sentiments in any point which is therein delivered.'

[2] In Stillingfleet's *Irenicon* and King's *Enquiry into the Constitution, Discipline, Unity and Worship of the Primitive Church*, the presbyterate and episcopate of the apostolic age were identified, thus making presbyterian ordination valid. This had also been the view of the learned Archbishop Usher, as indeed of many medieval schoolmen (cf. J. Perrone, *Praelectiones Theologicae* (1842), ii, 484; P. Battifol, *Etudes d'histoire et de theologie positive* (1904), 267–80; W. Telfer, *Journal of Eccl. Hist.*, iii, 1–13). See also G. Every, *The High Church Party*, 4 ff.; N. Sykes, *The Church of England and Non-episcopal Churches in the 16th and 17th centuries* (1948); N. Sykes, *Old Priest and New Presbyter* (1956).

[3] *Letters*, vii, 321.

[4] *Op. cit.*, viii, 377.

[5] E.g. S. G. Dimond, *The Psychology of the Methodist Revival* (1926); Humphrey Lee, *John Wesley and Modern Religion* (1931); Grant Cell, *The Rediscovery of John Wesley* (1935); J. E. Rattenbury, *The Conversion of the Wesleys* (1938).

It is plain that the experience of conversion meant far less to Wesley than the Moravians had taught him to believe that it should,[1] and that in subsequent years he was sporadically subject to despair and depression. What John Wesley's conversion provided, even if in form and outward expression the terminology was spiritual and theological, was a psychological reassurance.[2] His confidence and faith in the truth of what he was preaching gave him such strength, such dynamic impetus, that he could now move forward into the life of evangelism which took him in the next half-century to every corner of the British Isles. It made it very plain that while he was still a fellow of Lincoln and remained so until his marriage in 1751, yet the links which bound him to Oxford were now so tenuous that they hardly affected the great work on which he was now to engage. Wesley's life work would take him further and further away from the University and College in which he had been brought up, and which had in more senses than one made him the man that he was.

[1] 'It is very doubtful', the Moravian Bishop Latrobe said in 1785, 'whether John ever knew himself as a sinner or the Lord as his Saviour.'

[2] Cf. Evelyn Underhill's comment: 'The sinner's conflict . . . as a rule is only resolved and harmony achieved through the crisis of conversion breaking down resistance, liberating emotion and reconciling inner enmity with outer stimulus. There is, however, nothing spiritual in the conversion process itself.'

CHAPTER XV

Epilogue

IN his old age John Wesley could certainly look back to his life with some satisfaction. He had instituted a great religious and humanitarian movement, and in spite of continuous persecution and hostility, he had become a respected and venerated figure. 'The scandal of the Cross is ceased', he wrote in 1785, 'and all the kingdom, rich and poor, Papists and Protestants, behave with courtesy—nay and seeming goodwill! It seems as if I had wellnigh finished my course, and our Lord was giving me an honourable discharge.'[1] Occasionally in his later years he had looked back to the comparative tranquillity and youthful enthusiasm of his Oxford days. 'Let me be again an Oxford Methodist', he wrote to his brother Charles in 1772. 'I am often in doubt whether it would not be best for me to resume all my Oxford rules, great and small. I did then walk closely with God and redeem the time. But what have I been doing these thirty years?'[2] There were clearly times in after life when he wished he was still a fellow of Lincoln. He could not return to Oxford without a feeling of nostalgia. 'I love the very sight of Oxford,' he said in his *Plain Account of Kingswood School* (1781), 'I love the manner of life; I love and esteem many of its institutions.' In 1778 he spent an hour walking around the Colleges, and visiting Christ Church,

'. . . for which I cannot but still retain a peculiar affection. What lovely mansions are there! What is wanting to make the inhabitants of them happy? That without which no rational creature can be happy—the experimental knowledge of God.'[3]

Five years later, in July, 1783, he found the appearance of Oxford improved in everything 'except religion'; he compared Christ Church Hall to the Stadthuis at Amsterdam and found it 'loftier and larger', and St. John's and Trinity gardens, where he had wandered so long ago with Mrs. Boyse and Serena, the Parks, Magdalen walks and Christ Church

[1] *Letters*, vii, 277.
[2] *Op. cit.*, vi, 6.
[3] *Journal*, vi, 213.

meadow far superior to the Dutch gardens.[1] His love for Oxford remained undimmed.

In old age he retained many of the characteristics of the young man who had disputed in the schools and lectured in Lincoln Hall, who had sat with the prisoners in the Castle and had sipped his glass of wine in many a Senior Common Room. He had indeed for long put away most of the diversions which once entertained him. In trenchant fashion he condemned some of the crueller contemporary sports such as cock-fighting as 'foul remains of Gothic barbarity', but he was less censorious about those who hunted. 'Let those who have nothing better to do, still run foxes and hares out of breath. . . .'

'It seems', he continued, 'a great deal more may be said in defence of seeing a serious tragedy. I could not do it with a clear conscience, at least not in an English theatre, the sink of all profaneness and debauchery, but possibly others can . . . balls or assemblies . . . though more reputable than masquerades . . . have exactly the same tendency. So, undoubtedly, have all public dancings . . . of playing cards I say the same as of seeing plays. I could not do it with a clear conscience. But I am not obliged to pass sentence on those that are otherwise minded.'[2]

He had, however, in fact grown mellower and more tolerant with age, while at the same time retaining many of the characteristic practices of his Oxford life, regular devotion and Bible-reading. To the end he remained careful, precise, clean[3] and neat in his person, and was busy until his last days.[4] His cast of mind was still academic, and personally, academically and spiritually his indebtedness to Oxford remained incalculable.

When he visited the city in 1764 he recalled that he had had many pupils there, and

'I took some pains with them, but to what effect? What is become of them now? How many of them think either of their tutor or their God? But, blessed be God, I have had some pupils since who will reward me for my labour.'[5]

Much research would be required to follow all those whom he had known

---

[1] *Op. cit.*, vi, 432.

[2] Sermon on 'The More Excellent Way' (LXXXIX).

[3] Cf. 'Mend your clothes, or I shall never expect you to mend yourselves.'

[4] 'John Wesley's conversation is good,' Dr. Johnson exclaimed, 'but he is never at leisure. He is always obliged to go at a certain hour.' (Boswell's *Life of Johnson*, ii, 176.)

[5] *Journal*, v, 101.

at Oxford to their journey's end; but at least the majority thought of their God if they gave comparatively little thought to their tutor, since most of those who had been in any way intimately associated with the Wesleys were ordained. A country living was the eventual destination of the majority of his early associates; Richard Watkins of Wadham at Clifton Campville, Christopher Holland at Chippenham, Thomas Paget at Mells, Thomas Waldegrave at Washington in Sussex. The list could be largely prolonged. Some had died comparatively young, Shuckburgh in 1730, Hylton in 1739, Kinchin in 1742, Matthew Robinson in 1745. None had made a very significant or effective mark on the life of the Church. James Hervey had achieved some fame as a pious writer, but his Calvinistic views had latterly led to a breach with his former tutor. Yet there is nothing to suggest that Wesley's former friends and associates did not pass their lives in the quiet performance of their duties. At the little villages of Thorp Arch and Walton Christopher Atkinson laboured with unwearying patience for a quarter of a century, from 1749 to 1774. Even the tombstone of John Whitelamb, whose death had been unregretted by his preceptor and brother-in-law, declared that he was 'worthy of imitation'. The inscription on the tablet in memory of Matthew Horbery, who could have been elected President of Magdalen had he so wished, in Standlake Church spoke of his

'. . . eloquent and pathetic discourses from the pulpit, his learned and ingenious writings in defence of the Catholick faith,[1] his unaffected piety and benevolence of heart . . . the amiable simplicity of his whole life and conversation.'

Mural eulogies are perhaps no very happy guide to character; but Wesley's teaching and friendship may have harboured more than in later age he had foreseen or realized. It would be a disagreeable spiritual and social experience to have a high-powered evangelist in every parish.

Wesley's greatest disappointment had been his erstwhile pupil and brother-in-law, Westley Hall. He was for some time closely associated with the brothers, and after his mother's death in 1742 John invited Hall and his wife to live with him at the Foundry; but Hall had become a Moravian and removed to Salisbury, whence he sought to persuade his wife and her brothers to 'renounce the Church of England'.[2] Wesley was

---

[1] M. Horbery, *Works*, 2 vols. (1828).

[2] '1743, August 11. From ten to two, I got with my sister Hall in Salisbury. She stands alone. Every soul of her husband's Society has forsaken the ordinances of God; for which reason she refuses to belong to it.' (*Journal of Charles Wesley*, i,

the more surprised, when visiting Salisbury in 1746, to receive an invitation from Hall to preach. 'Was his motive only, to grace his own cause?' he asked. 'Or rather, was this the last gasp of expiring love?' Thenceforward his career was one of combined eccentric religiosity with moral turpitude of the gravest character. His eloquence attracted a following and enabled him to seduce his female disciples. Always brazen and self-confident, he found ample evidence for polygamous behaviour in the Scriptures. For a time the West Indies formed a congenial environment for amorous dalliance and evangelism; but at long last he returned home. His wife, the long-suffering Patty, behaved with exemplary patience throughout her husband's career. He died at Bristol on 3rd January, 1776.

'God', John Wesley wrote, 'had given him deep repentance. Such another monument of Divine mercy, considering how low he had fallen, and from what height of holiness, I have not seen, no, not in seventy years! . . . It is enough, if, after all his wanderings, we meet again in Abraham's bosom';

but whether Westley Hall would be an acceptable companion even there is a matter of opinion.

The contacts with the household at Stanton and their friends had long ended. There can have been comparatively little chance of their survival after words had passed between Charles Wesley and Varanese's mother, Mrs. Kirkham, at Gloucester in 1735.

'I dined with her [Mrs. Drummond] and several of the friends, particularly Joseph Martin. . . . My heart was enlarged, and knit to them in love. I went to the field at five. An old intimate acquaintance [Mrs. Kirkham] stood in my way.'

'What Mr. Wesley', she asked crisply, 'is it *you* I see? Is it possible that you who can preach at Christ Church and St. Mary's should come hither after a mob?' Charles Wesley cut her short in the unctuous way that he occasionally adopted towards his critics: 'The work which my Master giveth me, must I not do it.'[1] Mrs. Kirkham died in 1750.[2] Her

---

333; cf. i, 399.) On his father's death Hall inherited Hornington Manor and from his Mother he inherited her home in Fisherton. See John Wesley's *Letters*, ii, 54–7, 110–14; Maldwyn Edwards, *Family Circle*, 148–50.

[1] Charles Wesley, *Journal*, i, 164.

[2] Daniel Sandford writing on 10th November, 1750, said, 'at present she [Mrs. Chapone] is under a very heavy affliction from the loss of her mother, who died last week. . . . I don't doubt but that her excellent sense and great Piety will soon break thro'.' (*Ballard MSS.*, xliii, 108–9.)

daughter, Sally Chapone, lived another fourteen years, abundant as ever in good works and admired by all her friends. Her particular protégé had been Mrs. Elizabeth Elstob, to whom she had been introduced by her friend, the amateur scholar George Ballard.[1] In a disinterested way Mrs. Chapone invoked the help of Mary Pendarves, who handed her letter to a Mrs. Poyntz through whom it eventually reached Queen Caroline.

'Mrs. Poyntz said she [the Queen] knew no more than what the letter told, but that Mrs. Chapon was a friend of ours. The Queen said she never in her life read a better letter, that it had touched her heart, and ordered immediately an hundred pounds for Mrs. Elstob.'[2]

Later she tried to secure a post for her at a charity school founded by Lady Betty Hastings, but the position was filled before Sally's friend, Mr. Hastings, could approach Lady Betty. Mrs. Elstob went to Bath, where she was befriended by Dr. Oliver and eventually became governess to the children of the Duke and Duchess of Portland; here she renewed her acquaintance with the 'incomparable Mrs. Pendarves, in every way accomplished by Nature and Genius . . . an Honour and Ornament to her sex.' The eighteenth-century was profuse in its use of adjectives but common opinion established the cultivated minds and genuine goodness of the former friends of Wesley. Sally Chapone was a busy woman, the wife of a local schoolmaster of limited means,[3] and inconvenienced by the necessity of moving house on more than one occasion,[4] and a good mother;[5]

---

[1] The son of poor parents, he was apprenticed to a stay-maker and made gowns and mantuas, Mrs. Chapone being one of his customers. He taught himself Anglo-Saxon, and Lord Chedworth and some of the followers of the hunt, who used to stay in his neighbourhood at Campden in Gloucester, provided him with an annuity which enabled him to pursue his studies. In 1750 he went as a clerk to Magdalen, Oxford, and became a bedell. He suffered from the stone (for which Mrs. Chapone sent him prescriptions) and died, aged 49, in 1755.

[2] Lady Llanover, *Autobiography and Correspondence of Mrs. Delany*, i, 264.

[3] 'A pretty large family and a precarious income', Sally told Mrs. Elstob, 'leaves me little room for generosity except it be that of the heart.'

[4] 'Endeavouring to get an house, to shelter my family in being turned out here, in a manner too cruel to admit of a comparison.' (12th March, 1742.) Cf. *Autobiography and Correspondence of Mrs. Delany*, i, 453, 488-9.

[5] Cf. 25th October, 1745: 'My younger son is going abroad, I thank God, in an advantageous post'; 3rd July, 1749: 'My son arrived in London from Jamaica but when see him I don't know as business at the Admiralty keeps him in London.' There was also a younger daughter, Sally. Cf. p. 221.

but she found time to read and write.[1] She was indignant when her brother, Bob Kirkham, returning from a visit to Oxford in 1743, told her that

'. . . he heard a whole room full of [undergraduates], deny that thing was or could be written by a woman, which he himself knew in fact was so. Oxford is the seat of liberal education, but they strongly imbibe some unusual sentiments, of which this is a specimen.'[2]

At Oxford Kirkham had visited Ballard, whose work on *Memoirs of Several Ladies of Great Britain, who have been celebrated for their writings or skill in the learned languages, arts and sciences*, published in 1752, he sought to dedicate to Mary Delany (as she had now become). Mrs. Delany took six copies and among the other subscribers was her sister, now Mrs. Dewes, who kept up her friendship with Sally Chapone. In 1753 Anne Dewes was drinking the waters at Cheltenham, staying with the Chapones, being 'in an ill state of health'.

Mary Pendarves married Dr. Patrick Delany, who became Dean of Down in 1743. Gracious and charming, sociable and refined, she was a welcome friend to George III and his Queen. Edmund Burke described her as 'the highest-bred woman in the world and the woman of fashion of all ages'. She outlived her husband by twenty years and died on 15th April, 1788. It was indeed a cultivated and pleasing circle that Wesley had so long ago charmed by his presence. 'Conversation', Sally Chapone reminded Elizabeth Elstob, 'is the proper entertainment of a thinking person.' They must all have read of their former friend's growing reputation, but they would have shaken their heads gravely and agreed with what Mrs. Delany in her old age told Miss Hamilton on 14th December, 1783:

'These brothers joined some other young men at Oxford, and used to meet of a Sunday evening and read the Scriptures, and find out objects of charity to relieve. This was a *happy beginning*, but the vanity of being singular and growing *enthusiasts* made them endeavour to gain proselytes and adopt that system of religious doctrine which many reasonable people thought pernicious.'[3]

---

[1] 'I knew that she was the author of Hardships of English Law, &c., I did not mention it to you because I thought it was a secret.' (14th December, 1741.) In 1734 Wesley corrected Varanese's 'Essay on Laws', probably the same work.

[2] *Ballard MSS.*, xliii fol. 135.

[3] *Autobiography and Correspondence*, vi, 175.

Had either Mrs. Delany or John Wesley remembered the occasion when he sought her advice in the summer of 1731 as to whether he was 'too strict, with carrying things too far in religion'?[1] John Wesley had by 1790 moved far from the pleasant drawing-room of Stanton rectory. Even Epworth would soon be no more than an abiding memory, 'Epworth', as he wrote on 26th June, 1784, 'which I still love beyond most places in the world.' On his occasional visits there he renewed some of his former contacts.[2] When he preached at Epworth Cross on 19th April, 1752, he found only a small congregation because many had gone to attend the funeral of Richard Popplewell, of Temple Belwood, who had died three days earlier; 'emphatically poor, though while he lived he possessed (not enjoyed) at least a thousand pounds a year'.[3] He visited George Stovin and his former pupil, Mr. Pindar; the Maws received occasional mention in the *Journal*.[4] Yet in 1751 he found 'a poor, dead, senseless people' misled by the vilification by 'some of our preachers' who 'had diligently gleaned up and retailed all the evil they could hear of me'. He celebrated his eighty-sixth birthday at Epworth:

'How little have I suffered yet by the "rush of numerous years!" It is true, I am not so agile as I was in time past. I do not run or walk so fast as I did; my sight is a little decayed . . . I find likewise some decay in memory, with regard to names and things lately past; but not at all with regard to what I have read or heard twenty, forty, or sixty years ago; neither do I find any decay in my hearing, smell, taste or appetite.'

He was at Epworth once more on Sunday, 4th July, 1790, when he again attended the services in the church; though he preached, as had become

---

[1] *Letters*, i, 92 ff.

[2] H. J. Foster, 'In the Isle of Axholme', *W.H.S. Proc.*, v (1906), 196–205.

[3] See entries in the *Journal* for 8th July, 1748, and 20th July, 1774; 12th May, 1744, 22nd February, 1747, 20th May, 1753.

[4] In 1788 he had noted that the rector, Mr. Gibson, preached a 'plain, useful sermon' and read the 'prayers with seriousness': 'but I was sorry to see scarce twenty communicants, half of whom came on my account. . . . What can be done to remedy this sore evil? I fain would prevent the members here from leaving the Church: but I cannot do it. As Mr. Gibson is not a pious man, but rather an enemy to piety, who frequently preaches against the truth, and those that hold and love it, I cannot, with all my influence, persuade them either to hear him, or to attend the sacrament administered by him. If I cannot carry this point even while I live, who then can do it when I die? And the case of Epworth is the case of every church, where the minister neither loves nor preaches the gospel; the Methodists will not attend his administrations. What then is to be done?'

his custom, at the market cross. If Epworth meant anything, it embodied the precious memory of his mother, who died full of faith on 23rd July, 1742,[1] and the affection of his brother and sisters, only one of whom, the cheerful and indomitable Patty, outlived him.[2]

John Wesley had remained a fellow of Lincoln College until his marriage with Molly Vazeille in 1751 obliged him to resign; but his contacts with the College and the University had steadily weakened. Although he retained his rooms in College, the rooms to which he had moved in 1737,[3] and continued to draw his stipend, the entries in the College register only refer to his annual application for leave on 6th November, a request which was freely granted. When he was in Oxford he visited the colleagues whom he had known when he was a resident, more especially the Rector, Dr. Isham, Vesey and Hutchins; but he made no new friends among the governing body. He attended prayers in the Chapel and sat in the College garden, once correcting there the proofs of his *Collection of Psalms and Hymns*. In the summer of 1741 he made good use of the College Library, reading Bishop Bull's *Harmonia Apostolica*, and taking down the works of Episcopius by mistake he read with growing indignation of the doctrinaire intolerance disclosed by the proceedings of the Synod of Dort:

'I wonder not at the heavy curse of God which so soon after fell on our Church and nation. What it is that the *holy Synod* of Trent, and that of Dort did not sit at the same time; nearly allied as they were, not only as to the *purity of doctrine* which each of them established, but also as to the spirit wherewith they acted, if the latter did not exceed.'[4]

The sermon which he had originally intended to deliver before the University shows the measure of his disillusion with contemporary Oxford. 'With grief of heart I speak it,' he had written, 'that scarcely is the form of godliness seen among us. We are all indeed called to be saints, and the very name of Christians means no less. But who has so much as the appearance?' It may be urged that

[1] 'I found my mother', he wrote on 21st July, 1742, 'on the borders of eternity; but she has no doubt or fear, nor any desire but, as soon as God shall call her, to depart and be with Christ.'

[2] Of his brothers, Samuel died in 1739, Charles in 1788; of his sisters, Mary had died in 1734, Kezzy in 1741, Emily in 1771?, Sukey in 1764, Hetty in 1750, and Patty in 1791; the date of Nancy's death is uncertain.

[3] See Appendix 3.

[4] He had been reading the canons of the Council of Trent in the College garden at seven in the morning. A few days later he read an account of Calvin and Servetus in the Bodleian Library.

'. . . we have public prayers both morning and evening in all our Colleges . . . even during their continuance, can it be reasonably inferred from the tenor of their outward behaviour, that their hearts are earnestly fixed on Him who standeth in the midst of them? Do we keep the rest of the Sabbath-day holy? Is there no needless visiting upon it? No trifling, no impertinence of conversation? Are there not many among us found to eat and drink with the drunken? And even as to the hours arranged for study, are they generally spent to any better purpose? Not if they are employed in reading (as is too common) plays, novels,[1] or idle tales, which naturally tend to increase our inbred corruption, and heat the furnace of our unholy desires seven times hotter than it was before? How little preferable as the laborious idleness of those who spend day after day in gaming or diversions, vilely casting at that time the value of which they cannot know, till they are passed through it into eternity.'

He went on:

'How many lazy drones . . . how few of the vast number who have it in their power, are truly learned men. Not to speak of the other eastern tongues, who is there can be said to understand Hebrew? Might I not say, or even Greek? A little of Homer or Xenophon we may still remember; but how few can readily read or understand so much as a page of Clemens Alexandrinus, Chrysostom or Ephrem Syrus? And as to philosophy . . . how few do we find who have laid the foundation—who are the masters even of logic, who thoroughly understand so much as the rules of syllogizing; the very doctrine of moods and figures!'

He concluded:

'Is not the very notion of religion lost . . . is it not utterly despised? Is it not wholly set at nought and trodden under foot?'

Wesley was apparently dissuaded by Lady Huntingdon from preaching this outspoken indictment of men who were still his colleagues but instead rewrote his sermon on the 'almost Christian', the man who had the 'outside of the real Christian . . . does nothing which the gospel forbids' and yet lacks the reality of the saving faith.[2] The sermon was delivered at St. Mary's on 25th July, 1741.

During the course of the next ten years he made occasional appearances

[1] Wesley himself abridged and edited Henry Brooke's novel, *The Fool of Quality*, because it 'perpetually aims at inspiring and increasing every right affection, at instilling gratitude to God, and benevolence to men'. (Preface to *The History of Henry, Earl of Moreland*, 1781.) Cf. *Works*, xiii, 137; Tyerman, *John Wesley*, iii, 172 ff.

[2] *Sermons of John Wesley*, ed. Sugden, i, 53 ff.

in the city and University,[1] but the sermon which he delivered at St. Mary's on 24th August, 1744, constituted the turning-point in his relation with the academic world. It was listened to with hushed attention by a crowded church. 'Never', said his brother Charles, 'have I seen a more attentive congregation. They did not let a word slip them. Some of the Heads stood up the whole time, and fixed their eyes on him.' The sermon certainly created a furore. William Blackstone described it as 'curious', and thought much of its content unnecessarily insulting.[2] Benjamin Kennicott, the Hebraist, who was then an undergraduate at Exeter, believed that objection might reasonably be taken to the outright criticism which he made of the University.

'I liked', he wrote, 'some of his freedom; such as calling the generality of young gownsmen "a generation of triflers" and many other just invectives. But, considering how many shining lights are here that are the glory of the Christian cause, his sacred censure was much too flaming and strong, and his charity much too weak in not making allowances. . . . This, and the assertion that Oxford was not a Christian city, and this country not a Christian nation, were the most offensive parts of the sermon, except when he accused the whole body (and confessed himself to be one of the number) of the sin of perjury. . . . Had these things been omitted, and his censures moderated, I think his discourse, as to style and delivery, would have been uncommonly pleasing to others as well as to myself.'

Two-thirds of the sermon were in content unexceptionable. Wesley began with a description of the activity and influence of the Holy Spirit in the early Church, considered the growth of Christianity and drew a picture of the Christian community in which the Holy Spirit was actively at work. 'Having thus briefly considered Christianity, as beginning, as

---

[1] The College account books show that in 1740 he drew Commons for three and a half weeks; in 1741 for four and a half weeks; in 1744 for two and a half weeks. Thereafter, apart from a few days in 1749, and a week in 1751, he did not 'battel' in College, even when he visited Oxford.

[2] Hurst, *History of Methodism*, ii, 602. 'We were last Friday entertained at St. Mary's by a curious sermon from Wesley the Methodist. Among other equally modest particulars he informed us, 1st That there was not one Christian among all the Heads of Houses: 2ndly, that pride, gluttony, avarice, luxury, sensuality, and drunkenness were the general characteristics of all Fellows of Colleges, who were useless to a proverbial uselessness. Lastly, that the younger part of the University were a generation of triflers, all of them perjured, and not one of them of any religion at all.'

going on, and as covering the earth, it remains only', he told his listeners, 'that I should close the whole, with a plain, practical application.'[1] His 'plain, practical application' created resentment. He began by asking where a Christian country in the full sense of the word existed and replied by saying, 'Let us confess we have never yet seen a Christian country upon earth.' He went on: 'It is utterly needful that some one should use great plainness of speech towards you.' With the slight touch of arrogance which so often is a feature of prophetic utterances, he asked 'And who will use this plainness, if I do not? Therefore I, even I, will speak.'

Oxford was not a Christian city.

'Are we, considered as a community of men, so "filled with the Holy Ghost", as to enjoy in our hearts, and show forth in our lives, the genuine fruits of that Spirit? Are all the Magistrates, all Heads and Governors of Colleges and Halls, and their respective Societies (not to speak of the inhabitants of the town) "of one heart and one soul"?'

By a series of rhetorical questions, he showed only too plainly that the Heads of Houses were not obvious depositories of the Holy Spirit.

'Do you continually remind those under your care, that the one rational end of all our studies, is to know, love, and serve "the only true God, and Jesus Christ, whom He hath sent. . . . Do you labour therein with all your might? exerting every faculty of your soul, using every talent which God hath lent you, and that to the uttermost of your power"?'

When he came to consider the fellows of the Colleges, he did not stop short at rhetorical questions. He reminded his congregation that many of them were in Holy Orders and so entrusted with a special responsibility. 'Do we forsake and set aside, as much as in us lies, all worldly cares and studies. . . . Do we know God? Do we know Jesus Christ?' It could hardly be disguised that many among his congregation might well be embarrassed by the pertinent thrusts made so directly at them.

Nor were the undergraduates spared. They lacked respect for their superiors; they wasted their time, 'either in reading what has no tendency to Christianity, or in gaming—or in—you know not what'. They behaved unseemly in church; they did not keep the Sabbath. They were sometimes drunken and sometimes unclean. They were given to swearing. These things were not said directly but the questions were so phrased

[1] *Sermons.*, i, 104.

as to leave no doubt in the listener's mind that this was the preacher's opinion.

'May it not be one of the consequences of this, that so many of you are a generation of triflers; triflers with God, with one another, and with your own souls? For, how few of you spend, from one week to another, a single hour in private prayer! How few have any thought of God in the general tenor of your conversation. Who of you is in any degree acquainted with the work of His Spirit, His supernatural work in the souls of men? Can you bear, unless now and then in a church, any talk of the Holy Ghost? Would you not take it for granted, if one began such a conversation, that it was either hypocrisy or enthusiasm? In the name of the Lord God Almighty, I ask, what religion are you of? Even the talk of Christianity, ye cannot, will not bear.

'O, my brethren, what a Christian city is this! "It is time for Thee, Lord, to lay to Thine hand!"'

It was at this point, Benjamin Kennicott tells us, the congregation felt that it had been given a 'universal shock'. They were 'words full of such presumption'. As the preacher joined his three companions, his brother, Piers and Meriton, outside the Church, 'for of the rest none durst join himself to us', he must have realized that the silence of the congregation was the silence of disapproval. 'I preached', he wrote in his *Journal* that evening, 'I suppose the last time at St. Mary's. Be it so. I am now clear of the blood of these men. I have fully delivered my own soul.' After the service the Beadle came to tell him that the Vice-Chancellor, Dr. Hodges, the Provost of Oriel, had sent for the notes of his sermon.[1] He sealed them up and 'sent them without delay, not without admiring the wise providence of God. Perhaps few men of note would have given a sermon of mine the reading if I had put it into their hands, but by this means it came to be read, probably more than once, by every man of eminence in the University.' In the early afternoon he left Oxford and never occupied the University pulpit again.

Many felt that the sermon might have more immediate consequences. 'I hear', Kennicott wrote, 'the Heads of Houses intend to show their resentment.' 'His notes were demanded by the Vice-Chancellor,' Blackstone commented, 'but on mature deliberation it has been thought

[1] If the sermon contained anything contrary to the doctrine of the Church of England, the Vice-Chancellor was empowered to demand a copy, which he could then submit to the professors of Divinity; the preacher could be suspended from preaching again before the University unless he withdrew the statement to which objection had been taken.

proper to punish him by a mortifying neglect.' This was probably the wiser course. Much later, in 1781, he compared the comparatively soft treatment meted out to him with that which the dissenting preachers had to endure in 1662. 'They were turned out of house and home, and all that they had; whereas I am only hindered from preaching, without any other loss; and that in a kind of honourable manner; it being determined that, when my next turn to preach came, they would pay another person to preach for me. And so they did twice or thrice, even to the time that I resigned my fellowship.'

He last visited Oxford as an official fellow of the College in response to a request from the Rector to cast his vote at the election of an M.P. for the University. There were three candidates, Sir Roger Newdigate, a Warwickshire landowner who opposed Walpole, Sir Edward Turner, brother-in-law of the Master of Balliol, and Robert Harley, the second son of the third Earl of Oxford. Isham, who was a friend of Turner's, hoped that Wesley would vote for his candidate as the majority of the fellows of Lincoln were in favour of Newdigate. In spite of a severe frost and slippery roads, Wesley travelled to Oxford to do what he held to be his duty to the Rector. When he arrived at the schools to vote he did not find 'the decency and order' which he expected, but there was no abuse of himself or of his friends. 'I was much surprised, wherever I went, at the civility of the people—gentlemen as well as others. There was no pointing, no calling of names once, nor even laughter.' Since Newdigate was elected by a large majority[1] his journey was in some sense vain. Less than three weeks later he married Molly Vazeille and was obliged by the College statutes to resign his fellowship.

He visited Oxford a number of times in the remaining forty years of his life, but the connection was no longer a vital one. Since 1738 his main objective in going there had been to stimulate the Methodist society and his visits to the College had been largely incidental. After 1751 he had no contact with his colleagues of earlier years, though in March, 1761, he spent an evening with Richard Hutchins, who had succeeded Isham as Rector. 'His openness and frankness of behaviour were both pleasing and profitable. Such conversation I want; but I do not wonder it is offensive to men of nice ears.'[2] The Methodist society continued to have a nucleus of young graduates and undergraduates in addition to the townspeople who had for some time constituted the majority of its members. In

[1] Newdigate, 184; Harley, 126; Turner, 67.
[2] *Journal*, iv, 440.

October, 1769, he spent an hour talking 'quite agreeably with a few young serious students'.[1] On 31st November, 1780, he commented approvingly on their good behaviour: 'nor could I observe one smiling countenance, although I closely applied these words, I am not ashamed of the gospel of Christ'.[2] It was, however, among the townspeople that the Methodist cause was consolidated. The churches were closed to Wesley and he preached in a room in James Mears' house in St. Ebbe's. In October, 1769, as the proprietors had locked the doors of the local dissenting meeting-house, he preached in Mears' garden 'to such a congregation as I had not had in Oxford since I preached in St. Mary's Church'.[3] On later occasions he used the new preaching house, 'a lightsome, cheerful place',[4] which housed the Methodist congregation until a new one was built, much to the wrath of Dr. Tatham, the Rector of Lincoln, in 1818.[5] Methodism made sure and steady progress in Oxford. On 17th October, 1771, Wesley described his congregation as 'deeply attentive hearers';[6] on 12th October, 1776, the congregation was larger than any he had had at Oxford for twenty years, 'for seriousness or number', and was more than the room could hold.[7] In 1771 he had commented, 'So all the seed sown here has not fallen either on stony or thorny ground.'[8] Such is indeed the impression left by the visits in his later years. On 31st November, 1780, 'we had such a congregation at noon in Oxford as I never saw there before: and what I regarded more than their number, was their seriousness'.[9] Two years afterwards, on 15th October, 1782,

'I had seen no such prospect here for many years. The congregation was large, and still as night, although many gentlemen were among

[1] *Journal*, v, 346.

[2] *Op. cit.*, vi, 299.

[3] *Op. cit.*, v, 345.

[4] On 14th July, 1783. According to J. J. Moore (*Earlier and Later Nonconformity in Oxford*, 1875) the first chapel was built on a plot of land in New Inn Hall Street, leased from Brasenose College in 1760. It is curious that Wesley should not have made use of this if the chapel was built as early as this, more especially as he had difficulty in finding a place to preach in during his visit in 1769.

[5] The foundation of the New Chapel was laid in 1817. Dr. Tatham, a consistent opponent of the Methodists and a fierce controversialist, urged the workers to refuse to build the chapel; 'it is monstrous', he said, 'to build so large a Chapel in Oxford'.

[6] *Journal*, v, 433.

[7] *Op. cit.*, vi, 80.

[8] *Op. cit.*, vi, 158.

[9] *Op. cit.*, vi, 299.

them. The next evening the house would not contain the congregation; yet all were quiet, even those that could not come in.'[1]

In 1783 the congregation and society had 'increased in zeal as well as in number'.[2] In 1787 the house was filled as a result of a downpour of rain, 'filled, and not overfilled. I found great liberty of speech in enforcing the first and great commandment; and could not but hope there will be a great work of God here, notwithstanding the wisdom of the world.'[3] On 15th October, 1788, he wanted only a 'larger room. Many young gentlemen were there, and behaved well. I hope some of them did not come in vain.'[4] The last time he preached at Oxford was 29th October, 1789. He found that as notice of his coming had been given out previously, without his knowledge, he had a 'very serious congregation'. In the evening 'such a multitude of people pressed in that they hindered one another from hearing. I know not when we have had so noisy a congregation; so that by their eagerness to hear they defeated their own purpose.'[5] He was only to visit the city once more. On Tuesday, 2nd November, 1790, he came by chaise to Oxford *en route* for Witney but on his return he broke the journey to stroll through the familiar streets.[6] Five years earlier he had penned what might be called his epitaph on the place when he wrote: 'I once more surveyed many of the gardens and delightful walks. What is wanting but the love of God to make this place an earthly Paradise?'[7]

It might seem an epitaph, but what Wesley could not measure himself was the indelible influence which the University had had on him. He readily admitted that the stipend from his fellowship had given him the means to employ his time as he thought best. It was the licence that he received from the University which gave him the right to officiate throughout the kingdom. He was stating no more than the truth when he told Bishop Butler in 1739 that 'being ordained [priest] as Fellow of a College, I was not limited to any particular cure, but have an indeterminate commission to preach the word of God in any part of the Church of England'. Yet more than that, in the kind of man that Wesley became, in

---

[1] *Journal*, vi, 374.
[2] *Op. cit.*, vi, 454.
[3] *Op. cit.*, vii, 334.
[4] *Op. cit.*, vii, 442.
[5] *Op. cit.*, viii, 20–1.
[6] *Op. cit.*, viii, 111.
[7] *Op. cit.*, vii, 119.

every facet of his mind and every feature of his personality, the influence of Oxford as well of Epworth was manifest. It was something in many ways intangible, and it cannot be overlooked.

By the end of February, 1791, the busy life was almost over. He died on 2nd March, 1791, and his friends standing by sang with genuine understanding:

> Waiting to receive thy spirit,
> Lo! the Saviour stands above;
> Shows the purchase of His merit,
> Reaches out the crown of love.

Wesley's Reading, 1725-34

THIS list has been compiled from the entries in Wesley's diaries. It is naturally an incomplete index to the books read by John Wesley during the period 1725-34, and many of the titles are doubtful.

1725

Classical Literature:

Horace, *Epistles, Odes, Epodes, De Arte Poetica*
Juvenal, *Satires*
Virgil, *Eclogues, Georgics, Aeneid*
Terence, *Andria, Eunuchus, Heautontimorumenos, Adelphi, Phormio, Hecyra*
Works by Cicero and Cornelius Nepos; Xenophon; *Iliad*; Epictetus; Plutarch
Philippus Cluver, *Italia Antiqua.*

Religion:

J. E. Grabe, *Spicilegium SS. Patrum ut et hereticorum seculi post Christum natum*, 2 vols., 1714
John Goodman, *A Winter-Evening Conference between Neighbours* (1686), 11th ed., 1722
The Government of the Tongue, by the author of the *Whole Duty of Man* (R. Sterne? Lady Packington?), 6th imp., 1713
A Gentleman Instructed in the Conduct of a Virtuous and Happy Life, William Darrell, 6th ed., 1716
John Norris, *Practical Discourses upon several divine subjects*
G. Smalridge, *Sixty Sermons*
P. Sarpi, *History of the Council of Trent*, trans. by Sir Nathaniel Brent, 1676
R. Fiddes, *A General Treatise of Morality*, formed upon *The Principles of Natural Reason only*, 1724

W. Wake, *The Principles of the Christian Religion explained in a brief commentary upon the Church Catechism*, 1699

Bishop Atterbury, *Sermons and Discourses on several subjects and occasions*, 2 vols., 1723

John Ellis, *Defence of the Thirty-nine Articles of the Church of England*

H. Grotius, *Annotationes in Novum Testamentum*, 1641–6

Isaac Watts, *On Predestination*

George Hickes, *On Schism* [*The Constitution of the Catholic Church and the nature and consequences of schism*], 1716

F. Hutcheson, *Inquiry into Ideas of Beauty and Virtue*, 1725

Archbishop Sharp, *Sermons*

John Jackson, *The Duty of Subjects towards their Governors*, 1723

Thomas à Kempis, *Christian Pattern, or a Treatise of the Imitation of Jesus Christ*, ed. Dean Stanhope, 10th ed., 1721

H. Ditton, *A Discourse concerning the Resurrection of Jesus Christ*, 1714

Works by Bishop George Bull, Berkeley, Whiston, Thomas Bennet, and Samuel Clarke; *The Gentleman's Religion*.

General:

Samuel Butler, *Hudibras*

John Dryden, *Palamon and Arcite*

G. Fracastoro, *Syphilis; or A Poetical History of the French Disease*, trans. Nahum Tate, 1686

R. Johnson, *Aristarchus Anti-Bentleianus*, 1717

Charles Boyle, *Dr. Bentley's Dissertations on the Epistles of Phalaris and the Fable of Aesop Examined*, 1698

Sir S. Garth, *The Dispensary, a poem*, 9th ed., 1725

A. Cowley, *Essays*

G. Burnet, *History of His Own Times*; *The History of the Reformation of the Church of England*

Daniel Le Clerc and James Drake, *The History of Physick, an account of the rise and progress of the art*, 1699

John Milton, *Paradise Lost*

The Guardian; *The Spectator*

George Herbert, *The Temple*

Thomas Salmon, *A Review of the History of England*, 2 vols., 1724

Halley, *On Magnetism and Gravity*

J. Keill, *Principia* [*An Introduction to Natural Philosophy*, 1720?]

Robert Boyle, *On Chemistry*

Leonard Welsted, *Epistles, Odes, &c.*, 1724–5
Henry Lee, *Anti-Scepticism*, 1702
Life of Mireways
G. Cheyne, *New Theory of Fevers*, 4th ed., 1724
Matthew Prior, *Poems*
The Great Atlas
John Dennis, *Remarks upon Mr. Pope's Translation of Homer*, 1717
Marcus Vida, *Art of Poetry*, trans. Christopher Pitt, 1725
The Gentleman's Library
Works by Sir Francis Bacon and Betterton.

Plays:

By Lord Lansdowne; by Nicholas Rowe, *The Ambitious Stepmother*,
1700, *The Fair Penitent*, 1703, *The Tragedy of Jane Shore*, 1714;
Nathaniel Lee, *Theodosius or the Force of Love, a Tragedy* 1680.

1726 and part of 1727

Classical Literature:

Horace, *Odes, Epodes*, etc.
Virgil, *Eclogues*
Juvenal, *Satires*
Anacreon; Xenophon; *The Odyssey*; Cornelius Nepos; Terence.

Religion:

Zosimus; Chrysostom
Justin Martyr, *First Apology*, ed. Grabe, 1700
Edward Reynolds, *Sermons*
Robert Parsons, *Christian Directory*
Edward Synge, *On Toleration*
Humphrey Prideaux, *Connection between the Old and New Testaments*,
1716–18
G. Cheyne, *Philosophical Principles of Religion*, 1726
James Gardiner, *Practical Exposition of the Beatitudes*, 1713
N. Tate and N. Brady, *New Version of the Psalms*, 1696
Nathaniel Spinckes, *Collections of Meditations and Devotions*, 1717
Bishop Atterbury, *Sermons*
William Lowth, *Directions for the Profitable Study of the Scriptures*, 1718
Fenelon, *On Simplicity*

Works relating to Bishop Atterbury's dispute with Hoadly

Francis Bugg, *A narrative of the conference at Sleaford in Lincolnshire between Francis Bugg and Henry Pickworth, August 25, 1701*

Works by John Norris, William Beveridge, Samuel Clarke and Bishop Sprat.

General:

Vertot, *Histoire des Revolutions arrivées dans le gouvernement de la Republique Romaine*, 3 vols., 1719

G. Burnet, *History of the Reformation of the Church of England*

Milton, *Paradise Lost*

Rapin, *Reflections on Eloquence*

William Walsh, *Poems*

Dryden, *Miscellany Poems*

Lilburn's Trial

The Spectator

State Trials, ed. T. Salmon, 1719

Spenser, *Faerie Queene*

Duke of Buckingham, *Poems*

Thomas Parnell, *Poems*, 1721

Erasmus Lewis, *Poems*

Prideaux, *Life of Mahomet*

Godfrey of Bouillon

Charles Johnson, *A General History of Pyrates*, 1726

The History of Lilly's Life and Times, written by himself and prepared for publication by Charles Burman, 1715

The Life of General Monk

Swift, *Gulliver's Travels*; *The Battle of the Books*

John Dennis, *A Defense of Sir Foppling Flutter*, 1722

Collier, *Essays*; *A Short View of the Immorality and Profaneness of the English Stage*

Charles Cotton, *Poems*

Christopher Schleiber, *Philosophia Compendiosa*; *Metaphysica*

The Count of Gabalis, or the Extravagant Mysteries of the Cabalists, trans. by P. Ayres, 1680

William Somerville, *Occasional Poems*

William Whiston, *Euclid*

Sir Isaac Newton, *Opticks*, 1704

Clarendon, *History of the Rebellion*

Adventures of Aristonous
Works by Sir Walter Raleigh, Kenelm Digby.

Plays:

Shakespeare, *Othello, Henry IV, Richard III, King Lear, Julius Caesar,
Henry V*
Ben Jonson, *The Silent Woman; The Alchemist*
Congreve, *The Way of the World*
Nicholas Rowe, *The Royal Convert,* 1707, *The Tragedy of Lady Jane
Grey,* 1715
C. Molloy, *Half Pay Officers,* 1720
Thomas Otway, *The Orphan,* 1680, *Venice Preserved,* 1682
Wycherly, *The Plaindealer,* 1676
Beaumont and Fletcher, *The Elder Brother*
William Taverner, *The Artful Husband,* 1717
Thomas Southerne, *Oronooko,* 1696, *The Fate of Capua,* 1700
Possibly Sir George Etherege, *The Man of Mode,* 1676
The Duke of Buckingham, *The Rehearsal*
Paul Scarron, *The Whole Comical Works*
The Drummer.

1729 (incomplete)

Classical Literature:

Works by Horace; Themistocles; Terence (*Andria, Eunuchus*); Ovid,
Metamorphoses.

Religion:

G. Smalridge, *Sixty Sermons*
T. Sherlock, *The Trial of the Witnesses of the Resurrection of Jesus,* 1729;
Atterbury, *Sermons*
P. Browne, Bishop of Cork, *Procedure, Extent, and Limits of Human
Understanding,* 1728
à Kempis, *The Christian Pattern*
Norris, *Of Human Understanding*
A. Horneck,[1] *The Happy Ascetick; or the Best Exercise . . . to which is
added, A Letter to a Person of Quality, concerning the holy lives of the
Primitive Christians,* 6th ed., 1724

[1] Horneck was presented by Lincoln College to the chaplaincy of All Saints',
Oxford.

J. B. S. Jure, *The Holy Life of Monr. de Renty, a late Nobleman of France
and sometime Councellor to King Lewis the 13th,* trans. E. S. Gent, 1658
Edward Lake, *Officium Eucharisticum, a preparatory service to a devout and
worthy reception of the Lord's Supper,* 1673
Norris, *Essay towards the Theory of an Ideal and Intelligible World,* 1701
Jeremy Taylor, *Holy Living and Holy Dying*
Sermons by Norris and Trappes
Works by Barrow, Ken, and Wake.

General:

Edward Young, *The Last Day,* 1714
Samuel Wesley (jun.), *The Story of the Three Children,* 1724, *The Pig
and the Mastiff,* 1725, *The Iliad in a Nutshell; or Homer's Battle of the
Frogs and Mice,* 1726; *The Prisons Open'd,* 1729; *Ars Cogitandi*
Pope, *The Dunciad*
Dryden, *Miscellany Poems, Amphytrion, The Spanish Friar, Don Sebastian*
Collier, *Short View of the Immorality and Profaneness of the English Stage*
Voltaire, *Essay on the French Civil Wars*
Prior, *Poems*
Fontenelle, *New Dialogues of the Dead* (J. Dryden—Modern Novels,
vol. xii, 1692)
Ignoramus
Reflections on Learning
George Herbert, *Poems*
Aldrich, *Artis Logicae Compendium.*
Works by Bargaxone and Locke.

Plays:

Nicholas Rowe, *Tamerlane,* 1702; possibly Lord Lansdowne's *She
Gallants; Almo.*

1730

Classical Literature:

Terence, Plays (inc. *Heautontimorumenos*); Horace, *Epistles*; Juvenal,
Satires; Ceaser, *De Bello Civili*; Cicero, *De Natura Deorum*; Lucretius;
Anacreon; Phaedrus; Virgil.

Religion:

St. Augustine, *Confessions*
Justin Martyr, *First Apology*

Jeremy Taylor, *Holy Living and Holy Dying*
à Kempis, *The Christian Pattern*
William Law, *A Serious Call to a Devout and Holy Life*, 1729
Life of de Renty
R. Lucas, *Enquiry after Happiness*, 1685
Joseph Mede, *Works of the Pious and Profoundly Learned Joseph Mede*
Bishop of Cork, *Of Human Understanding*, 1728
The Second Spira
William Hamilton, *The Exemplary Life and Character of James Bonnel Esq.*
John Norris, *On Humility*
D. Waterland, *Advice to a Young Student*, 1730
William Beveridge, *Private Thoughts*
John Norris, *On Christian Prudence*
Jean la Placette, *The Christian Casuist or a treatise of conscience*, trans. by
   B. Kennett, 1705
Heylin, *On the Sabbath*
Sanderson, *On the Sabbath*
The Country Parson's Advice
Thomas Browne, *Religio Medici*
Case of Infant Baptism
Berkeley, *Of Passive Obedience*
Henry Stebbing, Tracts against Bishop Hoadly, viz.: *The meaning and*
   consequences of a position of the . . . Bishop of Bangor concerning sincerity
   asserted, 1719; *Remarks upon a position of the . . . Bishop of Bangor*
   concerning religious sincerity, 1718
Life of Bishop Bull.

General:
  Walton, *Four Lives*
  Sanderson's *Logic*; *Arithmetickal Logic*; *The Usefulness of Mathematics*
  Stephen's *Letters*
  Lewis, *Poems*
  Edward Young, *On the Passion*
  Works by Milton, Addison and Vertot
  Swift, *Gulliver's Travels*; *Proposal.*

Plays:
  Shakespeare, *Timoleon*
  James Miller, *The Humours of Oxford*

G. Lillo, *The London Merchant or the History of George Barnwell*, a
tragedy[1]
James Thomson, *The Tragedy of Sophonisba*, 1730.

1731

Classical Literature:

Works by Horace, Virgil, Sallust, Ovid (*Metamorphoses, Epistles*), Cornelius Nepos, Cicero (*De Natura Deorum, Tusculan Disputations*),
Anacreon.

Religion:

St. Augustine, *Confessions*
St. Bernard, *Meditations*
The Christian Monitor
Henry Scougal, *The Whole Duty of Man*
Atterbury, *Sermons*
John Kettlewell, *An Office for Prisoners* (with a preface by Robert
Nelson), 1697
Mary Astell, *Serious Proposal to Ladies*, 1694
Edward Welchman, *Articuli XXXIX Ecclesiae Anglicanae Testibus e
Sacra Scriptura*, 1713
Charles Wheatley, *The Church of England Man's Companion, or a Rational
Illustration of the Harmony . . . and Usefulness of the Book of Common
Prayer*, 1710
Thomas Bennet, *Directions for Studying*, 1714
Life of Archbishop Usher
John Norris, *On Human Understanding, On Christian Prudence*
Edward Synge, *Tract on Toleration*
Helps for Penitents
Gentlemen Instructed
Archbishop King, *De Origine Mali*
Works by Bishop Bull and Beveridge.

General:

G. Langbaine, *Ethices Compendium*, 1721
Sanderson, *Logic*

[1] Lillo's play was published in 1731. This entry may then refer to *An Excellent
Ballad of George Barnwell*, 1720; but Wesley's dates are not always impeccable—and
the lists were in some cases compiled much later—and he did very much like a
tragedy.

Vertot, *Histoire des Revolutions*
Elizabeth Elstob, *Anglo-Saxon Homilies*
Burnet, *Travels*
Francis Fuller, *Medicina Gymnastica, or a Treatise concerning the power of Exercise with respect to the Animal Economy, and the great necessity of it in the Cure of Several Distempers,* 6th ed., 1728
The Guardian
Samuel Wesley, *Homer's Battle of the Frogs and Mice,* 1726; *The Battle of the Sexes,* 1724
Essay on Woman
Walton, *Lives*
D. Waterland, *Advice to a Young Student*
Ignoramus
Life of Lord Rochester
Life of Dr. Moore.

Plays:

William Hatchett, *The Fall of Mortimer,* an historical play revived from Mountfort, 1731
D. Mallet, *Eurydice,* 1731
Lord Lansdowne, *The Jew of Venice,* 1701
Theophilus Cibber, *The Lover,* 1730.

1732
Classical Literature:

Works by Horace (*Odes*), Caesar (*De Bello Civili*), Sallust (*African War*), Velleius Paterculus, &c.

Religion:

Thomas à Kempis, *Christian Pattern*
Ephrem Syrus on Repentance
William Law, *Serious Call to a Devout Life; Christian Perfection*
Theologica Germanica
Francis Lee, *Memoirs of the Life of Mr. John Kettlewell,* 1718
Robert Nelson, *On the Sacraments*
Thomas Bennet, *On the Common Prayer*
The Decay of Piety
Adamson, *On Self-Murder*
Pierre du Moulin, *On Contentment*
Life of de Renty

John Johnson, *The Propitiatory Oblation in the Holy Eucharist*, 1710

William Cave, *Primitive Christianity, or the Religion of Ancient Christians in the First Ages of the Gospel*, 1672

Samuel Clarke, *Practical Essays upon Baptism, Confirmation and Repentance*

Brevint, *The Christian Sacrament and Sacrifice*

Tillotson, *Sermons*

J. Scandret, *Sacrifice the Divine Service, from the Covenant of Grace to the consummation of the Mystery of Man's Redemption*, 1707

P. Heylin, *Devotional Tracts*

Juan de Castiniza, *The Spiritual Conflict*, revised by Richard Lucas, 2nd ed., 1710

Robert Burhill, Commentary on Job (MS. commentary in library of Corpus Christi, Oxford)

Simon Patrick, *Advice to a Friend*

A Short Account of the Life of Lieutenant Illidge who was in the Militia of the County of Chester near fifty years, by Matthew Henry, 1710

Nathaniel Spinckes, *Collections of Meditations and Devotions*, 1717

William Spurstowe, *Meditations*

G. Perier, *Life of Pascal*

John Scott, *The Christian Life*, 1681

William Beveridge, *Private Thoughts upon Religion*, 1709

John Goodman, *Winter Evening Conferences*

Robert Nelson, *A Companion for the Festivals and Fasts of the Church of England*

Joseph Stennett, *An Answer to Mr. David Russen's Picture of the Anabaptists*, 1704

John Stearn, Bishop of Clogher, *Tractatus de Visitate Infirmorum*, 1697

John Rogers, *The Necessity of Divine Revelation and the Truth of the Christian Religion, an answer to the Deistic Writings of Anthony Collins*, 1727

The Strength and Weakness of Human Reason

John Norris, *On Schism*

King, *Against the Dissenters*

An Account of the sufferings of the Persecuted Protestants in the Archbishopric of Salzburg, 1732

Bishop Bull against Bossuet

Letter from a Resident to a Corresponding Member

John Ray, *The Wisdom of God Manifested in the Words of Creation*, 1691

An Office of Intercession
On the Crucifixion of Christ
D. Waterland, *Advice to a Student*
S. Clarke, *Essays*
Norris, *On Christian Prudence*
William Law, *Letter on Resignation*
J. Johnson, *Sermons*
Norris, *On Schism*
The Wiles of Satan
Works by Richard Baxter, Edmund Calamy, Bishop Sanderson,
    George Fox, and C. Bartholine.

General:

Vertot, *The history of the revolutions of the Roman Republic*
Spenser, *Faerie Queene*
Locke, *Essay on Human Understanding*
Sanderson, *De lege Poenali*
Weston, *Shorthand*
Character of the Times
Account of Noises
Bishop Berkeley, *Alciphron.*

Plays:

Shakespeare, *Macbeth.*

1733

Religion:

Lactantius, *de Morte*
Vincent of Lerins, *Commonitorium*
St. Francis de Sales, *Introduction to a Devout Life*
P. Heylin, *Devotional Tracts*   *1.732*
Richard Lucas, *Practical Christianity*, 1690
The Life of Ambrose Bonwick, 1729
Daniel Waterland, *The Nature, Obligation and Efficacy of the Christian
    Sacraments considered*, 1730
W. Reeves, *Sermons*, 1729
George Hooper, Bishop of Bath and Wells, *Discourse on Lent*, 1695
John Ray, *Three Physico-Theological Discourses*, ed. Wm. Derham, 4th
    ed., 1732

William Derham, *Physico-Theology, or a Demonstration of the Being and Attributes of God from his works*, 1711-12

Anthony Horneck, *The Happy Ascetick, or the Best Exercise*, 6th ed., 1724

Joseph Hall, Bishop of Exeter, *Contemplation on the New Testament*, 1662

The Second Spira

Alonso Rodriguez, *A Treatise of Humilite*

The Country Parson's Advice

John Norris, *Spiritual Counsel*

Jeremy Taylor, *Golden Grove*

Bishop Ken, *Manual*

Thomas Deacon, *The Doctrine of the Church of Rome concerning Purgatory*, 1718

Theologica Comparativa cum Adjectis

Gottfried Arnold, *Historia et Descriptio Theologiae Mysticae seu Theosophicae arcae et reconditae*, 1702

Young, *Sermons*

John Pearson, *Exposition of the Creed*

Mary Astell, *A Serious Proposal*

Bona, *Principia Vitae Christianae*

John Kettlewell, *Measures of Christian Obedience*, 6th ed., 1714

John Rogers, *A Discourse of the Visible and Invisible Church of Christ*, 1719

The Worthy Communicant

Clement Ellis, *The Self-Deceiver plaintly discover'd to himself, or the serious Christian instructed in his duty to God*, 1731

John Norris, *Miscellany*

William Lowth, *Directions for the Profitable Study of the Scriptures*, 1708

W. Wake, *Apostolic Epistles*

Robert Drew, *Admonitions and Cautions to discharg'd Debtors: a sermon preached . . . on the occasion of the Act for the Relief of insolvent debtors*, 1725

William Wollaston, *Religion of Nature delineated*, 1724

Henry Compton, Bishop of London, *Episcopalia, or letters to the clergy of his diocese*, 1686

Life of Bellarmine

Life of de Renty

Duppa, *Holy rules and helps to devotion, both in prayer and practice, with prayers before and after the Sacrament*, 7th ed., 1704

Richard Kidder, *A Discourse concerning Sins of Infirmity and Wilful Sins*

Sermons by Dr. Cockman, Dr. Secker, Dr. Knight, Mr. Anderson, Dr. Trappes, Dr. Lucas

Franck, *Manuductio ad lectionem Scripture Sacrae,* 1706

Fenelon, *The Maxims of the Saints, explained concerning the Interior Life,* 1698; *Pastoral Letter concerning the Love of God,* ed. Robert Nelson, 1715

A. H. Franck, *Nicodemus, de Cognicione Christiani*

The Retired Christian

The Practice of Piety

The Art of Contentment

Account of the Methodists

Dupin, *A Compleat Method of Studying Divinity,* 1724

The Bull Unigenitus

Bale, *On Public Prayer*

The Interior Christian

William Wogan, *Letter on Baptism*

Account of Salzburg

Prayer for Celibacy

Hopkins, *On Reproof*

Exhortation to Household

Valdesso, *The Hundred and Ten Considerations of Signior J. Valdesso: treating of those things which are most profitable, most necessary, and most perfect in a Christian profession,* trans. G. Herbert, 1638

Joannes Bona, *Manuductio ad Coelum: or a Guide to Eternity,* trans. Sir Roger L'Estrange, 6th ed., 1712

Jurien, *A Plain Method of Christian Devotion,* trans. W. Fleetwood, 28th ed., 1724

Fr. Courayer's Speech.

General:

William Higden, *View of the English Constitution . . . with respect to Allegiance and Oaths*

John Wynne, Bishop of Bath and Wells, *Abridgement of Locke's Essay on the Human Understanding,* ed. 1731

Sir Thomas More, *In defence of Erasmus*

Leonard Lessius and Lewis Cornaro, *A Treatise of Health and Long Life*

Bishop Bossuet, *An Introduction to, or a Short Discourse concerning Universal History,* R. Spencer, 1730

Le Clerc, *Metaphysics*
Rapin, *History of England*
Schumann, *On Female Learning*
Malebranche, *Recherches.*

1734

Classical Literature:

Cicero.

Religion:

H. Scougal, *Life of God in the Soul of Man*
John Norris, *On Christian Prudence*
Savonarola, *De Simplicitate Vitae Christianae*
Confessio Ecclesiae Orientalis
Bishop Wilson, *Principles and Duties of Christians,* 1707
The Christian's Way to Knowledge
H. W. Ludolf, *Reliquiae Ludolfianae: the pious remains of H.W.L.,* edited
    by A. W. Boehme, 1712
A. H. Francke, *Nicodemus: or a treatise against the fear of Man, done into*
    English by A. W. Boehme, ed. 1731
A. H. Francke, *Pietas Hallensis, or an abstract of the marvellous foot-steps of*
    divine providence attending the management and improvement of the Orphan
    House at Glaucha near Halle, 1716
A. H. Francke, *Manuductio ad lectionem Scripture Sacrae*
W. Wake, *Apostolic Fathers*
Charles Daubuz, *A Perpetual Commentary on the Revelation of St. John,*
    1730
Josiah Woodward, *An earnest persuasive to the observance of the Lord's*
    Day, 1712
William Cave, *Primitive Christianity*
Malebranche, *Recherches*
Motives to bear Afflictions
Antoine Godeau, Bishop of Grasse and Vence, *Pastoral Instructions and*
    Meditations, ed. B. Kennet, 1703
Francis de Sales, *Introduction to a Devout Life*
William Burkitt, *Expository Notes on the New Testament,* 1729
Roger Laurence, *Letters*
J. Guther, *Trial of a Saving Interest*
Account of the S.P.C.K.

J. Woodward, *Fair Warning to a Careless World*

A. H. Francke, *De Cognicione*

Francis Fox, *The Duty of Public Worship proved*, 1727

Vida, *Christiados libri sex* (1535), edit. E. Owen, 1725

Jeremy Taylor, *Opuscula*

M. Tindal, *Christianity as Old as Creation*, 1730

William Wall, *The History of Infant Baptism*, 3rd ed., 1720

Robert Parsons, *Christian Directory*

William Law, *Christian Perfection*

Ancient Devotions

George Monro, *Essay on Education, shewing the necessity and advantage of reading Christian authors in grammar schools*, 1712

A. H. Francke, *Nicodemus*

Patrick Delany, *The Doctrine of Abstinence from Blood defended*, 1734

Christian Sacrifice

A. W. Boehme, *Several Discourses and Tracts for promoting the common interest of true Christianity*, 1717

Nathaniel, Marshal, *The Penitential Discipline of the Primitive Church*, 1714

The Life of Ebenezer Yokton, An Exact Entire Mystic

William Reeves, *Apologies of Justin Martyr, Tertullian and Minucius Felix in Defence of the Christian Religion with the Commonitory of Vincentius Lirinensis concerning the Primitive Rule of Faith*, 2 vols., 1716

A Sure Guide to Contentment

Spiritual Retreat

Bishop Wilson, *A Short and Plain Instruction for the Lord's Supper*, 1733

The Sincere Convert

Letters of Francis Xavier

John Pearson, *Exposition of the Creed*

Trappes, *Sermons*

Thomas Burnet, *One Theory of the Earth containing an account of all the changes which it had already undergone or is to undergo till the Consummation of All Things.*

General:

Spenser, *Faerie Queene*

Collier, *Essays*

Milton, *Paradise Lost.*

Wesley's Income from his Fellowship

EVERY fellow was entitled to certain allowances when he was in residence, some of which continued even when he was on leave of absence (8s. for the laundress, 4s. for the barber, 3s. for vinegar, 1s. 8d. for brawn and oysters, 2s. for fishing, 3s. 4d. for dividend, 4s. 1d. for Broad Street, and poundage). As against this he had to pay his battels when in residence and his share of Common Room expenses; when he was out of residence the nominal annual sum he had to pay amounted to £1 12s.

Every fellow of the College was entitled to an annual payment of £10 as a result of Lord Crewe's benefaction, and to his share of the fines for the renewal of leases. It was the general practice in the management of estates to grant a lease for a number of years at a small yearly rent (the 'reserved rent') on condition that the lessee paid down a substantial sum, called a 'fine', at the time of obtaining the lease. This fine was treated as ordinary income of the year in which it accrued and was divided among the Rector (who took a double share) and the fellows in that year. Thus a year in which a considerable lease was granted (viz. Rowland Winn's in 1742-3) made a great difference to the money value of a fellowship in that year. The sums mentioned below do not include additional payments for College office (£20 a year as Moderator), or Combe preacher (3s.) or for tuition; nor ordinarily do they include the rental of an absent fellow's room. Details exist for only some of the years.

1726	Wesley owed the Bursar 11s. 11½d.
1730-1	£42 1s. 9½d.
1731-2	£57 0s. 1¾d.
1733-4	£39 6s. 11d.
1734-5	£54 12s. 4½d.
1735-6	£7 5s. 0d. (as a result of repayment of a loan of £15).
1737-8	£24 17s. 7¾d. Plus allowances.

1738–9	£38 5s. 6d.	He received room rent from Charles Allicock of £2 10s.; and a similar sum from John Robinson; and of 15s. from Thomas Griffiths.
1739–40	£34 10s. 6½d.	
1740–1	£18 11s. 3¼d.	
1741–2	£25 17s. 3½d.	
1742–3	£80 2s. 8d.	(Winn's fine, £32.)
1744–5	£30 17s. 1¾d.	Plus rental of £8 for his rooms.
1745–6	£28 4s. 4d.	
1746–7	£27 19s. 10¾d.	
1747–8	£27 12s. 3½d.	
1749–50	£38 3s. 1½d.	

cellent Way" VI. 4. "One of them had £50 a year. He lived on £28, & gave away 40/-. The next year received £60 ... The third year he received £90 ... The fourth year he received £120 ..."

Could be 1727, 1728, 1729, 1730 of Wesley. But — might be another colleague.

John Wesley's Rooms in Lincoln

EVERY fellow of an Oxford College had the right to a set of rooms in his College, free of rent, irrespective of whether he was actually in residence or not. If he was on leave of absence, he was entitled to the rent of his rooms if they were occupied by other members of the College. At Lincoln the rooms were allocated to the fellows at the College Chapter day meeting on 6th May. The fellows ordinarily occupied rooms on the first floor of the two quadrangles and the garret rooms above them.

At the Chapter day meeting on 6th May, 1726, John Wesley was allocated, or rather chose, the rooms previously occupied by his friend, Thomas Bayliff, rooms with which he must already have been familiar. There was also a garret room which had been let at an annual rental of 12s., and had been occupied for the first half of 1726 by Mr. Berdmore. The list of cubicula or chambers makes it possible to identify the position of Wesley's set. The Bible Clerk's room was the smallest room in the Chapel quad (A) and was situated on the ground floor. Opposite to it and separated by a staircase was a room occupied in 1726 by a young graduate Mr. Swinburn, and latterly by a Mr. Berkeley. Wesley selected the room that was located over this room (B). Its windows looked into the Turl and into the Chapel quad, and here Wesley lived and taught until he left for Georgia.

While he was away in Georgia, a change occurred. During his absence his room was occupied by Mr. Allicock, who entered the College as a commoner in October, 1735. The list of cubicula for 1736–7 shows Charles Allicock in Wesley's rooms (which are so named) for the last two quarters of the year, and a note in the battels book shows that £2 10s. or a half-year chamber's rent was actually paid to Wesley on 9th March, 1736.

Next year there was a change in the allocation of rooms. Resident fellows often occupied their sets for some years but changes occurred as new fellows were elected or older fellows, no longer in residence, gave up better sets. William Smith lived in the room over the buttery (C) from

PLAN OF LINCOLN COLLEGE IN THE EIGHTEENTH CENTURY

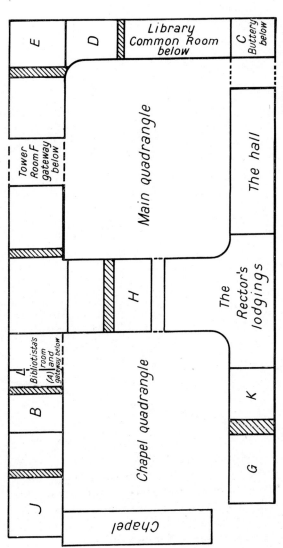

A. Bibliotista's Room
B. Wesley's Room 1726-37
L. Wesley's Room 1737-51
H. The room known as the Wesley Room.
Except for Room A, all rooms referred to are on the first floor.

VI A GROUND PLAN OF LINCOLN COLLEGE

May, 1731, until Toynbee took it over in May, 1750. Mr. Vesey occupied the pleasant set of rooms by the Common Room stairs and opposite the Library (D). Next to him, in the north-west corner, Mr. Chapman lived from May, 1737 (E). The room over the present lodge and main gateway, the Tower room (F), was long in the possession of Richard Hutchins until, having moved to the rooms east of the Chapel (G), he was followed there by Samuel Adams. Mr. Farrer had rooms in the centre of the south side of the first quad (H), and after his death was succeeded by William Smith. Michael Robinson had rooms west of the Chapel (J) from May, 1731, while Lewis Fenton was placed next to the Rector's Lodgings (K).

In May, 1737, John Wesley moved to rooms opposite to his existing set, placed immediately over the Bible Clerk's room (L). Whether Wesley actually lived in these rooms for long is a doubtful question. He himself said that on one of his visits to Oxford he came back to the rooms that he had left when he went to Georgia,[1] and in 1740-1 he paid room rent of £1 5s. to the Bursar, presumably for rooms he had occupied elsewhere in the College while drawing the rental of his own rooms; this could refer to the use of his old rooms in 1739. In 1739 John Robinson, a gentleman commoner of the College, paid him £2 10s. for two quarters' rent. In 1744-5 they were occupied by the younger Duncombe, who had both the rooms on the first floor and the garret (except for the first quarter), for which he paid £8 rent. When Wesley (or rather his agent, William Evans) drew his stipend in October, 1746, the chamber rent due on 6th November, 1745, was given to him. Whether John Wesley lived much in this second set of rooms or not, they were the rooms which he possessed until his resignation in 1751.

Neither of these sets is, however, the set of rooms traditionally associated with John Wesley. These rooms are on the first floor of the south side of the front quad and would appear to have been occupied by another fellow, Mr. Farrer, from May, 1736, until 1750. It seems impossible to say with absolute certainty who was living in them between 1729 and 1736, but it was certainly not John Wesley.

How then did this long-held traditional belief develop? There is no clear solution to the problem; but the tradition had developed[2] by the time that John Morley came to Lincoln as an undergraduate; 'for many

[1] He visited Oxford for ten days on 8th December, 1739, and noted that he 'came into my old room at Oxford, from which I went to Georgia'. (*Journal*, ii, 324.)

[2] There is nothing to indicate that the two Lincoln undergraduates of Wesley's time, John and Charles Westley, occupied these rooms.

terms I was lodged in Wesley's rooms'.[1] 'The last time I met John Morley', Sir Robert Perks wrote to the Rector of Lincoln in 1926, 'he spoke
to me about his early days at Oxford; and told me that talking one day to
John Bright he said that when at Oxford he had occupied the same rooms
as John Wesley—"Well, Morley," said Bright, "precious little good it
seems to have done you."' Subsequently this set of rooms became part of
the junior library of the College until the building of the present library
in 1906.

The belief that these rooms were the actual set occupied by John Wesley
was so firmly established that when a scheme was put afoot to commemorate the two-hundredth anniversary of his fellowship, these rooms eventually became the centre of the proposed memorial. The College had in
fact done nothing to commemorate its most distinguished fellow, but in
1926 it readily approved the suggestion to place a bronze bust in the
window of what was believed to be Wesley's rooms. The memorial was
an outcome of a resolution passed by the Wesleyan Methodist Conference to subscribe towards the bust as 'an outward and visible sign of
Wesley's attachment to Lincoln, and of the fulfilment by his Methodist
children of a filial duty'. The bust, a reproduction of the bust in the
National Portrait Gallery, long, if wrongly, reputed to be the work of
Roubillac, was unveiled by Mr. Walter Runciman on Sunday, 28th
March, 1926, following a commemorative service in the College Chapel
at which a sermon had been preached by Dr. J. H. Ritson, the President
of the Wesleyan Methodist Conference.

Among those present on this occasion was the American Methodist,
Bishop Eben S. Johnson, whose imagination was seized with the possibility of restoring Wesley's supposed rooms as a permanent memorial. It
was reckoned that the cost would be between £1,000 and £1,200.
Bishop Johnson put this proposition to the Bishops of the Methodist
Episcopal Church at their semi-annual meeting at Washington in the
early summer of 1926. They appointed a commission under the enthusiastic chairmanship of Bishop J. W. Hamilton. The idea of founding
a scholarship or a fellowship at Lincoln as a fitting memorial to Wesley
was mooted, but rejected owing to the appeals then being made in American Methodist colleges, especially the American University at Washington with which Bishop Hamilton was closely connected, for endowment

---

[1] *Recollections* (ed. 1921), 6. 'For many terms I was lodged in Wesley's rooms,
sometimes ruminating how it was that all the thoughts and habits of my youthful
Methodism were so rapidly vanishing.'

funds. The rooms were repanelled in sixteenth-century linen-fold oak, taken from the drawing-room of a dismantled castle, and furnished in eighteenth-century style.[1] The work was done under the supervision of Bishop Hamilton's brother, Wilbur D. Hamilton, who also painted a replica of Wesley's portrait by Romney, then housed in Philadelphia. The necessary funds were contributed by Methodist Church people throughout North America. The rooms were opened in the presence of Bishop Hamilton and his brother on Monday, 10th September, 1928. After Bishop Hamilton's address, the Rector, Mr. J. A. R. Munro, reminded his listeners that 'it was [Wesley's] Fellowship in Lincoln College . . . which provided him an independent livelihood and enabled him to devote himself to his evangelistic work and to the organization of his Society'. In his reply, Dr. J. A. Sharp affirmed that the years of John Wesley's fellowship at Lincoln were the formative years of his life.[2]

The conclusion that the rooms in which Wesley lived and worked were not in fact the rooms so pleasantly and generously restored in his memory cannot seriously detract from the value of the tribute. The memorial commemorates Wesley's connection with the College rather than his residence in a particular set of rooms. Whether it is an adequate commemoration of the man who 'stirred the heart of England' is another matter. It is to be hoped that there may be one day an endowment for a Wesley Fellowship which would be an apt and fitting reminder of the man who was for twenty-six years a fellow of Lincoln and who in a continuous series of publications which flowed from his pen, as in his last will and testament, described himself for sixty-six years as a fellow or former fellow of Lincoln College.

[1] The furniture included Chippendale chairs, a secretaire-bookcase of the same period, a Queen Anne bureau-bookcase, an old English writing-table with Bramah locks, drawers and cupboard by Gillow, and an English bracket-clock in a mahogany case by William Stanford of Yarmouth, dated 1780.

[2] For a detail of the ceremony see *John Wesley's Rooms in Lincoln College, Oxford, being a record of their reopening on the 10th September 1928 after restoration by the American Methodist Committee* (1929). The rooms are open to the public at scheduled hours; since 1954 they have been occupied by a fellow of the College as it was felt that it was more appropriate to commemorate John Wesley by rooms continuously in use than by preserving a museum piece.

INDEX

Sermons, ..., 1013.

Selena, p.224